The Symptom Path to Enlightenment:

The New Dynamics of Self-Organization in Hypnotherapy: An Advanced Manual for Beginners

Ernest Lawrence Rossi, Ph.D.
C.G. Jung Institute of Los Angeles, U.S.A.

Including A Chapter On
The New Dynamics of Human Nature
With
Otto Rössler, Ph.D.
University of Tübingen, Germany

Edited by: Kathryn Lane Rossi, Ph.D.

PALISADES GATEWAY PUBLISHING
PACIFIC PALISADES • CALIFORNIA

Library of Congress and Publication Data

Rossi, Ernest Lawrence
    The Symptom Path to Enlightenment: The New Dynamics of Self-Organization in Hypnotherapy: An Advanced Manual for Beginners/Ernest Lawrence Rossi
        p. cm.
    Includes biographical references and index.
    ISBN 0-9651985-0-2
    1. Medicine, Psychosomatic. 2. Behavior and psychotherapies. 3. Hypnotism — Therapeutic use. 4. Psychobiology. 5. Nonlinear dynamics and chaos theory.
    I. Rossi, Kathryn Lane, editor. II. Title

Cover design by Kathryn Rossi.

Published by
Palisades Gateway Publishing
505 Palisades Drive
Pacific Palisades CA 90272
Phone (310) 230-1067 Fax (310) 230-1486
email: Rossi@earthlink.net
Ernest Rossi Home Page: http://home.earthlink.net/~rossi

Manufactured in the United States of America

10 9 8 7 6 5 4 3 2

I thank the following scientific researchers and publishers who generously gave permission to utilize their graphs, equations and words:

R. Abraham, C. Shaw & Aerial Press for their illustrations of Rössler's attractor from *Dynamics, The Geometry of Behavior, Part Two: Chaotic Behavior, 1983.*

G. Brandenberger, A. Meier-Koll and Springer-Verlag for figures that appeared in Lloyd & Rossi, (Eds.) *Ultradian Rhythms in Life processes, 1992 and* Sturis et al. for their graph of ultradian oscillations of insulin, C-peptide & glucose appearing in *Diabetologia, 1992.*

Murray, A., Solomon, M, & Kirschner, M. (1989). The role of cyclin synthesis and degradation in the control of maturation promoting factor activity. *Nature*, 339, 280-286.

J. & M. Shawe-Taylor and JKB Sutherland, Publisher, for their four illustrations of the process of *Consciousness as a Linear Phenomenaon, 1996.*

I thank the *European Journal of Clinical Hypnosis* for their excellent editing of four of my papers that now appear in an updated form as part two of this book. I especially thank my co-authors Brian Lippincott and Arlene Bessette for their contribution of case histories to our papers *The Chronobiology of Mindbody Healing: Ultradian Dynamics in Hypnotherapy: Parts one & two* in the *European Journal of Clinical Hypnosis* in 1994 and 1995 which appears as the last chapter of this book.

Thanks as well to *Hypnos, Swedish Journal of Hypnosis in Psychotherapy and Psychosomatic Medicine* and Journal of European Society of Hypnosis for the three graphs that originally appeared in Rossi, E., Periodicity in Self-Hypnosis and the Ultradian Healing Response, 1992.

Contents

Boxes, Figures and Tables

Other Books by Ernest Lawrence Rossi

Palisades Gateway Publishing

New in 1998! *Dreams, Consciousness & Spirit: The New Dynamics of Self-reflection and Healing, Third Edition* Rossi

The 20 Minute Break: Ultradian Healing Response Rossi & Nimmons, 1991(Tarcher) Now at Palisades Gateway Publishing!

W. Norton

The Psychobiology of Mind-Body Healing: New Concepts of Therapeutic Hypnosis, Revised Rossi, 1993

Mind-Body Therapy Rossi & Cheek, 1988

Springer/Verlag

Ultradian Rhythms in Life Processes: A Fundamental Inquiry into Chronobiology & Psychobiology Lloyd & Rossi, Eds., 1992

Brunner/Mazel

The February Man: Evolving Consciousness and Identity in Hypnotherapy Erickson & Rossi, 1989

Irvington

Hypnotic Realities Erickson & Rossi, 1976

Hypnotherapy: An Exploratory Casebook Erickson & Rossi, 1979

Experiencing Hypnosis Erickson & Rossi, 1981

The Collected Papers of Milton H. Erickson on Hypnosis (4 volumes) Erickson & Rossi, Eds., 1980

   Vol. I: *The Nature of Hypnosis and Suggestion*

   Vol. II: *Hypnotic Alteration of Sensory, Perceptual & Psychophysiological Processes*

   Vol. III: *Hypnotic Investigation of Psychodynamic Processes*

   Vol. IV: *Innovative Hypnotherapy*

The Seminars, Workshops and Lectures of Milton H. Erickson

   Vol. 1. Healing in Hypnosis Rossi, Ryan & Sharp, Eds., 1984

   Vol. 2 Life Reframing in Hypnosis Rossi & Ryan, Eds., 1985

   Vol. 3 Mind-Body Communication in Hypnosis Rossi & Ryan, Eds., 1986

   Vol. 4 Creative Choice in Hypnosis Rossi & Ryan, Eds., 1991

Acknowledgments

The author wishes to acknowledge the guidance and support of colleagues who have made important contributions to the many new concepts presented in this book. Foremost among these is Otto Rössler of the University of Tübingen who provided generously with his time, inspiration and hospitality in our discussions about the possibilities of applying nonlinear dynamics to a deepening of our understanding of psychodynamics. Thanks to Frederick Abraham for his careful reading and incisive comments on these ideas as presented in Chapter Two. All misconceptions and errors in this area, of course, are mine. Thanks are due to Pedro Marijuan and the University Carlos III of Madrid and the University of Zaragoza for their leadership in sponsoring the Foundations of Information Science from which I received much more than I gave. Portions of Chapter Three were freely adapted from my paper The Psychobiology of Mindbody Communication: The Complex, Self-Organizing Field of Information Transduction which was published in *BioSystems* in 1996. My many discussions with Tom Stonier have provided a continuing source of inspiration for exploring the far reaches of theory and speculation in the application of information theory to psychobiology.

I thank the *European Journal of Clinical Hypnosis* for their excellent editing of four of my papers that now appear in an updated form as part two of this book. I especially thank my co-authors Brian Lippincott and Arlene Bessette for their contribution of case histories to our papers *The Chronobiology of Mindbody Healing: Ultradian Dynamics in Hypnotherapy: Parts one & two* in the *European Journal of Clinical Hypnosis* in 1994 and 1995 which appears as the last chapter of this book. Thanks as well to *Hypnos, Swedish Journal of Hypnosis in Psychotherapy and Psychosomatic Medicine* and Journal of European Society of Hypnosis for the three graphs that originally appeared in Rossi, E., Periodicity in Self-Hypnosis and the Ultradian Healing Response, 1992.

I acknowledge with deep appreciation the support of the staff of *Psychological Perspectives: A Journal of Global Consciousness Integrating Psyche, Soul and Nature*, published by the C. G. Jung Institute of Los Angeles, that has provided editorial space for the initial expression of many of the ideas for this book as they emerged in my mind over the past ten years.

Special thanks to the peer reviewers of this manuscript: Haraldur Erlendsson, David Jarvis, Bruce Gregory, Peter Bloom, Norma and Philip Barretta, and Diane Siegmund. Much of the inspiration of this volume derives from the continuing support and cooperation of the Milton H. Erickson family and Jeffrey Zeig, Director of the Milton H. Erickson Foundation of Phoenix, Arizona.

Foreword

By the year 2001 the great Human Genome Project will be completed — we will have a clear map of all our genes — a potential guide to our future evolution. How will we find the wisdom needed to guide us through this critical turning point in human destiny?

Two hundred years of the history of hypnotherapy from its origins in Mesmerism to Charcot, Janet and the current methods of Milton H. Erickson have recorded observations that we recognize today as evidence for the wave nature of human intelligence and communication on all levels of society and consciousness even to the molecular level in the expression of our genes. The new permissive approaches taught in this book extend these insights in a way that can help everyone learn how to utilize their own natural mindbody wisdom to facilitate their own development.

While it is apparent that we all influence each other all the time, many academic authorities acknowledge that their current theory and research in hypnotic suggestion has reached an impasse. This impasse is related to the loss of the deep tradition of healing we read about in historical hypnosis. In this book the Non-linear Dynamics of Self-Organization and Adaptive Complexity Theory is proposed as a new orientation that will help us break out of this impasse to achieve a more comprehensive understanding of how we can facilitate the essence of problem solving and healing in hypnotherapeutic work.

Current research supports the view that a major source of stress and psychosomatic illness may be found in the chronic abuse of our natural mindbody rhythms of activity and rest. It is hypothesized that these adaptive rhythms are an expression of virtually all the self-regulating systems of mind and body —the central nervous system, the autonomic, endocrine and immune systems — at all levels from the molecular-genetic to the cognitive-behavioral and the dynamics of family and social systems.

In this book the mysteries, problems and paradoxes of hypnosis are resolved in a manner that is consistent with these new truths of modern chronobiology. We now recognize how we all experience natural mindbody rhythms every hour and a half or so throughout the day in our capacity for optimal performance in work, learning and sports, for example. In this book we learn how to achieve excellence in all these areas with *"high phase hypnosis."*

We also learn how to recognize the natural mind body signals of our normal need to take a break for brief periods of rest and recovery throughout the day to avoid chronic stress, fatigue and associated psychosomatic problems such as tension, headaches and pain as well as the many types of addiction. We learn practical methods of self-hypnosis that can facilitate deeply healing states of comfort and relaxation that we now call *"low phase hypnosis."*

Evidence is presented for the view that most of our current approaches to holistic healing such as hypnosis, meditation, imagery, ritual, prayer, and biofeedback share a common denominator in facilitating our natural rhythms of activity and rest. This is particularly true of the 20 minute *Ultradian Healing Response* that coordinates the major systems of mindbody self regulation every 90-120 minutes throughout the day. It is precisely these natural psychobiological peaks and troughs that are utilized in our new approaches to high and low phase hypnosis.

The profound implication of this new point of view is that we do not have to suggest or program humans in hypnotherapeutic work — people undergo spontaneous phase transitions in the naturally creative flux of their mindbody that are the real foundation of problem solving and healing. The new ideo-dynamic approaches presented in this book utilize this naturally adaptive capacity to facilitate creativity, problem solving and healing in a very permissive manner that respects everyone's individuality. We find to our surprise that psychological problems and symptoms are actually mindbody signals of potentially creative phase transitions taking place in our lives. With a bit of wisdom we can learn how to use our so-called problems as *The Symptom Path to Enlightenment.*

Several of the peer reviewers of this book emphasized that it is actually several books in one. They strongly recommend that the reader be advised that *Part Two: New Approaches to Creative Hypnotherapeutic Work* could stand alone as *A Practical Introductory Manual To Modern Permissive Hypnotherapy.* Many students and practicing psychotherapists may want to read it first for its refreshingly simple, innovative approaches to facilitating problem solving and healing in hypnotherapy by utilizing the patient's own creative resources.

The more theoretically inclined reader will find *Part One: The New Dynamics of Hypnotherapeutic Work* is a challenging introduction to an entirely new vision of psychology and its current evolution via Self-Organization and Chaos Theory in Chapters One and Two. These new insights are explored in relation to the mindbody problem as it comes up in psychotherapy in general and hypnotherapy in particular. Some fascinating leading edge thinking about the possible relations between mind, information, energy and matter are discussed in Chapter Three. As most readers will appreciate, just how these concepts are to be integrated is still not well understood. Part One of this book is presented only as a introduction to some of the interesting issues that are involved. A well-developed, verifiable scientific theory is not attempted at this time. At best, this book can only make some suggestions about the kinds of research we may need to explore questions in this area in the future. A glossary has been provided to help readers with the important task of relating many new concepts of the current "non-linear revolution" that is taking place in scientific theory and research to the traditional frameworks of hypnotherapy.

A new concept of Hypnotherapeutic Work is introduced in Chapter Four that addresses many of the problems and paradoxes of current theory by clarifying the psychobiological distinction between "High Phase Hypnosis" that is most useful for optimizing human performance in work with an outer world focus versus "Low Phase Hypnosis" that is more appropriate for facilitating therapeutic problem solving and healing within the more personal inner world of identity, emotion and meaning. Many new practical approaches to creative hypnotherapeutic work are then explored in the second half of this book.

Part 1:
The New Dynamics of
Hypnotherapeutic Work

Chapter One:
The Symptom Path to Enlightenment

It is the theory which decides what can be observed.

Albert Einstein

Too long hypnosis has been misrepresented as the handmaiden of psychiatry and the stepchild of psychopathology. History records that hypnosis began more than two hundred years ago before the advent of modern psychology, psychiatry and psychoanalysis. In fact, a careful reading of history helps us understand how most schools of psychotherapy have their roots in hypnotherapy (Edmonston, 1986; Ellenberger, 1970; Zilboorg & Henry, 1941). From this historical perspective we can regard hypnosis as the mother of most of the psychotherapies in practice today. Yet, many of her children do not recognize her any longer. Indeed, some even scorn her as they scamper about proclaiming perennial pagan panaceas with pseudo-scientific posturing.

In this book we will go somewhat beyond simply correcting these misconceptions. We will explore how it may be possible to reformulate the foundation of hypnosis from first principles. We will investigate how hypnosis can be understood in terms of the currently evolving mainstream of mathematics, physics and biology that is becoming known variously as the *Science of Self-Organization, Synergetics, Non-Linear Dynamics, Adaptive Complexity and Chaos Theory*. We will introduce this new foundation with case examples from ancient and modern sources illustrating what we mean by the *Science of Self-Organization* in human development in general, and hypnotherapy in particular.

In this chapter many of the basic terms of modern *Dynamics* will be introduced by placing them in *italics* in the familiar contexts of interesting clinical case histories that will be easily understood by students and psychotherapists. In the next chapter we will add the more technical scientific meaning of these terms. To a surprising extent we will find that the basic concepts of the new *Non-linear Dynamics of Self-Organization and Complex Adaptive Systems* often overlap with similar psycho-*dynamic* concepts commonly used in therapeutic hypnosis and depth psychology. Indeed, a guiding sentiment of this book is that this overlap is no coincidence. The stumbling and sometimes controversial half-truths of historical hypnosis can be viewed as anticipating on a phenomenological level many of the concepts that the new *non-linear dynamics* now formulates more precisely with mathematics.

The major goal of the new *Science of Self-Organization* is to uncover the basic patterns, relationships and laws of nature that are shared in common by all *adaptive complex systems* in the sciences and humanities. It is interesting to note that the source of this currently evolving trend to seek unifying relationships on many levels may be traced to the French mathematician, Henri Poincaré, about a century ago when he was grappling with deep problems in the *non-linear dynamics* of physics. This was within the same time frame that Sigmund Freud and Carl Jung were developing their psycho*dynamics* to account for deep problems of human psychology and culture. It is only now, with a one hundred year perspective, that we can finally recognize their common ethos and divine the possibilities of their creative union for dealing with the ever growing problems of *adaptive complexity* we face in modern life. But let us first go back more than a century earlier to the generally acknowledged sources of hypnotherapy in religious exorcism and emotional crisis.

Exorcism and Crisis: Life On The Edge of Chaos

Father Johann Joseph Gassner, who is regarded as one of the most astonishing healers of all time, was famous for his exorcisms of evil in private and public rituals throughout central Europe. In 1775 one of his public exorcisms was witnessed by eager crowds and officially documented by a notary public and Abbe Bourgeois whose description goes as follows:

> The first patients were two nuns who had been forced to leave their community on account of convulsive fits. Gassner told the first one to kneel before him, asked her briefly about her name, her illness, and whether *she*

agreed that anything he would order should happen. She agreed. Gassner then pronounced solemnly in Latin: "If there be anything preternatural about this disease, I order in the name of Jesus that it manifest itself immediately." *The patient started at once to have convulsions.* According to Gassner, this was proof that the convulsions were caused by an evil spirit and not by a natural illness, and he now proceeded to demonstrate that he had power over the demon, whom *he ordered in Latin to produce convulsions in various parts of the patient's body; he called forth in turn the external manifestations of grief, silliness, scrupulosity, anger, and so on, and even the appearance of death. All his orders were punctually executed.* It now seemed logical that, once a demon had been tamed to that point, it should be relatively easy to expel him, which Gassner did. He then proceeded in the same manner with the second nun. After the seance had ended, Abbe Bourgeois asked her whether it had been very painful; she answered that *she had only a vague memory* of what had happened and that she had not suffered much. (Ellenberger, 1970, p. 54, Italics are ours).

In this remarkable early record we find many of the important features that ancient and modern methods of healing share with the emerging science of self-organization. Having convulsive fits wherein a part or the whole of the body shakes and vibrates rapidly with an apparent loss of control is a profoundly human experience of emotional and spiritual transition that goes back to Biblical times. In modern *non-linear dynamics* this *shaking and vibration* is now recognized as being highly characteristic of *critical periods of transition* from one level of equilibrium or performance to another in any complex system from a steam engine to human athletics (Thelen & Smith, 1994; Kelso, 1995). Gassner's utilization of the nuns' own religious belief system, his initial request for obedience, his solemn demands and his taking over control of the nun's emotional state and symptoms are all typical features of modern hypnotherapy that uses each of these techniques in a more subtle manner (Erickson & Rossi, 1979).

Another inspired but deeply flawed step toward modern hypnotherapy was evident in the approach of the German physician Franz Anton Mesmer, who describes his early ideas in his doctoral dissertation in 1766 as follows:

According to the familiar principles of universal attraction ascertained by observations which teach us how the planets mutually affect one another in their orbits, how the sun and moon cause and control the ocean tides on our globe and in the atmosphere, I asserted that those spheres also exert a direct action on all the parts that go to make up animate bodies, in particular on the nervous system, by an all-penetrating fluid. I denoted this action by the INTENSIFICATION AND THE REMISSION of the properties of matter and organic bodies, such as gravity, cohesion, elasticity, irritability, and electricity.

11

I maintained that just as the ultimate effects, in respect of gravity produced in the sea the appreciable phenomena which we term ebb and flow, so the INTENSIFICATION AND THE REMISSION of the said properties, being subject to the action of the same principle, cause in animate bodies alternate effects similar to those sustained by the sea. By these considerations I established that the animal body, being subjected to the same action, likewise underwent a kind of ebb and flow. I supported this theory with different examples of *periodic revolutions*. I named the property of the animal body that renders it liable to the action of heavenly bodies and of the earth ANIMAL MAGNETISM. I explained by this magnetism the periodical changes which we observe in sex, and in a general way those which physicians of all ages and all countries have observed during illness. (Tinterow, 1970, p 34-35, Italics are ours.)

The capitalization of the basic *dynamics* of "intensification" and "remission" that appears in Mesmer's original document emphasizes the central significance he attributed to these complementary processes. Today we would say there is a natural turning on and off (Mesmer's ebb and flow) of complementary biological processes on all levels from gene expression and cellular biochemistry up to respiration, cardiac dynamics and consciousness itself (waking and sleeping). All the balanced systems of the body are connected by *"critical phase transitions"* between one state and the other. The autonomic system, for example, shifts or *bifurcates* between its arousal phase (sympathetic system dominance that corresponds to Mesmer's "intensification") and its relaxation phase (parasympathetic system dominance that corresponds to Mesmer's "remission") *periodically* throughout the day. Mesmer then went on to report an important early case that led him to distinguish between metal magnets and "animal magnetism." Notice Mesmer's continuing recognition of the *periodicity* of the *phase transitions* in the expression and alleviation mindbody symptoms as the "ebb and flow to which animal magnetism subjects the human body." In the next few chapters on the new *dynamics of self-organization* we will find that *periodicity and phase transitions* and are key characteristics of *deterministic chaos* in all life processes as well as hypnotherapeutic work.

While most of us today would dispute the validity of the concept of animal magnetism, we will find that Mesmer was correct in emphasizing the significance of the periodic relationship of an "ebb and flow" between symptoms and their alleviation. As Henri Poincaré, the originator of *modern dynamical systems theory* pointed out: "The aim of science is not things themselves, as the dogmatists in their simplicity imagine, but the relations among things; outside these relations there is no reality knowable." (Poincaré, 1905/1952, p. xxiv) Poincaré goes on to point out that the careful expression of these *relations* is the essence of mathematics. That is why mathematics is so valuable for science; it helps us understand the relationships of transition and change that are the essence of knowing. While mathematics is not required for this clinical introduction to the *dynamics of hypnotherapeutic work*, later chapters will illustrate in special boxes some elementary mathematical relationships that may be useful guides for students and researchers interested in exploring this area.

Mesmer describes one of his early cases as follows:

> It was chiefly in the years 1773 and 1774 that I undertook in my house the treatment of a young lady, aged 29, named Oesterline, who for several years had been subject to *a convulsive malady, the most troublesome symptoms of which were that the blood rushed to her head and there set up the most cruel toothache and earache, followed by delirium, rage, vomiting, and swooning.* For me it was a highly favorable occasion for observing accurately that kind of ebb and flow to which ANIMAL MAGNETISM subjects the human body. The patient often had beneficial crises, followed by a remarkable degree of alleviation; however, *the enjoyment was always momentary and imperfect.*
>
> *The desire to ascertain the cause of this imperfection* and my own uninterrupted observations brought me time and time again to the point of recognizing Nature's handiwork and of penetrating it sufficiently to forecast and assert, without hesitation, the different stages of the illness. (Tinterow, 1970 p. 36-37, Italics are ours.)

The quixotic nature, fantastic range, unpredictability and dramatic *instability* of the "troublesome symptoms" reported by Mesmer's patient are an often mentioned and are a characteristic feature of the problems that hypnotherapy has always dealt with. The historical as well as the modern scientific literature certainly agree when Mesmer says, "The patient often had beneficial *crises,* followed by a remarkable degree of alleviation; however, the enjoyment was always momentary and imperfect." Like Mesmer, modern researchers seek "to ascertain the cause of this imperfection." A major proposal of this book is that precisely here, in this "imperfection," we will find both the source of the notorious unreliability of the so-called "suggestion and placebo cure" as well as their future possibilities for healing when they are better understood. As we shall see, *instability* characterized by large and irregular *critical fluctuations* in behavior is a fundamental feature of life's ability to creatively adapt to changing circumstances. *Critical points of transition* or *crises* are now well recognized in all *self-organizing systems* that have been carefully studied in physics, biology and the psychosocial sciences (Kelso, 1995; Kruse & Stadler, 1994; Vallacher & Nowak, 1994).

In the current parlance of *complex adaptive systems* theory this *instability,* that is so characteristic of *phase transitions,* is called *"living on the edge of chaos."* The nature of life is not as stable as we would like to imagine. The long time scale of adaptive biological evolution, as well as those flashes of insight that we all admire in ourselves, are only possible because life is perpetually poised on the creative brink between stasis and *chaos.* Non-living systems, like a rock, are static and rigid so they break when *perturbed* by the inevitable *fluctuations* of a changing environment. Psychological crises and psychosomatic symptoms, on the other hand, are significant signatures of potentially *creative phase transitions* in human development and the evolution of consciousness. In this sense The Symptom Path to Enlightenment is more than a metaphor. In the second half of this volume we will explore the new *ideo-dynamic* approaches to hypnotherapy that utilize symptoms as natural guides to the behavioral *instabilities* that are typical of creative life transitions.

Imagination, Faith and Hope: The Harmony of Healing

A more carefully articulated understanding of the nature of the phenomenology of human experience in terms of imagination, faith and hope entered the history of hypnosis to correct Mesmer's misconceptions about a mysterious magnetic force pervading the universe that could be used by the therapist for healing. In 1784 King Louis XIV of France assembled an outstanding group of leading academicians and investigators, including the famed chemist Lavoisier and Benjamin Franklin, whose empirical investigation concluded that there was no evidence of "animal magnetism." They reported instead:

> The uninterrupted observation of ages proves, and the professors of physic acknowledge that nature alone and without our interference cures a great number of persons. (Tinterow, 1970, p 93). ... *The imagination of sick people has unquestionably a very frequent and large share in the cure of their diseases.* With its effect, we are otherwise not acquainted except through general experience. Though it has not been traced in positive experiments, it should seem reasonable not to admit doubt. It is a well-known adage, that in psychic as well as religion, men are saved by faith. This faith is the product of the imagination. *In these cases the imagination acts as a gentle means, and it acts by diffusing tranquillity over the senses, by restoring the harmony of the functions, by recalling into play, every principle of the frame under the genial*

influence of hope. Hope is an essential constituent of human life; the man that yields us one contributes to restore to us the other. (Tinterow, 1970, p 125, italics are ours.).

This early recognition of the role of the patient's imagination, faith, and hope in the healing process was a deep recognition of the patient's role that is still not sufficiently appreciated even today (Dossey,1982,1995; Siegel, 1986, 1989,1993). It represents a profound shift of the locus of the holistic healing agent from the outside to the inside. That is, it recognized that the source of holistic healing resided not in any mystical powers of an external therapist or healer, but rather within the attitudes and inner world emotions and skills of the patient. We could call it the first official recognition of client centered therapy. In the language of our new *self-organizing dynamics theory* we could say that the various inner states we call "imagination, hope, and faith" represent *basins of attraction* that are more likely to lead to "restoring the harmony of functions" in mindbody states of healing. The basic question remains, however. How is mind related to body in sickness and health?

Further understanding of the role of the patient's imagination, hope, and faith in facilitating mindbody healing was promoted by another prominent physician, John Elliotson, writing in what we may regard as the first professional journal of hypnosis, *The Zoist, A Journal of Cerebral Physiology and Mesmerism and their Application to Human Welfare* in 1843. "The faculties of the brain — the mind — are the highest objectives in the universe that man can study; and in as much as its power over the faculties of the body at large, and especially over the brain and whole nervous system, is immense, it is therefore capable of application to prevent and remove suffering, and to cure disease, far beyond the means hitherto possessed by the arts of medicine." (Tinterow, 1970, p. 194). These words were an early recognition of the essential role of mindbody communication within the patient as an agent in healing.

During this same period the Scottish physician, James Braid, in his book, *The Power of the Mind over the Body*, in 1846 helped to introduce the term "hypnotism" for this new field of healing. He is also credited with defining the healing process with a new term: "psychophysiology." In his own words:

> With the view of simplifying the study of reciprocal actions and reactions of mind and matter upon each other... the condition arose from influences existing within the patient's own body, viz., the influence of concentrated attention, or dominant ideas, in modifying physical action, and these dynamic changes re-

acting on the mind of the subject. I adopted the term *"hypnotism"* or nervous sleep to this process... And finally as a generic term, comprising the whole of these phenomena which result from the reciprocal actions of mind and matter upon each other, I think no term more appropriate than *'psychophysiology'*. (Braid in Tinterow, 1970, p. 369-372, italics are ours).

It usually comes as a bit of a surprise for modern students when they learn that it was Braid, the same physician who popularized the term "hypnotism," who apparently coined the word "psychophysiology" to describe how hypnotism achieved its therapeutic effects. We could go on multiplying similar examples in their own words of how the early pioneers of hypnosis (e.g., Esdaile, Charcot, and Bernheim) struggled to understand the essence of hypnotherapeutic suggestion as the mechanisms and processes whereby mind and body interacted and communicated with each other. Because theory and experimental techniques were not available for exploring the parameters of mindbody communication in these early years, however, the psychophysiology of the pioneers of therapeutic hypnosis remained a theoretical hope and clinical promise rather than a well documented science and reliable method of therapy. We will update the psychobiological basis of hypnosis later in Chapter Four where we will explore the *wave* nature of consciousness and being in terms of the *periodicity* and *oscillations,* that are a natural *dynamic* of *self-organizing* and *adaptive complex systems.* For now, let us review a few very well documented historical cases of psychophysiological *periodicity* and *oscillations* in the *dynamics* of mental illness obviously associated with stress, and its resolution with hypnotherapy.

Post Traumatic Stress Disorder: Sensitivity To Context and Initial Conditions

One of the most dramatic clinical case histories probing the source of mental ills in emotional trauma and their cure by hypnotherapy was recorded by the brilliant Pierre Janet in France in 1889. We will recount his case of Marie in detail because it clearly documents the psychobiological basis of trauma and stress on memory as well as the *periodic dynamics* of symptom formation and its resolution by hypnotherapy.

At the age of 19 Marie was brought from her home in the country to the hospital of Le Harve because she was considered to be hopelessly insane. Marie experienced periods of *"convulsive attacks and delirium which usually lasted for a few days."* After a period of observation Janet reported that her sickness consisted of *"periodical manifestations which occurred regularly at the time of her menstruations.* " Marie's mood and personality underwent a spontaneous transformation just before the beginning of each menstruation. She became depressed and gloomy and suffered various pains, nervous spasms with shivering throughout her body. Within a day of its beginning, however, the menstruation suddenly stopped and Marie experienced a *"great hysterical crisis"* with tremors and sharp pain. Although these attacks were violent, they never lasted very long. During her delirium Marie would utter cries and speak of "blood and fire" and acted as if she was trying to escape flames. At other times during her delirium she would apparently regress emotionally, play as a child and generally create havoc in the ward. Janet reported that *"This delirium and the violent body contortions alternated with short periods of rest during 48 hours."* The attack would end with Marie vomiting blood several times before she came back to normal. After a day or two of recovery, Marie would again become her usual quiet herself and when questioned she apparently *"remembered nothing"* of her bizarre suffering. Between these monthly attacks she experienced "contractures" or rigid positions in her arms, shifting patterns of anesthesias in various parts of her body and apparent blindness in her left eye.

During the eighth month of her hospital stay Janet asked her "Look here, explain to me now what happens when you are going to be sick." Marie was never able to give a clear answer and *"seemed to have forgotten most of the events about which I asked her."* It then occurred to Janet to put Marie into a deep somnambulic condition: *"a state wherein it is possible to bring back seemingly forgotten memories."* With persistent questioning Janet finally was able to learn *"the exact memory of an incident which had hitherto been only very incompletely known."*

Marie was not prepared for her first menstruation at thirteen. She experienced great shame and told no one about it. About 20 hours after the beginning of her menstruation she secretly went outside and plunged herself into a shockingly cold bucket of water to clean herself. The cold shock to her system stopped the menstruation and *"in spite of a violent shivering,"* she was able to go back into the house with her secret intact. She was sick for a while, however, and experienced a few days of delirium.

The menstruation did not reappear until five years later! With further hypnotic detective work Janet came to this conclusion:

17

"Every month, the scene of the cold bath repeats itself, brings forth the same stopping of the menstruation and a delirium...until a supplementary hemorrhage takes place through the stomach. But, in her normal state of consciousness, she knows nothing about all this, not even that the shivering is brought forth by the hallucination of cold. *It is therefore probable that this scene takes place below consciousness, and from it the other disturbances erupt.*" This is one of the earliest concise descriptions of the dynamics of repression, psychosomatic symptom formation and the amnesia that often accompanies some forms of post-traumatic stress disorder.

Janet now describes how he "tried to take away from somnambulic consciousness this fixed and absurd idea that the menstruation was stopped by a cold bath." That is he tried to use direct suggestion to free Marie of her symptoms but this approach did not work. After some further exploration he stumbled upon a more successful method: "I was able to succeed only thanks to a singular means. *It was necessary to bring her back, through suggestion, to the age of thirteen, put her back into the initial circumstances of the delirium, convince her that the menstruation had lasted for three days and was not interrupted through any regrettable incident. Now, once this was done, the following menstruation came at the due point, and lasted for three days, without any pain, convulsion or delirium.*" Janet age regressed Marie to a period just before her trauma and had her re-experience her first menstruation in a healthy way. How well did this reframing of reality work?

Further hypnotic revivification of her early years suggested that many of the bizarre psychosomatic symptoms she experienced during her attacks were a repetition and acting out of scenes from real life when, for example, she witnessed an old woman killing herself by falling down stairs. The blood, of which she always spoke during her crisis apparently was memory from this scene. Janet reports how he then reframed this early trauma "through bringing the subject back by suggestion to the moment of the accident, I succeeded, not without difficulty, to show her that the old woman had only stumbled but had not killed herself." After this the attacks of terror with screams of blood and fire did not recur.

In a similar manner Janet systematically investigated Marie's other symptoms. He usually found that Marie experienced a traumatic memory that remained terrifying because there was no one who could correct her misconceptions. In regard to the blindness of the left eye, for example, Marie could recall nothing while in her normal awake state. Janet then reports: "During somnambulism, I make her play the chief scenes of her life at the time, and I see that the blindness starts at a certain point on the occasion of a trifling incident. She had been compelled, in spite of her cries, to sleep with a child of the same age who had impetigo on the entire left side of her face. Some time later, Marie developed an almost identical impetigo, in the same place. Then plagues appeared again several times at about the same time of year and were finally cured; but no one noticed that, hence forward, she had an anesthesia of the left side of her face and was blind in the left eye! ... I put her back with the child who had so horrified her; I make her believe that the child is very nice and does not have impetigo...After two re-enactments of this scene...she caresses without fear the imaginary child...and when I wake her up, Marie sees clearly with the left eye."

Five months after this hypnotherapeutic work Marie gave up even slightest signs of hysteria. Janet summarizes: "I do not attach to this cure more importance than it deserves, and do not know how long it will last, but I found this story interesting as showing the importance of fixed subconscious ideas and the role they play in certain physical illnesses, as well as in emotional illnesses." Marie was retired to her home apparently cured but she later experienced tragic relapses in her unsupportive sociocultural environment and had to return to the hospital where Janet was again successful in hypnotherapeutic efforts with her.

There is much to be savored in this classical case that is central to the *dynamics of self-organization.* There is above all, the important role of the original traumatic experience of her first menses with no preparation, and the trauma of plunging herself into a bucket of cold water, which somehow stressed her normal hormonal process of mindbody communication for five years and replaced it with a plethora of violent and difficult to understand symptoms. Its easy to recognize a *general sort of determinism* in Marie's psychophysiological stress but it would be *impossible to predict* the exact details of her symptoms and apparently strange states as she experienced them. This kind of *determinism in general* that is so complex that *it is impossible to predict in detail* is an important characteristic of so-called *"Chaos Theory"* in all self organizing *systems.* In this sense Chaos Theory describes real life as we all experience it.

Science may say that *theoretically* everything in nature is *strictly determined* according to exact mathematical laws of cause and effect. In practice, however, most of us are a little more relaxed about it. We know that in the world of practical reality *we really cannot predict everything in detail* (or we could all get rich betting on the horse races). In the next chapter we will learn that this is the essential difference between the *Linear Dynamics* of classical mathematical science of the past few centuries where we learned some general laws of what we can predict in nature versus the new *Non-Linear Dynamics* of Chaos Theory where we now recognize that even though we can understand a process in general, *we may not be able to predict its behavior in detail.* We know that in general we will help our children if we can give them a good education, but we know that we cannot predict with any exactness how they will actually turn out!

It was in an effort to see through these complexities that Janet, and later pioneers such as Sigmund Freud and Carl Jung, developed "psychodynamics." As we shall see in the next chapter, however, the "psychodynamics" of psychoanalysis could not be expressed in mathematical terms as the *non-linear dynamics* of Henri Poincaré can. Because of this psychoanalysis was not accepted as a genuine science. Academic psychology in the same time period followed, instead, the statistical approach of Galton, which often developed in the direction of giving up on determinism all together in certain areas of human behavior. This statistical approach to psychology achieved great scientific acceptance, but at the price of giving up determinism.

We are today in a period of confusion and transition in the psychosocial sciences. What is determinism and to what degree can we use this to predict behavior? What is really random (stochastic or statistical) and how do we best cope with it? Now, the new *non-linear dynamics of chaos theory* has introduced a third possibility: there is much in physics, biology and psychology that is deterministic but so complex that we cannot predict it. It is *chaotic* to our limited perception, but it is not really random or confused in the all knowing eye of God. Does knowing that deterministic chaos governs behavior help us understand it and guide in any way better than if we know it is purely random?

Aye, that is the question that motivates the new methods of hypnotherapy that we develop in the second half of this volume. We will find, in keeping with recent developments in the study of deterministic chaos in everything from engineering systems and the weather to cardiac dynamics, that it is possible to predict and modulate deterministic chaos but only to a very limited degree. Like the weather, we can sometimes predict and even modulate *local conditions* for a brief period but long term predictions and absolute control is impossible. This will keep us humble, indeed, in our tendency toward hubris in presuming to control, manipulate and program human behavior.

Returning to the case of Marie, there were other "trifling incidents," as Janet calls them, that lead to other apparently mysterious symptoms. In all this, we note the sensitivity of the human psyche to emotional stress, particularly early life stress, or what is called *"sensitivity to initial conditions"* and history *(hysteresis)* in *nonlinear dynamics.* No, that was not a misprint. A fascinating feature of nonlinear dynamics is that the history of the behavior of a complex system is important for its transitions from one mode of expression to another. This historical feature is called *"hysteresis"* in non-linear dynamics. The etymology is fascinating. Does the *non-linear dynamics of hysteresis* have anything to do with human *hysterical* behavior? They both involve *history, unpredictability* and *large shifts or fluctuations in the amplitude of the response* or behavior of a *complex system* during *critical phase transitions.* We will use this association between *hysteresis* (in the sense of critical transitions of a complex system) and *hysterical or highly aroused symptomatic behavior* as an opportunity for facilitating healing and problem solving in part two of this book. We will learn to recognize and utilize the patient's symptoms as a path to healing and sometimes even enlightenment.

The *periodicity and recurrence* of Marie's symptoms is another characteristic *pattern of non-linear dynamics.* Her periodic hysterical crises would be called emotional *"basins of attraction."* Her fixed ideas are *"fixed point attractors"* in the new parlance of *chaos* that will be presented in technical detail in the next chapter. We can empathize with Janet's dilemma when he initially found that *direct suggestions did not work* when he says "therapeutic suggestions, notably suggestions concerning her menstruation, had nothing but bad effects and increased the delirium." Janet's suggestions were apparently accessing what we would today call the "state dependent memory, learning and behavioral encoding" of her symptoms, but direct suggestion only made them worse. Janet was a pioneer in recognizing that direct suggestion does not cure so much as set up the conditions (in this case age regression) for the reliving of early trauma and the facilitation of mindbody communication that could eventuate in symptom resolution. That is Janet was able to use suggestion to change the *context* of Marie's subjective experience from the present to the past by so-called "age regression." Non-linear systems are as sensitive to *changes in the contexts of their ongoing dynamics* as they are to initial conditions. One such psychosocial context that facilitated Marie's therapy, of course, was her rapport or transference with Janet that enabled her to re-experience and reframe her traumatic early experiences in a new therapeutic context. This became the basis of Joseph Breuer and Sigmund Freud's *Studies of Hysteria* (1895/1955) published almost ten years later wherein they describe the cathartic method and the transference that was to become the early foundation of psychoanalysis.

We are approaching one of the central subtle mysteries of hypnotic suggestion: How does it work and what are the contrasting roles of patient and therapist in the process? Another of Janet's early cases, a women named Justine, helps us understand these issues. Justine was a forty-year old married woman who came to the out-patient service of the Salpêtrière in 1890. For a number of years she had a morbid fear of cholera and would shout, "Cholera ... it's taking me!" as she fell into a hysterical crisis. Janet found that once the crisis was over *Justine seemed to have forgotten everything but the idea of cholera.* As was the case with Marie, a *spontaneous amnesia was characteristic of the state-bound dissociation between her hysterical states and normal consciousness.* Janet found that when the crisis was over, Justine had apparently forgotten everything but the idea of cholera itself with which she remained preoccupied. Janet treated Justine as an out-patient for three years during which he used hypnosis to trace her morbid fear of death to her childhood experiences of helping her mother, who was a nurse, attend patients dying of cholera.

Here again Janet found that direct suggestion was of little value to Justine particularly during her hysterical crisis when she appeared to be in a self-induced trance. Janet used a more dramatic approach by playing along with her private drama during her crisis. When, for example, Justine cried, "Cholera! He will take me," Janet responded with, "Yes, he holds you by the right leg!" When she responded by pulling back her leg, Janet pressed on with, "Where is he, your cholera?" to which she answered, "Here! See him, he's bluish, and he stinks!" In this way Janet developed a dialogue with the self-entranced Justine. Continuing in this manner Janet gradually transformed Justine's hysterical crises into hypnotic states during which he had a good rapport with her. He could then induce hypnosis more directly in a controlled manner to engage further hypnotherapeutic transformations. In his description of his approach Janet insisted, contrary to the belief of his day, that strong commands and direct suggestions administered to the hypnotized patient were of little value. He never believed in the myth that hypnotized patients could be programmed like automatons. He found that the most effective approach was "substitution." This usually involved the use of more indirect suggestions that led to a gradual therapeutic transformation or what we would today call a "reframing" of her inner realities. Janet found that all this was not enough for a more permanent cure of psychological problems, however. The more complete solution of the patient's problem required the development of a fuller capacity for attention and "mental synthesis" in the patient. Janet gradually found it was useful, for example, to train Justine with a series of remedial school exercises in arithmetic and writing. By the end of the third year, Justine was apparently normal.

In this case we witness the gradual evolution of hypnotherapy from its initially precarious and unreliable method of "direct suggestion" to "psychological analysis" and finally "psychological synthesis." In "synthetic reconstruction" Janet even included "elementary school exercises!" Obviously Janet was trying to teach the patient to learn something, to do some sort of *inner work* to help herself. He found that direct suggestion is of limited value in shifting the patient's pathological *"basins of attraction"* that swallow up current life experience into the rather fixed symptoms, delusions and hallucinations of the past.

The reliving of symptoms and psychological analysis is more effective in destabilizing the patient's symptoms, the patient's *periodic fixed attractors,* in the shift from illness to health. Janet used synthetic approaches to inner work, wherein suggestion could utilize her hallucinations, ("Yes, he holds you by the right leg!") to facilitate the possibility of Justine therapeutically reorganizing her inner experience. Janet pioneered the indirect approaches of "psychological implication" and hypnotherapeutic work that facilitate the patient's own natural processes of *self-organization* and healing

(Erickson, Rossi & Rossi, 1976; Erickson & Rossi 1979; Rossi, 1986/1993).

The case of Justine confirms it is not direct suggestion, per se, that cures, but rather the synthetic process of reframing memories and self-reorganization. Some form of arousal, activity and inner work is evident in Justine's obvious emotional crisis during this period of creative inner work. Janet provided hints for the course of this inner work, but Justine had to seize upon it at some level and make it a living experiential reality by re-synthesizing her inner world so that instead of terror she experienced laughter. This is not direct suggestion in the currently popular misconception of hypnosis as a process of programming someone's mind while they are in some sort of blank, automaton-like state. Rather, Janet's innovations anticipated Milton H. Erickson's later work of offering the patient creative possibilities for inner work. The second half of this book is devoted to the further development of these approaches to facilitating the patient's own inner creative work in as non-directive a manner as possible so that the locus of control, problem solving and healing remains within the patient rather than the therapist.

Suggestive Therapeutics: Phase Transitions Of The Ideodynamic

Hippolyte Marie Bernheim was a French physician whose rich documentation of hypnotherapeutic induction and ten thousand clinical case histories (Zilboorg & Henry, 1941) summarized much of what was known in his day. He also consolidated the idea that therapeutic suggestion was a useful medical procedure. Hypnotic induction could lead people through varying levels, or degrees, of hypnotic depth with observable changes in behavior as well as altered states of mind. He begins his classic volume on *Suggestive Therapeutics* with this conception.

> I proceed to hypnotize in the following manner. I begin by saying to the patient that I believe benefit is to be derived from the use of suggestive therapeutics, that there is nothing either hurtful or strange about it; that it is an ordinary sleep or torpor which can be induced in everyone, and that this quiet beneficial condition restores the equilibrium of the nervous system, etc. (Bernheim, 1886/1957 p. 5-9)

In his later descriptions, however, Bernheim emphasized that hypnosis was probably not genuine sleep, but a fascinating *complexity* of *transition states* between waking and sleep that were easy to recognize by the experienced therapist even though they were an important transition to the popular medical view of hypnosis, even today, "that this quiet beneficial condition restores the equilibrium of the nervous system." His recognition of different degrees or depth of hypnosis also contributed a source of inspiration for the development of modern research scales of hypnotic susceptibility.

Some subjects experience only a more or less pronounced dullness, a heaviness in the lids, and sleepiness. This occurs in the smallest number of cases; it is the first degree of M. Liébault. This sleepiness may vanish as soon as the operator's influence is withdrawn. In some cases it lasts for several minutes, in other's longer, an hour, for instance. Some subjects remain motionless. Others move a little, and change their position, but still remain sleepy. At the following séances, this condition may pass to a more advanced degree, though often one cannot go beyond that first attained. For example, in the case of a woman, I induced more than a hundred times a sleepiness lasting from half an hour to an hour, but only this somnolence of the first degree. ...

In the second degree, the patients keep their eyes closed. Their limbs are relaxed, they hear everything that is said to them as well as what is said around them, but they remain subject to the inclination to sleep. Their brain is in the condition called by magnetizers, hypotaxic, or charmed.

This degree is characterized by suggestive catalepsy.

By this word the following phenomenon is meant. If, as soon as the patient falls asleep, the limbs being relaxed, I lift his arm, it stays up: if I lift his leg, it remains uplifted. The limbs passively retain the positions in which they are placed. We call this suggestive catalepsy, because it is easy to recognize that it is purely psychical, bound up in the passive condition of the patient, who automatically keeps the attitude given just as he keeps the ideas received. ...

In the third degree of drowsiness is more pronounced. Tactile sensibility is diminished or destroyed. Aside from suggestive catalepsy, the patient is capable of making automatic movements. I move both arms, one about the other. I say, "You cannot stop," The arms keep up the rotation for a longer or shorter time or indefinitely. The patient hears everything that is said around him.

In some cases this automatic rotation follows the impulse given to the arms. The verbal suggestion is not necessary. In cases of this degree, suggestive contracture can also be brought about.

The fourth degree is characterized, in addition to the preceding phenomena, by the loss of relationship with the outer world. The patient hears what the operator says, but not what the others around him say. His senses are only in communication with the operator. They are, however, susceptible of being put into relationship with any one.

The fifth and sixth degrees — characterized according to M. Liébault, by forgetfulness, upon waking, of all that has happened during sleep — constitute somnambulism. The fifth degree is light somnambulism. The patients still remember in a vague sort of way. They have heard some things confusedly; certain memories awake spontaneously. Destruction of sensibility, suggestive catalepsy, automatic movements, hallucinations caused by suggestion, — all these phenomena of which we shall speak later in greater detail, reach their greatest expression.

In deep somnambulism, or the sixth degree, the remembrance of all that has happened during the sleep is absolutely destroyed and cannot revive spontaneously.

We shall see later that these memories can always be revived artificially.

The patient remains asleep according to the operators will, becoming a perfect automaton, obedient to all his commands.

This division of hypnotic sleep into several degrees, is purely theoretical. It permits us to classify each patient influenced, without making a long description necessary. There are variations and cases intermediary between the several degrees. All possible transitions may be noticed from simple drowsiness and doubtful sleep to the deepest somnambulism. ... Each sleeper has, so to speak, his own individuality, his own special personality. I only wish to emphasize that the aptitude for realizing suggestive phenomena is not always proportional to the depth of sleep. (Bernheim, 1886/1957 p. 5-9)

Notice how Bernheim's emphasis on dullness, heaviness and sleepiness is in striking contrast with the earlier reports about the work of Gassner, Mesmer and Janet where excitement and emotional crises were a dramatic part of the therapeutic process. Bernheim recognized and even quoted Braid's earlier descriptions of how he varied the patient's psychophysiological state of arousal and relaxation as follows.

These manipulations are based upon this fact, that the cataleptiform rigidity of a limb produces, according to Braid, an acceleration of the pulse, which becomes small and wiry. This acceleration of the pulse caused by the effort to hold the limbs stretched out for five minutes, is much greater in the hypnotic than in the normal condition. If the muscles are made to relax while the subject is still under the influence of the hypnosis, the pulse declines rapidly to its rate before the experiment, and even below it. (Bernheim, 1886/1957 p. 205)

In spite of this clear recognition of the combination of activation and relaxation in Braid's method, Bernheim apparently preferred to follow his teacher Liébault's emphasis on sleep and a verbally commanding approach to therapeutic suggestion. In Chapter Four we will review more recent research that indicates that there is an important and entirely natural place for both activation and relaxation in hypnotherapy. Today, of course, most clinicians are wary of too much patient activation and are, indeed, actually fearful of precipitating emotional crises in our litigious society. They vastly prefer quiet, safe relaxing approaches. The creative oriented ideo-dynamic approaches to hypnotherapeutic induction and problem solving that are presented in the second half of this book avoid the excessive emotional activation and crises of the past. These new "fail-safe" approaches are simply a utilization of the normal psychobiological waves of activity and rest that take place in everyday life.

Bernheim's description of the patient becoming "a perfect automaton" in the state of somnambulism described as the sixth degree is, the chilling but ever popular image of hypnosis most often portrayed in the media. Somnambulism is now recognized as a relatively rare state, however and it is much more an exception than the rule in therapeutic and experimental hypnosis. It is common only in the popular imagination. Bernheim emphasizes different degrees of amnesia which patients experience, as well as their varying reactions, to give a more realistic picture. Bernheim sought to explain the *dynamics* of hypnosis as follows:

> The one thing certain is, that a *peculiar aptitude for transforming the idea received into an act* exists in hypnotized subjects who are susceptible to suggestion. In the normal condition, every formulated idea is questioned by the [conscious] mind. ... If there is a cause, the mind vetoes it. In the hypnotized subject, on the contrary, the transformation of thought into action, sensation, movement, or vision is so quickly and so actively accomplished, that the intellectual inhibition has not time to act. When the mind interposes, it is already an accomplished fact, which is often registered with surprise, and which is confirmed by the fact that it proves to be real, and no intervention can hamper it further. If I say to the hypnotized subject, "Your hand remains closed," the brain carries out the idea as soon as it is formulated. A reflex is immediately transmitted from the cortical center, where the idea induced by the auditory nerve is perceived, to the motor center, corresponding to the central origin of the nerves subserving flexion of the hand; — contracture occurs in flexion. There is, then *exaltation of the idio-motor reflex excitability, which effects the unconscious transformation of the thought into movement, unknown to the will.*
>
> The same thing occurs when I say to the hypnotized subject, "You have a tickling sensation in your nose." The thought induced through hearing is reflected upon the center of olfactory sensibility, where it awakens the sensitive memory-image of the nasal itching, as former impressions have created it and left it imprinted and latent. This memory sensation thus resuscitated may be intense enough to cause the reflex act of sneezing. There is also, then, *exaltation of the idio-sensorial reflex excitability, which effects the unconscious transformation of the thought into sensation, or into a sensory image.*
>
> In the same way, the visual, acoustic, and gustatory images succeed the suggested idea.
>
> The mechanism of suggestion in general, may then be summed up in the following formula: *increase of the reflex idio-motor, idio-sensitive, and idio-excitability.* (Bernheim, 1886/1957 p. 137-8, Italic mostly ours.)

The idea that the basic *dynamics* of hypnotic suggestion involves "transforming the idea received into an act" may be regarded as one of the earliest expressions of the theory of *information transfer or transduction* between mind and body as the essence of healing in hypnotherapy (Rossi, 1986/1993). The fascinating implications of this idea in terms of modern *adaptive complexity theory* will be explored in Chapter Two and Three, where current speculations about the nature of life as a *self-organizing process* wherein information "captures" or "computes" matter and energy at the *edge of chaos* are discussed.

Loss of the Historical Identity of Hypnotherapy in Modern Research

The detailed descriptions of the *phase transitions* of hypnotic experience by Bernheim and others then led to many early qualitative descriptions of "hypnotic depth" (Davis & Husband, 1931). These early qualitative scales eventually inspired the pioneering psychologists of our era such as Clark Hull, Ernest Hilgard and H. J. Eysenck who investigated the dynamics of hypnosis experimentally. They all began by trying to define the domain of suggestion with behavioral tests and observable responses that could be easily measured in a quantitative manner. This led to the creation of the well known hypnotic susceptibility scales, which were presumed to be instruments that would be useful for measuring the essence of therapeutic suggestion as a behavioral and psychosocial process. After more than a generation of intensively active research, however, this has not proved to be the case.

In response to criticism about the clinical adequacy of these scales (Weitzenhoffer, 1980), Hilgard (1981, p. 25) has acknowledged "Hypnotic susceptibility or hypnotizability refers to hypnotic talent, that is the ability to respond to hypnotic suggestions under appropriate circumstances." These scales, in fact, have been extremely valuable for identifying hypnotic talent under experimental laboratory conditions but their clinical usefulness in hypnotherapy has remained controversial (Gruenewald, 1982; Sacerdote, 1982). *These modern research scales of hypnotic susceptibility appear to have lost all connection to the psychophysiological foundations of hypnosis that were emphasized by the fathers of hypnotherapy.* Academic researchers who tended to standardize these scales of hypnotic susceptibility on college students and normal populations lost touch with the *emotional crises and phase transitions* that made up the essence of therapy in historical hypnosis. Modern hypnosis became a study of normative psychology rather than the desperate transforming experiences between sickness and health, sanity and insanity, life and death itself in historical hypnosis.

After three generations of research with these behavioral scales of hypnotic susceptibility, however, we seem to have reached an impasse and a series of paradoxes (Balthazard & Woody, 1985). Naish, for example, has recently summarized the situation as follows: "As [hypnotic] susceptibility is normally assessed, a high scorer is one who *produces* the behavior, the *reason* for its production remains unknown... The claim was frequently made that cognitive processes are involved in the production of 'hypnotic' effects. However, the exact nature of these processes generally remained obscure." (Naish, 1986, p. 165-166). Obscure, indeed! The heart, essence and context of historical hypnosis in the desperate psychophysiology of illness, emotional crises and transitions to health had been lost altogether.

The basic impasse and emerging paradox of current hypnosis research is that a remarkable number of the highly respected researchers who developed and utilized these scales of hypnotic susceptibility are now reporting that, whatever hypnosis may be, its domain cannot be limited to the behavioral or psychosocial processes as defined by these scales. Ernest Hilgard, for example, recently summarized and defined the domain of hypnosis with these words, "The first point is that hypnotic behavior cannot be defined simply as a response to suggestion... Although hypnotic-like behaviors are commonly responses to suggestion, the domain of suggestion includes responses that do not belong within hypnosis, and the phenomena of hypnosis covers more than specific responses to suggestion." (Schumaker, 1991, p. 45-46). Hilgard seems to be saying that the domain of hypnotic suggestion and the behavioral responses to it as currently defined are not adequate or complete. So, what is missing?

From our historical perspective, we propose that what is missing from the domain of current suggestion theory as it has been developed by behaviorally oriented researchers like Hilgard is precisely the *psychophysiological phase transitions* that the fathers of hypnosis described with their many outlines of the changing degrees of hypnotic depth. A major goal of this book is to reconnect with the psychophysiological foundations of hypnosis that have been lost to most modern researchers. In one recently edited volume, for example, the editor (Schumaker, 1991, p. 19) asks, "Are we progressing toward a biology of suggestion?" Aye, back to the future! As we have seen, Braid defined the domain of hypnosis as "psychophysiology" back in 1855. Having lost its psychobiological roots, it is no wonder that much current research in hypnosis seems to be impoverished in its understanding of the role and potency of hypnotherapeutic work. Having cut suggestion from its psychobiological foundations, current psychological research in hypnosis apparently lost itself altogether in the "statistical byways of unreliability."

H. J. Eysenck summarizes this loss of the reality and role of suggestion in hypnotherapeutic work most pungently as follows: "There is no single, unitary trait of suggestibility, no one uniform type of reaction to different kinds of suggestion in human subjects. There are several, or possibly many different suggestibilities which bear no relation to each other. These are uncorrelated and, in turn, correlate differentially with other cognitive and emotional variables. This finding is of considerable interest and importance... It does make books containing in their title the word 'suggestibility' of rather doubtful value!" (Eysenck, 1991, p. 87). Once again, we have a clear admission by a leading, behaviorally oriented researcher, that the domain of hypnotic suggestion has fallen into a muddle of correlated and uncorrelated "cognitive and emotional variables" when it is limited to these behaviorally defined domains. One wonders if Eysenck really would have us throw out the baby with the bath water by proscribing any more books about "suggestibility."

The paradox of our leading researchers beginning their careers by defining hypnosis as behavioral responsiveness to suggestion and then, after a lifetime of research, turning around and saying, in effect, (1) hypnosis cannot be operationally defined simply as responsiveness to suggestion, and (2) there is no unitary human trait of suggestibility, must give all thoughtful students and clinicians pause. Balthazard & Woody, for example, have stated, "Although a fair amount of factor analytic work has been done with the hypnosis scales (see Balthazard & Woody, 1985, for a review) this work appears to be at an *impasse* methodologically, and it has failed to yield any consistent picture of the mechanisms that underlie performance on the hypnosis scales." (Balthazard & Woody, 1992, p. 22, Italics added here.)

Kirsch and Lynn (1995) have recently summarized the current status of opinion in an authoritative paper in the *American Psychologist* as follows.

Is there a uniquely hypnotic state that serves as a background or gives rise to the altered subjective experiences produced by suggestion? Having failed to find reliable markers of trance after 50 years of careful research, most researchers have concluded that this hypothesis has outlived its usefulness. Nevertheless, most clinicians still believe that hypnosis is a unique state with casual properties (see Kirsch, 1993); as do some influential theorists (e.g., Fromm, 1992; Nash, 1991; Speigel & Speigel, 1978; Woody & Bowers, 1994). Because the state hypothesis is an existential rather than a universal proposition, it cannot be disproved, but can, in principle, be verified. As E. R. Hilgard (1973) noted, "The fact that no signs are now present, or that none are likely to be found, does not deny the possibility that some subtle indicators will be eventually uncovered" (p. 978). Kirsch and Lynn (1995, p. 854).

The presence of paradoxes in science is usually taken as an important clue that there is something wrong with current theory and practice; an important transition and expansion is usually required before further progress can be made. Paradoxes frequently point to places where theory and practice need to be revised in some fundamental way. Paradox usually inspires investigators to plan and execute new directions in research to resolve the paradox.

In the following chapters we will present evidence that the source of the current impasse in the traditional approach to hypnosis as an altered state is in the inappropriate use of over-simplified *linear models* to study complex human experience. As an alternative, we will present the new *non-linear* approaches of *self-organization theory* to the ever shifting *"critical phase transitions"* that describe the human experience of hypnotherapeutic work. That is, we will focus on a new understanding of hypnotherapy as process of continuous *dynamic* change called *"phase transitions"* rather than the rather static view of hypnosis as an altered state.

We will explore, in particular, the recent findings of the *"Synergetics"* school that is now developing new conceptual and experimental non-linear approaches to the classical phenomena of hypnosis and suggestion. But for now let us focus on a creative alternative to direct suggestion as the essential dynamic of hypnotherapy in the clinical work of Milton H. Erickson and others.

Suggestion and Self-Organization In Creative Hypnotherapeutic Work

If direct suggestion is not the major mechanism of hypnotherapy, what is? The late Milton H. Erickson explored this question through out his long career as an innovator and teacher of hypnotherapy. In his very first professional paper on hypnosis titled, "Possible detrimental effects of experimental hypnosis," published in 1932, when he was thirty-one years old, for example, he acknowledges the limitations of so-called "hyper-suggestibility" as follows.

The first of these theories of possible detrimental effects centers around the question of the development of hypersuggestibility. ... In the writer's own experience, upon which it unfortunately will be necessary to a large extent to base the elaboration of these various questions, *hyper-suggestibility was not noticed*, although the list of individual subjects totals approximately 300 and the number of trances several thousand. Further, a considerable number were hypnotized from 300 to 500 times each over a period of years. ... *Far from making them hyper-suggestible, it was found necessary to deal very gingerly with them to keep from losing their cooperation*, and it was often felt that they developed a compensatory negativism toward the hypnotist to off-set any increased suggestibility. Subjects trained to go into a deep trance instantly at the snap of a finger would successfully resist when unwilling or more interested in other projects... *In brief, it seems probable that if there is a development of increased suggestibility, it is negligible in extent.* (Erickson, 1932/1980, pp. 495, Italics are ours.)

In a profoundly important later paper on "Hypnotic Psychotherapy" the more mature Erickson, at the age of forty-seven, summarizes his observations on the "Role of Suggestion in Hypnosis" as follows.

The next consideration concerns the general role of suggestion in hypnosis. Too often the *unwarranted and unsound assumption is made that, since a trance state is induced and maintained by suggestion, and since hypnotic manifestations can be elicited by suggestion, whatever develops from hypnosis must necessarily be completely a result of suggestion and primarily an expression of it.*

Contrary to such misconceptions, the hypnotized person remains the same person. His or her behavior only is altered by the trance state, but even so, that *altered behavior derives from the life experience of the patient and not from the therapist.* At most, the therapist can influence only the manner of self-expression. *The induction and maintenance of a trance serve to provide a special psychological state in which patients can re-associate and reorganize their inner psychological complexities and utilize their own capacities in a manner in accord with their own experiential life.* Hypnosis does not change people nor does it alter their past experiential life. It serves to permit them to learn more about themselves and to express themselves more adequately.

Direct suggestion is based primarily, if unwittingly, upon the assumption that whatever develops in hypnosis derives from the suggestions given. It implies that *the therapist has the miraculous power of effecting therapeutic changes in the patient*, and disregards the fact that *therapy results from an inner re-synthesis of the patient's behavior achieved by the patient himself*. It is true that direct suggestion can effect an alteration in the patients behavior and result in a symptomatic cure, at least temporarily. However, such a "cure" is simply a response to the suggestion and does not entail that re-association and reorganization of ideas, understandings, and memories so essential for an actual cure. *It is this experience of re-associating and reorganizing his own experiential life that eventuates in a cure, not the manifestation of responsive behavior which can, at best, satisfy only the observer.*" (Erickson, 1948/1980, pp. 38. Italics are ours.)

Notice the important distinction that Erickson carefully makes between the use of suggestion to (1) induce and maintain trance versus, (2) the therapeutic benefits that derive from it when he says, "*Too often the unwarranted and unsound assumption is made that, since a trance state is induced and maintained by suggestion, and since hypnotic manifestations can be elicited by suggestion, whatever develops from hypnosis must necessarily be a completely a result of suggestion and primarily an expression of it.*" What else is there besides direct suggestion? His answer finally comes 16 years later when he was finally ready to describe the essential mechanism of hypnotherapy, "*Therapy results from an inner re-synthesis of the patient's behavior achieved by the patient himself.*" And again, "*It is this experience of re-associating and reorganizing his own experiential life that eventuates in a cure, not the manifestation of responsive behavior which can, at best, satisfy only the observer.*" These passages make it apparent that Erickson was rediscovering Janet's synthetic approaches as the essential *dynamics* of hypnotherapeutic work.

Hypnosis has always had its "observers." The public crowd is always mesmerized by hopes for the miraculous behind what it does not understand. If it is not God, or magnetic forces from the universe, or even "animal magnetism" that heals, perhaps it is at least imagination, hope and expectation. If these alone are not sufficient for some "patients" perhaps what they need are powerful "psychosocial cues" manipulated by the hypnotherapist as a sort of new age social programmer. That's it! The mind is a computer and the body a slave! We can program the neurons of mind just like the silicon chips of a computer and the healing of the body magically follows. A major premise of this book is that this is false analogy and "magical thinking" indeed.

The realistic alternative to the mirage of magical thinking that pervades so much of the current psychotherapeutic scene is to understand the genuine *psychobiological dynamics of creative inner work* within the patient as the essence of healing and problem solving. What is the nature of this creative inner problem solving and healing work? Erickson calls it the *"experience of re-associating and reorganizing his own experiential life that eventuates in a cure."* Henri Poincaré's introspections on his own creative process of problem solving in mathematics led him to describe this inner work in four stages as (1) Data collection, (2) Incubation, (3) Insight, and (4) Verification. These four stages then became the basis of later experimental research on the creative process for more than half a century by psychologists (Hadamard, 1954; Rossi, 1972/1986/1998). These four stages of the creative process become the corner-stone of our psychosynthetic approach to problem solving and healing in hypnotherapy in Chapter Six.

The Symptom Path to Enlightenment:
More than a Metaphor

Current research programs led by psychologists such as J. A. Scott Kelso, Director of the Center for Complex Systems at Florida Atlantic University, in the areas of sensory-perceptual learning and spatio-temporal patterns of brain activity now view creativity itself as a *phase transition* to a more *complex process of adaptation* in everyday life (Kelso, 1995, p 26). This central concept of creativity as a *phase transition,* a period of *flux or chaos* between an older established order of the personality to a newer and more complex level of adaptation, was anticipated around the turn of this century by Richard Maurice Bucke, the medical superintendent of the asylum for the insane in London, Canada. In his classic volume on *Cosmic Consciousness,* Bucke (1901) assembled many ancient and modern examples of profoundly moving experiences whereby mental symptoms of neurosis, psychosis and social maladjustment turned out to be signals of the transition stage of *critical fluctuations* in personality dynamics as the person shifted uncertainly from a lower to a higher, or more *complex,* level of human development. Here is one example from the Bible to give a flavor of what Bucke meant by the evolution from our ordinary "normal" state of existence through a precarious *phase of transition* to a state of enlightenment or what he called "cosmic consciousness."

One of Bucke's earliest and most stirring examples comes from the Bible which describes how a young man, Saul, with an "ardent and impetuous nature" began as a persecutor of the small groups of believers in Christ after his crucifixion. While he was on his way to Damascus, a little way outside of Palestine, bent on these persecutions he had this "conversion experience" that led him to transform his life so that he was eventually called, Saint Paul.

As he journeyed it came to pass that he drew nigh unto Damascus: and suddenly there shone round about him a light out of heaven: and he fell upon the earth and heard a voice saying unto him, 𝕾𝖆𝖚𝖑, 𝕾𝖆𝖚𝖑, 𝖜𝖍𝖞 𝖕𝖊𝖗𝖘𝖊𝖈𝖚𝖙𝖊𝖘𝖙 𝖙𝖍𝖔𝖚 𝖒𝖊? And he said, Who art thou, Lord? And he said, 𝕴 𝖆𝖒 𝕵𝖊𝖘𝖚𝖘 𝖜𝖍𝖔𝖒 𝖙𝖍𝖔𝖚 𝖕𝖊𝖗𝖘𝖊𝖈𝖚𝖙𝖊𝖘𝖙: 𝖇𝖚𝖙 𝖗𝖎𝖘𝖊 𝖆𝖓𝖉 𝖊𝖓𝖙𝖊𝖗 𝖎𝖓𝖙𝖔 𝖙𝖍𝖊 𝖈𝖎𝖙𝖞, 𝖆𝖓𝖉 𝖎𝖙 𝖘𝖍𝖆𝖑𝖑 𝖇𝖊 𝖙𝖔𝖑𝖉 𝖙𝖍𝖊𝖊 𝖜𝖍𝖆𝖙 𝖙𝖍𝖔𝖚 𝖒𝖚𝖘𝖙 𝖉𝖔. And the men that journeyed with him stood speechless, hearing the voice, but beholding no man. And Saul arose from the earth; and when his eyes were opened, he saw nothing; and they led him by the hand into Damascus. And he was three days without sight, and did neither eat or drink. (From the Bible, Acts, 9, as quoted by Bucke, 1901, p.114)

Bucke goes on to summarize what is known of how this conversion experience led to the recreation of Saul's personality into its opposite: a new life dedicated to the spirit so that he was later to become Saint Paul. At this point we can only wonder whether this fascinating type of transition from one state to a polar opposite is in any way related to what is today called "dual personality," or the shifts between the manic and depressive phases of bipolar disorders. From the perspective of our currently developing *non-linear dynamics theory of self-organization,* these *phase transitions* are called *"bifurcations,"* where by a personality can shift between two or more *"basins of transition"* to different states of consciousness called *"attractors."*

Bucke outlines about a dozen characteristics of this phase transition of the personality such as an intellectual illumination, moral elevation, added charm, more distinct individuality, and even changes in physical appearance. Bucke richly documents how religious figures such as the Buddha, Mohammed, Moses and Christ, as well as philosophers and poets such as Francis Bacon, William Blake and Walt Witman and a host of ordinary people from everyday life experienced such dramatic personality transitions. It is interesting to note how Bucke described the transition states of many of these ordinary folks as "Lesser, Imperfect and Doubtful Instances" that sometimes hung on for hours, days, months or years in what he called a

"Twilight" between the old personality and the new. The dynamics of facilitating these *transition phases* between the old and the new, particularly with people who present themselves as patients in psychotherapy, is what I call "The Symptom Path to Enlightenment."

The Basic Ideas

This chapter surveyed some of the most noteworthy phenomenological discoveries of historical hypnotherapy that are consistent with currently evolving concepts of the new sciences of *Self-Organization and Complex Adaptive Systems*. These concepts present us with a rare opportunity to recreate the foundations of hypnosis from the first principles that it shares with mathematics, physics, biology, the psychosocial sciences and the humanities in general. They enable us to take some initial, though admittedly speculative steps toward a synthesis of the sciences of mind, consciousness and behavior.

(1) *While it is apparent that we all influence each other all the time, many authorities acknowledge that current theory and research in hypnotic suggestion has reached an impasse. Our point of view is that this impasse is related to the loss of the psychobiological foundations of healing in historical hypnosis. The Nonlinear Dynamics of Self-Organization and Adaptive Complexity Theory is proposed as a new orientation that will help us break out of this impasse to achieve a deeper understanding of how we can facilitate the essence of problem solving and healing in hypnotherapeutic work.*

(2) *There is a deep correspondence between the psycho-dynamics of historical hypnosis and the Non-linear Dynamics of Chaos and Self-organization Theory that suggests that they both derive from a common archetypal foundation. Bernheim's statement, "I only wish to emphasize that the aptitude for realizing suggestive phenomena is not always proportional to the depth of sleep" is a clear recognition of what is today called "Non-linear Dynamics in Complex Adaptive Systems of Self-organization." There is no simple, proportional, cause and effect relationship between suggestion and most of the interesting clinical and creative features of hypnotherapy. We will explore the application of the technical language of non-linear dynamics to reformulate the foundations of hypnotherapy in the next few chapters.*

(3) *The flow of information and communication between mind and body is an essential path of problem solving and healing in*

hypnotherapy. Bernheim's special view of the nature of the "ideo-motor and ideo-sensorial reflex excitability" in "transforming the idea received into an act" is one of the earliest expressions of the theory of psychobiological information transduction and communication as an essential vehicle of healing in hypnotherapeutic work. Chapter Three will be devoted to an exploration of the relations between matter, energy and information in our current efforts to understand "What is Life?" There we will review the fascinating idea that life is a process of Self-Organization wherein information is able to enfold matter and energy in evolutionary processes that are today called "Complex Adaptive Systems."

(4) *Time and non-linear periodicity is a window into the new psychobiology of mindbody communication and healing. Current research on the chaotological (chaos theory) and chronobiological aspects of hypnosis that opens the possibility of a new understanding of the natural dynamics and phase transitions in human development are reviewed in Chapter Four. The practical implications of these studies for creating new approaches to hypnotherapeutic work that can facilitate problem solving and healing at all levels from mind to gene will be presented in the second half of this volume.*

Chapter Two:
The New Dynamics
Of Human Nature

Chaos thus represents the greatest challenge to the mind — to break out from the prison of appearances...Miraculously, the ancient dualistic thinking in connection with the word "chaos" and the modern developments in chaos theory are not at odds with each other.

Otto Rössler, 1995

A child playing on a sunny beach lets a handful of sand slowly trickle through her fingers to make a sweet little pile that forms all by itself. She does not realize that her little sand pile, with a *critical slope* of about 34 degrees, is a simple example of spontaneous self-organization in nature. If she carefully lets another handful trickle down on top of the first, the sand pile will grow a little higher but the slope will remain the same because a tiny series of little avalanches will follow a *power law* maintaining the developing sand pile in a precise 3-dimensional cone pattern of self-organization. This natural pattern of self-organization in nature contains the secret of the new dynamics of human nature. What are the psychodynamics of how our consciousness and personality evolve naturally without our trying to push or pull them in one direction or another? How are we created in nature independently of the illusion of human will?

To see the world in a few grains of sand is more than a poetic metaphor. Per Bak and Kan Chen (1991) suggest that sand piles illustrate *self-organized criticality,* a kind of generic "domino effect" that accounts for the *cascade* of avalanches that continually sculpts the sand pile. If the sides of the cone momentarily grow too steep or too shallow, the number and size of the avalanches will spontaneously adjust themselves. The child made the sand pile, to be sure, but it was nature's dynamics that shaped it just so. Bak and his colleagues carefully study the *dynamics* of *composite systems* of sand piles as a simple model of more *complex systems* such as earthquakes, ecosystems, the stock market and the human brain with about 10^{12} neurons. These are all examples of *self-organized criticality* that require no programming or master organization chart from the outside to tell them how to work. They are simply following nature's laws from within. Bak and Chen describe their ideas as follows:

> We propose the theory of self-organized criticality: many composite systems *naturally evolve to a critical state* in which a minor event starts a chain reaction that can affect any number of elements in the system. Although composite systems produce more minor events than catastrophes, chain reactions of all sizes are an integral part of the dynamics. According to the theory, the mechanism that leads to minor events is the same one that leads to major events. *Furthermore, composite systems never reach equilibrium but instead evolve from one metastable state to the next.* (Bak & Chen, 1991, p. 46, Ital. are ours).

> One might think of more exotic examples of self-organized criticality. Throughout history, wars and peaceful interactions might have left the world in a critical state in which conflicts and social unrest spread like avalanches. Self-organized criticality might even explain how information propagates through neural networks in the brain. It is no surprise that brainstorms can be triggered by small events...(ibid., p. 53)

The power laws that describe the dynamics of earthquakes, economic markets and ecosystems are just as fundamental in human perception where they relate our subjective experience ("just noticeable differences") to the objective intensity of a stimulus — the loudness of sound or the brightness of light for example. These power laws are of essence in the hidden autonomous processes of self-organization of human experience on many levels. But what has all this to do with psychotherapy in general and hypnotherapy in particular? *Critical States!* There has been a great deal of controversy about defining hypnosis as an "altered state" or "relaxed state" or "somnambulistic state" or, as we will review in Chapter Four, "hypnosis as the relative entrainment of any of the dynamical variations of our natural circadian (~daily) or ultradian (less than 24 hours) rhythms of consciousness and being." What Bak and his colleagues contribute with their theory of self-organized criticality is the implication that all complex systems such as the human brain never really reach "stable equilibrium." Instead our brain is in continual *evolution from one metastable state* to the next.

We have all been misguided a bit about the traditional idea of stable equilibrium and the concept of homeostasis: the view that the physiological ideal of life is to remain in a "normal" stable unchanging state (Rossi, 1994a). The new view of life as perpetually balanced on the edge of *self-organized criticality* has important implications for hypnosis. It means that our 200 year hypnotic fascination with changing mental states — however we wish to conceptualize them — is no perverse pursuit of the strange and bizarre in human nature. Our interest is as normal as apple pie. Only now is main-stream science beginning to catch up with us. The new science of self-organization, proposes to explain with numbers, maps, graphs and computer models how we were right all along: *human nature is an ever shifting dynamic of metastable states in self-organized criticality on the edge of creative adaptation.*

Self-Organized Criticality and Attractors In Hypnotherapy

There are many other profound implications in Bak's concept of self-organized criticality for hypnosis and psychotherapy. The late Milton H. Erickson, MD, the founder of the American Society of Clinical Hypnosis, continually reminded us of the "domino effect" in life as well as in psychotherapy. Seemingly little, insignificant events in everyday life — a little inspiration here, a discouraging word there — can sometimes be amplified into profoundly important changes in the course of a person's life, particularly when they are teetering on a critical edge of some change or other. During these periods a casually administered hypnotherapeutic suggestion that can initiate even the smallest behavioral change — a mere grain of sand in the cascade of typical daily activity — can set off a domino effect of greater and greater changes that eventually become an avalanche of life transformation.

As we shall see, the domino effect is a characteristic feature of the *nonlinear dynamics* of the *self-organization* in human experience. It is related to our extraordinary *sensitivity to initial conditions* where tiny differences in the beginning of a relationship, for example, can lead to vastly different outcomes while, paradoxically enough, the exact reverse could also be true: apparently *catastrophic* outside events such as the loss of family and fortune can sometimes leave us unmoved within the core of our character. This is called *insensitivity to initial conditions* by Fred Abraham (1995 a and b). It is precisely these disproportionate cause and effect relations in human affairs that the traditional type of *linear* thinking in psychology has been unable to cope with. As folk wisdom would have it, "With some people, you just never know!"

Milton H. Erickson also liked to explore the disproportionate effects of what he called a "yo-yoing of consciousness" (Erickson and Rossi, 1979). From our new perspective we would now call this a subjective experience of a "critical phase transition in consciousness" as patients go into or out of hypnotherapeutic trance. Erickson would induce a deepening of trance during the initial hypnotic induction, for example, by counting from one to twenty and suggesting that the patient would go deeper with each number so a very deep trance would be experienced by the time they heard "twenty." Later, to awaken the patient from trance, Erickson would count backwards from 20 to one with trance "lightening" with each count. The critical phase transition in consciousness was experienced when Erickson mischievously reversed the count when he came about half way from 20 to one. Erickson would solemnly intone, "20, 19, 18, 17, 16, 15, 14, 13, 12, 11," with the tone of his voice going from deep base to a lighter and lighter tone as the numbers got smaller and smaller. During this count down the patient presumably moved from trance closer and closer to normal waking consciousness. When he reached 10, however, Erickson would pause for an extra second or two and then, instead of going down to nine as the patient expected, Erickson suddenly switched back upward by continuing with, "11, 12, 13, 14..." with a correspondingly deeper tone to reinducing trance depth. Sure enough, most patients would later report they experienced "a jerk and turn about" as they suddenly felt themselves unexpectedly falling back into a deeper trance with a mild sense of confusion.

When questioned about it later many patients did not even know why they suddenly felt themselves propelled back into a deeper trance. Why did Erickson do this, quite apart for his own obvious interest in the clinical exploration of the trance experience? He explained that many patients who experienced hypnotherapy for the first time did not believe they were really in trance. Somehow their consciousness did not recognize its own altered state, Erickson claimed, until he "jerked it around a bit" to convince the patient that an altered state was indeed being experienced. As far as I am aware this simple and elegant approach to altering consciousness has never been documented scientifically. There could be no better documentation of our basic thesis that the essence of hypnotherapy is a utilization of the creative instability of the brain and mind precariously poised on the edge of chaos between the "attractors" we label as "altered states, attitudes, emotional complexes, expectations, images, obsessions, compulsions, symptoms, or habits" and the possibility of creating new and better states of "self-organization" and "identity."

"Attractor" is a new concept from self-organization theory that corresponds to the essence of what traditional hypnosis and depth psychology have always been concerned with: What is the hidden or archetypal source of those repetitive but puzzling aspects of mind and behavior that seem to have no rational meaning? Why do we make the same mistake in choosing the wrong job or partner or way of saying and doing things? Why do we repetitively experience bizarre fetishes, compulsions, addictions and habits we would rather not have? On the positive side we want to know what it is that drives some creative people to explore and make new discoveries that seem to have a similar theme in art, music and drama. "Oh, its a sign of an *unconscious complex*," we say from a traditional psychoanalytic point of view. Yes, precisely, but after one hundred years of psychoanalysis how shall we conceptualize "unconscious complexes" in terms of current leading edge thinking in mathematics, physics and biology? Our basic idea is that these unconscious complexes that are the source of the *irrational psycho-dynamics* of human experience and behavior in depth psychology correspond to the *nonlinear dynamics* of modern theory. "Unconscious complex" and "Archetypal pattern" in depth psychology means, very roughly, the same thing as "Attractor" in the nonlinear dynamics of chaos theory. What psychology gains by exploring this correspondence is the possibility of developing a new unifying theory and methodology for describing behavior on many levels in a quantitative manner.

Attractors describe the long-term behavior of dynamically changing systems in biology and the depths of the human psyche as well as social and cultural institutions. A person's life, for example, may be stuck at **fixed point attractor** (e.g. depression or other apparently fixed symptom). One may be caught up in a **periodic attractor** such as a bipolar mood disorder, or one may be going around in repetitive circles getting nowhere that are called **limit-cycle attractors**. The most interesting life is one that manifests **chaotic or strange attractors** which involve continually changing, novel experiences within a creative framework. Much more about the dynamics and meaning of these attractors later in this chapter.

The world of *nonlinear dynamics* introduces a new way of helping us understand and facilitate in a practical manner the critical phase transitions between the attractors that are the essence of creative hypnotherapeutic experience. These new concepts help us explore the dynamics of the new and unknown that shapes human experience as well as some of the very real limitations of human knowledge that the philosophy of science has made us aware of. It also exposes us to entirely new mathematical models and metaphors for exploring the more puzzling questions our evolving mind and behavior. The nonlinear dynamics we shall survey briefly in this chapter will provide us with the possibility of generating a fresh understanding of what we mean by the so-called "unconscious dynamics and complexes" within us as well as how the "forces of our psychosocial environment" interact with it to shape our cognition and behavior. So, what are these *nonlinear dynamics* that we should be so mindful of them (Ford, 1988)?

A Nonlinear World: The Source of Multiple Possibilities

Let us continue to compare and contrast the new nonlinear *dynamics* of self-organization theory with the traditional psycho-*dynamics* of hypnosis and depth psychology. It is interesting to note, for example, that on one level they are both qualitative and best expressed with pictures and intuitive diagrams without numbers of any sort. This qualitative approach to nonlinear dynamics, complexity and chaos theory is grounded in the *qualitative topological mathematics* invented by Poincaré. Poincaré's *topological* approach to *nonlinear mathematics* is "qualitative" because much of it uses pictures and intuition as well as numbers and mathematical equations to portray *dynamics* of how things change in virtually all the sciences from physics, chemistry and biology to ecology, psychology, sociology, economics and more.

It is precisely because *nonlinear dynamics* uses pictures that it can serve as a convenient and easily comprehensible foundation unifying all the sciences and humanities. While some mathematical formulae are placed in special boxes in this and later chapters, it is not entirely necessary for clinicians to understand the math to comprehend and apply the new dynamics of self-organization in a creative manner in their daily practice. An elementary understanding of some of the more important features of nonlinear dynamics will help clinicians read the scientific literature with a deeper understanding, however. In particular, it will help clinicians understand why many of their most interesting and intuitive psychodynamics seem to disappear when the researcher tries to validate them with experimental controls and statistics.

From this new point of view the basic conceptual problem between clinicians and researchers is the shadow that falls between the *clinical complexity of nonlinear reality* versus the *simple linear models* that have been used in research. Clinical psychodynamics attempts to formulate, often with literary metaphor, the nonlinear twists and turns of the mind and behavior. Most of the academic researcher's traditional methods, however, have been over-simplified with linear models. The linear net with a large regular mesh of statistical holes usually fails to capture the slippery nonlinear eels of human psychodynamics. It's just easier for researchers to deal with linear mathematical models where one and one make two, nothing more and nothing less. One cause leads to one proportional effect. But human affairs are never that simple!

Nonlinear mathematics, on the other hand, helps us understand the natural complexity of human affairs. It clarifies, for example, how one equation can have two or more solutions. Thus we say *nonlinearity is the source of multiple possibilities.* Sally Goerner, a past president of The Society for Chaos Theory In Psychology and the Life Sciences, expresses this well in the context of outlining the current nonlinear revolution from the classical theory of reductionism in science to an understanding of the constructive emergence of the new dynamics of relationships (inter-dependence) and communication in chaos theory.

But there is another concept that is also critical to the nonlinear revolution: inter-dependence. Popular chaos literature often confounds inter-dependence and nonlinearity, but actually they are not related. Nonlinearity has to do with proportionality. Inter-dependence has to do with whether or not two things mutually effect each other (or, in mathematical terms, whether or not the two are functions of one another). A conversation is an inter-dependent (also called interactive) communication between two people — both people are affected, and the exchange becomes a reciprocating mutual effect system. ... *Independent systems like linear systems are actually just useful idealizations. In the real world there are no truly linear systems and there are not truly independent systems — not even soliloquies. The notion of truly independent systems has also tended to create erroneous assumptions about how the world (vs. our models) works...*

How does this relate to a new vision of things? Classical approaches such as calculus and linear approximations first broke down when people tried to make their models more realistic, which meant including nonlinear inter-dependent aspects that had been there all along. The classic example of this is the three-body problem. Newton established the classical vision of precise prediction by applying equations of motion to the solar system. He did this using a simple two-body model; he looked at the effects of a massive body, the sun, on individual smaller bodies, the planets, taken one at a time. Chaos was first discovered when people tried to increase the precision of the model by adding the effects of just one more body (say, a moon or another planet). This model of the solar system is a three-body problem. The problem was that this minutely more sophisticated model could not be solved by approximation methods and had unexpected behaviors that did not appear in the two-body model. The three-body problem exhibits chaos. *Newtonian predictability is an illusion of the simpler model.* (Goerner, 1995, p. 20-21 in Robertson & Combs, 1995, Italics are ours.)

Linear relationships as illustrated in Box 2.1 are those where we can add up all the parts or their effects to get a sum that is a true picture of the whole. If Mary has one apple and Kathryn gives her one more then Mary has two apples. In more technical language we say that linear systems are those in which the output is additive or proportional to the input. In linear systems the whole really is *merely* the sum of the parts. Most relationships in psychology, however, are nonlinear systems where the whole is *more* than the sum of its parts. A little bit of extra motivation may help a person perform a task better but sooner or later there comes a *critical point* beyond which more motivation will make the person too hyper and decrease performance efficiency (Box 2.1). We touched on this idea before with Bak's concept of *self-organized criticality* and Erickson's counting approach that often exposed the critical moment of transition into and out of hypnotherapeutic trance. Nonlinear systems have special "critical" areas where a small change in values can lead to *disproportionate effects*. These disproportionate effects are usually visible and grab human attention because they are important in the real world. Our sensitivity to the nonlinear was obviously selected for in evolution because it has great survival value.

What is actually going on in these "disproportionate effects in nonlinear systems?" *Phase transitions in self-organization!* Think of water getting colder and colder. As water passes through a *critical transition zone* — 33° F to **32° F** to 31° F — it freezes. That is, it goes through a physical phase transition, a spontaneous self-organization into the crystallized form we call ice. Or think of the loss of this *self-organization* that takes place as water gets hotter and

hotter when it goes through the *critical phase transition zone* — 211°
F to **212° F** to 213° F — it begins to boil and turn into steam. From
ice to water to steam are critical areas of phase transition in one of
nature's most common nonlinear systems. As it moves from the
more organized solid state of ice to the fluid state of water to the
nebulous state of steam and finally water molecules floating through
the atmosphere it becomes less and less organized. It is important to
recognize that apart from God and the laws of nature there is nothing
telling water what to do. But is this merely an another example of the
relatively simple *physical laws* of nature that are in contrast to the
complexities of human psychology?

Nonlinear Dynamics in the Imagination of Depth Psychology

There is no programming involved or directed organizing action
in the physical and biological world. Nature follows its own inherent
laws of matter, energy and information. We would now like to understand the corresponding natural dynamics of human psychology and
culture. We no longer believe in the figments of our imagination
such as the lovely cherubs blowing the wind over land and sea from
the corners of ancient maps as an entirely satisfactory source of
causation in human destiny.

How can we create models of human experience just as we do
with the rest of the natural world? What is meant when we say that
science deals with *Dynamical Systems of interacting phenomena that
change over time?"* There usually are two basic features of Dynamical Systems: (1) a definition of the state of the *components* or
variables of the system that can often be pictured — such as the
continents and oceans on a map of the globe — and (2) a *rule or set
of rules* for describing the *dynamics* — the changing patterns of
behavior of the system as a whole over time. At its physical scientific
best the *components* of the dynamical system are well defined variables such as mass, size and temperature. The *rules* are usually
mathematical equations, particularly differential equations, that tell
how the dynamical system changes over time.

The Symptom Path to Enlightenment

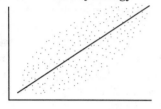
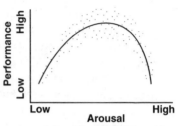

One way of understanding Self-Organized Dynamical Systems is to recognize how they are made up of one or more parts that can "communicate" with each other with feedback loops as illustrated below. These feedback loops form a kind of reciprocal or *circular causation* which is the fundamental process in the shift from linear to nonlinear dynamics.

A Linear system of causation that is almost impossible to find in the natural world. It usually is created artificially in the laboratory where it can be studied.

A Nonlinear feedback loop of Circular causation illustrating Poincaré's four stages of the Creative Cycle in Psychotherapy (From Rossi, 1972/1986/1998).

Virtually all living dynamical systems, of course, are made up of multiple feedback loops and circular causation that makes it very difficult to untangle the simple cause-effect relationships that are the ideal of linear mathematics. This is why we have such puzzlement about cause and effect in psychology — which came first the chicken or the egg? In fact, now we can say that whenever we are confronted with such a circular causation puzzle or paradox, we are entering the area of nonlinear dynamics! Even if we cannot entirely sort out, predict and control these circular dynamics, the nonlinear approach usually gives us a more realistic picture of the inherent individuality of Complex Adaptive Systems such as human personality and social structure.

Above all, the Complex Adaptive Systems approach to Self-Organization helps us avoid the tragic illusion of linear control with direct suggestion, programming, and manipulation of humans in personal and professional relationships. The implications for any ethical theory of suggestion and the facilitation of optimal change in therapeutic hypnosis are obvious.

But If suggestion is not the programming, manipulation and control over the experience and behavior of another, then what is it? Our tentative answer: *"hypnotherapeutic work" is the facilitation of the subject's own healing and problem solving capacities in the Self-Organizing Phase Transitions they courageously allow themselves to experience at their subjective Edge of Personal Chaos."* The Ideo-dynamic approaches to hypnotherapeutic work in Part Two of this book facilitate *creative experiences* where the ultimate locus of control remains within the subject rather than the therapist (Bloom, 1990) .

How are such dynamical systems expressed in the depth psychology that evolved out of the traditions of historical hypnosis? How do we learn to recognize the natural nonlinear dynamics of the human mind and affairs? There is much to imply that the nonlinear dynamics and phase transitions of physical nature are so important for evolutionary survival that our mind magnifies them by projecting anthropomorphic attributes and imagined motivations into them. You trip when walking along a forest path because a "nasty root caught your foot." A bad spirit or impulse from another more unconscious part of your personality made you do something silly or worse.

Most psychodynamics from psychoanalysis, in fact, could now be recognized and understood as efforts to conceptualize the subtle nonlinear dynamics and phase transitions of our inner experience. So subtle are these inner dynamics, in fact, that we may speculate that the subjective qualities, the *qualia of consciousness* (e.g. hot, cold, color, pain, trance etc.), may have evolved to enhance our sensitivity to nonlinear dynamics. The so-called "psychological mechanisms of defense," for example are actually significant nonlinear shifts and phase transitions of attention and behavior in dynamically ambiguous situations. Consciousness itself is the mind's most sensitive means of focusing our attention on shifting nonlinear dynamics of nature. This could be at least a partial answer to the "Hard Problem" of why the subjective experience (the "qualia" or qualities of consciousness) evolved and what their primary function are (Chambers, 1995; Güzeldere, 1995).

This hypothesis about the relationship between consciousness and the nonlinear gives us a new way of exploring Erwin Schrödinger's view of the nature of consciousness. Schrödinger, who was the pioneering physicist who created the wave equation of the basic dynamics of quantum theory in the 1920s, had a special view of consciousness that still stands as a challenge to current thinkers. "Schrödinger finds a specific role of consciousness in relation to biological evolution. He understands consciousness as the guardian of anomalies, unusual events and other novelties that are not yet shifted to unconscious knowledge and eventually to genetic memory." (Havel, 1996, p. 50). Recent research on the subjective experiences of consciousness in hypnosis has developed a methodology that may contribute to the future exploration of these hard questions about the necessity of consciousness in coping with the nonlinear dynamics of nature (Pekala, 1991, 1995 a & b).

We can see in this line of thinking an entirely new theory of the dynamics of science, art and the humanities as well as depth psychology. The delight children take in hearing stories and reading fairy tales could now be understood as a dim realization of their value as cautionary tales. What is actually of value here? Teaching tales (and are there really any other kind?) focus children's attention on learning about the illogical and irrational that are the manifestation of nonlinear dynamics in human experience. Of course, the same may be said of "adult entertainment" of all sorts and levels. Why do we spend so much time with the arts - myth and saga in literature, music, dance? Why sit transfixed in front of the TV tube and now the internet? We are continually entranced with the ever-changing nonlinear dynamics of stories that stir us to *wonder*. *Wonder* itself may be understood as an experience of being momentarily transfixed and hopefully transformed in a state of creative incubation coping with the nonlinear, irrational dynamics of life and nature.

Could the so-called *"irrational"* be irritating to many of us precisely because it is arousing us to an awareness of the *"nonlinear"* dynamics in human experience that are important for us to recognize for our survival? Our *irritation* with the *irrational* could be nature's way of arousing us to the dangerous nonlinearity's of things changing in the real world including our own consciousness and being. Having a mood or feeling about something still only partially understood is a natural manifestation of the psychobiological process of evolving consciousness. Having an *intuition* is a presentiment of a nonlinear, dynamical *emergence* in our experience. Likewise we can now recognize in fantasies and dreams the operation of the nonlinear dynamics of the psyche wherein we find ourselves unwittingly exploring and experimenting with the spontaneous emergence of new patterns of self-organization whether we like it or not. *Perhaps dreams themselves evolved as a way of confronting consciousness with subtle nonlinear dynamics of the unconscious that we would not otherwise know how to recognize.* We can easily recognize in all this the foundation for a new meta-psychology of hypnosis and psychoanalysis.

It seems paradoxical, but it is true that nonlinear dynamics which are the root of self-organization and the *emergence of the new* as well as the beautiful and meaningful in human experience, are also the root of the warped, weird and irrational. Until now the very term *emergence* has been associated with attitudes and states of mystical befuddlement. It is therefore time for us to seek a more precise understanding of the meaning of *emergence* for good or ill with the new tools of nonlinear dynamics on the creative edge of chaos.

The traditional classical approach of linear science, where natural aspects of the world are isolated and reduced to fragments that can be portrayed in simple models, breaks down when we study the emergence or synthesis of wholes on whatever level: a whole society, person, brain, neuron, energy flux or genetic matrix of an individual cell. The naturally nonlinear nature of the world consists of many layers of systems where everything seems to be related to everything else. It is precisely this nonlinear inter-relatedness and inter-dependence of everything that leads to the emergence of the new so that we say, "The whole is more than the sum of the parts." There is something so profoundly different in this shift to the nonlinear world view in all fields from math and physics to psyche that we expect it will continue to shatter many of our previous conceptions of nature as we get a better grasp of the new dynamics of self-organization. Here we will focus on what is probably the most important issue for deepening our understanding of psychotherapy in general and hypnotherapy in particular. Above all is the concept of mind and human experience perpetually in transition on the creative edge. As we shall soon understand, it is precisely here in the phase transition from one state to another that the essence of the creative inner work of hypnotherapy is to be found.

Life on the Creative Edge:
The New Dynamics of Human nature

In retrospect we now realize that we could view the entire 200 year history of hypnosis as an ever puzzling effort to understand the relations between strange, irrational (nonlinear!) dynamics of illness, normal health, creativity and extraordinary human capacities. In particular, we have always been interested in how to facilitate the transitions of mind and behavior. How to solve psychological problems and heal the ill? How to facilitate motivation and change from the lesser to better states of mind and behavior? Indeed, is it really possible to facilitate extraordinary abilities? While scientific research has led us to become ever more modest in these pursuits, there remains the ever tantalizing core of well documented case histories, as we reviewed in Chapter One, that continually spurs us on. If only we had a clue to the real dynamics of human nature, surely we could make vast improvements.

A clue! A clue! Aye, that's the issue! Does the new self-organization theory with its beckoning conception of life and mind computing at the *creative edge of chaos* really provide us with such a clue about the phase transitions associated with hypnotherapy? Today there are a number of different versions of the evolution of chaos and self-organization theory in providing new tools for understanding the phase transitions of physics, biology, mind and behavior. To gain an orientation to the fundamental questions involved it will be interesting to follow the discovery paths of three pioneers of our generation, Mitchell Feigenbaum, Stephen Wolfram and Christopher Langton. Each of these young men in their twenties made a fundamental discovery about the nonlinear transitions between order and chaos. Order and chaos have traditionally been considered as opposites in science as well as everyday life. Since biblical times chaos was understood to be the dark irrational face of nature where the rational, linear laws of light were lost or corrupted somehow. Each of our pioneers found evidence that a deeper understanding of nonlinear dynamics will be of essence for any breakthrough in understanding nature, life and mind in the future.

The recent fascination with the mathematics of nonlinear dynamics between order and chaos has its source in the fact that a very simple equation can have more than one answer. That is, some equations, as most of us found to our confusion in high school, have multiple solutions. Solving the simple equation $x^2 = 4$, for example, produces two solutions: $x = 2$ and $x = -2$. In Box 2.2 we extend the exploration of a similar quadratic equation in a process commonly called *feedback, recursion, or iteration* (Strogatz, 1994). While each of these three terms have different connotations, we use them here to describe a basic mathematical operation that is important for modeling life dynamics. You take the answer from the first equation and feed it back into the same equation to get a new answer and keep doing this over and over again. What do you find? Is there any lawfulness in this feedback process? Are there any patterns in the series of iterated answers you get or are they random? The surprising answer demonstrated by Mitchell Feigenbaum in 1975, while he was still a graduate student in physics, is that you will find both order and chaos in the pattern of answers you get to this simple process of iteration. That is, from the mathematical point of view, order and chaos are not opposites as is commonly supposed. They are both stages of a more general process of modeling complexity or self-organization in numbers and nature.

Box 2.2: Dynamics, Feedback and Iteration: Feigenbaum Bifurcation

The word *bifurcation* simply means a sudden change in the pattern or number of solutions to an equation as a parameter is varied. In the equation below the letter "a" represents a "control parameter" that acts as a kind of control valve on the expression of the equation. The value of the parameter at which the bifurcation takes place is called, logically enough, *a bifurcation point or bifurcation parameter value* (Nusse and York, 1994). A *bifurcation diagram* is made by plotting a parameter on one axis and a phase variable on another. The essential dynamics of a Feigenbaum bifurcation diagram is illustrated by a branching tree where each branch represents an answer or "choice" in the series of solutions to an equation obtained by a process of feedback or iteration. *Choice?* Does this have anything to do with human choice? Mathematical bifurcation is a natural consequence of the way numbers work with feedback or iteration. This model helps us understand how many physical and chemical systems in nature and virtually all complex biological and psychological systems involve multiple processes of feedback. Since mind and behavior obviously utilize information feedback on many levels we naturally wonder whether such bifurcation models can illustrate anything interesting about human choice points on conscious or unconscious levels.

That is the controversial question that we would like to explore with one of the most well known equations used to demonstrate nonlinear dynamics: the logistic equation that was originally proposed as a model of population dynamics where feedback prevents populations of bacteria, plants and animals from growing infinitely because of environmental limitations of food supplies and space as well as the presence of predators. Can the logistic equation also be used to illustrate any facets of the population dynamics of ideas, awareness or consciousness? In the logistic equation

$$x_1 = a \, x_0 \, (1 - x_0)$$

the initial value (x_0) is fed back into the equation to get first solution (x_1). This first solution is then fed back into the equation to get the second solution x_2 as shown below.

$$x_2 = a \, x_1 \, (1 - x_1)$$

Continuing this feed back process leads us to a series of solutions that are illustrated in the bifurcation diagram illustrated below. The first long stem coming down from the top represents a series of solutions that then branches or "bifurcates" as indicated and from each of these two branches we see two more bifurcating again and so on. This is called the "period-doubling regime" on the path to chaos. Notice that the branches get shorter and shorter as they move down until a threshold is finally reached, that is now called the *Feigenbaum point*, after the fourth bifurcation where the system falls into chaos illustrated as the dark but structured smudge. There is a ratio that quantifies the period doubling path to chaos that is found to be true of many different equations when they are iterated. This ratio is called *Feigenbaum's Constant* which converges to a value of 4.6692... The ratio obtained is made up of the lengths of any two successive branches. The *Feigenbaum's Constant* is now regarded as important in dynamics theory as the number Pi is to geometry.

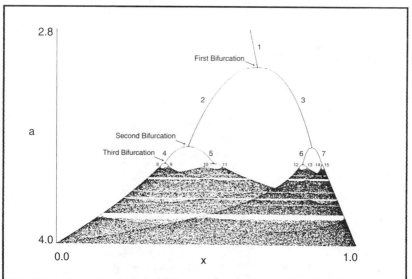

This Illustration of the Logistic bifurcation diagram was made with *Dynamics* software by Nusse and York (1994).

While the Feigenbaum point marks the onset of "deterministic chaos," it is not really random. *Deterministic Chaos only looks random because of the limitations of human perception.* If we zoom in on any small portion of the diagram with a computer we will find that the overall picture is reproduced again in the smaller portion that we blow up. This is called the *"fractal"* or *"self-similar"* aspect of the equation on all scales. Notice that when we look at the diagram we can easily see about seven paths clearly as labeled. If you are really talented you might spot more, as many as 15, if you count the next lower bifurcating level carefully. But after that the distribution of paths seems to be a chaotic smudge with some vague structure and blank spaces on from about the middle to the bottom of the diagram. Kihlstrom (1980) found that 15 items was the upper limit for post-hypnotic memory in low as well as highly susceptible hypnotic subjects but they achieved that level of performance differently.

A number of classical studies in psychology confirm that seven units (plus or minus two) is, in fact, the usual limit of human perception (Miller, 1956). Sperling (1960), for example, found that people could remember about seven letters over a 1-second interval. He called this the *iconic trace.* Neisser (1967) found that the auditory trance, which he called *echoic memory,* had similar characteristics. Recall how telephone numbers in most developed areas also have seven digits. Is the number seven as a band-width in human sensory-perceptual studies and the seven paths we can see easily in the bifurcation diagram simply a coincidence? Or is it another example of the seemingly unreasonable effectiveness of mathematics in modeling human experience in the most unexpected ways? Research extended to other sensory and perceptual levels of human experiencing is now needed to confirm the relevance of the number seven and the Feigenbaum point in human awareness.

Does the birfucating diagram illustrate anything else of interest about human awareness and perhaps conscious-unconscious dynamics in general? Notice the "bubbles" that appear in the bifurcating diagram below for the more complicated two variable equations of the Henon system.

$$(x,y) \longrightarrow (1.25 - x^2 + ay, x)$$

This illustration of the Henon bifurcation diagram was made with *Dynamics* software by Nusse and York (1994).

Quite apart from the mathematical rational for these bubbles which is beyond the scope of this volume, why do such bubbles appear? To continue our metaphor, are these bubbles "islands of consciousness or awareness" surrounded by deterministic chaos that human perception is too limited to discern clearly? Do the bubbles represent a few groups or levels of the laws of nature that we can discern in the vaster darkness that surrounds human understanding. The physicist John Archibald Wheeler (1994) has described such limitations in our perceptions of the laws of nature and how we can cope with them. The pioneering depth psychologist Carl Jung has described "islands of consciousness within the unconscious" that might be modeled by these bubbles. One can only wonder whether these bubbles are akin to dreams, fantasies and creative inspirations that seem to bubble up spontaneously from the nonlinear dynamics of the unconscious.

Ernest Hilgard (Hilgard and Hilgard, 1983) reports experimental research in hypnosis that provides evidence for a "hidden observer" that is able to verbally report on what is being experienced (e.g. pain) on a deeper level even when the conscious personality does not report the experience of pain. Is this hidden observer and, perhaps more generally, the dissociated experiences of multiple personality being illustrated in the bubbles in the birfuraction diagrams? Is not pain and, indeed, all "symptoms" to be understood as forms of *in*formation, messages or awareness that bubbles up from the unconscious (deterministically chaotic) levels of the body?

Has consciousness itself evolved as a practical method of coping with the deterministic chaos of living experience? Could this be part of the answer to the "hard question" of why consciousness has evolved (see the special issue of the *Journal of Consciousness Studies,* vol. 2, 3, 1995 devoted to "Explaining Consciousness — The Hard Problem). Consciousness, according to this intuition, is a sort of amplifying lens or mirror that allows us to sort out or linearize various aspects of nonlinear experience that are necessary for survival.

At present we can only speculate about whether the significance of the number seven in gambling and many mantic and mystical belief systems could have the same source in the limitations in our sensory-perceptual-cognitive awareness that may be illustrated in the bifurcation diagrams. Seven items are about as much as we usually can hold in consciousness so we feel we know them and we are comfortable with them. When consciousness has to juggle more than seven items, dimensions or levels, understanding seems to become chaotic, dark, fearful, *unconscious* and perhaps *unreal* though we may have dim *intuitions* of other levels that seem to be in the realm of *prophesy.* What are the mathematical implications and predictions of the bifurcation diagrams regarding human experience that could be tested experimentally? The problem is that apart from the types of intuitions reported here, at the present time the connection between the bifurcating diagrams and human experience is not well understood but remains an area of pioneering research (Rössler 1992 a &b; Vallacher and Nowak, 1994; Guastello, 1995). In the second half of this volume we will explore practical approaches to utilizing the natural bifurcations (or dissociations) of hypnotherapeutic experience to facilitate creative choice points in problem solving and healing.

Even more surprising was the discovery that there is a well defined path or route which leads from order to chaos that is described as *"universal"* (Feigenbaum, 1980). It is universal because the same abrupt changes between order and chaos, usually called *"bifurca-tions,"* can be found in many apparently different equations and processes of nature. When the series of iterated answers to different equations are graphed they all have features in common with the Feigenbaum diagram illustrated in Box 2.2. Peitgen, Jürgens & Saupe (1992, p. 587) have said, "The Feigenbaum diagram has become the most important icon of chaos theory. It will most likely be an image which will remain as a landmark of the scientific progress of this century."

The universality in the appearance of the Feigenbaum numbers in many complex systems of a different nature allows the prediction of the onset of turbulence in dripping faucets as well as torrential rivers, the oscillations of liquid helium, electric circuits and the fluctuations of insect and animal populations (Shaw, 1984). There are a number of fascinating though highly speculative views about the possible significance of the *Feigenbaum Point* for psychology, sociology and the humanities in general. Merry (1995, p. 37) suggests, for example, that the *Feigenbaum Point* is where systems cascade into chaos *"where infinite choices create a situation in which freedom has no more meaning."*

Could we generalize this to say that emotions, imagery, behavior and cognition and, yes, even psychosomatic symptoms that have lost their meaning have somehow fallen into the chaotic regime within "experiential space" where even our sense of reality teeters off the edge of understanding or rationality? Does this suggest that beyond the *Feigenbaum Point* inner experience may fall into a sense of "unreality" where we lose our sense of self-control? Put another way, does the Feigenbaum point signal the division between *primary process* (irrational) versus the *secondary processes* (*rational, ego processes*) as defined in psychoanalysis? In this sense, would the Feigenbaum point represent the limit of our sense of voluntary ego control over our mental experience and behavior? If highly hypnotizable subjects report a sense of *involuntaryness* in their experience and behavior does that mean they have moved toward the creative edge of the nonlinear dynamics of a chaotic realm (the unconscious) wherein they cannot predict what they will experience next? Would this be equivalent to saying they are on a creative edge between the unconscious and conscious where problem solving and healing might take place that is usually outside their normal range of self-help? At the present time we have no answers to these fascinating questions.

The physicist uses the route to chaos as a way of describing turbulence in nature (fast moving water flowing over rocks, air turbulence behind an airplane etc.). Do we have another analogy here between physics and psychology by saying that *the subjective experience of confusion or disorientation is the turbulence of the mind moving past the Feigenbaum point into chaos?* How would we actually measure such a *Feigenbaum Points* of inner experience? We could go on and on with such questions that are intuitively provocative but which we at present do not know how to answer. Until we develop new methodologies to test hypotheses about the relationship between the mathematical formalisms of chaos theory and human experience we really do not have a new science of the dynamics of human nature. We still do not know whether the *Feigenbaum Point* is simply a provocative metaphor for psychology or a major breakthrough into the possibility of formulating new mathematical models of human experience with conceptual as well as predictive power.

What other intuitions do we have that the nonlinear dynamics of the chaotic regime of the brain-mind make up what we call the "unconscious?" Is this why during those brief moments of introspection as we are falling asleep or awakening we occasionally glimpse what from our conscious perspective seems to be a confused plethora of inchoate images, feelings, thoughts and what not? Are there circumstances when consciousness gets caught in the chaotic realm so that the person experiences a "dissociation" and/or a sense of "identity loss?" Is this what some cultural and spiritual traditions call a "loss of soul?" These concepts are so new that we will need to stretch our imagination to learn how we can use them in hypnotherapy and personality dynamics. Obviously this will be a rich area for exploring new ways of reconceptualizing the foundation of hypnosis and psychotherapy from the same universal principles that govern other complex systems in mathematics, physics, biology and ecology.

One path to exploring these dynamics is illustrated by the work of Stephen Wolfram. In the 1970's he was studying at the Princeton Institute for Advanced Study where he wondered how one could isolate and explore the most basic rules and dynamics for generating archetypal patterns or complex systems on a computer. That is, are there general rules that lead to the formation of *adaptive complex systems*? Are there general rules, for example, at the molecular-genetic level within the cell that also govern the complexity of neural networks in brain, the dynamics of personality as well as the total ecological system of a planet?

Wolfram made the question manageable by investigating the simplest processes possible, which were called "cellular automata," in a computer. Cellular automata are essentially short programs that use simple rules of how basic elements or creatures, usually in the form of pixels of light on a computer screen, will interact together to create more complex forms. It is important to understand that the computer programmer does not know ahead of time just what complex forms will *emerge*. As in the famous "Game of Life" invented by the English mathematician Conway, the programmer is usually surprised by the structures and movements that evolve in a deterministic but unpredictable way. The game of life is precisely determined by the rules, but the behavior that evolves spontaneously from the rule is so unexpected that at least one investigator has called it "The Science of Surprise" (Casti, 1994). Remember this "Science of Surprise!" In the second half of this volume "surprise" will be found to be one of the most important features of genuinely creative hypnotherapeutic responses to the new non-verbal "ideodynamic" approaches that are introduced.

Wolfram found that regardless of the specific rules he programmed into his computer, only four classes of structure, pattern, behavior or response evolved over time. They are similar to the archetypal patterns described above as solutions to nonlinear equations. In Class I the structures would evolve for a little while and then either disappear or fall into a fixed, static and homogeneous state; they are said to possess "fixed points." In Class II the structures evolve into a fixed finite size, forming patterns that repeat themselves indefinitely; they are called "periodic or limit cycles." Class III structures are called "chaotic" because, while they are precisely determined by the rules, they never repeat their pattern exactly; they are also called "strange or chaotic attractors." While these first three classes were known from previous work, Wolfram recognized the great significance of Class IV complex structures that grow, evolve, reshuffle and contract in very complex irregular patterns. These Class IV structures evolve very long lived "transients," such as the "gliders" found in "The Game of Life" that never seem to settle down.

Class IV structures are therefore somewhat between the Class II patterns that freeze into fixed structures or the same repeated (periodic) behavior, on the one hand, and the total chaos of Class III behavior on the other. These class IV patterns of complex dynamics are now called "Living on the edge of chaos." This seminal idea emerged in published form initially in Christopher Langton's 1986 paper, Studying Artificial Life with cellular Automata" where he wrote of "the onset of chaos" and in Norman Packard's 1988 paper, "Adaptation Toward the Edge of Chaos."

Box 2.3: The Logistic Path to Chaos and Self-Organization

It probably will come as a profound relief to most readers to learn that when we graph the series of iterated or feedback solutions of even simple formulas, such as the logistic equation, that model complex adaptive systems in physics, chemistry, biology and the psychosocial sciences, they are found to exhibit only three or four basic patterns. These patterns are so fundamental that they have been called "archetypal dynamics" of nature. Because these mathematical models are abstractions, they are never seen in a pure form in nature. They are usually seen with many variations and combinations complicated by "noise" as they interact with all sorts of natural forces. Here is an illustration of four stages of the logistic equation written with slightly different notation from Box 2.2 where its bifurcation dynamics were illustrated. The parameter **"a"** functions like a control knob whose changing values lead the logistic equation through a series of at least four stages from a fixed point to limit cycles and quasi-periodicity to chaotic behavior.

$$x_{i+1} = a x_i (1 - x_i), \ 0 < a < 4$$

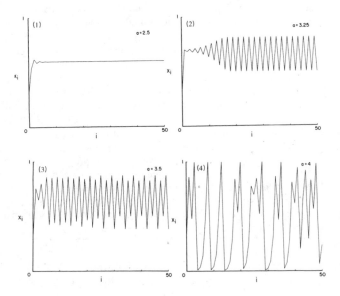

Time series illustrating solutions of the logistic equation as the parameter "a" is varied: (1) A fixed point or steady state a=2.5; (2) a cycle of period two at a=3.25; (3) a cycle of period four at a=3.5; (4) chaos at a= 4.

(1) *The Fixed Point or Steady State Attractor* is typical of all systems that move toward a final resting place. A rock that rolls down a cliff and then comes to a final resting place on the bottom has reached a fixed point. Biological systems, on the other hand, do not really have any such final fixed point resting state except death. Some textbooks, however, refer to the relatively constant internal milieu of biological systems that we call *homeostasis* as a steady state that is supposed to be

ideal for maintaining life. The relatively constant steady state of *blood pressure*, for example, that is usually restored to equilibrium after a perturbation (any disturbance) achieves a steady state. Sometimes *rigid or fixed symptoms* and *stereotyped behaviors* have been called steady state attractors.

(2) *The Periodic or Limit Cycle Attractor* is most common in biological and ecological systems with obvious rhythms: predator-prey oscillations in the relative number of rabbits and foxes over many seasons, for example. The circadian rhythms of waking and sleeping; heart beat; respiration; digestion and the pulsate flow of most hormones are all approximately or *relatively periodic*. As we will find in Chapter Four, however, when examined closely most of these rhythms are actually *quasi-periodic* or *chaotic*. The nonlinear dynamics of these rhythmical systems introduces a flexibility into living systems that is a fundamental aspect of their adaptive complexity. When adaptive complexity breaks down, for whatever reason, Glass and Mackey (1988) describe *the shift from normal to abnormal temporal biological organization as a dynamical disease*. From this point of view psychosomatic dysfunctions would be signals of a breakdown in psychobiological communication that reduces it from the more complex chaotic attractors (type 4 described below) to the more simple periodic or limit cycle attractors.

(3) *The Quasi-periodic Cycle Attractor* are found when two or more rhythms of different periods interact to produce oscillations that never repeat themselves exactly: many physical systems such as two coupled pendulum, the biological systems mentioned above and the brain itself (Albano et al., 1987) move in and out of quasi-periodicity. Vallacher and Nowak (1994) note that social attitudes and group dynamics can shift in a manner that may be periodic, quasi-periodic or chaotic.

(4) *The Chaotic or Strange Attractor* is the most interesting nonlinear dynamic found in nature: the weather; fluid turbulence; electric circuits; chemical systems; molecular dynamics at the cellular-genetic level; predator-prey oscillations under certain environmental conditions; social dynamics in animals and humans under most conditions; the personal dynamics mind, personality, emotions and behavior under all conditions. Merry (1995) has described how identifying and coping with the growing complexity and intensifying deterministic chaos of the modern world is the most basic challenge of biological and social evolution.

Christopher Langton was a pioneer who helped organize the first conference on complex systems and artificial life at the newly developing Santa Fe Institute, even before he got his Ph.D. He wanted to know the what, how and why of Wolfram's classes of computer automaton behavior. Was it all simply abstract mathematics and computer patterns or could it be related to the real world? Langton, of course, was aware that simple *parameters* in dynamical system could shift the systems behavior in wondrous ways. He began to explore the effects of changing what he called the "lambda parameter" on the evolution of Wolfram's classes of computer creature behavior. The biochemist, Roger Lewin, described Chris Langton's moment of discovery in this way.

By accident, Chris had honed straight in on Wolfram's class four region, the region where maximum computational capability resides ... Chris referred to this no-man's-land as "the onset of chaos." But, he realized, this wasn't just an unreal, Alice in Wonderland world. It was the real world. He began to see the switch from order to chaotic regimes in dynamical systems as analogous with phase transitions in physical systems, the switch from one state to another; from the solid state to the gaseous state, for instance, perhaps with a fluid intermediate state. The notion of analogous phenomenology between universal computing and these physical phase transitions wormed its way into Chris's mind. Here was a shift from abstract computation to the reality of the physical world. (Lewin, 1992, p. 50-51)

Langton was now able to conceptualize the world of mathematics and computer automata as well as physics and biology as nature "computing" on the narrow edge of chaos. Of special interest for our study of the state transitions of consciousness and being in hypnotherapy was Langton's study of *first and second order phase transitions* in his "Life at the Edge of Chaos" paper (Langton, 1992). He formulates the basic question and answer in this way.

In living systems, a dynamics of information has gained control over the dynamics of energy, which determines the behavior of most non-living systems. How has this domestication of the brawn of energy to the will of information come to pass? (Langton, 1992, p. 41)... We expect that information processing can emerge spontaneously and come to dominate the dynamics of a physical system in the *vicinity of a critical phase transition*. (Langton, 1992, p. 81. Ital. are ours.)

First order phase transitions are those most commonly found in physical systems. First order transitions take place fairly quickly at a *critical phase transition point* as described above by Bak, for example, in earth quakes and the stock market. Water freezes all at once at 32° F, for example, or turns into steam at 212° F. Temperature is a control parameter that forces the water molecules to make a quick choice between the relatively firm order of ice, the more fluid order of water or the relative chaos of steam.

Second order phase transitions are much less common in purely physical systems. Second order phase transitions are slower as is characteristic of many life processes where the behavior of molecules seems to combine order and chaos. The physicist Waldrop describes Langton's insights about the transition zone between order and chaos when freezing takes place with an ever-changing dance of submicroscopic arms and fractal filaments of ice throughout water at 32° F in this way.

Order and chaos intertwine in a complex, ever-changing dance of submicroscopic arms and fractal filaments. The largest ordered structures propagate their fingers across the material for arbitrarily long distances and last for an arbitrarily long time. And nothing ever really settles down.

Langton was electrified when he found this: *"There* was the critical connection! *There* was the analog to Wolfram's Class IV!" It was all there. The propagating, glider-like "extended transients," the dynamics that took forever to settle down, the intricate dance of structures that grew and split and recombined with eternally surprising complexity — it practically defined a second-order phase transition. (Waldrop, 1992, p. 230)

Langton describes the deep relations between second-order phase transitions in nonlinear mathematics and computation in ways that seem to suggest that they may be characteristic of the psychodynamics of consciousness and personality as well.

First, the existence of computability classes is explained by the fact that the phase transition separates the space of computations into an ordered and a disordered regime, which we refer to as the halting and the non-halting computations, respectively.

Second, the dynamics in the vicinity of a second-order transition gives rise to the phenomenon of *critical slowing down*, and therefore the transients along the way to ultimately periodic (halting) behavior can diverge to infinity, which explains the existence of undecidability, as characterized by Turing's famous Halting Problem.

Alan Turing's famous halting problem has to do with the fundamental reality of undecidability in human experience. As a logician of genius he found that there is an unresolvable uncertainty about whether a computer will ever stop or halt in trying to solve some problems. It turns out that it is impossible to predict whether or not a computer will ever halt even when it is given very simple programs. This was one of the original proofs of the idea that there are important limits on our ability to predict the behavior of deterministic systems as well as to prove things with logic (Robinson, 1995). *The only way to find out is to try it out.* Does this not seem similar to many dilemmas of human experience?

I hypothesize that Turing's halting problem may provide us with mathematical models of our inability to predict human mental processes and behavior. As such these models become an important rational for the development of the ideodynamic, approaches to hypnotherapeutic work presented in the second half of this volume. *The important idea is that it is impossible to expect the psychotherapist to know how to suggest, program or predict exactly what is right for the patient.* The therapist's role is to engage patients in genuinely creative ideodynamic experiences *live* wherein patients can experience the natural but essentially unpredictable evolution of their own consciousness and behavior. From another perspective this can be seen as a deeper rational for what Carl Rogers (1980) called "client-centered therapy."

Kelso, (1995, p. 133) has emphasized how *critical slowing down* is a predictor of upcoming nonlinear transitions on many of levels of human sensory-perceptual experience. In hypnotherapeutic work the most obvious manifestation of *critical slowing down* may be the general slowing of the psychomotor behavior that is observed during hypnotic induction. Is the phenomenon that the hypnotherapist calls *"relaxation"* an example of dynamical *critical slowing down* during the moment of *psychological phase transition* to the so-called hypnotic state? In Chapter Six I will offer some speculations on the significance of what appears to be an initial increase in eyelid fluctuations and then a critical slowing down during hypnotic induction.

Critical slowing down in the vicinity of second order phase transitions may thus be a new way of signaling the shifts in consciousness and problem solving that are so typical of hypnotherapeutic work. For now it is important to learn to recognize some of the different levels of critical phase transitions ranging from mathematics to nature, life and mind that are on the leading edge of research today (Langton, 1989; Langton et al. 1992; Langton, 1995).

Dynamical Systems of Nonlinear Mathematics:
Order ➤ "Complexity" ➤ Chaos

Wolfram's Computer Cellular Automata Classes:
I. Fixed Point ➤ II. Periodic ➤ IV. "Complex" ➤ III. Chaotic

Langton's Physics of Transition of Matter
Solid ➤ "Phase Transition" ➤ Fluid

Turing's Undecidability Theorem in Computation
Halting ➤ "Undecidable" ➤ Non-halting

Evolution Computing on the Edge of Chaos:
Too static ➤ "Life/Intelligence" ➤ Too noisy

The concept that *evolution* is a process of "life" and "intelligence" self-organizing itself by *"computing on the edge of chaos"* is a numinous idea that deeply motivates a crowd of creative workers at the Santa Fe Institute Studies in the Sciences of Complexity in New Mexico (Kauffman, 1995; Langton, 1989, 1995; Zurek, 1990). This is a deep vision of life precariously balanced on the edge of chaos, always in danger of falling off into too much order and rigidity on the one hand, and too much chaos on the other. Langton's and Packard's original versions of optimizing computation or creative adaptation and change at the edge of chaos has been challenged by others (Coveney and Highfield, 1995; Crutchfield and Young, K.,1990; Mitchell, Crutchfield, & Hraber, 1994) and adapted in different ways (Kaufmann, 1994, 1995; Kelso, 1995: Kruse and Stadler, 1990) but it remains as a central concept in the dynamics of self-organization theory on many levels from the origin of life in *autocatalytic molecular systems* to the evolution of genes, cells and the operation of the human brain, mind and behavior. Kauffman (1994, p. 101) summarizes its current status with this statement.

> Order is not the result of [evolutionary] selection alone. Perhaps most intriguing is the complex regime located at the phase transition between order and chaos. It is an interesting speculation that systems in the complex regime can carry out and coordinate the most complex behavior, can adapt most readily, can build the most useful models of their environments. The bold working hypothesis is that Complex Adaptive Systems adapt to and on the edge of chaos. The more general question is whether Complex Adaptive Systems evolve to a preferred position on the order-chaos axis, perhaps within the ordered regime near the edge of chaos.

In the next chapter we will present further evidence that suggests that evolution itself is this process of life learning how to organize more and more of its own parameters, so that it has a better chance of maintaining a creative existence on the edge of deterministic chaos.

The Growth Process in Dreams and Psychotherapy

How is this related to the process of transition, change, adaptation, growth, creativity and synthesis in psychotherapy? In the previous chapter we cited examples of the earliest forms of psychotherapy in the rituals of exorcism and Mesmerism wherein it appears, in retrospect, as if emotional crises and catharsis were the high point of extreme stress and transition that we would today recognize as "adapting (computing or problem solving) on the edge of chaos." In 1972 I outlined and illustrated clinical examples of Buck's view that "mental problems and developmental blocks" were manifestations of a transition phase in the evolution of consciousness. The drama of our dreams and "psychological dysfunctions" were conceptualized as "symptoms of development" that I now recognize as essentially similar to the basic ideas of this chapter (Rossi, 1972/1986/1998).

Developmental Blocks➔ Symptoms of Development ➔
Enlightening Experience

In this early paradigm I described psychological problems ranging from depression, confusion and anxiety to dissociation, a sense of unreality and even acute psychosis as symptoms of development that could be conceptualized as transition states to original experiences of mind. Such transitional psychological experience, with good fortune and the help of creatively oriented psychotherapy, could lead to new patterns of identity and behavior. Poincaré's four stages of the creative cycle was used as a model for growth in psychotherapy. This path to original experience and self-creation was described by Carl Jung as the process of *"individuation."* More recently Guastello (1995, p. 328), an industrial psychologist and current president of the Society for Chaos Theory in Psychology and the Life Sciences, summarized the relationship between creativity and chaos as follows.

> Virtually all known process dynamics concerning creativity and innovation are nonlinear: insight and tenacity, output over a professional life span, output over a professional cross section, the evolution of the creative personality, the impact of feedback channels in a group or organizational context, the economic assimilation of creative work, and organizational response to an already chaotic environment. Chaos and creativity have a mutual causation structure: Chaos promotes creativity. Creativity is a self-organizational process that reduces complexity. Creative work induces more chaos in the social and economic environment. Thus creative systems exist at the edge of chaos.

On a deeper level these creative chaotological dynamics of the evolution of personality are akin to what C. G. Jung called the *transcendent function*: the psychosynthetic activity of integrating unconscious and conscious dynamics in the process of individuation. Some recent proposals for integrating the dynamics of the conscious and unconscious, the rational and irrational, the linear and nonlinear are outlined in Box 2.4. This is the broad background for a host of new ideo-*dynamic* approaches to facilitating the transitional states on the edge of chaos from illness to health, *The Symptom Path to Enlightenment,* that will be presented in Part Two of this book.

The Symptom Path to Enlightenment

Box 2.4: **Conscious and Unconscious, Rational and Irrational, Linear and Nonlinear.**

Another fascinating historical parallel between the psychodynamics of depth psychology and the nonlinear dynamics of Chaos Theory is in their efforts to bridge the great polarities of human experience. These polarities have been described in a variety of ways in different cultural traditions as: the Conscious vs. Unconscious; the Rational vs. Irrational; the Apollonian vs. Dionysian; the Yang vs. Yin; and now the Linear vs. Nonlinear.

In Freud's psychodynamics the relation between the conscious and unconscious, the ego and the id, was epitomized by the *psychoanalytic mechanisms of defense* such as rationalization, repression, displacement, projection and sublimation (Freud, 1946). For Jung the relationship between the conscious and unconscious was described as the transcendent function defined in this way.

"There is nothing mysterious or metaphysical about the term 'transcendent function.' It means a psychological function comparable in its way to a mathematical function of the same name, which is a function of real and imaginary numbers. The psychological 'transcendent function' arises from the union of conscious and unconscious contents." (Jung, 1960, p. 69).

For Jung the transcendent function was mediated by a special form of self-confrontation via inner imagery and dialogue that he called *"Active Imagination."* Prior to these efforts from depth psychology were the labors of philosophers and logicians such as George Boole, who laid the groundwork for modern symbolic logic with his celebrated treatise *"An Investigation of the Laws of Thought on Which Are Founded the Mathematical Theories of Logic and Probability,"* (Boole, 1854/1958). Boole formulated the laws of the linear and rational thought as they are perceived in conscious human experience. What he left out was the nonlinear and irrational of human experience, precisely what is of most interest in portraying the emergence of the self-organizing processes of nature and mind. Our focus on nonlinear dynamics is thus an approach to formulating the laws of the irrational in human experience to complement Boole's focus on the laws of rational logic.

I propose that the nonlinear dynamics of human experience are most readily observed in transition between the unconscious and consciousness that we describe as the dreams (rapid eye-movement sleep) at night as well as the semi-autonomous experience of fantasy when we are awake. I outlined the subjective experiences of psychological growth and signs of the evolution of consciousness in dreams in about two dozen hypotheses that are described and illustrated with clinical case material elsewhere (Rossi, 1972/1986/1998). More recently a number of investigators have developed new systems of bridging the gap between the rational and irrational on the borderline between psychology and nonlinear science. J. & M. Shawe-Taylor (1996), for example, have described consciousness as a linear phenomenon. From our perspective their theory provides an opportunity to deepen our understanding of at least one major function of consciousness: mediating the transition between the nonlinear and the linear. It is close to what Freud called "rationalization." The Shawe-Taylor theory is that the essential function of consciousness is to transform the nonlinear dynamics of the unconscious into a linear conscious system of relationships. Why has this transformation evolved in nature? Recall that the long term behavior of nonlinear systems is very difficult or impossible to predict.

Consciousness has the Herculean task of remapping, transducing, transforming or reframing, if you will, the natural nonlinear dynamics of our unconscious physical and biological nature into the linear, rational and at least somewhat more predictable dynamics of our subjective experience .

Consciousness, of course, is only partially successful in this heroic task. As we all know, we are continuously engaged in an unceasing Sisyphean struggle to make sense of the world. It is all to easy to fall into the irrational and chaos in the negative sense of unpredictability. What is most interesting about the Shawe-Taylor theory of the *linearization function of consciousness* is the evidence they marshal for it from research on (1) artificial neural networks in neuroscience and (2) Aaron Beck's (1976) version of Cognitive Therapy. In brief they conceptualize Beck's Cognitive Therapy as an exercise in facilitating the linearization function of consciousness in correcting the errors and unpredictability of the nonlinear dynamics of nature and mind.

The linearization function of consciousness by J.M. Shawe-Taylor (1996) is illustrated in the following four conceptual graphs of the nonlinear "errors" the mind is prone to.

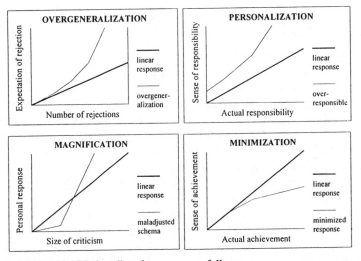

Beck (1987, 155-156) describes these errors as follows:

There are a number of typical conceptual or inferential errors found in psychopathology.

Selective abstraction consists of focusing on a set of details taken out of context. In this process the person may ignore salient features of the situation and conceptualize the entire experience on the basis of a single set of data. Thus the depressed patient may single out the negative and exclude the positive aspects of a situation, the anxious person may focus exclusively on symbols of danger, and the paranoid person may selectively extract instances of abuse.

Arbitrary inference is the process of drawing a conclusion without evidence to support it, or in face of evidence which is contrary to it. *Overgeneralization* is the process of using a single incident to draw general conclusions considered operative across all situations. *Magnification and minimization* refer to the polarized assessment of events, skills etc. For example, a patient may magnify the difficulty of a task and minimize his ability to accomplish it. *Personalization* is the tendency to relate external events to oneself when there is no basis for making such connections. *Dichotomous thinking* refers to the patient's tendency to interpret on an either-or, black-and-white basis. The depressed person sees himself exclusively as competent or incompetent, as a success or failure.

How to correct such "errors" of the natural nonlinear dynamics of mind is perhaps one of the most important basic issues distinguishing the various schools of psychotherapy. In Part Two of this book we will explore how therapists can engage many of the classical techniques of traditional hypnotherapy within a new context of a highly permissive, non-directive approach to the nonlinear but highly creative dynamics of human experience.

Strange Attractors and The New Dynamics Of Human Nature

The new dynamics of human nature take a special direction in the approach of Otto Rössler who explores how dynamical systems of strange attractors may be studied as models of self-organization in the real world on all levels from social interaction and mind to the molecular. Being a professor of Theoretical Chemistry at the University of Tübingen in Germany, Rössler's early work focused on the molecular and biological levels. How are energy, structure and information related? Rössler used the metaphor of a wind sock on an airfield to determine the direction of the wind. As the wind blows in, it is trapped so that a portion of its energy is converted into useful information for an observer. The energy of the wind becomes self-organized into doing useful work and evolving information on all levels from the quantum to the human brain (Rössler, 1994 a). Otto Rössler developed the idea that the squeezing and folding dynamics of strange attractors could serve as mathematical models of how real molecules evolve into *autocatalytic sets* of self-organizing biological systems that are at the origin of life (Rössler, 1971, 1983). Autocatalysis is a *cooperative cycle* of interactions between molecules that facilitate (catalyze) each other's formation in a cyclic manner that is characteristic of life. As noted above, complex cycles are one of the major archetypal forms of strange attractors in which the nonlinear dynamics of life is manifest.

Eigen then coined the term *"hypercycle"* for the next essential stage in the evolution of life whereby a small circle of genes spontaneously fall into a fortuitous "replication cycle over which a catalytic feedback loop is superposed" (Eigen and Winkler-Oswatitsch,1992). This is the beginning of *"cooperative"* behavior that made replication, the conservation of information and the perpetual evolution of higher life forms possible (Eigen, 1971; Eigen and Schuster, 1977; Eigen and Winkler, 1981). We will explore this fundamental role of attractors in the evolution and creative transformations of information in the basic rhythms of life processes in the next two chapters where they will lay the foundation for our new approach to hypnotherapeutic work in the second half of this book.

Are there any general principles governing cooperative and competitive behavior on all levels from the molecular-genetic to the mental and social? Could such general principles be modeled with the dynamics of systems of differential equations? Soon after the initial publication of the presence of chaos in a system of differential equations by the meteorologist-mathematician Lorenz (1963, 1993), Rössler (1976) formulated a simpler system that has become one of the most widely studied models of a strange attractor (Box 2.5).

Box 2.5: Rössler's Attractor and The New Dynamics of Human Nature
Rössler (1976) formulated what is generally recognized as the simplest model of a strange attractor that utilizes the stretch and fold dynamics from the following system of differential equations.

$$x' = - (y + z)$$
$$y' = x + ay$$
$$z' = b + xz - cz$$

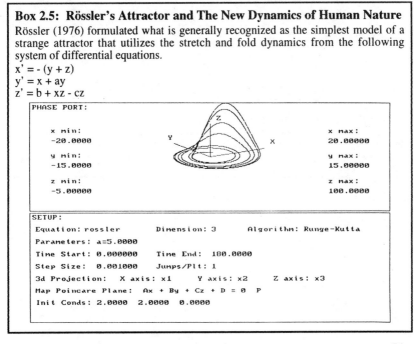

```
PHASE PORT:

   x min:                                          x max:
    -20.0000                                        20.00000

   y min:                                           y max:
    -15.0000                                        15.00000

   z min:                                           z max:
    -5.00000                                        100.0000
```

```
SETUP:
Equation: rossler        Dimension: 3        Algorithm: Runge-Kutta
Parameters: a=5.0000
Time Start: 0.000000     Time End: 180.0000
Step Size: 0.001000      Jumps/Plt: 1
3d Projection:   X axis: x1      Y axis: x2      Z axis: x3
Map Poincare Plane:   Ax + By + Cz + D = 0   P
Init Conds: 2.0000    2.0000    0.0000
```

The above illustration of Rössler's Attractor was made with *Phaser* (Koçak, 1989) one of the simplest and most useful software packages for studying dynamical systems. Notice that when the trajectory moves to the outer part of the attractor it is stretched. Even though the vertical z-axis has a much larger scale, the curve stretches upward above much more than it does on either the x-axis or y-axis. It then folds down toward the y-axis to complete the **stretch and fold** cycle so typical of strange attractors.

The stretch and fold cycle is one of the most important characteristics of strange attractors that makes them so useful for modeling living systems that have a natural periodicity or cycle boundary within which they operate. All living systems, by definition have this important property of going through cycling phases (though chaotically, never exactly) until they are dead. You go to sleep, but after a time you cycle back to wakefulness; you breathe in, but after a time your system cycles back through breathing out. Life experiences can *stress* your system so that you must *stretch* yourself to deal effectively with a problem until you can safely *cycle back* and *return* to *relaxation*. The same stretch and fold dynamics will be seen to apply to the four phase creative dynamics of hypnotherapeutic work we will present later in the second half of this volume. A more detailed illustration of the stretch and fold dynamics of Rossler's attractor by Abraham and Shaw (1992) is presented below.

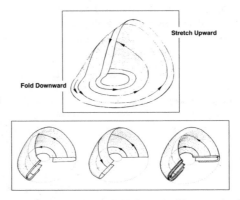

These three iterations of the stretch and fold dynamic illustrate the *fractal* complexity of strange attractors (that will develop folds within folds *ad infinitum*) that enables them to stay within certain recognizable boundaries though never repeating any cycle exactly. Preliminary investigation indicates that hypnosis has a fractal structure (Endo et al., 1995).

Could Rössler's strange attractor be a mathematical model for the apparent fractal union of fire and water in this ancient Indian painting? Notice the characteristic fractal interlacing of the fingers of the fire and water. This image has been used as a symbol of the union of polar characteristics in human nature (Jung, 1966). It surely mimics the romantic "attraction of opposites" between people as well (Norma Barretta, personal communication). Does fractal geometry (Mandelbrot, B. (1977) model dimensions of human experience and symbolism in the same sense as it models outer nature?

Rössler's (1995, 1994 b) recent meta-psychological insights into the nature of the stretch and fold mixing dynamics of chaotic or strange attractors makes them intriguing models for human consciousness and experience.

In Eastern thinking, Hun Tun (Kon Ton) means mixing and chaos and is also the name of the first Emperor who possessed and needed no sense organs to see clearly. Up to this day, "Kon Ton" refers to a state of mind beyond illusion....

Chaos thus represents the greatest challenge to the mind — break out from the prison of appearances.

In the west, chaos occupies a similarly elevated position in the hierarchy of thought. The pre-Socratic philosopher-scientist Anaxagoras adhered to a duelist view related to that of his Eastern predecessors. The whole cosmos is chaos originally — a perfect mixture which existed for an infinitely long time....

The mind is able to unmix the perfect mixture in a process that is still unfinished. The unmixing is accomplished, very specifically, by a "recurrent" (prechoretic, that is, "around going") motion which, so it is made clear, is neither closed nor periodic....

The most surprising feature...is the presence of an "internal explosion" — an exponential separation of neighboring positions as one follows up two that originally lie on two closely adjacent spiral paths. The explosion, however, stays "bounded" due to the repetitive back-folding. No loss of efficiency ever occurs (as would be unavoidable with an ordinary explosion). One therefore suddenly wonders: is this the essence of chaos — a never-stopping internal explosion? (Rössler, 1995, p. 5-7)

An internal explosion, indeed! Are the profound *emotional crises of historical hypnosis* as well as our new *ideo-dynamic* approaches to emotional catharsis and problem solving presented in the second half of this book also manifestations of such chaotological internal explosions? Are these internal explosions the source of the subtle states of psychobiological arousal that are an initial phase of the creative processes that we facilitate in hypnotherapeutic work? Each such creative breakthrough would pierce through yet another veil of Maya in the perpetual unmixing of chaos to help us break out of the prison of appearances. The simplicity and mystery of our current limited understanding of the relationships between chaos, science and projections of our own mind are hinted at further by Rössler as follows.

Chaos is a maximally simple phenomenon as we saw — a gentle entanglement of smooth, locally parallel hairlines in 3-space. Its ubiquitous occurrence in real-life systems involving three interacting variables is a direct consequence of this simplicity. Yet, apart from its usefulness in explaining empirical phenomena, chaos also provokes genuine fascination in children and adults alike. Is there an explanation for this phenomenon as well?

The fascination may have to do with a not-so-obvious fact. Chaos reflects in the real world the existence of the transfinite.

The transfinite object which "lives" in chaos is the long line of topology. The latter defies imagination to such an extent that even most mathematicians are unfamiliar with its existence. (Rössler, 1995, p. 8)

But is all this really enough or are there further frontiers beyond ordinary chaos that are in the future of the new dynamics of human nature?

Chaos lives in three dimensions, just as oscillation (periodic recurrence) lives in two. The difference is that the necessary limitation of amplitude is no longer (as in a planar limit cycle) accomplished *within* the two dimensions of the flow containing the expanding spiral, but by the flow engaging — at least temporarily — a third variable and dimension. This principle is so simple that analogs are bound to exist in higher dimensions. Most of these are yet to be discovered....

This principle generates hyperchaos. Hyperchaos consists of a trajectorial tangle in 4-space in which exponential divergence occurs not just in one direction as in ordinary chaos but in two. It is the most straightforward generalization of chaos, exhibiting many new properties. Nevertheless there is reason to believe that a radically different type of dynamical behavior also may arise under a similar condition. It would differ from chaos as much as chaos does from a limit cycle. This postulated flow ("X-attractor") has yet to be found. (Rössler, 1995, p. 10)

What are these "many new properties" that may be found in *hyperchaos*? Will they contain hints about how we may model the more hidden or "unconscious" aspects of human nature that we now have only dim psychoanalytic intuitions of? Will hyperchaos thus prove to be yet other example of the unreasonable effectiveness of mathematics in helping us break out of the prison of appearances? At this time we can only speculate that it is here, on the frontier of hyperchaos, that the new psychological dynamics of human nature may be developed.

What happens when the equations that model strange attractors are coupled together (Rössler, 1976)? Could they model patterns of human interaction on mental, behavioral and social levels as well as the molecular-genetic (Abraham, 1995 b)? Rössler (1987, p. 236-7) discusses the possibilities of using simple systems of differential equations to model strange attractors as *optimizers* of brain, psychological and social interaction as follows.

...there is the case of two coupled optimizers. Gregory Bateson was struck by the finding that small social systems like families possess dynamical properties (manifested by a spontaneity and apparent "will" of their own) that are not among the intentions of any subsystems (family members) involved.... Recently, the idea was proposed that logical paradoxes (one of Bateson's pet subjects) might be understood entirely in dynamical terms. Logical reasoning does have its dynamical aspects and is performed by dynamical systems. Nevertheless, it appears that there is also a certain risk involved in one's trying to apply dynamics too readily to human beings and their characteristic rationality. Reason and chaos are poles not only in Anaxagora's theory. In the present context, the point is that autonomous optimizers are exceedingly hard to make rational. In order to be rational, they would have to cease optimizing, that is, to give up their own nature.

This does not mean that the solution might not lie with dynamics. The great advantage of looking at optimizers from a dynamical point of view is that the possibility of "function changes" (Rosen's word for bifurcation) arises naturally. Interacting optimizers, like any dynamical system, are subject to bifurcations, specifically, symmetry-breaking ones....Is it possible for an optimizer to shed its very nature of being an optimizer (that is an autist) and become a cross-optimizer (an altist)? The answer is yes.

An altist knows good (he invents "meaning good" in the transition); he also is rational. An independent second bifurcation of the triggering (rather than symmetry-breaking) type may lead to the acceptance of evil. A third interactional bifurcation of similar standing may also exist (illustrating Bateson's principle that there are situations in life in which it is immoral not to become insane). These three possibilities are, at the time being, still slightly beyond the reach of science, that is, ordinary understanding.

Within this very broad context Rössler (1987, p. 229) has stated, "Understanding autonomous optimizers is, of course, what psychiatry is all about." He thus builds a bridge between the mathematical dynamics of coupled strange attractors and human dynamics in professional as well as personal relationships. While a deeper exploration of this theme remains for future research, the new ideodynamic approaches to facilitating problem solving and healing presented in the second half of this book take an initial step to

75

utilizing Rössler's concepts of bifurcations and symmetry-breaking in the altist optimization of hypnotherapeutic work.

The New Psychodynamics of Strange Attractors

A basic question now arises in the use of the new dynamics of nonlinear systems of self-organization by psychotherapists at this early stage in its development. Are they using the concept of chaotic attractors, also called strange attractors, simply as an interesting metaphor of complexity in psychology or are these new dynamics really contributing to a new world view of the nature of psychotherapy and how it should be done? At the present time it appears as if psychologists are using nonlinear dynamics in both ways; most often as an evocative and heuristic metaphor but also as a fundamentally new approach to theory and research (Abraham and Gilgen, 1995; Robertson, 1995; Robertson and Combs, 1995; Smith and Thelen, 1993; Tschhacher, Schiepek & Brunner, 1992). Here are a few interesting heuristic metaphors of the connections between classical psycho*dynamics* and nonlinear self-organization *dynamics* theory that now need to be explored further in clinical practice and research (Rossi, 1989a).

Chaotic attractors have a *self-generative quality.* Mathematically, they are calculated by processes of iteration (or recursion) whereby the output of the first step is used as the input for the next. This reminds us of the archetypal image of the uroboros — the snake swallowing its own tail symbolizing a process of self-generation as an essence of life. Strange attractors also have a *self-reflective aspect* called "fractals," wherein self images are reflected on infinitely large and small scales of time and space. This could be a basic mechanism in the fundamental process of self-reflection and identity formation in human development (Rossi, 1972/1986/1998). The mathematician Ralph Abraham (1995a, p. 60), a pioneer in nonlinear dynamics, has written "Chaotic attractors consist of fractal (infinitely folded) sets of states, over which the model system moves, occupying different states in a sequence called a *trajectory,* or time series." There have been many artistic, literary, and psychological intuitions of consciousness and personality as made up of many layers of an onion, each enfolded or repeating on many levels. The recognition of an artist's individual style and themes are perhaps the most obvious manifestations of fractal dimensions of human experience. The artistic images of Eschler wherein we see the same images and relationships repeating on many levels is one example. Freud's concept of the "repetition compulsion" is another. The sense of deja vu, the belief in past lives, and multiple personality are more speculative examples of how the fractal dimension may be manifest in human experience. In a fascinating aside, Abraham (1995b, p. 160) has commented on the fractal nature of deep layers of human intuition as follows.

> Carl G. Jung (1875-1961) came late in his life to some fractal awakening, expressed in his book *Answer to Job* (1952). This presents an astonishingly bold psychoanalysis of the god Yahweh, in which good and evil are combined in a fractal binary. Further, his concept of *enantiodroma* (oscillation) admits a Lewinian model (Abraham, Abraham & Shaw, (1990, p. vol. 3, p.11).

One begins to wonder, in this context, whether the concept of God itself is a strange attractor, a fractal whose infinite dimensions of omnipresence and omniscience can both enlighten and ensnare us on all levels. Current cultural ideas surrounding the concept of the strange attractor and fractals in human experience are provocative and evocative of many levels of awareness and self-transformation on which most mortals maintain but a tenuous hold. One might even go so far as to postulate there are certain human concepts and experiences whose strange attractor-fractal nature belong to a special class of metapsychology much as the concept of *complementarity* holds a special status in physics (Wheeler, 1995) and the concept of the *continuum* and *infinity* has in mathematics (Robertson, 1995). The concept of the double bind in psychology that has pathological as well as therapeutic consequences on many levels would be an example to study carefully in this regard (Erickson and Rossi, 1975; Rossi and Jichaku, 1992).

The self-organizing aspect of strange attractors are incredibly robust and creative. Hit a crystal with a hammer and it is shattered forever; hit a life form and it may be hurt but it has a self-preservative aspect that attempts recovery. This robustness is not rare; it is a direct outcome of how nature's complex systems organize themselves. This self-organization responds *creatively* to environmental changes rather than the robot-like stimulus-response model of yesteryear's behaviorism. The creative aspect of strange attractors has led Prigogine and Stengers (1984) to propose that these robustly creative processes of nature lead us to *la nouvelle alliance*: a new, mutually synergistic alliance between the sciences and the humanities.

One's initial impression of the images of strange attractors is that they look like mandalas of which Jung (1959, p.10) wrote, "We know from experience that the protective circle, the mandala, is the traditional antidote for chaotic states of mind." In fact, the new science of chaos deals with the basic issue of how order is created in nature. The organizing aspect of strange attractors led Gleick to write: "Nature was *constrained*. Disorder was channeled, it seemed, into patterns with some common underlying theme" (1987, p. 152). Although these patterns have a common theme, closer inspection reveals that, like snowflakes, no two individuals are the same. In fact, for the first time there is mathematical language that clarifies how the individual can play a decisive role in irrevocably changing the whole society of which he/she is a part."

The psychoanalytically suggestive aspects of chaotic or strange attractors are seductive, indeed. Who would not immediately intuit, for example, that obsessive thoughts are a manifestation of a chaotic attractor on the cognitive-emotional level? The compulsively repetitive patterns of anxiety, phobias, and depression — each with their seemingly infinite variations on a central circular theme— would seem to be psychobiological problem solving efforts gone astray. They are all examples of a new theory of psychopathology: *Psychological and psychosomatic problems are all manifestations of falling into an inappropriate attractor rather than remaining on the creative edge of chaos.* In Jungian terms this is generalized as the fundamental psycho*dynamic* problem of "inflation" or "identifying with the archetype." If we believe psychotherapy and depth psychology are oriented toward constructive *change*, then we definitely have an ally in the new science of self-organization because it deals with, above all, the essentials of the dynamics of flux and identity on the creative edge of what we may call adaptive chaos.

On other levels, we can conceive of social processes, rites and rituals as broadly based strange attractors. Religions, cultural practices and philosophies are all subject to the same dynamics of the new science of deterministic chaos that can do justice to their common features as well as their uniqueness. The dynamics of social stability, peace, and war are the basic subject matter of the study of chaos and catastrophe (Thom, 1972). Why do we have chaos and catastrophe in the first place? Up to now this has been a metaphysical question closed to empirical science. The science of catastrophe initiated by Thom illustrates how chaos and change are not so much philosophical principles as the way nature actually works. Langton describes the general process as follows.

Living systems can perhaps be characterized as systems that dynamically *avoid* attractors. The *periodic regime* is characterized by *limit-cycle* or *fixed-point attractors*, while the chaotic regime is characterized by strange attractors, typically of very high dimension. Living systems need to avoid either of these ultimate outcomes, and must have learned to steer a delicate course between too much order and too much chaos — the *Scylla* and *Charybdis* of dynamical systems.

They apparently have done so by learning to maintain themselves on extended transients — i.e., *by learning to maintain themselves near a "critical" transition*. Once such systems emerged near a critical transition, evolution seems to have discovered the natural information-processing capacity inherent in near-critical dynamics, and to have taken advantage of it to further the ability of such systems to maintain themselves on essentially open-ended transients.

Of course, climbing out of one attractor just pushes the problem back to a higher-dimensional phase space, in which the system is again in the basin of some attractor. It is therefore possible to view evolution as a repeated iteration of the process whereby a system climbs out of one attractor into a higher-dimensional phase space, only to find itself in the basin of a higher-dimensional attractor, a process that gives evolutionary significance to the phrase "out of the frying pan, into the fire!" (Langton 1992, p. 85, Italics mostly ours.)

We may generalize these concepts into a deeper and broader understanding of just what the hypnotherapeutic enterprise has been trying to do since its beginning in the healing temples of Egypt to the exorcism of Father Gassner, healing in the emotional crises and chaos of Mesmerism, the early cathartic therapy of Sigmund Freud and the shock and surprise methods of Milton H. Erickson (Rossi, 1973a). The hypnotherapist arranges conditions so that healing can take place when patients find the courage to move out of the stagnant *fixed points* and out-moded *limit cycles* that are the chief dynamical characteristic of "problems" and "symptoms." If you stop to think about it for a moment, you realize that on this is the simplest possible model of what problems and symptoms actually are: they are either (1) *fixed points* of maladaptive behavior wherein patients feel stuck so they cannot move ahead or (2) they are limit cycles or circular patterns of behavior the patient does not know how to change.

We may speculate that the phase transitions from one level of adaptation and consciousness to another are expressions of Langton's idea that adaptive complex systems can move from one basin of attraction to another. Rössler (1992b) has speculated how "interactional bifurcations" in social experience are a basic dynamic in facilitating the evolution of "ultraperspective" implied in those developmental jumps of human consciousness in acts such as "showing courtesy, devising a joke, trading, making a commitment, asking an opinion, conceiving of benevolence." In the second half of this volume we will explore how Poincaré'sfour stage creative process can facilitate the mutual evolution of such ultraperspective in hypnotherapeutic work.

The Current Paradigm Clash in Linear and Nonlinear Science

It is evident that we have raised more questions than we have answered in this introductory chapter on current developments in linear and nonlinear science. But they are stimulating questions! If anything is clear it is that we are not yet clear about how to approach some of the fundamental issues involved in applying the new possibilities to psychology. At the present time there is a wide range of scientific opinion about the roles and relative importance of linear and nonlinear science on all levels from mathematics and physics to biology and psychosomatic medicine. It may therefore be appropriate to end this chapter with a pair of quotations illustrating this clash of paradigms.

> More generally, the question arises as to the applicability of chaos in various fields ranging from physics, chemistry and biology to economics... It is still unclear whether chaotic behavior is associated with pathology or healthy conditions in physiology...Besides the nonlinear dynamics of the brain...a case in point is the heart, whose rate exhibits a variability that has been analyzed in terms of chaos; the source of this variability appears to lie in neurohumoral control of the heart...Suppressing this control may prove more detrimental than suppressing chaotic dynamics per se, which may be a marker of the multiplicity of controls exerted on the heart rhythm. At the cellular level, the latter rhythm, as shown by the study of models for electrical activity in cardiac pacemaker tissues..., appears to be of the limit cycle type. What can be said at this point is that the function of chaos in physiology remains largely unclear, compared to the well-established roles for periodic phenomena. (Goldbeter, 1996, p. 511).

This conservative opinion by Goldbeter, who is one of the international pioneers in the nonlinear dynamics of biochemical and living systems, suggests that the basic strategy of living systems is to control chaos. This view certainly has merit as his research on the cellular level documents. In some suspensions of living cells (*Dictyostelium*), for example, the presence of a small number of cells that have a regular periodicity will often suppress the chaotic rhythms in the rest of the cells and entrain them so that the cells with the chaotic rhythms adopt the regular periodicity. Indeed, as we have seen in this chapter, one of the most interesting speculations about the function of human consciousness is its role in transforming some of the apparently non-predictable aspects of nonlinear dynamics into linear and predictable phenomena.

Most workers in nonlinear dynamics, however, acknowledge that chaos per se is not the desideratum in living systems and psychology. Rather it is believed that *Life balanced and computing on the Edge of Chaos* (not in it) opens the possibility for new insights into the dynamics of *complex adaptive systems* where evolution and change rather than stasis make a positive contribution to survival. This belief is well expressed by Orsucci of the Institute of Psychiatry at Rome University "Tor Vergata' in a recent featured article in the pioneering newsletter of the Society For Chaos Theory in Psychology and The Life Sciences.

> The strong and "natural link" which psychosomatics has with the "nonlinear field" is evident, so we can say that psychosomatics belongs to nonlinear science "from its birth." As psychosomatics is based on the borderland between different domains, psychosomatic research is founded on the discovery of correlations and isomorphisms. In other terms we could say that "in psychological systems most oscillators, from neurons, to neuroendocrines, to sexual, appetitive, sleep, and personal changes are coupled with related biological and environmental oscillators."... The benefit which psychosomatics could receive adopting the theoretical framework and the analytical techniques of nonlinear science is potentially vast...
>
> We know that studies in biology and medicine revealed the presence of nonlinear dynamics in living systems. Ary Goldberger...discovered that healthy hearts show more variability in their beating than do sick ones. A loss of complexity in cardiac rhythm could be a predictor of sudden death, and the frequency spectrum could be used to prevent heart attacks and seizures...The roots of cardiac complexity may be found in the structure of the heart, as well as in the structure of nervous systems which control it. The single neuron and nerve-nets should be understood according to fractal geometry. As Goldberger says, "if you accept that our anatomies are fractal, it's only a small leap to say the day-to-day workings of these systems is fractal." He reaches a conclusion which could be of great interest for psychosomatic medicine: "Healthy systems don't want homeostasis. They want chaos." (Orsucci, 1995, p. 9-10).

In the following chapters we will continue to explore the "potentially vast" contributions nonlinear science may make to a deeper understanding of the dynamics of psychology in general and hypnotherapy in particular. We will attempt to balance the provocative and heuristic nature of our current understanding of nonlinear dynamics with a bit of ballast from the history of psychotherapy and our hopes for its future.

The Basic Ideas

1. *The new sciences of Self-Organization and Adaptive Complexity model human nature as an evolving nonlinear dynamic of multistable states on the critical edge of deterministic chaos. Creative adaptation and evolution itself are optimal at this edge of chaos. We accept this as an updated description of the historical interest of hypnotherapy in altered states and phase transitions (emotional crises, catharsis etc.) on the creative edge of chaos in the experience of healing and problem solving.*

2. *Bifurcation points (critical phase transitions) of mathematical iteration (recursion, feedback) are a useful metaphor and model for the evolving psychobiological dimensions of consciousness and problem solving in hypnotherapy. The ever ongoing, iterated solutions to these equations provide four basic patterns for the dynamics of problem solving in psychology: (1) Fixed Point or Steady State Attractors; (2) Periodic or Limit Cycle Attractors; (3) Quasi-periodic Attractors and (4) and Chaotic or Strange Attractors. These patterns are so pervasive in the fundamental dynamics of all living systems that they have been called "archetypal patterns" of mind and behavior.*

3. *Nonlinear Self-Organization Theory proposes a new view of psychopathology: Psychological problems and psychosomatic symptoms are all manifestations of falling into inappropriate fixed points, steady states or periodic attractors rather than remaining on the creative edge of adaptive chaos. The ideo-dynamic, bifurcating, symmetry-breaking and polarity approaches to hypnothrapeutic work described later are all designed to facilitate optimal human experience and problem solving on the creative edge of development.*

4. *The experiences and behaviors that evolve spontaneously from nonlinear dynamics are so unexpected that they have been called the "The Science of Surprise." A major function of consciousness may be to transform the nonlinear, irrational, unconscious and difficult to predict dynamics of nature into the more linear, rational and predictable dynamics of human experience. Surprise rather than suggestion will be found to be one of the most characteristic dynamics of all genuine creativity in the new ideo-dynamic approaches that are the essence of hypnotherapeutic work introduced in the second half of this volume.*

5. *But If suggestion, programming, manipulation and control over the experience and behavior of another is not the essence of hypnotherapy, then what is? The answer we are working toward: "Hypnotherapeutic Work" is the facilitation of the subject's own healing and problem solving dynamics in the natural second order phase transitions they courageously allow themselves to experience on their subjective edge of creative chaos between the rational, linear dynamics of their conscious experience and the irrational, nonlinear dynamics of the unconscious.*

6. *Why did the linearization or rational function of consciousness evolve? Nonlinear processes are usually difficult and, indeed, most often impossible to predict. Consciousness evolved to linearize bounded bits and pieces of nonlinear nature so that the organism could predict important ranges of experience necessary for survival. Linearization is involved in transducing the nonlinear universe into sufficiently predictable patterns — just predictable enough to ensure survival. A prey animal, such as a deer or rabbit, for example, has to evolve just enough linear sensory-perceptual-motor organization to predict and avoid the trajectory of a predator pursuing it. Just as the mathematical process of linearization is always bounded within certain narrow limits in which it is effective (well defined), so consciousness is also bounded in its linearization and capacity to predict nature. The boundary conditions of the rational world view of western consciousness are implied by the paradoxes of logic and Gödel's Incompleteness Theorem, Turing's Halting Problem, the Uncertainty Principle in quantum physics and the Dynamics of Chaos in psychobiology, as we shall see in the next two chapters.*

Chapter Three:
What Is Life?
Matter, Energy and Information

Under what conditions can we expect a dynamics of information to emerge spontaneously and come to dominate the behavior of a physical system?

Christopher Langton

Schrödinger's famous little book, "What Is Life?" published over fifty years ago has been spectacularly successful in inspiring many developments in modern molecular biology, the unraveling of the genetic code and new insights into the quantum nature of life and mind. Now, fifty years later, a curious situation has arisen that is little understood. Concepts of mind such as "information" and "communication" are being introduced into the basic sciences of physics, biochemistry and biology at an accelerating rate. This is curious because few seem to recognize its major implication: we are shifting from a model of reductionism to constructivism in science. Schrödinger's plan for understanding life is now evolving into a new science of how the elements of physics, chemistry, biology and psychology can synthesize themselves into more Adaptive Complexities that we call "life" and "mind".

Our understanding of life is developing new perspectives wherein the concepts of information and communication are being recognized as the common denominator between nature, body and mind (Rossi, 1986/1993). How are the "physical processes" of matter, molecules and energy to be understood as the evolution of information and self-creation? How does information and communication feedback on matter and energy to create the autopoietic — the self-sustaining systems — we call life? The prospect of actually creating this new science of self-organization is more than can be accomplished by any single person or academic discipline. This was well recognized by Schrödinger when he wrote these words of "apology" in the preface of his book:

> We feel clearly that we are only now beginning to acquire reliable material for welding together the sum total of all that is known into a whole ... it has become next to impossible for a single mind fully to command more than a small specialized portion of it.
>
> I can see no other escape from this dilemma (lest our true aim be lost forever) than that some of us should venture to embark on a synthesis of facts and theories, albeit with secondhand and incomplete knowledge of some of them — and at the risk of making fools of ourselves. (Schrödinger, 1944)

With this caveat well in place we will embark on the open seas of current scientific speculation on how we can conceptualize the nature of life and mind in a manner that can provide more tools and insights for the daily work of the hypnotherapist. In this quest we will continue to draw upon the emerging sciences of self-organization, adaptive complexity and chaos theory in their exploration of the emerging relationships between energy, matter and information (Zurek, 1990). In particular we will take our inspiration from Christopher Langton when he says, "In living systems, dynamics of information has gained control over the dynamics of energy, which determines the behavior of most non-living systems. How has this domestication of the brawn of energy to the will of information come to pass?" (Langton, 1992, p. 41)

Transformations of Matter, Energy and Information

An approach to answering this question comes from the study of the thermodynamic relationships between matter, energy and information. A major source of inspiration in this area is credited to Ilya Prigogine who received the Nobel Prize in chemistry in 1977 for his experimental and theoretical contributions to the study of *non-equilibrium thermodynamics*. A system in nature is said to be in *thermodynamic equilibrium* when its temperature, matter, energy and dynamics are *symmetrical or uniform throughout*. Stir a spoonful of sugar in a cup of water and after a moment or two the system of sugar-water will be in thermodynamic equilibrium. It is the same throughout — every spoonful is like every other. The individual molecules of sugar and water are continually moving about within the solution — a state of *dynamic equilibrium* — but there is no systematic flow of matter, energy or information from one place in the solution to another. The random *movements of billions of molecules cancel each other out statistically* so we can also say we have a system in *stochastic equilibrium.* Most important of all for our study of mind, body and nature is the idea that nothing more can evolve out of this stochastic balance in thermodynamic equilibrium if it is a *closed system.* That is the system — our cup of sugar and water — is sealed off from the rest of the world somehow so that any further changes in temperature, matter, energy or information cannot take place.

We could at least approximate such a closed system, say, by placing our sugar water in a thermos bottle. The thermos bottle prevents the flow of heat from entering or leaving the system (only imperfectly, of course, in the real world). No change in heat energy or thermodynamics means the closed system is also in *entropic equilibrium.* The thermodynamic property of *entropy* is a measure of the disorder or randomness of all the parts of the system in a given state — a cup of sugar and water in our case. Organization, the opposite of randomness, can be defined as information. No organization or information can operate on a closed system, however. Isolated in its pristine purity, no changes, certainly no life or mind could evolve out of this isolated system. This isolated system is a clear illustration of the famous second law of thermodynamics: such systems evolve to a state of thermal symmetry where there is a maximum of entropy, loss of information and ability to do useful work. Nothing moves, nothing changes, nothing evolves.

How different the real world is from this artificially isolated system. *In the real world of ever shifting nature most things are not in thermodynamic equilibrium.* In the natural world practically everything is an *open system and far-from-thermodynamic-equilibrium.* Everything moves and changes. Far-from-equilibrium systems evolve from the continuous flow of free energy, matter and information into and out of the system. *All forms of life are classical examples of open far-from-thermodynamic equilibrium systems.* Prigogine (1980) calls any system, such as life, that maintains its equilibrium by using up energy a *dissipative structure.* They are dissipative in the sense that they *use high energy sources to do some form of useful work to create the information and organization of life at the cost of degrading or dissipating the high energy into a lower form energy* and returning it to the environment. This degraded or dissipated energy has been reduced to a more random state (that is, greater disorder, of higher entropy and lower information). *Life creates itself by doing the useful work of metabolizing food (burning up high energy sources) in order to increase its own information, complexity and self-organization.* Life is a far from equilibrium dissipative system.

The study of the nonlinear dynamics of life as a dissipative system brings the concepts of mathematics, physics and biology together with a newly intensified focus on how living systems operate. Dissipative systems theory does not provide us with all the answers, however. After all there are many non-living systems that are also dissipative. A car engine is dissipative in degrading the high energy form of fuel we call gasoline into the lower forms of waste carbon dioxide, water and noxious fumes. Even roller blades get hot as they dissipate energy and degrade it into the waste heat of friction. What is it that life does that makes it a truly unique dissipative system? What is the secret strength of its self-creation? How does it manage to continue to proliferate into ever more diverse forms with no central planner or programmer? Does life have any other general characteristics besides being a dissipitive system? Are there any more specific mechanisms of life as a dissipitive system that can help us understand more precisely just how it converts randomness into organization and information? Ah, yes, that at last is the crux of the matter. What is the essential mechanism by which life converts randomness into information?

Randomness, Life and Mind:
Stochastic Resonance and Noise

What are the phenomena and laws of nature that can account for the shift from randomness to the apparent order we observe in the world about us? What is the simplest observation we can make, the most primitive possible mechanism by which disorder is channeled into the extravagantly improbable organizations we call "life" and "mind?" The most recent answer comes in the phenomenon called *stochastic resonance.* Putting these two words together is actually oxymoronic. They mean opposite things. On the simplest level stochastic means statistical disorder or randomness. Resonance, to the contrary, means an organizing state where by two or more sympathetic vibrating physical systems (sounds, clock pendulums etc.) interact together in synchronization. Stochastic resonance therefore must mean something about how randomness is transmuted into order. How can this possibly take place?

Since its introduction in 1981, stochastic resonance has become a deeply researched phenomenon by physicists and biologists. They found that certain nonlinear systems, subject to weak input signals, have the property that presentation of stochastic forcing, or 'noise' can enhance information flow (Moss et al., 1994). A recent paper by Bezrukov and Vodyanoy (1995, p. 362) takes us to the leading edge of research in this area.

The presence of noise in a signal transduction system usually interferes with its ability to transfer information reliably. But many nonlinear systems can use noise to enhance performance, and this phenomenon, called stochastic resonance, may underlie the extraordinary ability of some biological systems to detect and amplify small signals in noisy environments. Previous work has demonstrated the occurrence of stochastic resonance in a complex system of biological transducers and neural signal pathways, but the possibility that it could occur at the sub-cellular level has remained open. Here we report the observation of stochastic resonance in a system of voltage-dependent ion channels formed by the peptide alamethicin. A hundred-fold increase in signal transduction induced by external noise is accompanied by a growth in the output signal-to-noise ratio. The system of ion channels considered here represents the simplest biological system known to exhibit stochastic resonance.

The concept of stochastic resonance helps us understand how the signals of life processes can be amplified by the random disorder of nonlinear mechanisms on many levels from the molecular in sensory neurons to the perceptual and conceptual . A few images of how noise or the random perturbations of a settled system could move it to another more organized state is illustrated in Box 3.1. *The important idea is that noise, random perturbations or disturbances to a life system can actually enhance the strength or amplitude of life's signals.* How odd this seems to us when the conventional idea has always been the opposite. Stochastic resonance is a means by which life has learned to convert the random energy of noise into organization and information on many levels from the molecular to the central nervous system (Moss, 1994).

Box 3.1: **Stochastic Resonance and Metastability in The Nonlinear Landscape of Life**

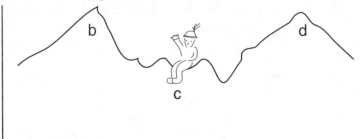

A person stuck in a relatively low metastable position in the "landscape of life." What kind of a shake-up will be necessary to move him on to the higher peaks to the right or left? A metaphorical earthquake or a random slip or fall would be like stochastic resonance moving him one way or another. Hypnotherapeutic work might utilize any or all such random life events to facilitate his progress.

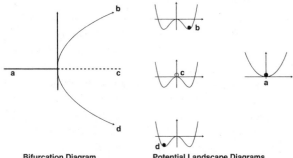

Bifurcation Diagram   Potential Landscape Diagrams

The correspondence between the bifurcation type diagram from Box 2.2 and the "potential landscape" diagram that moves from the pictorial image of the "landscape of life" above to a more mathematical model of the differential equation

$$dx/dt = x^2 + \lambda$$

where λ is a control parameter. The dark balls represent stable positions or solutions (a, b and d) while the white ball (c) is the unstable or vanishing mathematical solution when the system moves past the bifurcation point at "a." We hypothesize that this "vanishing mathematical solution" models how a previously stable level of adaptation at "a" disappears with changing life circumstances measured by the parameter λ. The parameter λ could reflect the degree of emotional security or stress as measured by standardized scales. People are perpetually shifting through the landscape of their lives: hung up for a while and then shaken up by events so that they move out of a previously stable position at "a" to different levels of adaptation. It is precisely at the unstable bifurcation points (the unstable white ball at "c") that hypnotherapeutic work may be more effective in facilitating a creative shift to a new stable position at either "b" or "d."

Current research is exploring the dynamics of "taming spaito-temporal chaos with disorder in the laboratory (Braimen et al., 1995). Kelso (1995) reports on an extensive series of experiments documenting how stochastic resonance is a fundamental dynamic that can be used to modulate human perception, memory and learning. He proposes "that to retain flexibility the nervous system should live near, but not in, mode-locked behavior" (Kelso, 1995, p. 223). Indeed, stochastic resonance is now seen as a central dynamic in shifting life processes and the phase transitions of mind from one metastable state to another. Maladaptive behavior and symptoms can be understood as being locked or stuck in one mode or state attractor for too long a time. Does this sound familiar? Yes, these are the same ideas that were introduced in the previous chapter where we introduced the *self-organization and adaptive complexity model human nature as an ever evolving nonlinear dynamic of multi-stable states on the critical edge of deterministic chaos.* The essence of the *psychopathology of maladaptive behavior* is being stuck too long in one state. The essence of optimal behavior is great skill in adaptively shifting between many states as needed. The essential dynamic of psychotherapy is to facilitate such adaptive skills and even the creation of new states of consciousness and being (Rossi, 1972/ 1986/ 1998).

Amplifying Information in Hypnotherapy

Is it too big a jump to go from the utilization of noise by stochastic resonance to amplify signals and information on the molecular, sensory, perceptual and the memory-learning levels to the facilitation of psychotherapy? Surely we do not introduce noise into psychotherapy, or do we? The late Milton Erickson certainly took a pixie-like enjoyment in introducing quite a bit of noise in the form of ambiguity, confusion, not-knowing and even shocks and surprises into his hypnotherapeutic work (Rossi, 1973). In fact my very first published paper about Erickson's approaches was an effort to puzzle out how he used confusion, shock and surprise to shake up certain symptoms and rigidly set patterns (or "limit set" attractors as described in Chapter Two) of dysfunctional behavior (Rossi, 1973). I had earlier described in great detail the creative process within dreams by which many patients could breakout of their problems, but Erickson was doing it in the most unusual ways. From this new perspective, I now wonder if stochastic resonance could account for the efficacy he found in introducing the noise of confusion, shocks, surprises and pattern interruption to break up a patient's problems (that is, the patient's maladaptive fixed point or limit cycle attractors) in his practical hypnotherapeutic work.

Erickson was very intuitive in his hypnotherapeutic work with patients. He certainly never wrote or spoke of the concept of "noise" to amplify responses as a formal technique in his work but a careful study of what he actually did suggests it. One of Erickson's favorite hypnotic induction techniques was hand levitation. He carefully explained to me that for hand levitation to work the patient had to have a certain amount of "muscle tonus" in his arms and hands. It was the activation of the patient's unique system of expectations and inner resources for healing and problem solving that was important rather than the idea that the patient was falling under the suggestive influence of the therapist as is indicated in his following explanation.

In the induction of hypnosis you make one thing contingent on another because your subject cannot analyze your suggestions for their logic. He cannot and does not have the time to recognize that *the suggestions are fallacious* in so many ways. You are here utilizing the fact that we have a lifetime of experience in responding to *false contingencies and false relationships*. The suggestion you give the patient is only a suggestion to do something, possibly produce hand levitation. Just possible. If there is something else he prefers to do, let him do it. Do not try to restrict him to hand levitation. That is false and that is wrong. *Your attitude should be completely permissive.* (Ital. ours, Erickson and Rossi, 1980)

Erickson's use of "false contingencies and false relationships" certainly appears to be a clear example of how he utilized the noise of cognitive confusion to activate a patient's particular dynamics for problem solving. This is particularly evident in his use of hypnosis to deal with pain problems. Erickson (1980b) outlined eleven approaches to dealing with pain problems. Most of them seek to scramble or distort, dissociate and reframe the experience of pain by utilizing such false relationships that can never-the-less enable the patient to experience relief and comfort. For the new perspective of nonlinear dynamics we could say that pain is a "limit set" attractor that is disrupted by such disruptive hypnotherapeutic techniques. More recently Harold Crasilneck has documented how a half-a-dozen of these approaches can be condensed into a single hypnotherapeutic session in what he calls the "Bombardment technique in problems of intractable organic pain." He acknowledges that while "it is difficult to speculate how the Bombardment Technique affects the patient's pain perception...Some of the observed efficacy...may be in its utilization of a broad array of techniques that allow the patient to

maximize   their   individual   psychophysiological   strengths."
(Crasilneck, 1996, p. 28)

As their personal dynamics are activated, it is very typical to see
patients sweating from the obvious psychophysiological activation of
their sympathetic system in hypnotherapeutic work (Rossi & Cheek,
1988). This leads us to hypothesize that many of the traditional therapeutic techniques of hypnosis and many other holistic methods utilize
arousal and the dynamics of stochastic resonance to non-specifically
facilitate healing and problem solving. For example, it is well
recognized that the presence of an audiences in hypnotic demonstrations seems to enhance the intensity of the therapeutic experience
for the patient (recall the public rituals of Father Gassner and Mesmer
in Chapter One). It is said that the audience adds "energy" to the
hypnotherapeutic work. What is this energy? What else could it be
than the emotional arousal and expectation experienced by the patient
in front of a large group. Some people like to have a radio or TV on in
the backround when they are studying. Is it possible that any
fascinating fantasy or cockeyed, irrational idea that stimulates
imagination, hope and faith may function as a healing placebo in the
appropriate context of expectancy? Indeed, why not take a step
further and say that perhaps our enduring fascination with magic and
all the mantic methods of divination (astrology, tarot, I Ching, etc.)
are actually marginally useful forms of noise, that is, stochastic
resonance, that evoke or arouse the person to do some random form of
inner search that sometimes leads to problem solving and healing.
Could this be the role of the *irrational* but emotionally provocative
rituals, myths and fairy tales that we use in politics, religion, drama
and teaching? In sum, is the *irrational* channelled by stochastic
resonance in ways that can facilitate the evolution of human
consciousness by provoking emotional arousal, random search and
inner work until we stumble upon a useful connecting link or
interpretation we call a solution?

How can we use these fundamental concepts from the mathematics, physics and biology of life's basic dynamics such as
stochastic resonance, amplification and information transduction to
reformulate the foundations of hypnotherapy from first principles? An
approach to this far reaching question can be explored by updating
what we actually know about the dynamics of energy, matter and the
psychobiology of mindbody communication today (Rossi,
1986/1993). In the next section we will trace the pathways of

93

information transduction and amplification from the molecular-genetic level to the dynamics of mind and behavior as presented in the literature of psychobiology and hypnosis. The research literature on four levels: (1) the molecular-genetic-cellular, (2) neuroendocrinological, (3) neural networks and the brain and (4) state-dependent memory, learning and behavior will be outlined together with suggestions for future research on a practical program for exploring the psychobiology of mindbody communication and its implications for the psychotherapeutic arts of the future.

Information Transduction as the Molecular-Genetic Basis of Life

In the most general outline we can trace three stages in the evolution of our current conceptions of the nature of life: (1) the original Greek theory of the universe and life itself as essentially matter that was epitomized by Democritus's phrase, "in reality there is nothing but atoms and space" (Durant, 1933); (2) the conception of life as vitalism or, as we would call it today, essentially *energy*, thermodynamics and the ability to do work (Leff and Rex, 1990); (3) our emerging conception of life as essentially the transduction of *information* and communication in the new sciences of complexity and self-organization (Kauffman, 1993, 1995; Zurek, 1990). It is interesting that we can trace these three fundamental conceptions even in the recent history of our understanding of the role of proteins in life processes. Originally the albuminoids, called "proteins," were thought of as the structural or *material* substance of life (Kordon, 1993). Proteins were later recognized as playing an essentially *energetic* role as enzymes catalyzing the metabolism of the cell and most recently proteins are viewed as *informational and computational* processors at the molecular-genetic-cellular level (Bray, 1995; Marijuan, 1995).

Even with all this phenomenal progress in our understanding of life processes at the molecular-genetic-cellular level, however, the precise relationships between the material, energetic and informational views of life remain enigmatic. It took almost two thousand years to realize that what we now call "energy" was equivalent to matter as immortalized in Einstein's famous equation: $E = MC^2$. It is only within our generation that some scientists are now speculating about the possible equivalence of matter, energy and information.

John Archibald Wheeler, one of our greatest living physicists, baldly states "Information Has Mass" and discusses current views about the equivalence of mass and information in this way.

It from bit. Otherwise put, every it — every particle, every field of force, even the space-time continuum itself — derives its function, its meaning, its very existence entirely — even if in some contexts indirectly — from the apparatus-elicited answers to yes or no questions, binary choices, *bits.*

It from bit symbolizes the idea that every item of the physical world has at bottom — at a very deep bottom, in most instances — an immaterial source and explanation; that what we call reality arises in the last analysis from the posing of yes-no questions and the registering of equipment-evoked responses; in short, that all things physical are information-theoretic in origin and this is a *participatory universe.* (Wheeler, 1994, p. 296) ... A brave new proposal of Bekenstein is now the subject of exploration by more and more investigators: that there is no device whatsoever that will store a given number of bits of information which does not have a product of mass and linear dimensions — expressed in appropriate units — which is at least as great as that number of bits. Information is not dreamlike nothingness. What an incentive to put "information" into the center of our thinking about physics! And to ask, is information the foundation for all we see and know (Wheeler, 1994, p.179)?

The idea that information has mass seems even more surprising than Einstein's idea that mass and energy are equivalent. Tom Stonier (1990) takes another step in exploring the relationships between mass, energy and information. He places information at the center of physics, biology and psychology in his study of the relationship between thermodynamics and information in the work of Ludwig Boltzman, Erwin Schrodinger and Claude Shannon. Stonier (1990, p. 51) calculates that "One entropy unit equals approximately 10^{23} bits of information." It now remains one of the most challenging frontiers in this area to integrate Stonier's equation of information and energy with Einstein's equation of energy and matter to obtain an experimentally verifiable formula for the equivalence of the three basic concepts of matter, energy and information in the evolution of life and mind.

The concept of information allows the cosmologist Frank Tipler (1995, p. 124) to define life in a succinct manner: "I claim that a 'living being' is any entity which *codes information* (in the physics sense of this word) with the information coded being preserved by *natural selection.*" Notice how this association of *information* with *natural selection* brings Tipler's definition of life in line with Darwinian evolution as well as mathematics and physics. But is it consistent with our understanding of biology? Tipler is well aware that his definition will require some adjustments in current biological views of life.

> This definition of "life" is quite different from what the average person — and the average biologist — would think of as "life." In the traditional definition, life is a complex process based on the chemistry of the carbon atom. However, even supporters of the traditional definition admit that the key words are "complex process" and not "carbon atom." ... What is important is not the substrate but the pattern, and the pattern is another name for *information*.
>
> But life of course is not a static pattern. Rather it is a dynamic pattern that persists over time. It is thus a process. But not all processes are alive. The key feature of the "living" patterns is that their persistence is due to feedback with their environment: the information coded in the pattern continually varies, but the variation is constrained to a narrow range by this feedback. Thus life is, as I stated, information preserved by natural selection. (Tipler, 1995, p. 124-125).

Tipler's working definition of life is thus entirely consistent with our new awareness of the biological significance of patterns, feedback, iteration and the Nonlinear Dynamics of Self-organization Theory we presented in the last chapter. How all this actually operates in the flow of information between the environment, the mind-brain and the body is the subject of our next section on the psychobiology of mindbody communication.

The Neuroendocrine Information Loop Between Brain and Body

We may begin our survey of the psychobiology of mindbody communication with the locus of information transduction in the limbic-hypothalamic-pituitary system that has been proposed as a major mediator of information transduction between the brain and the body. Papez (1937), among others, traced the anatomical pathways by which emotional experience of the brain was presumably transduced into the physiological responses of the body in a circuit of brain structures that are now generally recognized as the limbic-hypothalamic-pituitary system. The Scharrers (1940) and Harris (1948) then made microscopic observations suggesting how secretory cells within the hypothalamus could mediate molecular information transduction between brain and body. These cells transformed the essentially electrochemical neural impulses of the cerebral cortex that putatively encoded the phenomenological experience of "mind" and emotions into the hormonal messenger molecules of the endocrine system that communicated with (regulated) the body.

This neuroendocrine channel of communication composed of hormonal "molecular messengers," also called "informational substances," is currently believed to modulate the action of neurons (the neuromodulators) and cells at all levels from the basic pathways of sensation and perception to the regulation of the homeostatic processes of life on the molecular-genetic-cellular levels. It has been proposed that informational substances of the endocrine, autonomic and immune systems mediate stress, emotions, memory, learning, personality, behavior and symptoms in a manner that provides a new pragmatic understanding of the mindbody problem in "psychological time" (Rossi, 1992a & b). That is, the domain of psychological time in minutes and hours relates the basic rest activity cycle of human behavior to the processes of mindbody information transduction and communication mediated by the slower neuroendocrine communication system (Rossi, 1986/1993). This original, slower loop of information transduction by messenger molecules contrasts sharply with the evolutionary more recent form of rapid mindbody communication mediated by neurons (the central and peripheral nervous system) in small fractions of a second that are briefer than the phenomenological span of conscious human attention (Libet, 1993; Lloyd & Rossi, 1993; Rossi & Lippincott, 1992). In its bare essentials, this psychobiological approach to understanding the molecular basis of mind, memory, learning, and psychosomatic medicine in the therapeutic arts is based on four interlocking hypotheses about the operation of the complex system of cybernetic information transduction between mind, neuro-endocrinal system and genes as follows (Rossi, 1986/1993).

The Neuroendocrine Information loop between Brain and Body

Hypothesis One: Localized neuronal networks of the brain are modulated by a complex dynamic field of informational substances: Information and meaning in the complex field of mindbrain dynamics.

The extracellular fluid of the brain makes up about 20% of the brain's volume. Schmitt (1984) has noted that informational substances can diffuse as much as 15 mm from the extracellular fluid to any site within the cerebral cortex of the adult human brain. There would thus be ample intercellular space for the dynamic interplay of many kinds of informational substances to diffuse from release points throughout the body to receptors on or in the neuronal networks of the cerebral cortex and other loci of the brain that encode the phenomenological experiences of mind and behavior. In the simplest case, a 15-square mm neuronal network could be turned on or off by the presence or absence of a specific informational substances that modulate the phenomenology of mind in psychological time. That is, the activity of neuronal networks and the psychological experience they encode would be "state-dependent" aspects of mind and behavior dependent on the presence or absence of a specific complex of informational substances. There are potentially thousands of informational substances interacting with hundreds of different receptors on the brain neurons. This means that the state-dependent neuronal networks are ever-changing dynamic structures, as they would certainly have to be in order to function as the psychophysiological basis for the phenomenology of mind, emotions, and behavior.

If we are willing to grant that information is encoded within the neuronal networks of the brain via protein modulated changes in the Hebbian synaptic connections (that is synaptic neural connections that grow stronger with activity), then we could say that meaning is to be found in the complex dynamic field of informational substances that continually contextualize the information of the neuronal networks into new patterns of meaning. Freeman (1995), for example, has pointed out how oxytocin is a hormonal informational substance released during childbirth and lactation that encodes certain types of memory and learning as well as unlearning (forgetting) that would provide a survival advantage during evolution. Oxytocin in concert with a complex of other messenger molecules in the extracellular fluid of the brain makes up the ever changing dynamical field of meaning that is expressed in the phenomenological experience of "mind" and intentional goal directed behavior during childbirth and the nursing period.

Hypnotherapists often report interesting case histories of how they accidentally evoke long forgotten state-dependent memories. Milton Erickson, for example, was consulted by women who ostensibly wanted hypnosis to help her recover memories of giving birth to her first child. In this case, that was carefully recorded verbatim, the woman was fairly successful in recovering with the help of hypnosis some details of the birth of her first child three months earlier (Erickson & Rossi, 1979, p. 282-313). This case is particularly interesting because, in the process of the revivification of these memories of childbirth, she also "accidentally" recovered previous traumatic life experiences she had forgotten for many years. As she recovered the experience of these early trauma with Erickson, she was now able to reorganized a significant portion of her emotion life that led to a surprising maturation of her personality in a very short period of time. In discussing the unexpected development of this case Erickson noted that the common conception of hypnosis as a method of direct suggestion or programming "is a very uninformed way" of doing therapy (Erickson & Rossi, 1979, p. 288). Hypnotherapeutic work often involves therapy on two or more levels. There is (1) the patient's conscious "presenting problem" (the problem they present to the therapist such as this patient's wish to recover childbirth memories) and (2) other more unconscious, "state-dependent" problems they do not know how to articulate (such as this patient's own early life traumas). The therapist's direct suggestion or so-called programming is usually focused on the patient's conscious presenting problem only. The depth oriented hypnotherapist, however, can also help patients engage in those more general non-directive exploratory approaches that tend to evoke state-dependent (or state-bound) memories that leads to an opportunity to resolve deeper problems. In this particular case the resolution of the deeper early life trauma led to a significant "maturation" in the woman's personality and world view.

An important research frontier for the scientific documentation of state-dependent memory will require the use of modern brain imaging methods such as the PET (positron emission tomography) scans and MRIs (magnetic resonance images) to document the presence of hormonal messenger molecules in complex mind-brain fields of information transduction and communication during therapy. Ideally, for example, researchers would be able to image the brain during hypnotherapy to determine whether oxytocin was in fact released in certain brain fields during the recovery of the childbirth memories. An excellent beginning has been made by a number of research teams (Decety et al., 1994; Stephan et al., 1995) providing evidence of how the loci of mental processes such as *imagined hand movements* are similar yet different from the brain loci of real hand movements. In the future such imagery methods may provide the most direct evidence of the locus and dynamics of how informational substances can diffuse through the extracellular fluid to sites within the cerebral cortex to modulate the neural synaptic vesicle cycle that mediate the neural networks of the brain in memory, learning and behavior (Sudhof, 1995). In Part Two of this book we will explore the use of a number of new of ideo-dynamic hand movements that can be used for hypnotherapeutic induction and problem solving. The investigation of these new approaches via brain imaging methods will provide a genuinely scientific foundation for a hypnotherapy of the future.

Hypothesis 2: State-dependent memory, learning, and behavior are encoded in human experience by informational substances in these localized neuronal networks of the brain.

There is now excellent experimental evidence in animals that the diffusion of informational substances between cells is responsible for encoding memory, learning, and behavior (Shashoua, 1981; Frederickson et al., 1991). The rate of release of these informational substances into the extracellular fluid is increased during intensive learning experiences. This is precisely what one would expect if critical phase transitions are a period of heightened arousal in memory and learning as Langton's theory would predict. This training results in long-term memory and learning that can be abolished when the informational substances are removed from the extracellular fluid by the administration of antisera that block their ability to bind to neural receptors.

The research that makes such state-dependent memory, learning and behavior (SDMLB) so significant is that in the past 25 years we have learned that it is not only drugs that can lead to a partially reversible amnesia. We now know that dozens of the body's own natural molecules are modulating memory, learning, and behavior in a state-dependent manner (Cahill et al., 1994; Freeman, 1995; McGaugh, 1983). This is the new basis of the psychobiology of memory and learning, particularly in relationship to emotions, stress and trauma (Rumelhart, 1995). In particular, we now know that the stress hormones, the same information substances that are responsible for mediating psychosomatic problems are at the same time modulating memory and learning in humans (Izquierdo, 1984, 1988; Rossi, 1986/1993).

The implications of this finding that stress hormones and many other information substances are involved in memory and learning are profound. I have summarized the research literature that indicates that most forms of learning (Pavlovian, Skinnerian, imprinting, sensitization, etc.) are now known to involve information substances, also called neuromodulators or *"messenger molecules"* (Rossi, 1986/1993). Insofar as these classical forms of learning use information substances associated with a wide range of phenomenological states and phase transitions, they *ipso facto* have a state-dependent

100

component. (Rossi & Cheek, 1988). A series of researchable hypotheses detailing how information substances modulating the activity of neural networks that encode memory and learning that could be the basic process of mind/brain information transduction in hypnotherapeutic work has been published elsewhere (Rossi & Cheek, 1988, pp. 50-68). A number of exemplary clinical cases of how such knowledge can provide hints of practical hypnotherapeutic approaches are presented in Chapter Eight of this book. It is important to note that this model of mindbrain communication is a two-way street; it shows how molecules of the body can modulate mental experience as well as how mental experience can modulate the molecules of the body. This is the basis for emphasizing the hypothesis that state-dependent memory, learning, and behavior (SDMLB) is the common denominator that bridges the mindbody gap — the so-called Cartesian dichotomy between mind and body." SDMLB enables us to escape the reductionistic trap of maintaining that mind is nothing more than the matter of Democritus's molecules. The state-dependent concept has recently been generalized as new foundation for understanding the life histories of a species in evolutionary ecology (McNamara & Houston, 1996).

Stress and The mind-gene connection

Hypothesis 3: The molecular-genetic basis of memory, learning, and behavior is modulated by informational substances; The mRNA test of mindbody communication and healing.

Kandel and his coworkers have found that informational substances can facilitate the molecular-genetic basis of memory, learning, and behavior. In pioneering papers, Kandel (1983, 1989) proposed how these molecular-genetic mechanisms could account for many of the classical phenomena of acute and chronic human anxiety and neurosis. Kandel's theoretical and experimental work is the clearest expression of the possibilities of the "mind-gene communication" that was originally formulated independently by Rossi (1986/1993) as the molecular basis of psychosomatic medicine in the psychotherapeutic arts.

The most comprehensive experimental demonstration of how the psychosocial processes of mind and behavior are related to genetic expression is developing in the field of psychoneuroimmunology. As one of the pioneers in this field has emphasized recently, "the exchange of information between the brain and the immune system is bidirectional" (Ader, 1996, p. 15). The clearest documentation is provided by current research that traces the effects of psychological stress experienced by medical students during academic examinations on the transcription of the Interleukin-2 receptor gene and Interleukin-2 production (Glaser et al., 1990, 1993). I have previously outlined the loci at the cellular-genetic level where Glaser and others have found evidence for the effects of psychological stress (Rossi, 1986/1993). These researchers have measured how information transduction is modulated by psychological stress throughout the main cellular-genetic loop of information transduction particularly at these sites: (1) the primary messengers (ACTH, cortisol, epinephrine, etc.), which trigger (2) secondary messengers (cAMP) that (3) mediate gene transcription which eventuates in (4) mRNA (messenger RNA) production and (5) protein synthesis that leads to the formation of (6) other informational substances and receptors on the cell surface. Proliferating evidence is now outlining how psychological stress can modulate the cellular-genetic level (Glaser et al., 1993). The general time parameters for one complete loop of mind-body communication is about an hour and a half or so (one ultradian cycle). These psychobiological rhythms may provide a new window on how the phenomenological experiences of mind and consciousness are related to processes at the molecular-genetic-cellular level (Rossi and Lippincott, 1992; Rossi, 1994b & c).

The most obvious research frontier of the future in this area is to document how a positive psychotherapeutic intervention designed to reduce psychosocial stress could lead to a facilitation of the expression of the Interleukin-2 receptor gene — essentially the reverse of the Glaser protocol outlined above. Glaser's research gains even more profound significance for a general theory of mindbody communication and healing when we realize that other independent medical researchers (Rosenberg and Barry, 1992) have found that interleukin-2 is a messenger molecule of the immune system that tells certain white blood cells to attack pathogens that cause diseases and even cancer cells. The purely medical research represented by Rosenberg and the holistic medicine represented by Glaser have found the same bottom line of mind-gene communication in the developing field of psychoimmunology. I propose that this will become the new criterion for evaluating all forms of holistic mind-body healing in the future — biofeedback, massage, meditation, imagery, active imagination, hypnosis, prayer, ritual or whatever (Dossey, 1982,1995; Siegel, 1986, 1989). Whatever the holistic method, we can test whether it has really facilitated mindbody communication and healing simply by taking a blood sample to determine whether gene transcription actually took place with the very easy and reliable test of whether mRNA is made so that new proteins could be synthesized for growth, healing and new consciousness (Rossi, 1996a, b, c).

Yes, even God would have to pass our mRNA-Gene test if she came down from the clouds to heal a lame child's withered limb. When we do our mRNA (messenger RNA) test on the child's miraculously healed limb we will expect to find evidence that all the normal mRNA-gene transcriptions are operating as they do in a normal limb. Or do you really believe that God would heal the limb by placing some sort of special spiritual substance in there to make the withered limb work? Would God really show her hand by transcending the normal mRNA-Gene transcription method of operation that she uses in all other living creatures here on earth? Actually, I would enjoy witnessing such a sign!

Hypothesis 4: Informational Substance-Receptor communication systems are the psychobiological basis of state-dependent mindbody processes in everyday life as well as psychoanalysis and the therapeutic arts.

Over the past 40 years, psychopharmacologists have used the classical state-dependent memory and learning experimental paradigm to assess the psychological and behavioral effects of psychoactive drugs, which we now know are mediated by informational substance-receptor systems in humans as well as in animals (Cahill et al., 1994; Overton, 1978). Of central significance for our working hypothesis is the fact that when animal or human subjects are given memory/learning tasks while under the influence of many psychoactive drugs that mimic or modulate informational substance-receptor systems, there is a varying degree of amnesia and apparent loss of learning when the drug has been metabolized out of the system. That is, when memory/learning is encoded under drugged conditions, it tends to become state-dependent or statebound to that psychobiological condition; such memory/learning behavior becomes dissociated or apparently "lost" after the drug is metabolized. Re-administering the drug reestablishes the original encoding condition and typically results in some gain of memory/learning.

What is most interesting about these experiments in state-dependent memory and learning is that they enable us to study the parameters of "reversible amnesia," which have been important criteria in understanding the phenomenology of psychoanalysis and therapeutic hypnosis (Rossi, 1986/1993, 1994b). Just as most experiments in state-dependent memory and learning demonstrate that this "reversible amnesia" is only partial (that is, there is usually some memory/learning available even in the dissociated condition after the drug is out of the system) so most of the hypnotic literature documents that hypnotic amnesia is usually fragile and partial in character. A full amnesia that is completely reversible is relatively rare in state-dependent memory/learning experiments as well as in psychoanalysis and therapeutic hypnosis. In the historical literature of hypnosis and psychoanalysis this same fragile and partial character of reversible amnesia may have been responsible for many of the puzzling and paradoxical features of memory that remain the source of continuing controversy that challenges the validity of the various theories of depth psychology.

One of the most interesting clinical examples of reversible state-dependent memory is in the recent reports of unilateral and alternating unilateral lachrymation and its association with depression and pain relieved with hypnotherapy (LePage et al., 1992; LePage & Schafer, 1995).

This is the story of Yolande, a 29-year-old woman who sought treatment from one of the authors (KEL) on referral from her primary physician. Although she wanted help with her life which was in complete disarray, and from her depression, the root of her problems manifested itself during her second visit. While in a hypnotic trance easily induced by a combination eye roll, progressive muscle relaxation and regression, *she was observed to be crying only from her left eye associated with concurrent pain in her right shoulder, back, neck and head.* This pain occurred only in the proximity of her parents. She revealed that she always sat with her mother on the left — at the table, in the lounge room, or in the car ...

The key traumatic event occurred at the age of eight when her stepfather was "belting" her, a regular action of both the stepfather and mother, associated with parental fighting which often involved guns. The patient was running away from her stepfather when he caught her, picked her up and hit her on the right shoulder and back regions. She slid across the table and hit the right side of her head, neck and shoulder on a solid kitchen cupboard. She described severe right-sided headaches while in high school at her ages of 14 and 15. After leaving home and high school at the age of 15 she was symptom free for 10 years.

At the 11th interview and after the stepfather's death, she reported one week of *left headache, shoulder and neck pain* plus a drawing-down feeling of her left eye. She had been without pain from the time of her stepfather's death until she awakened with the opposite side pain the morning her parents' wedding anniversary just prior to this eleventh visit for therapy. This pain disappeared in her hypnotic trance during that therapy session and never returned ... Her pain syndrome is completely gone and her crying is normal. After her last visit, she had a diamond stud inserted onto her left nostril. She saw this as an act of rebellion and a way of declaring her individuality. (LePage & Schafer, 1995, p. 119-121).

The authors explain the very revealing psychodynamics of this case and others as manifestations of state-dependent memory as described by this author (Rossi, 1986/1993) and others (Fischer, 1971 a, b & c; Fischer & Landon, 1972; Swanson & Kinsbourne, 1979; Weingartner, 1978). In the next chapter we will review related research on the state-dependent dynamics of many functions of the left and right cerebral hemispheres, the basic ultradian rest activity cycle, the nasal cycle and their associations with a variety of personality dynamics, stress, dissociative and healing processes on many levels in everyday life as well as hypnotherapy.

Since the earliest days of psychoanalysis it has been noted that a sudden fright or shock could evoke "hypnoidal states" that were somehow related to dissociated or neurotic behavior (Rossi, 1992a & b). A nonlinear dynamics model of how these sudden changes could take place is presented by Thom's (1973, 1983) Catastrophe theory of change (see Box 3.2). I have hypothesized that such "hypnoidal states" are phenomenological expressions of the rest phase of ultradian rhythms. The basic dynamic is that significant psychosocial stimuli may lead to altered levels of arousal in informational-receptor messenger-molecule systems that can encode and release memory, learning, and behavior in a state-dependent manner (Rossi, 1987, 1990a & b). This leads us to the view that the highly individualized and continually changing character of the "software" of the para-synaptic informational substance-receptor communication systems can account for many of the phenomenological vagaries of human memory and behavior in life in general as well in the therapeutic arts.

These hypothesized relationships between informational substance-receptor systems, state-dependent memory and learning, stress, and traumatically encoded mindbody problems suggest a new research frontier for the psychobiological investigation of many classical psychoanalytic concepts such as *repression, dissociation, and emotional complexes.* The foundations of psychoanalysis rest upon the phenomena of reversible amnesia associated with emotional trauma. Jung's concept of the "feeling-toned complexes" as the source of psychological problems had its original experimental validation with the word association test, in which gaps or time lags in the associated process suggested the presence of blocks, repressions, or dissociations in the mind. Informational substance-receptor systems provide a researchable model of how neural networks and cellular processes that encode psychological problems can be blocked or facilitated by endogenous antagonists or agonists on the molecular level and vice versa — how mental processes can modulate molecular processes (Rossi, 1990b).

A new paradigm of such research has been provided recently by Cahill et al., (1994) who compared the effects of the beta-adrenergic receptor antagonist propranolol hydrochloride on the long term memory for an emotionally arousing and emotionally neutral short story. Their results supported their hypothesis that the enhanced memory associated with emotional experiences involves activation of the messenger molecules of the beta-adrenergic system. It would require only a simple extension of their method of telling subjects short stories to apply their approach to documenting the activation of similar messenger molecule-receptor systems in the arousal phase of psychotherapy that is presumably mediated by the neuroendocrinal system (Rossi, 1987, 1995a & b).

Catastrophe Theory: Critical Phase Transitions on the Edge of Chaos

The abrupt suddenness of many experiences of state-dependent memory, *repression, dissociation, and emotional complexes* has never been adequately modeled in depth psychology. A profound problem for the scientific description of psychological as well as natural life events is how to mathematically model the abrupt critical points of change we see all about us. Rapid unexpected changes can be dangerous so they are often called catastrophes: earthquakes, heart attacks, war, emotional moods, the straw that breaks the camel's back etceteras. One of the most interesting yet still controversial mathematical models of the abrupt dynamics of critical points of change is the Catastrophe Theory of Thom (1975, 1983). Thom believes that chaos theory is a subset of catastrophe theory while other authors claim the reverse. However their relationships may eventually be conceptualized, chaos and catastrophe are intimately related. A recent text by Strogatz (1994) provides the most lucid introduction to these dynamics for the budding student of dynamics.

The basic idea of catastrophe theory is contained in the Classification Theorem which states (with many careful qualifications) that given a maximum of four control parameters, all abrupt discontinuous dynamics of change can be modeled by one of seven elementary topological forms. In psychology these models have been used to describe the dynamics of qualitatively distinct but related behaviors and the abrupt shifts that take place between them: bipolar disorders and mood shifts; arousal and fatigue; high versus low reaction time, job performance, stress, illness, accidents, social unrest, etc. (Box 3.1). The two relatively stable states of behavior are mediated by an important *Cusp Point,* (mathematically called the *point of degenerate singularity*) where *behavior is ambiguous and in the process of change.* The cusp point is obviously of greatest interest in any dynamics of psychotherapy and psychological change. From the cusp comes radically different potentials and polarities of human experience and behavior. What are the dynamics that govern the shifts between the various states? How do we learn to recognize and facilitate the critical cusp points in psychotherapy?

Research will be needed to determine, for example, whether certain phases of *emotional arousal, anxiety, phobia and ambivalence are actually characteristic of cusp point behavior* in *critical transitions* from problematic to more adaptive behavior. It is precisely here that conventional psychotherapeutic wisdom may fail. Trying to relax and calm patients down to help them get rid of their painful phase of emotional uncertainty may actually interfere with the patient's creative process. In the second half of this volume we will illustrate in great detail how the therapist can learn to recognize these critical transition periods and help patients utilize their painful arousal and uncertainty to facilitate the four basic phases of the creative cycle.

Box 3.2 **The Dynamics of Catastrophe Theory:**
The Critical Change Point

The most common of the seven elementary models of Thom's Catastrophe Theory used in psychology appears to be the *Cusp Catastrophic Response Surface* illustrated below.

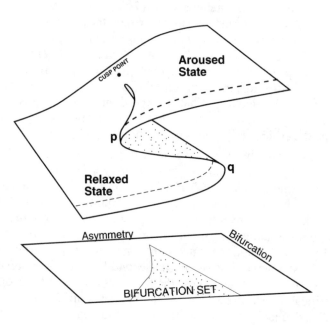

Visualize this cusp catastrophic response surface as a two dimensional sheet with a fold in it. It models two relatively stable states of behavior and an important *Cusp Point,* (mathematically called the *point of degenerate singularity*) where *behavior is ambiguous and in the process of change.* As illustrated, mathematically the shifts between the two stable states are modeled by two processes: (A) Asymmetry and (B) Bifurcation. The change process is smooth and orderly at low values of (B) Bifurcation, for example, but there is a sudden jump or fall (catastrophe) at higher values as indicated. The cusp surface models a complex interaction between (A) and (B) given by the differential equation

$$df(y)/dy = y^3 - by - a.$$

The phenomenon of *hysteresis* (is it related to the hysteria of historical hypnosis?) is illustrated above by the different points at which a dramatic shift in behavior occurs. If behavior is moving in the direction of left to right, the sudden shift up takes place at point **q** when behavior shifts from a relaxed to an aroused state. It is interesting to wonder whether this sudden up shift in arousal or level of consciousness can be used to model the ah-ha or Eureka experience of sudden insight in the future. If behavior is moving in the right to left direction the sudden shift down does not take place until the point **p** reached. This may model many apparently paradoxical psychological patterns when behavior suddenly changes when least expected depending upon the history of the situation. Hysteresis deftly incorporates the very important dimension of personal history in the psychoanalysis of behavior. How people respond in any social situation obviously depends upon their history of experience with that situation. If you are coming from the left that represents a relaxed state you will not reach arousal until you reach point **q**. If you are coming from the right that represents an aroused state you will not shift to relaxation until you reach point **p**. There is an asymmetry between arousal and relaxation that has obvious implications for hypnotherapeutic work. Erickson, for example, was highly sensitive to where patient's were on this arousal-relaxation continuum. His naturalistic and utilization approaches to hypnotic induction utilized the patient's current state of relaxation or arousal rather than beginning at some hypothetical ground zero point of relaxation (as in the standardized induction used in the Stanford and Harvard hypnotic susceptibility scales) and going from there (Erickson, 1958/1980. 1959/1980).

The basic question of hypnotherapeutic work becomes how do we access the cusp point and facilitate optimal choices for problem solving and healing there? Is the process of hypnotic induction actually a means of seeking the flexible potential for change centered at the cusp point? When the traditional hypnotherapist seeks to have a patient go deeper and deeper into a profound hypnotic state is it the critical cusp of potential flux and change (the mathematician's point of degenerate singularity) that is being sought? I hypothesize the answer is yes to all these questions. The traditional hypnotherapist, however, has a different interpretation of this cusp point. The traditional view has been that at this cusp point the patient's mind was a *blank slate on which the therapist's words could be written so that behavior could be programmed.* Alas, as we have seen in Chapter One, the foremost researchers in hypnosis today recognize that this traditional model of suggestion does not work.

The *Cusp Catastrophic Response Surface* model, by contrast, reveals that the critical dynamics of hypnotherapeutic work involves optimizing potentials for change at rather precarious points of ambiguity in human experience and behavior. We may hypothesize that the cusp point is the source, the matrix, the original chaos out of which consciousness, problem solving and healing emerge.

Obviously a gentle therapeutic tap at the cusp point could profoundly alter behavior for good or ill.

But let us persist and ask, precisely how? Research demonstrates that the EEG can reliably record readiness-potentials for behavior up to about half a second before subjects say they have made a conscious decision to voluntarily behave in such and such a way (Libet, 1993). Does hypnotherapeutic work access this readiness potential for voluntary action in such a way that the patient receives a sense of security or conviction about the appropriateness of certain potential paths of problem solving and healing? Does this experience of the cusp point (before voluntary decisions seem to take place) coincide with the peculiar sense of *involuntaryness* that often accompanies successful behavior change and healing in hypnosis? Is this the source of the paradox of why the traditional lore of historical hypnosis emphasizes the importance of involuntryness while so much academic research insists that sense of the involuntary is an illusion (Sarbin and Coe, 1972)?

Let us be bold and ask further speculative questions. Does the experience of *intuition* or "Letting go and letting God" actually imply that some people are sensitive to this nascent cusp point of subjective experience where important feelings, perceptions, cognitions are still in involuntary flux of emergence? Is this the state that some schools of meditation try to facilitate by "stopping the chattering of the monkey mind" with inner focusing, mantras, koans or rituals etc.? Is this why people are usually quiet and still for a moment before they make an important decision so they may "collect their thoughts," for example, before speaking or acting? Is this why fools are rash? Libet (1993) has speculated that here, in fact, is the role of consciousness in decision making. Consciousness does not make decisions. Consciousness merely has the role of inhibiting the acting out of inappropriate choices.

Question people about this quiet moment of "collecting their thoughts" and they will often surprise you by saying their mind is actually blank or seems so. Is this akin to the so-called *blank state* of hypnosis? Is this why traditional hypnotherapists like it? Is this the source of their mistaken magical notion that they can suggest and program all sorts of things into patients when they are in the blank state of hypnosis? Is this, in fact, what magic is? Do we delight in magic because it succeeds, even for only a moment, in helping us access that involuntary cusp point between imagination and reality where the profound as well as the ridiculous may take place?

In Chapter Two we learned that the highest intensity of information processing in nature on the physical, biological and psychological levels takes place *near critical phase transitions*. We can now recognize a connection between Thom's Catastrophe Theory with its cusp points of critical change and Langton's critical phase transitions between different states. The critically important points of change, by their very nature, are usually precariously balanced on a narrow edge of chaos. That is, the informational "computation" of life and mind can only take place in a narrow range of conditions in space and time. That is where, for example, it is hypothesized that a very special "local medium" (e.g. a microscopic cell of life) facilitates the evolution of information processing, growth and complexity at the expense of an increase in "global entropy" in the rest of the universe. Langton (1992) describes these conditions thus:

> Now, Nature could not have been so beneficent as to have maintained this medium near a critical phase transition for very long. This means that the nascent information dynamics must have gained control over some parameters that allowed them to maintain *local* conditions near the phase transition while *global* conditions drifted away from the phase transition. Of course, there must be many parameters that could push such systems away from their vital transition point, and many of these probably varied widely, destroying a large proportion of these early information-processing systems. Evolution can be viewed as the process of gaining control over more and more "parameters" affecting a system's relationship to the vital phase transition. (Langton, 1992, p. 85)

Most of the interesting equations that model physical as well as biological, psychological and social systems have a small number or adjustable values, or parameters as Langton describes above. As we have seen, it is these parameters of nonlinear equations that determine the behavior of the system by tracing its path. As one or more critical parameters vary over a range of values the various types of attractors (fixed point, limit cycle, quasi-periodic and chaotic) become manifest in determining the changing behavior of the system. In this way we achieve a potentially marvelous economy in our models of behavior: the same equation can describe many different patterns of behavior as the system bifurcates and evolves over a wide range of attractors (typical behavior patterns). The synergetics school of self-organization has emphasized some special insights into the nature of "order" and "control" parameters that are of particular interest to the hypnotheapist.

The Symptom Path to Enlightenment

The Synergetics of Life and Mind

Hermann Haken, who is a mathematical physicist and specialist in lasers, has inspired a new school of *Synergetics* over the past twenty-five years to study the dynamics of how self-organizing systems create themselves. Haken and his followers emphasize theory and research designed to reveal how self-organizing systems evolve through the complex interplay of cooperation and competition in their order and control parameters. At the present time there are almost seventy volumes in the Springer-Verlag series on synergetics edited by Haken covering a vast range of applications in all the sciences and, increasingly in the psychology, sociology and even the humanities. While this school has been based in Europe, for the most part, there now are important contributions coming from American sources such as that of J. A. Scott Kelso at the Center for Complex Systems at Florida Atlantic University (Kelso, 1995).

Most theorists speak only of "control" parameters that determine the behavior of the system from the outside. A temperature gradient, for example, a range of decreasing temperatures from hot to cold, is a *control parameter* that decreases the motion of water molecules so they pass through an evolution of phase transitions and increasing order from *steam* to *liquid* water and finally *ice. Notice that a control parameter is something that pushes the system from the outside.* Temperature can effect different systems in different ways, however. How a system responds to an outside control parameter such as temperature depends upon the *internal dynamics of its order parameters.* There is something about the nature and structure of the inherent *"order parameters"* of water molecules that determines its self-organizing behavior under pressure from the outside *"control parameter"* of temperature. Haken (1992) has described the concept of order parameters in social systems in this way.

> In a nation, the national language plays the role of an order parameter that lives much longer than the individuals. When a baby is born it is subjected to language. He or she learns it, and eventually, carries the language further. Quite clearly, an individual may be subjected to several order parameters, such as family, school, language, culture, religion, political party, and so on. (Haken, 1992, p. 35)

Clearly, Haken is using the concept of order parameters to indicate how psychosocial variables may be expressed mathematically and integrated with the dynamics of mind-brain-body. Kruse and Stadler (1990, p. 210) utilize the Gestalt concept of the natural instability (metastability or multi-stability might be alternate descriptions as illustrated in Box 3.1 above) of all brain-mind-perceptual systems to generalize Haken's theory of order parameters in psychology to account for the role of suggestion and the dynamics of psychosomatic interactions in this way.

1. Phenomena of cognitive instability [All the classical phenomena of hypnosis] are macroscopic properties of the microscopic instability of nervous processes ... thoughts and expectations are order parameters which govern the activity of the whole system if it is operating close to instability points. Therefore, the various relations between systemic instability, cognitive multi-stability and suggestibility may be seen as an indirect support of the self-organization metaphor of brain-mind interaction.

2. Phenomena of instability in cognitive systems are not a failure or breakdown of normal functioning but the phenomenological representation of an underlying basic mechanism of order formation. Therefore as a methodological tool and as an empirical and theoretical object of research this class of phenomena is of central importance in cognitive sciences.

3. An interaction between self-organization theory, e.g. synergetic simulation and psychological research, might allow the elaboration of an integrative model for the phenomenal diversity of cognitive multi-stability and suggestion effects.

We could generalize this by adding that cognitive and belief systems as well as imagery, sensations, emotions, and personality constructs such as ego, self, identity, etc. could also function as *order parameters* in the dynamics of the self-organizing psyche. Perhaps perception, awareness and consciousness itself could be conceptualized as order parameters. Traditional depth psychology is essentially an effort to understand how the psycho*dynamics* of such internal order parameters organize the mind, behavior and fate of the person.

How, then, does hypnotherapeutic suggestion fit into the interaction between order and control parameters? Hypnotherapeutic suggestion, as conventionally conceived, is something imposed on a subject from the outside. The traditional hypnotist tries to program or manipulate the subject from the outside. Such suggestion coming from the *outside* therefore must be a *"control parameter."* This makes good sense because traditional direct hypnotic suggestion has always been thought of as a way of manipulating and *controlling* the mind and behavior of the subject. "Hypnotic induction" is thought of as a manipulative procedure for altering the state of subjects so their internal experience and external behavior can be *controlled* by the therapist.

What is it that the hypnotherapist actually tries to control? Well, obviously, the awareness, consciousness, sensations, imagery, emotions, cognitions, identity, behavior etc. of the subject. That is, the traditional hypnotheapist tries to use suggestion from the outside to manipulate the subject's personal internal *"order parameters!"* Traditional direct suggestion attempts to seize control of a subject's internally self-organizing *"order parameters"* and convert them into *"control parameters"* that can be manipulated by the hypnotherapist on the outside. This seems so simple an inference that one may wonder why it is emphasized so strongly here.

This distinction between order and control parameters in the dynamics of hypnotherapy is emphasized because it may enable us to write differential equations describing the process of hypnosis for the first time (Rossi, 1994a, b; 1995c). In the next chapter I illustrate how such mathematical models may be developed to investigate chronobiological relationships between order and control parameters in hypnotherapeutic work. The theory and actual research practice of how order and control parameters may be explored for the creation of new mathematical models in neuroscience have been described by a growing number of workers. Freeman (1995), for example, has modeled the chaotic dynamics of the self-organization of sensation and perception in the olfactory bulb and discussed its implications for understanding brain, cognition and behavior. Smith & Thelen (1993) and Thelen & Smith (1995) have presented detailed models of a dynamical systems approach to human development, cognition and behavior. Tschhacher et al., (1992), have edited a volume on self-organization in clinical psychology and a number of others have made some initial contributions to the synergetic approach to suggestion and hypnosis (Kruse & Gheorghiu, 1992; Kruse & Stadler, 1990; Kruse et al., 1995).

Kruse & Gheorghiu (1992) use the dynamics of self-organization theory to conceptualize the efficacy of hypnosis and suggestion as a natural consequence of the essential instability (or multi-stability) of the cognitive construction of individual reality. Kruse et al., 1992, p. 114) say " ... hypnotic induction may be one efficient therapeutic intervention to enhance the intra-systemic instability of a person and the well-defined expectations induced by ritual behavior sequences can be used to stabilize or destabilize the reality constructions." They utilize the basic Gestalt assumption that perception is *adaptively ambiguous* and "suggestion leads to a direct reduction of degrees of freedom without wasting conscious intellectual capacity in the disambiguation process" (Gheorghiu & Kruse, 1992 b, p. 131). This concept finds experimental support in the work of Unterweger et al.,

(1992) who found that highly susceptible hypnotic subjects did not have to work as hard as low susceptible's in dealing with the cognitive demands of passing items on The Stanford Hypnotic Susceptibility Scale.

Erickson's use of a two step approach in using (1) confusion, shock and surprise to initially destabilize a person's erroneous and rigid mental sets and then (2) a variety of other approaches to facilitate creative moments in hypnotherapy was described as follows (Rossi, 1973a, p. 19).

The relation between psychological shock and creative moments is apparent: a "psychic shock" interrupts a person's habitual associations so that something new may appear. Ideally psychological shock sets up the conditions for a creative moment when a new insight, attitude or behavior change may take place in the subject. Erickson has also described hypnotic trance itself as a special psychological state which effects a similar break in the patient's conscious and habitual associations so that creative learning can take place as follows.

"The induction and maintenance of a trance serve to provide a special psychological state in which the patient can re-associate and reorganize his inner psychological complexities and utilize his own capacities in a manner in accord with his own experiential life ... therapy results from an inner re-synthesis of the patient's behavior achieved by the patient himself ... It is this experience of re-associating and reorganizing his own experiential life that eventuates in a cure, not the manifestation or responsive behavior which can, at best, satisfy only the observer." (Erickson, 1948/1980, p. 38)

The implications of the nonlinear dynamics of self-organization theory in hypnotherapy has been explored by Revenstorf (1992, p. 119) in a manner that supports the richness of Erickson's diverse approaches. He uses the chaotic and essentially unpredictable paths of the logistic equation as a rationale for his basic thesis that "hypnosis and its chance effects cannot be explained by any of the classical schools of therapy; instead a non-theoretical heuristic point of view is stressed." He then describes Erickson's extremely flexible intervention with variable outcomes: "Hypnotherapy in this sense is meant to initiate an attentional shift in order to facilitate an internal search process which will enable the client to look at a problem not only from a different point of view but to correct a certain part of the experience" Revenstorf (1992, p. 129). New approaches to facilitating these internal search processes that can facilitate the essentially non-rational resolution of psychological problems and symptoms by patients will be discussed in detail in the second half of this book.

Kelso (1995) has recently presented in rich detail the history of his research program into the nonlinear order and control parameters of the self-organization of the brain and behavior that could well serve as one of the clearest and most useful paradigms of the new self-organizational dynamics for clinicians as well as researchers. He focuses on the significance of the natural self-organizational dynamics of brain, mind and behavior versus the currently popular programming concepts because they usually lead to an infinite philosophical regress of who or what is the top programmer.

Kelso's emphasis on the essential identity of the principles governing "overt behavior and brain behavior" is a direct outcome of his twenty year research program on the coordination dynamics of hand and body movements. As such it may have important implications as a model for the new ideo-dynamic approaches to hypnotherapeutic work that utilize the inherent multi-stability of brain and behavioral processes presented in the second half of this book. There we will illustrate and discuss the spontaneous ideo-dynamic hand and body movements as well as the organic and psychosomatic symptoms that function as the mindbody's own natural information and communication system in hypnotherapeutic work. There we will explore the deep and profoundly ethical question of whether the role of the modern hypnotherapist really is to try to change the patient's natural internal *order parameters* into *control parameters* that are to be programmed and manipulated from the outside. Following the inspiration provided above by Kelso, it will be seen that the truly creative and surprising experiences that are a natural result of the spontaneous self-organizing dynamics of the psyche do not require such manipulation, programming and control by the therapist.

The Basic Ideas

1. *We are shifting from a model of reductionism to constructivism in science; from analysis to synthesis in all forms of psychotherapy. This deeply integrative approach is taking us to the threshold of understanding the transformations of matter, energy and information as the essence of the hypnotherapeutic enterprise. Asking ideo-dynamic questions generates information that facilitates the patient's self-organizational processes of mindbody healing and problem solving in hypnotherapeutic work.*

2. *The phenomena of stochastic resonance indicate that noise, random perturbations or disturbances to a life system can*

actually enhance the strength of signals on many levels from the molecular to human perception, learning and behavior. Many of the traditional and Ericksonian therapeutic techniques of hypnosis as well as other holistic methods may be useful forms of stochastic resonance that non-specifically facilitate healing and problem solving.

3. *The distinction between order and control parameters in the dynamics of hypnotherapy may enable us to write differential equations modeling the process of hypnotherapeutic work in the future. This new understanding of order and control parameters has important practical implications in developing new ideo-dynamic approaches to psychotherapy. Hypnotherapeutic work utilizes the inherent instability of brain-mind-behavior systems to help patients access the order parameters of their phenomenological experience to facilitate their own process of creative change from the inside. (rather than the therapist attempting to access control parameters to manipulate the patient from the outside).*

4. *A focal issue of hypnotherapeutic work becomes how do we help patients access the Cusp Point of transition and change on their Catastrophic Response Surface to facilitate optimal choices for problem solving and healing? We hypothesize that the process of hypnotic induction is actually a means of seeking the flexible potential for change centered at this cusp point of transition in human experience. While the traditional hypnotherapist sought to have patients "go deeper and deeper into a profound hypnotic state," we reconceptualize this "deepening process" as a dynamical phase transition accessing the critical cusp of potential flux and change in the natural process of problem solving and healing.*

5. *The basic implication of Self-Organization and Adaptive Complexity Theory is that we do not have to suggest or program humans in hypnotherapeutic work. People undergo spontaneous phase transitions in the natural multi-stability of mind and all psychobiological systems of self-organization. The new ideo-dynamic approaches presented in the second half of this volume utilize this naturally adaptive multi-stability to facilitate the evolution of information, creativity, problem solving and healing.*

Chapter Four:
The Concept of
Hypnotherapeutic Work

You must be a chaos to give birth to a dancing star.

Nietzsche

The concept of hypnotherapeutic work that is being introduced in this chapter evolved gradually during three stages over the past twenty-five years. The first stage was in my initial explorations of the periodicity that was observed in Milton H. Erickson's approach to hypnotherapy (Rossi, 1981, 1982, 1986/1993). This led to the second stage consisting of clinical/experimental research assessing a series of hypotheses about the chronobiological (the biology of time) aspects of hypnotic susceptibility and self-hypnosis (Aldrich & Bernstein, 1987; Brown, 1991 a & b; Lippincott, 1992 a, 1993; Lloyd & Rossi, 1992; Osowiec, 1992; Rossi, 1992; Rossi & Lippincott, 1993; Saito & Kano, 1992; Sanders & Mann 1995; Sommer, 1993; Wallace, 1993; Wallace & Kokoszka, 1995). The current third stage is leading to a reinterpretation of all previous work in terms of the chaotobiological (deterministic chaos) dynamics of hypnotherapeutic work. In this chapter we will explore the view that it is the *patient's own internal hypnotherapeutic work* rather than the therapist's hypnotic suggestions or programming per se that is the essence of the efficacy of hypnosis in problem solving and healing. What the therapist says and does is very important in helping patients accessing the possibility of healing; what the patient actually does with the therapist's words is the essence of hypnotherapeutic work.

This idea of hypnotherapeutic *work* takes us to a deeper level of understanding the report of the 1784 commission of King Louis XIV

119

of France that concluded that the cures of Mesmerism were nothing more than the positive emotions of imagination, hope, faith coupled with suggestion. These positive attitudes, I would maintain, are not in themselves the healing agent (Dafter, 1996; Rossi, 1996b). Rather, such positive emotions are the most easily observable states associated with the more *hidden inner psychobiological work of optimizing mindbody communication and successful problem solving* that is the basic stuff of stress reduction and healing in hypnosis. We begin this chapter by telling the story of what we now know about the wave nature of human consciousness and experience. This will lead us into recent research about the psychobiological domain of hypnotherapeutic work on all levels of mindbody communication from cognition, emotion and behavior to the neuroendocrine and psychoimmune systems all the way down to the cellular-genetic level.

The Wave Nature of Consciousness and Being

The first real understanding about the wave nature of human consciousness and being began with our current era of scientific research into the periodicity of our dreams. Until recently, it was thought that sleep was simple rest. A profound revolution took place in 1953 when three researchers at the University of Chicago — Eugene Aserinsky, Nathaniel Kleitman, and William Dement — reported that every 90 minutes or so throughout the night, our sleep became a very active process for about 10 to 30 minutes. The brain-wave pattern as measured by the electroencephalograph (EEG) became very similar to the active pattern when we are awake. In addition, the sleeper's eyes moved rapidly under the closed eyelids, as if a moving scene was being observed. Indeed, it was found that when people were awakened during these Rapid Eye Movement periods (REM sleep), they reported that they were dreaming.

The REM dream cycle immediately became the touchstone for evaluating all past and present theories of the meaning of dreams as well as their role in mindbody performance, health and behavior. During REM periods, oxygen consumption increases and more blood flows to the brain than when we are awake. Our breathing, heart rate, blood pressure, and gastrointestinal movements are more variable than during wakefulness. Clearly, sleep and dreaming could not be a simple, passive process of rest and recovery. The highly active periods of REM sleep must involve some adaptive processes very important for survival as well as recuperation and rejuvenation. But exactly what are they? This remains as a leading-edge question even today, almost 40 years after Aserinsky, Kleitman, and Dement reported their discovery of dream sleep (Moffitt et al., 1993; Moffitt, 1995).

The mystery only deepened when it was later discovered that the 90-to-120-minute dream rhythm apparently continues even during the day, when we believe we are normally awake. Kleitman called this daytime rhythm the "Basic Rest-Activity Cycle" (BRAC) and originally described it as follows:

> Manifestations of a basic rest-activity cycle (BRAC) in the functioning of the nervous system were amply established by recording EEGs of sleepers ... The operation of the BRAC in wakefulness is not as obvious as it is in sleep; there are too many external influences that tend to disrupt or obscure the cycle. ... [Nevertheless], everyday observations support the view that the BRAC operates during the waking hours as well as in sleep. The now common "coffee-break" at 10:30 a.m. divides the three-hour office stint from 9:00 a.m. to noon into two 90-minute fractions. The relief obtained by some individuals from brief 10-to-15-minute catnaps perhaps represents a "riding over" the low phase of a BRAC, and postprandial [after lunch] drowsiness may be an accentuation of the same phase. (Kleitman 1969, pp. 34-47)

Kleitman maintains that the general public as well as most professionals have not yet grasped the deeper significance of these mindbody rhythms as a fundamental characteristic of the life process. In one of his last research papers titled, "Basic Rest-Activity Cycle — 22 Years Later," he supported this view with these words: " ... the cycle involves gastric hunger contractions and sexual excitement — processes concerned with self-preservation and preservation of the species — which led to the designation of the cycle as basic." (Kleitman, 1982, p. 314)

There have been three stages in the evolution of this new model of the wave nature of consciousness and being. The traditional view has been that consciousness has been a simple wave of increasing alertness peaking around mid-day and disappearing into the deepest levels of sleep at night. This was updated when we recognized the nightly variations in consciousness and arousal in REM dream sleep. A mathematical model of the wave nature of human consciousness that recognized its peaks and valleys while we are asleep and awake was then developed by Rutger Wever of the Max Planck Institute in Germany. Wever's has made detailed studies over the past 30 years of *circadian* (daily rhythms) and *ultradian* rhythms (faster rhythms that take place many times a day such as heart rate and breathing) in human subjects living in a controlled environment. These studies were carried out in "bunkers" in the side of a Sylvian hill at the Max Plank institute in Germany where his subjects lived for months at a time, isolated from all the normal cues that were thought to influence our mindbody rhythms. These cues from our environment — such as daylight, temperature, sounds and mealtimes — are called *Zeitgebers*. Zeitgebers are said to "entrain" or "synchronize" our internal mindbody "clocks" so that they can be continually adjusted to the changing seasons and demands of daily living.

One might object that the idea of "Zeitgebers" sounds rather like a rigid and mechanical way of looking at life. Wever insists, however, that just the opposite is the case (Wever & Rossi, 1992). He emphasizes that *personal relationships between people are actually the most significant "time givers."* In a modern society, we usually wake up and go to sleep not with the dawn of light and the setting of the sun, but with the cues we give each other — such as yawning, stretching, and acting sleepy as well as alarm clocks and the need to go to work. Although there is a great deal of research that supports Wever's ultradian model in Box 4.1, it is still theoretical in the sense that most of the data were collected under carefully controlled laboratory conditions isolated from the distracting influences of real life. More recent research exploring nonlinear dynamical systems in social psychology strongly supports the idea that "behavior is a wave" involving point attractors, limit cyclic attractors and strange attractors (Newston, 1994). Carefully designed studies to determine the extent to which Weaver's chronobiological model can fit a broad array of psychosocial behaviors have not yet been done, however. Until now no one has understood how chronobiology and depth psychology may be related. The rational for exploring the view that *chronobiological rhythms may provide us with a window into the psychodynamics of mindbody healing* is provided by a careful reading of the intuitions of many pioneers in hypnosis and depth psychology.

Box 4.1: Psychological Stress and Circadian Dyschronization

The significance of psychological stress in contrast to simple physical work on circadian mindbody rhythms has been emphasized by Wever (1988, p. 302) with his summary statement: "In contrast to physical work load, psychological or behavioral burdening of the subjects does seem to have an influence on human circadian rhythms, by lengthening the period and increasing the tendency toward *internal dyschronization*." Wever's third order differential equation for modeling the circadian sleep-wake oscillation is as follows

$$y''' + y'' + \varepsilon\,(y^2 - 1)\,y' + y = z$$

---

where z represents "all those external stimuli that control the generated oscillation." (Wever, 1984, p. 28-29). Wever's research, however, indicates that it is not solely environmental stimuli but rather other order parameters within the person (e.g., personality, motivation, stress) that may modulate the chaotobiological expression of mindbody oscillations of circadian rhythms. A phase portrait of his equation nicely illustrates the two strange attractors of sleeping and waking. The corresponding real time view of this equation, however, does not do justice to some well established facts about the ultradian dream rhythm. For example, the first dream period after sleep begins is the deepest. Thereafter the dream peaks go higher and higher as they approach closer and closer to the threshold of consciousness as the night progresses. In addition there are typically four or five dream periods nightly rather than the two or three modeled by the Wever equation. The more recent work of Strogatz (1986, 1994) serves as a transition from the early mathematical models to the current recognition of the chaotic dynamics of the circadian processes of mindbody rhythms. The rush of new empirical data in this area leads to the current challenge to develop more adequate mathematical models than what are illustrated here.

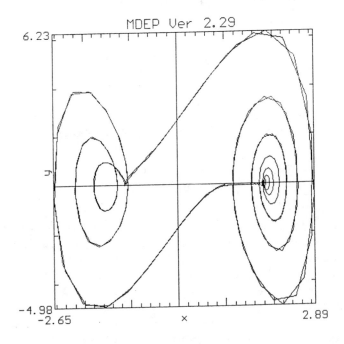

A phase portrait of the bi-phasic chaotic sleep-wake cycle as modeled by the Wever equation as drawn by the Midshipman Differential Equations Program (MDEP), Version 2.29. This software is available free from J. L. Buchanan, Mathematics Department, U. S. Naval Academy, 572 Holloway Rd., Annapolis, Maryland, 2144402-5002.

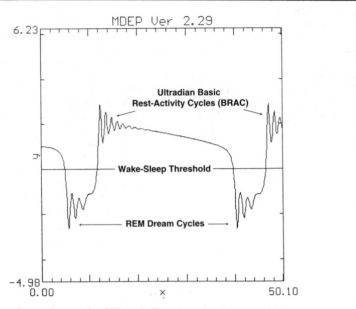

The above time series graph of Wever's Equation reveals some of its limitations in portraying the REM dream cycle drawn with MDEP software. Research indicates that we typically experience four or five major REM dream cycles per night with an ascending series of tops as we approach awakening in the morning. Wever's equation, however, shows only two or at most three peaks that are not in an ascending series.

Depth Psychology and the Wave Nature
of Human Experience

If the psychobiological wave nature of consciousness and being is really so important for adaptation and health why had no one recognized them before? Or had they? The founders of depth psychology — the great 19th-century French neurologist, Jean-Martin Charcot, Pierre Janet, an early pioneer of hypnosis, Sigmund Freud, and Carl Jung — all believed that conscious experience was rooted in our body. Unfortunately, the biology of their time was inadequate to understand the subtle relationships between mind and body. Yet in much of their work, we can find a trail of clues that suggest that they understood something about the wave nature of consciousness, stress and healing in everyday life as well as in the consulting room.

Charcot's "Hypnoid" State, Dreams and Hysteria

Jean-Martin Charcot was a professor of neurology and psychiatry in Paris a century and a half ago (Ellenberger, 1970). He believed that there existed a state of consciousness which occurred periodically, somewhere between sleeping and waking. He called it "hypnoid" and identified it as a source of hysteria and many psychological problems. He believed that this state was something like hypnosis, but could appear spontaneously during everyday life. He did not know why it appeared, but hypothesized that it was much like the experience of being caught up in a dream at night. At such times, he believed, any strong emotional stimulus could become imprinted on the mind in an unhealthy or a neurotic fashion. Particularly when we cannot rest, we become prone to highly-charged emotional states, anxiety, irritability, and depression. Charcot searched in vain to find a biological basis for such a hypnoid state. Another century of research was required before laboratory scientists coined the term *ultradian* and recognized that our nighttime dreams take place every 90 to 120 minutes when we sleep, while our daydreams follow the same rhythm when we are awake.

Janet's "Abasement" — A Lowering of Mental Energy

From Charcot, the trail led to one of his students — a brilliant physician named Pierre Janet — who would go on to become one of the most profound theorists and practitioners of hypnosis. Janet noticed that, at various times through the day, we experience periodic daily fluctuations in our mental status. These he termed *"abaissement du niveau mental,"* (a lowering of mental level). During these periods of *abaissement,* Janet found, our psyche seems to lose some of its capacity to synthesize reality into a meaningful whole. If we encounter a traumatic or strong emotional event during these periods, the mind lacks its usual ability to make sense of it and fit it properly into a meaningful, secure, whole (Ellenberger, 1970; Rossi and Smith, 1990). During *abaissement,* we tend to be emotionally vulnerable and easily overwhelmed; we can register the life experiences but cannot properly "digest" them. The emotional experience floats in our unconscious, unassimilated, in effect, jamming the gears of the mind. Janet hypothesized that such unassimilated experiences could become the seed of psychological or psychosomatic illness, obsessive thought patterns, phobias — all sorts of behavioral problems. Many chronic problems, he believed, were the result of the mindbody's continuing, frustrated effort to make sense of the original disturbing experience.

Janet believed that there was an underlying physiological source of the *abasements* during the day that were somehow associated with stress and exhaustion. One medical historian of this era summarized Janet's view:

> We do not know the exact nature of psychological forces. Janet never doubted that they are of a physiological nature, and seems to have believed that the day would come when they could be measured. He considered that these forces were, to a great extent, connected with the condition of the brain and organs. . .and differ from one individual to another. These forces can obviously be reconstituted in some way. "I don't know where these reserves are, but I do know that they exist," said Janet. One of the main sources of this reconstitution is sleep; hence the importance for the therapist to teach his client about the best way of preparing himself for sleep. The same could be said about the various techniques of rest and relaxation, *the distribution of pauses throughout the day*, of rest days during the month, and of vacations during the year. . .(Ellenberger, 1970 p.380, Italics added).

Does not the phrase, *"the distribution of pauses throughout the day,"* sound like Janet's anticipation of our new understanding of the wave nature of human consciousness? Many of Janet's ideas were adopted a generation later by Freud, when he formulated the foundations of psychoanalysis.

Freud's Psychopathology of Everyday Life

It was Freud's genius to recognize the essential connections between the sources of psychopathology and creativity in everyday life. In their early classic volume, *Studies on Hysteria*, Breuer and Freud recognized that the *hypnoid* state was somehow related to "abnormal states of consciousness" as well as the ordinary everyday "absence of mind" we all experience. They describe their puzzlement about these connections as follows:

> The longer we have been occupied with these phenomena the more we have become convinced that *the splitting of consciousness which is so striking in the well-known classical cases under the form of "double conscience" is present to a rudimentary degree in every hysteria, and that a tendency to such a dissociation, and with it the emergence of abnormal states of consciousness (which we shall bring together under the term "hypnoid") is the basic phenomenon of this neurosis."* (Breuer and Freud, 1885/1957, p. 12).

> ... Are hypnoid states of this kind in existence before the patient falls ill, and how do they come about? I can say very little about this, for apart from the case of Anna O, we have no observations at our disposal which might throw light on the point. It seems certain that with her, the auto-hypnosis had the way paved for it by habitual reveries and that it was fully established by an affect of

protracted anxiety, which, indeed, would itself be the basis for a hypnoid state. It seems not improbable that this process holds good fairly generally.

A great variety of states lead to "absence of mind" but only a few of them predispose to auto-hypnosis or pass over immediately into it. An investigator who is deep in a problem is also no doubt anesthetic to a certain degree, and he has large groups of sensations of which he forms no conscious perception; and the same is true of anyone who is using his creative imagination actively. . . (Ibid. p. 217-218).

Here we find a basic question about the wave nature of consciousness posed with perfect clarity: "...Are hypnoid states of this kind in existence before the patient falls ill, and how do they come about?" At that time it was speculated that the hypnoid state was caused by a traumatic experience or a "hereditary taint" or perhaps a combination of both. It would take another 50 years before researchers found that there is an entirely natural "absence of mind" that takes place for 10 to 20 minutes every 90 to 120 minutes or so throughout the day.

Freud's recognition that "a great variety of states lead to 'absence of mind'. . .and the same is true of anyone who is using his creative imagination actively..." was later elaborated by Carl Jung into a profoundly far-reaching theory of the evolution of mind and higher states of consciousness.

Jung's Transformation of Character and Consciousness

The relationship between Janet's *abaissement* and the symptoms of ultradian stress, healing, creativity, and the transformation of character were described by Jung as follows.

The *abaissement du niveau mental*, the energy lost to consciousness, is a phenomenon which shows itself most drastically in the "loss of soul" among primitive peoples, who also have interesting psychotherapeutic methods for recapturing the soul that has gone astray. ... Similar phenomena can be observed in civilized man. ... He, too, is liable to a sudden loss of initiative for no apparent reason. ... Carelessness of all kinds, neglected duties, tasks postponed, willful outbursts of defiance, and so on, all these can dam up his vitality to such an extent that certain quanta of energy, no longer finding a conscious outlet, stream off into the unconscious, where they activate other, compensating contents, which in turn begin to exert a compulsive influence on the conscious mind. (Hence the very common combination of extreme neglect of duty and a compulsion neurosis!)

This is one way in which loss of energy may come about. The other way causes loss, not through a malfunctioning of the conscious mind, but through a "spontaneous" activation of unconscious contents, which react secondarily upon the conscious mind. These are moments in human life when a new page is turned. New interests and tendencies appear which have hitherto received no attention, or there is a sudden change of personality (a so-called mutation of character). During the incubation period of such a change we can often observe a loss of conscious energy: the new development has drawn off the energy it needs from consciousness. This lowering of energy can be seen most clearly before the onset of certain psychoses and also in the empty stillness which precedes creative work. (Jung, 1954, p. 180-81)

Jung wrote what is probably the clearest description of the rhythmic or "wavelike character" of emotional complexes and imagery before the term *ultradian* came on the scene:

What then, scientifically speaking, is a "feeling-toned complex"? It is the *image* of a certain psychic situation which is strongly accentuated emotionally and is, moreover, incompatible with the habitual attitude of consciousness. This image has a powerful inner coherence, it has its own wholeness and, in addition, a relatively high degree of autonomy, so that it is subject to the control of the conscious mind to only a limited extent, and therefore behaves like an animated foreign body in the sphere of consciousness. The complex can usually be suppressed with an effort of will, but not argued out of existence, and at the first suitable opportunity, it reappears in all its original strength. Certain experimental investigations seem to indicate that *its intensity or activity curve has a wavelike character, with a "wave-length" of hours, days, or weeks. This very complicated question remains as yet unclarified.* (Jung, 1960, p. 96, Italics added)

I would submit that Jung's "very complicated question" is at least in part answered by our developing understanding of the ultradian wave nature of consciousness in stress and healing. Jung later went on to elaborate these ideas into a new theory of consciousness and the use of meditation and religious rituals to facilitate experiences of "a supernormal degree of luminosity" (Jung, 1960, p. 436). In all of this Jung went quite a bit further than anyone else in recognizing the rhythmic aspect of "higher consciousness" and healing.

We have come full circle, from the classrooms of 19th-century Paris and Vienna to our current exploration of the wave nature of consciousness. From the "hypnoid state" of Charcot and the *abaissement* of Janet as the source of psychopathology to Freud and Jung's recognition of its role in healing, creativity, and the evolution of consciousness. Each of these pioneers seemed to describe much the same phenomenon: there are special time periods of potential stress or healing that come on us naturally in daily life. Each described mindbody states when our balance of consciousness and capacities shift, rise and fall, leaving us not fully awake, nor quite asleep. All had glimpsed in it a "royal road" to our inner mindbody, holding the potential for pathology as well as personal growth. What those 19th-century physicians could not know because of the limitations of the biological sciences, 20th-century researchers could now explore in detail.

Milton Erickson'sCommon Everyday Trance: The Psychobiology of Self-Hypnosis

One of the first therapists to notice and actually utilize the wave nature of consciousness was Milton H. Erickson, MD, the eminent American psychiatrist and hypnotherapist. While most therapists saw patients for a 50-minute session, Erickson preferred to meet for an hour and a half or more. In over a half century of treating people, Erickson noticed that the mental-emotional equilibrium of his patients naturally varied during the course of their sessions. He claimed that people in everyday life also naturally drifted between subtle but distinct mindbody states. When he worked with patients for at least an hour and a half or two, he found, they were almost certain to go through distinct changes in their consciousness and states of being (Erickson, 1986; Rossi, 1986/1993).

During these lengthier sessions, for no apparent reason, the patient's head might start to nod rhythmically, eyelids would blink slowly, and then close over faraway-looking eyes. The body might go perfectly still, with fingers, hands, arms, or legs apparently frozen in an awkward position. Sometimes there was a subtle smile on the person's face or, more often, the features were passive and slack — what Erickson described as "ironed out." During his teaching sessions with me he often pointed out their rapidly quivering eyelids, furrowed brows, trembling lips or chin, and tears — the outward signs that his patients were intensely groping with private inner dramas. On some occasions, Erickson did nothing to direct people to go into trance; it just seemed to happen, sooner or later, all by itself. Erickson's sessions with patients seemed to be very subtle and indirect forms of hypnotherapeutic encounter wherein nature came in as an equal partner in ways that most observers could not yet understand.

Erickson always took advantage of the natural ebb and flow of consciousness that seemed to open and close like windows throughout his therapeutic sessions. Only when he observed that the patient's physical and mental processes were either *heating up* or *quieting down* would Erickson "facilitate hypnotherapeutic trance." Years of treating patients had taught him that during these naturally arousing or relaxing therapeutic periods, that usually lasted between 10 and 20 minutes, most people are able to gain better access to their emotions, intuitions, and deepest thoughts. Erickson would use these windows of inner access to help people learn to solve their own problems in their own way.

Erickson called these natural periods of healing *"The Common Everyday Trance"* because they appeared to be a normal feature of our daily lives as well as the consulting room. All of us have such moments of inner preoccupation during the course of our day, when we are in some in-between state of consciousness, neither fully awake nor quite asleep. The housewife staring vacantly over a cup of coffee in mid-morning, the student with a faraway look in his eyes in the middle of a lecture, the truck driver who blinks in mild surprise as he suddenly reaches his destination without any memory of the last 20 minutes, are all exhibiting the common everyday trance.

Although common, such brief periods of inner focus are clearly very special. During these quiet periods we can be more open and introspective. Our focus turns inward as our dreams, fantasies and reveries — the raw material of growth in everyday life as well as psychotherapy — become unusually vivid. Our natural Common Everyday Trance seems to be a period when the window between our conscious and unconscious opens a bit. Because the inner mind is the source of our deepest intuitions, people may be at their most creative and experience insights, fantasy, and intuitive leaps during these meditative moments. The Common Everyday Trance can also be a period of openness and vulnerability to outside influences; suggestions made during this time are sometimes more easily accepted. Erickson called his use of the common everyday trance his "naturalistic" or "utilization approach," because he believed he was simply helping people utilize their own natural inner resources to solve their own problems in their own ways during these periods.

This led me to speculate that Erickson's reputation for having an uncanny knack for facilitating deep hypnosis and resolving psychosomatic problems could be due, at least in part, to his unwitting utilization of our natural waves of consciousness — our natural circadian and ultradian mindbody rhythms. This became the seed in my mind for an entirely new theory of therapeutic hypnosis and self-hypnosis as well as mindbody communication and healing: *Excessive and chronic stress cause symptoms by distorting our normal ultradian/circadian rhythms; hypnosis could ameliorate these symptoms simply by providing an opportunity for these natural mindbody rhythms to normalize themselves.* Hypnotic suggestion might work because it *entrains* and *synchronizes* our natural ultradian processes of ultradian and circadian rest, restoration and healing. *The secret of transformation from illness to health to higher levels of performance and well-being lay in recognizing and facilitating a person's own creative resources during these natural windows of inner focus and rejuvenation that arise periodically for about 20 minutes every hour and a half or so throughout the day* (Rossi, 1982).

But precisely why are people so uncommonly accessible for therapeutic change during these special periods? In particular, how are they able to make curative connections between body and mind so readily? Term it the "Common Everyday Trance," "self-hypnosis," "relaxation," "meditation," "daydreaming," "imagery" or whatever, just what is going on during these special periods? The questions led me to explore the psychobiological sources of the wave nature of our consciousness from mind to gene and their relationships to stress and healing.

Stress, Healing and the Chaotic Wave Nature of Consciousness

There are four basic hypotheses at the heart of this new conception of stress, healing and the chaotic wave nature of consciousness as well as the essence of hypnotherapeutic work. They begin by locating the ultimate source of the wave nature of life in *(1) the periodic nature of the molecular-genetic-protein loop at the source of life in the cell cycle and (2) the consequent periodic brain-body loop of neuroendocrine self-regulation* and mindbody communication. These two basic hypotheses lead to the next two on the source and resolution of mindbody dysfunctions. *(3) traumatic life experiences or chronic stress can disrupt or desynchronize these natural mindbody rhythms and (4) hypnotherapeutic work can facilitate the adaptation of these complex mindbody rhythms for problem solving and healing.* Since I have already dealt in detail with the data that supports these hypotheses (Lloyd & Rossi, 1992 a & b, 1993; Rossi, 1986, 1987, 1986/1993; Rossi and Cheek, 1988; Rossi and Ryan, 1986), I will review here only the more recent types of research that provide support for a deep chronobiological conception of the wave nature of mind-gene communication in psychotherapy and hypnotherapeutic work.

1. The timing of the nonlinear dynamics of molecular-genetic expression at the cellular level are the ultimate source of chaotobiological rhythms of life and the wave nature of consciousness and being (Barinaga, 1995; Braiman, et al., 1995; Sehgal et al., 1995; Takahashi & Hoffman, 1995).

It takes time to create life. It takes time to grow, develop and go through the entire life cycle. The fundamental unit of all life is, of course, the cell — it takes about six trillion of them to make up the brain and body. Each of these cells has its own life cycle — birth, growth, maturity and death. Some nerve cells apparently last a lifetime, other cells such as those that make up the lining of the digestive system may last only a day before they are worn out, die and are replaced by others. Since most of the body needs new cells to grow, develop and replace those that are lost, there is a continuous *cell cycle* of birth, growth, and replication by cell division going on all the time. Some of the most profound advances in molecular biology over the past decade have had to do with fundamental discoveries about how the *recursive timing* of the *cell cycle* works at the genetic level.

The major breakthrough in this area began with the discovery that certain aberrations in the circadian cycle behavior of a wide variety of organisms ranging from bread molds to fruit fly's and rodents could be traced to mutations in certain genes. Konopka and Benzer (1971; Benzer, 1971) initially found that behavior as complex as the circadian cycle could be traced to a single gene now called *"per"* (for *per*iod). Current developments now trace the molecular source of ultradian and circadian rhythmicity to the communication loop between expression of the *per* gene, its messenger RNA and the clock protein it is translated into within certain pacemaker cells of the organism (Takahashe and Hoffman, 1995).

One of the clearest illustrations of the nonlinear ultradian rhythmic dynamics at the molecular-genetic level is presented in a series of graphs by Murray et al. (1989; 1991) that are reproduced here in figure 4.1. In this series of three graphs it can be seen that a typical 90-120 minute ultradian rhythm is fundamental in cell growth and division. The approximately 20 minute peak in Maturation Promoting Factor (MPF), the protein Cyclin and the H1 kinase enzyme act in concert to signal the final stage of genetic replication for cell division (mitosis) for growth and healing. A recent mathematical model of the cell cycle illustrating the nonlinear dynamics of a 20 minute rhythm as the fundamental time-frame for life at the cellular-genetic level is summarized in Box 4.2. I hypothesize that the ultimate source of chaotobiological rhythms of life and the wave nature of consciousness and being are these nonlinear dynamics of molecular-genetic expression at the cellular level. It is the class of these molecular-genetic dynamics that are responsive to psychosocial stimuli that we hope to entrain with hypnotherapeutic work.

If ultradian rhythms are so fundamental at the genetic level why is it that until recently it was the circadian rhythms that have been most emphasized? The more obvious 24 hour circadian rhythm was historically the first to be documented scientifically centuries ago by the astronomer, De Marian, when he found that the daily movement of the leaves of certain plants were "endogenous." That is, something going on inside the plant caused their circadian movement rather than the cues provided by the daily rising and setting of the sun because the movements continued even when the plants were placed in continuous darkness in a closet. More recent studies of the gradual development of the sleep-wake cycle in the human infant between the first and third month of life suggests that the circadian cycle evolves out of the gradual consolidation of a number of ultradian rhythms of the central and autonomic nervous systems (Hoppen-brouwers, 1992; Meier-Koll, 1992).

David Lloyd (1992) has cited his own original research on the molecular cellular level together with that of others supports the view that intracellular time keeping is due to epigenetic oscillations of an ultradian clock. "Epigenetic oscillations" in this context means the ultradian rhythms involved in the transcription and translation of the gene-protein loop as described above. This ultradian clock is the center of a broad orchestration of cellular activities in plants and animals consistent with the thermodynamics on the cellular and orgasmic levels. Brodsky (1992) has brought together a detailed summary of the ultradian circahoralian (approximately hourly) oscillations of proteins, enzymes, and the fundamental energy dynamics of cyclic ATP production at the cellular level that apparently exhibit fractal dynamics. He paints a broad picture of how these oscillations at the molecular-genetic-cellular level are apparently causally related to similar ultradian rhythms at the level of hormones in the blood plasma and a host of self-regulatory systems at the brain, body and behavioral levels to which we may now turn our attention. Table 4.1 summarizes some of the main classes of biological rhythms discussed by Brodsky that are related in varying complex patterns.

133

Box 4.2   A 20 Minute Mathematical Model of Ultradian Dynamics

Albert Goldbeter, who is a pioneer in the creation of new mathematical models of the nonlinear dynamics of chronobiological rhythms describes their scope as follows.

The role of biological rhythms are manifold. Well-known is the function of circadian rhythms in adaptation to the environment. If these endogenous rhythms and the periodic alternation of day and night with which they coincide did not exist, how would we see the passage of time? Also clear is the role of other periodic phenomena in the generation of rhythmical behavior in repetitive machines such as the heart or the respiratory system. The functions of other ultradian rhythms have recently been reviewed [Lloyd & Rossi, 1992]. The preceding discussion suggests that the provision of an *optimal mode of intercellular communication could well be a most important function of biological rhythms.... Frequency-encoded, rhythmic processes would be more accurate and versatile than those encoded by the sole amplitude of the intercellular signal...*(Goldbeter, 1996, p. 523, Ital. are ours).

Goldbeter's mathematical model of the 20 minute "mitotic oscillator" which is the essence of cell cycle in replication, growth and healing is illustrated below. Klevecz (1992) has presented evidence of how the dynamics at this cellular-genetic level could function as a tuner of the cell cycle. He sees these dynamics as a chaotic or strange attractor that could be modeled by a bifurcation diagram of Rössler's attractor. The details of the system of differential equations that generates Goldbeter's model (1996, pp. 419-438) may suggest how such ultradian dynamics on the cellular-genetic level could be integrated with apparently similar ultradian dynamics on the neuroendocrine level, psychosocial and the hypnotherapeutic levels in the future.

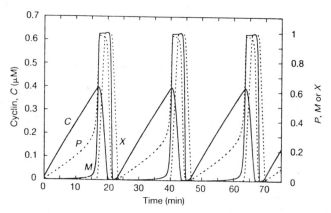

Illustrated are the dynamical interaction of four mediators of the mitotic oscillator where: P is the fraction of Cell Division Cycle (cdc25) phosphatase; M is the fraction of active cdc2 kinase; C is the cyclin concentration and X is the fraction of active cyclin protease.

Table 4.1: Biological rhythms classified by increasing period length that may be of significance in psychotherapy and hypnotherapeutic work.

Rhythm	Period
Neural	0.01 to 10 seconds
Cardiac	1 second
Respiration	4-5 seconds
Glycolytic (ATP energy)	several minutes
Biochemical	1 to 20 minutes
Cell Cycle (Mitotic cycle)	20 minutes (to 24 hours or more)
Enzyme & Protein Levels	20 - 90 minutes
Hunger	90-120 minutes
Hormonal	90-180 minutes (to 24 hours)
Circadian (sleep/wake cycle)	24 hours
Human Ovarian Cycle	28 days
Ecological	months to years

The current challenge is to explore how the biological rhythms of Table 4.1 are related to psychological behavior. Neural rhythms are obviously related to psychophysical responses such as reaction time, sensation and perception. Hormonal rhythms are now known to be related to a variety of behaviors such as sexuality, sleep-waking, the Basic-Activity-Rest and REM dream cycles as well as memory, learning and attention (Smith & Nutt, 1996). But are the glycolytic rhythms, that are fundamental in energy production at the cellular level every few minutes, related to the momentary shifts we actually experience throughout the day? When people take a short break for a few minutes now and then, for example, are they actually waiting for their glycolytic cycles to catch up?

2. The self-regulatory systems of the mind, brain and body (e.g., the autonomic system, the central and peripheral nervous system, the neuroendocrine system, the immune system) are coordinated by and serve the complex nonlinear genetic dynamics at the cell cycle level (Dawkins, 1989). Many of these self-regulatory systems are manifest in the observable behavior the Basic-Rest Activity Cycle (BRAC).

The most well documented facts about the nonlinear ultradian dynamics of all the major systems of self-regulation is currently evolving out of research in the time parameters of physiology, endocrinology and immunology. Traditionally the field of neuroendocrinology has been data rich but rather devoid of theory apart from the basic idea that the hormones flowing between brain and body were essentially messenger molecules coordinating development, metabolism, and homeostasis. The monumental research of Selye introduced a more dynamical conception of the role of the neuroendocrine system in the bodies response to trauma, emotional stress and other challenges to adaptation from the environment (Selye, 1976, 1982; Rossi, 1986/1993). More recent research is providing detailed data about the nonlinear dynamics of the pulsate flow of hormones in coordinating complex cybernetic loops of information transduction between mind, behavior, brain, body and gene (Haken and Koepchen, 1991; Lloyd and Rossi, 1992 b).

Hormones, now generally recognized as "messenger molecules," are produced within the nonlinear ultradian time parameters of gene transcription and translation and coordinate communication between genes and the self-regulatory systems of the mindbody interacting with the environment. In the simplest terms, hormones along with the nervous system are the connecting communication link between the genes and the environment. Hormones are the original, slower communication system developed by life at the single cell level. Hormones are usually released in a pulsate manner and operate within ultradian time parameters of minutes, hours, days, weeks, months and the seasons of the year. The nervous system, by contrast, evolved later to meet the needs for a more rapid communication system that operates to coordinate the relatively vast distances in large multicellular organisms with pulses (waves of depolarization) of less than a second. The phylogenetically older hormonal system regulates the nervous system at the molecular-genetic level and vica versa so that the adaptive responses of the modern organism is a marvelously complex coordination of the hormonal and nervous systems. Since our interest in this book is on the perceptible dimensions of the human time frame of psychotherapy over minutes, hours, days and weeks, our focus will be primarily on the hormonal systems of ultradian time outlined by the parameters of the 90-120 minute Basic-Rest-Activity Cycle (BRAC).

One of the clearest illustrations of the complex adaptive systems of ultradian dynamics on multiple levels of the mindbody is in the pulsate release of the hormones of the renin-angiotensin-aldosterone system in relation to the REM-NREM cycles of dream sleep

(Brandenberger, 1992). From a purely physiological point of view this is a key hormonal system regulating blood pressure, blood volume and sodium retention. From the psychobiological point of view, however, let us keep in mind that we are interested in the renin-angiotensin-aldosterone system only as an example of the ultradian communication dynamics between the genetic level where hormonal messenger molecules are made and the psychodynamics of the dream where at least some psychological life is made. With this caveat in place let us read what Brandenberger (1992, p. 128) has to say about this hormonal system in sleep and dreams.

> ...simultaneous monitoring of PRA [plasma renin activity] and the changes in the sleep stages gave evidence of a strong relation between PRA levels and the sleep cycles... NREM sleep is invariably linked to increasing PRA levels, and declining levels are observed when sleep becomes lighter; spontaneous and provoked awakenings blunt the rise in PRA normally associated with NREM sleep. So PRA curves exactly reflect the pattern of sleep stage distribution. When the sleep cycles are regular, PRA levels oscillate at a regular ultradian periodicity and for incomplete sleep cycles, PRA reflect all irregularities in the sleep structure.... It does not appear that this association can be broken. In normal men, modifying the renal renin content only modulates the amplitude of the nocturnal oscillations without disturbing their relation to the sleep stages..., and in the case of sleep disorders, such as narcolepsy or sleep apnea, the renin profiles reflect all disturbances of the internal sleep structure...

As illustrated in figure 4.2, the ultradian dynamics in the pulsate flow of plasma renin activity (PRA) can be profoundly altered by mind and behavior simply by delaying the onset of sleep for eight hours. I am not aware of any studies of the psychotherapeutic implications of this shift in the dynamics of the renin-angiotensin-aldosterone system but we do know that personality and behavior are related to blood pressure in marvelously complex ways. In the final chapter of this book a case is presented of narcolepsy that was apparently successfully treated with a hypnotherapeutic approach utilizing the ultradian healing response. It will be the task of future research to boldly go where no psychobiological theory has gone before in linking the mindbody-gene levels in this area. It would be most instructive to learn, for example, if the classical hypnotic induction approaches of the standardized hypnotic susceptibility scales that emphasize relaxation and even sleep can in any way modulate plasma renin activity and, by implication, its associated psychobiological dynamics on all levels from mind to gene.

Figure 4.3 illustrates a series of graphs of the ultradian dynamics of another major communication system of the mindbody arousal and relaxation mediated by adrenocorticotropin (ACTH), cortisol and beta-endorphin . As can be seen there are wide individual variations in the ultradian pulsate flow of ACTH and cortisol in terms of amplitude and time for the two subjects yet there is a recognizable similarity as well. There are usually major ultradian peaks of an hour and a half or so corresponding to the Basic-Rest-Activity-Cycle in the early morning hours between say 5 a.m. and noon with diminishing peaks thereafter in the afternoon hours. But even this may be highly variable. Notice how the subject J.L.R. has a major peak late at night around 10 p.m. (about 19 or 20 hours on the top graph). There is evidence that these peaks in hormonal messenger molecule communication correspond to variations psychosocial demands as well as psychosocial dominance (Sapolsky, 1990,1992).

Even more fascinating are the relationships between psychobiological arousal and relaxation mediated by the relationships between the pulsate ultradian flow of cortisol and beta-endorphin. As a result of gene transcription and translation the large protein "mother molecule" proopiomelanocortin (POMC) is initially produced in anterior pituitary cells of the brain (Rose, 1989). It is called a mother molecule because it gradually breaks down into about a dozen children molecules including ACTH and that have varying effects upon psychobiological arousal, memory, learning and relaxation (Brush and Levine, 1989; Buchanan et al., 1992). We witness the wisdom of nature here in an exquisite manner. The same mother molecule in the brain, POMC, is produced to regulate an entire cycle of (1) arousal via ACTH communicating a signal to the adrenal cortex of the body to produce cortisol to facilitate the dynamics of energy production and (2) relaxation by the coordinated release of beta-endorphin. The available evidence suggests that an entire 90-120 minute ultradian cycle of arousal, work optimum performance is initiated by the action of ACTH and cortisol and then brought to a natural conclusion by the release of beta-endorphin that can ease the pain of this work phase and promote a quiet resting phase to facilitate healing and the cellular dynamics of building up the restorative phase of the ultradian cycle in preparation for the next work phase.

Recall how the heart works to (1) produce a beat to pump blood and then (2) rests a bit to prepare for the next beat. Similarly respiration requires the initial effort of breathing in to get oxygen for the energy burn to drive metabolism and then a relaxation phase to exhale and prepare for the next inhalation. All basic life processes require alternating phases of (1) arousal and effort where energy is consumed and (2) a phase of so-called "relaxation" where the system is actually furiously busy building up energy (cyclic AMP) and supplies (enzymes and messenger molecules) at the genetic-cellular level for the next work cycle. We emphasize this basic two phase dynamic of arousal and relaxation because it will be found in the next section that these same alternating phases of arousal and relaxation are fundamental in the new conception hypnotherapeutic work that we are developing to resolve the paradoxes of current theory and practice first discussed in chapter one.

Iranmanesh et al. (1989, p.1023) have studied the complex periodic relations between the pulsate release of cortisol and beta-endorphin in men. While their number of subjects was small their intensive sampling of these hormones at 10 minute intervals over a 24 hour period provided enough data to document the existence of a the 20 minute feedback relationship in the activity of cortisol and beta-endorphin as follows.

> In five of the seven men, a negative cross-correlation was found between serum beta-endorphin and cortisol concentrations, when cortisol was considered to lead beta-endorphin by 20 or 30 minutes. Thus, whenever cortisol concentrations decreased, serum beta-endorphin concentrations increased, within 20-30 minutes. Correspondingly, whenever cortisol concentrations increased, serum beta-endorphin concentrations decreased 20 or 30 minutes later. These observations provide evidence for autofeedback of a lagged negative nature between cortisol and beta-endorphin in normal men.

It is just such data that I have proposed as being one of the psychobiological basis of the ultradian stress syndrome and the 20 minute ultradian healing response that will be discussed later in this chapter (Rossi, 1986/1993; Rossi and Nimmons, 1991).

3. Psychobiological stress engendered when we chronically interfere with our natural ultradian mind-brain-body-gene cybernetic loop of self-regulation by a traumatic and/or excessive chronic work load on physical, cognitive and emotional levels is a major etiology for psychosomatic problems and stress related dysfuntions of the immune system in psychoimmunology.

The six sets of illustrations 4.1 through 4.6 may be taken to illustrate how the complex cybernetic paths of information transduction and self-regulation from the cellular-genetic level to mind, behavior and hypnotherapeutic work are all connected. I hypothesize that these connections are a two way street. Just as the ultradian dynamics at the cellular-genetic level can modulate the neuroendocrine axis and behavior, so can mind and behavior ultimately modulate the messenger molecules that will eventually modulate gene expression. It is this great chain of consciousness and being that is the new foundation of hypnotherapy of the future. This will only be possible, however, if the appropriate resources are devoted to research on mindbody relationships in hypnotherapy rather than limiting research to the psychological-behavioral level alone as has been typical of most past work (Rossi, 1989b).

That the ultradian rhythms of growth, development and healing at the cellular-genetic level in figure 4.1 are directly related to the ultradian rhythms of the hormonal messenger molecules of the neuroendocrine system in figures 4.2 and 4.3 is evident from a knowledge of the basic fact that all hormones are ultimately products of gene expression. Gene expression and hormonal flow are all part of the same cybernetic brain-body loop of nonlinear information transduction. How this gene-hormone loop is associated with the mind-behavior loop, however, is even more complex and less well understood at this time. The transition from the gene-hormonal loop to the mindbody is evident in the next three figures 4.4, 4.5 and 4.6 that illustrate similar ultradian rhythms every hour and a half or two. The ultradian rhythm of the hormone insulin is a major player in the ultradian rhythms of glucose, the major fuel of the brain and body. Thus, people with diabetes take injections of insulin on an ultradian rhythm to regulate their blood glucose level for optimal ultradian rhythms of mindbody experience and well-being. That mind and behavior are intimately related to glucose utilization in the brain is well illustrated by recent research that documented how cognitive-behavioral therapy of patients with obsessive-compulsive disorder could actually modulate the metabolic utilization of glucose in the caudate nucleus of the brain as measured by positron emission tomography (Schwartz et al., 1996).

An area of psychobiological self-regulation where stress dynamics are evident on all levels from mind and behavior to gene is the field of psychoimmunology. The Glaser et al., (1990) research study documents how psychosocial stress of students encountering a week of medical exams interferes with the genetic expression of the inter-leukin-receptor gene was presented earlier in chapter three. Crabtree (1989) has summarized data on the wide range of periods required for the molecular-genetic operation of the immune system. They range from the short ultradian processes of about 5 minutes for secondary messengers from the cell surface to communicate across the cytoplasm to the genes to the more typical 90-120 BRAC periods before T-cells are committed to activation to the longer periods of a week or two for a complete cycle of making new antibodies to fight a major infectious illness.

A recent psychoimmunological study by Naliboff et al. (1996) of the effects of the ultradian time parameters of stress provides important insight into the operation of psychosocial factors on the cellular level as follows:

> Brief laboratory stressors such as mental arithmetic, vigilance tasks, or public speaking consistently lead to immune system changes including increased Natural Killer (NK) cell numbers and cytotoxicity, and in vivo decreases in proliferative response to mutogens PHA and ConA. The typical stressor for these studies lasts 5 to 20 minutes and we have previously shown a return to baseline for the immune measures one hour after the stress. The current study was designed to evaluate whether the physiological and immune system changes to these laboratory stressors would persist over a more extended period (60 minutes) of mild to moderate activation...

> The subjects were 15 healthy young men (age range = 19.28). Subjects were tested on two sessions. During one session subjects participated in the extended stressor consisting of a repeating series of five computer tasks (Stroop, paired-memory, vigilance, and two types of eye-hand coordination)...On a second session (order randomized) subjects watched a 60 minute video as a resting control...

> Results indicated significant increases in heart rate and skin conductance across the entire 60 minutes of the stressor compared to the control task, Significant increases in NK cell numbers, NK cell cytotoxicity, and numbers of CD8 T-cells were found 12 minutes into the stress task compared to the video. There was some decline in these measures at 60 minutes but overall they remained above the control task levels. CD19 (B cells) were decreased at 60 minutes during the stress task compared to the control task. There was a small but significant decrease in the proliferative response to PHA during the stress task. This study demonstrates the rapid immune changes during brief stress tend to last the length of stressors at least up to 60 minutes. (Naliboff et al., 1996, Abstract A. 13).

Similar ultradian time parameters have been used in most studies of stress, the immune system and hypnotherapy. Barabasz et al. (1996), for example found significant alteration of the immune system response as measured by B-cell and helper T-cells for highly hypnotizable subjects.

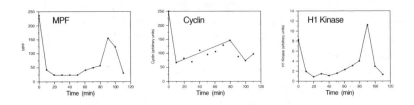

Fig. 4.1. The Cellular-Genetic Level. In this series of graphs it can be seen that a typical 90-120 minute ultradian rhythm is fundamental in cell growth and replication. The approximately 20 minute peak in Maturation Promoting Factor (MPF), the protein Cyclin and the enzyme H1 kinase act in concert to signal the final stage of genetic replication and cell division (mitosis) (From Murray et al., 1989). Some researchers believe this may be the basic ultradian pacemaker that sets all other levels such as the metabolic, neuroendocrinological, cognitive-behavioral and the socio-cultural as illustrated below.

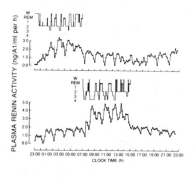

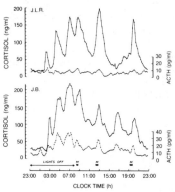

Fig. 4.2. The Endocrine-Behavior Level. An example of the interaction between the cognitive-behavioral and hormonal levels. The typical 90-120 minute ultradian rhythms in the pulsate expression of the endocrine renin-angiotensin-aldosterone system have their higher amplitude peaks shifted to the right by an 8-hour delay of the sleep-wake cycle in the lower graph. The small inset illustrates the relationship between plasma renin and the stages of waking consciousness, Rapid Eye Movement Sleep (REM Dreaming state) and the four major levels of sleep depth (From Brandenberger, 1992).

Fig. 4.3. The Neuroendocrine Level. Two profiles of the individual ultradian rhythms in ACTH and Cortisol in two subjects when blood samples were taken at 10 minute intervals over a 24 hour period (From Brandenberger, 1992). While there are obvious differences they both illustrate 90-120 minute pulsate rhythms with varying amplitudes. The lower profile, perhaps more typical, illustrates how these two hormonal messenger molecules that mediate states of arousal tend to their highest peaks in the early morning hours and gradually dwindle in the afternoon and evening when energy levels are lower.

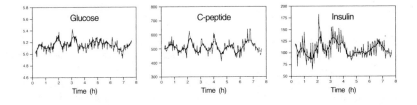

Fig. 4.4. The Endocrine-Energy-Metabolic Level. Blood Glucose (left), C-peptide (middle) and insulin (right) obtained at two minute intervals during an 8-hour fasting period have rapid 10-15 minute oscillations that are shown superimposed on the approximately 90-120 ultradian rhythms (Sturis et al., 1992).

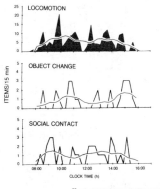

Fig. 4.5. The Behavioral-Social-Cultural Level. Time series illustrating the ultradian rhythms of the locomotion (about 80 minutes), object change (about 65 minutes) and social contacts (about 103 minutes) for the Indian child "Ram" in a naturalistic setting in a small village in India. Similar ultradian rhythms are found in a child of !Ko Bushmen and social synchronization in a village community of Colombian Indians as well as free play in highly urbanized children in Germany. (From Meier-Koll, 1992).

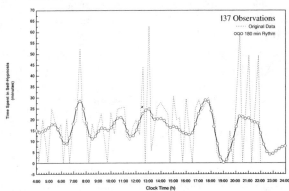

Fig. 4.6. The Cognitive-Behavioral Level. An illustration of the 180 minute ultradian rhythms of self-hypnosis recorded by 16 subjects in their diaries (From Rossi, 1992a). Similar rhythms are found in the time series of subjects who were instructed to simply enjoy an "ultradian healing response" whenever they felt a need to.

143

Currently, there is considerable scientific interest in the potential effects of psychological factors on the immune system. This has stimulated both new research and a reconsideration of previous data on the effects of relaxation, imagery, and hypnosis on immune function...

An audio-taped hypnotic induction was played while each subject sat alone in a quiet room. A positive suggestion, ... asked subjects to "imagine your white blood cells attacking and distorting germ cells in your body." The entire hypnosis session lasted 20 minutes. Subsequently, subjects were given instruction on rapid alert self-hypnosis... and instructed to practice twice daily during the week (total of 5 — 10 minutes per day required). One hour after hypnosis the second blood sample was obtained. At a one-week follow-up session, the self-report SCL-90-r was again administered prior to a second 25 minute hypnotic induction. The third blood sample was taken one hour after hypnosis...

The results of this study appear to show significant immunomodulation for subjects exposed to hypnosis as measured by B-cells and helper T-cells. Highly hypnotizable subjects exposed to hypnosis showed significantly greater T-cell counts in contrast to highly hypnotizable subjects exposed to REST [Restricted Environmental Simulation Therapy] relaxation only. In general, the results of the study demonstrate that hypnosis was specifically associated with an immune system alteration while a treatment known to produce significant relaxation effects (REST) with potential for immunoenhancement was not associated with similar positive immunomodulation. The finding that hypnosis can modify the production and/or activity of components of the immune system has far reaching implications for researchers and clinicians. (Ruzyla-Smith, et al., 1995, pg. 71-77).

Igor Todorov (1990) has integrated research on the molecular-genetic-cellular level that outlines the more general process of complex adaptation to physical trauma, shock and stress. The wave nature of the healing response at this ultimate cellular-genetic level is evident in three major cycles of gene expression and the production of their healing proteins. The initial M (Metabolism) phase are those produced within an hour to mobilize energy and form the first protein building blocks for healing. The next R (Ribosomal) stage proteins are produced within hours to facilitate the further process of translation in making the next set of healing proteins. The third N (Nuclear) stage takes dozens of hours to a day or more to access the DNA polmerase enzymes and other factors in the nucleus of the cell to complete the healing response.

This cycle of response to stress and trauma at the cellular level takes on particular significance in association with the recently developed "Danger Model Theory" of immune system function versus the traditional "Self/non-self Model." The self/non-self theory model, for which Peter Medawar and Frank Macfarland Burnet received the Noble Prize in medicine in 1960 emphasizes that early in fetal development the immune system "learns" how to distinguish between self and non-self tissues by automatically killing off any maturing T cells of the immune system that attack the "self" — the fetuses own tissues that are identified by a uniquely individual molecular signature (the major histocompatibility complex found on the surface of nearly all body cells). From that time on, the T cells of the immune system attack only foreign or "non-self" antigens that are molecular signals of the presence of things like bacteria and viruses that do not belong to the self.

The new "Danger model theory," formulated by Polly Matzinger and colleagues (Richardson, 1996; Ridge, Ephraim & Matzinger, 1996), by contrast, emphasizes that the immune system's antigen presenting Dendritic cells pick up danger signals from body cells that have been killed by stress and/or trauma. An apt, popular description of the process is provided by Richardson (1996, p. 85).

> Dendritic cells, the least-known type of antigen presenters, were tailor-made for this role of immune sentry. All tissues are laced with them: their long, fingerlike extensions — the dendrites — reach into every cranny of the body, forming a lacy network. Under normal circumstances they rest quietly. But when dendritic cells are activated by whatever it is that activates them, they get moving: they literally crawl through the tissue. And their typical destination is a lymph node.

> Soon the whole thing seemed clear to Matzinger. Maybe what activates dendritic cells, she thought, is danger — the danger as signaled by prematurely dying cells floating around the tissue. Maybe they provide the signal that prompts dendritic cells to sound the alarm. The scenario wasn't hard to imagine. Somewhere in a piece of tissue, a cell dies a nasty death — perhaps it is a skin cell burst open by a chicken pox infection. Viral proteins and skin proteins both spill out of the cell. A nearby dendritic cell, sensing the danger, somehow becomes activated and begins drinking up the dying cell's contents. Then it starts crawling toward the nearest lymph node.

> There, like a good APC [antigen presenting cell], the dendritic cell presents antigen — it displays viral proteins and skin proteins on its surface. The T cells that can recognize the tell-tale proteins bind to them, thus getting the first signal. But along the way to the lymph node, prompted somehow by the evidence of cell death it has absorbed, the dendritic cell has produced another substance on its surface, one of a group of molecules whose identity is still being worked out. That substance gives T cells the second signal: it tells them to get going. Multiplying rapidly, they fan out in search of virus-infected cells to kill. Eventually they eliminate the virus. A few of them remain as memory cells to respond more quickly the next time it invades. (Richardson, 1996, p. 85).

The current challenge to psychoimmunology is to integrate this new view of how the immune system works with research that relates psychological trauma and stress with Todorov's three fundamental cycles of the healing response at the cellular-genetic level. It would seem obvious that one way to do this would be to combine Todorov's analyses with the Glaser type research paradigm of the psychosocial-stress decrement of the immune system described above. As is typical of the medical research process, it is usually the case that we first establish how pathology works. Later we explore options for healing. In this case we are learning how psychobiological stress and trauma interact with the immune system: psychosocial stress can turn off gene expression required for the optimum functioning of the immune system in fighting disease. The next step would be to use hypnotherapy to turn off the psychosocial stress in order to turn the healing genes back on using the Ruzyla-Smith type paradigm. This would be the type of crucial evidence needed to document the dynamics of the new psychobiological foundation for hypnotherapeutic work from mind to gene as proposed by the author (Rossi, 1986/1993)..

4. The basic mechanism and psychobiological dynamics of hypnotherapeutic work is to entrain and utilize the information transduction loop on all levels between the cognitive-behavioral, neuroendocrine and molecular-genetic to facilitate these natural rhythms of activity, problems solving, rest and healing.

Some of the most interesting studies of ultradian rhythms on the cognitive-behavioral level have been done in laboratory and field studies of free-play in children in both urban and native settings illustrated in figure 4.5. Meier-koll (1992, p. 279) summarizes the deep perspective of this work as follows.

> In the preschool child ultradian cycles can be detected in time series of free playing and related activities. The child's spontaneous behavior roughly described in terms of exploratory and solitary phases seems to be organized according to the alternating half-phases of an ultradian 2 hour cycle. In both mentally handicapped children and adults, several stereotyped activities were found to be modulated according to ultradian periods. Additionally, the frequency of stereotyped hand waving determined separately for the right and left hand during daytime can reflect ultradian shifts in the relative predominance of one cerebral hemisphere compared with the other. Finally, social synchronization of individual, ultradian behavior cycles could be observed in a community of Colombian Indians living as hunters and gatherers. This suggests, that social synchronization of ultradian behavior cycles enables small groups of so-called primitive peoples to organize their daily life with respect to optimal cooperation and the economy of their physical efforts. As *Homo Sapiens* and some of his ancestors have developed on the sociocultural level of smaller hunter-gatherer

communities, one might speculate that socially synchronized behavior cycles served for the survival of early hominid groups.

Not only early hominid groups but current society utilizes the 90-120 minute basic rest activity cycle (BRAC) in many obvious ways. Important social meetings, business activities, sports and the movies usually take up one BRAC. If the meeting is to go on longer there is usually some arrangement to take a 15-20 minute break sometime in the middle. It has usually been assumed that these were simply convenient activity periods or that they were entirely conditioned by outer cues and circumstances. The balance of evidence according to Meier-Koll and others, however, is that while there certainly are conditioning social and physical cues (e.g. sunrise, sunset, artificial lighting), the ultradian rhythms of work, play, social and solitary activity are "endogenous." That is there is a built-in psychobiological component in ultradian rhythms that is entirely consistent with our basic assumptions that these endogenous rhythms are coordinated on all levels from the cognitive-behavioral level of hypnotherapeutic work to the genetic. Details about ultradian rhythms at the hypnotherapeutic level illustrated in figure 4.6 will be presented later in this chapter

How we are to create mathematical models of these endogenous rhythms that may help us utilize them to optimize both outer world performance as well as inner world healing is the now the task of interdisciplinary hypnotherapeutic research. Some paradigms for such research comes from recent chronobiological research on the synchronizing effects of light in psychobiology. From the Circadian, Neuroendocrine and Sleep Disorders Section of the Harvard Medical School comes a report on the practical implications of artificial light on the human circadian pacemaker (Boivin et al., 1996, p. 540) that has interesting implications for hypnotherapeutic research.

Since the first report in unicells, studies across diverse species have demonstrated that light is a powerful synchronizer which resets, in an intensity-dependent manner, endogenous circadian pacemakers. Although it is recognized that bright light (~7000 to 13,000 lux) is an effective circadian synchronizer in humans, it is widely believed that the human pacemaker is insensitive to ordinary indoor illumination (~50-300 lux). It has been proposed that the relationship between the resetting effect of light and its intensity follows a compressive *nonlinear function,* such that exposure to lower illuminances still exerts a robust effect. We therefore undertook a series of experiments which support this hypothesis and report here that light of even relatively low intensity (~180 lux) significantly phase-shifts the human circadian pacemaker. Our results clearly demonstrate that humans are much more sensitive to light than initially suspected and support the conclusion that they are not qualitatively different from other mammals in their mechanism of circadian entrainment.

A practical implication of this research is on the significance of reduced room illumination that was more popular with the hypnotherapeutic practice of the past before the current use of hypnotic susceptibility scales presumably standardized in full indoor illumination. Contrary to expectation from this study, an earlier report by Mann and Sanders (1995) found no apparent relationship between two different conditions of indoor light intensity and hypnotic trance depth. It is not known whether the two lighting conditions of this study made effective use of the nonlinear relationship between light and circadian pacemaker entrainment reported by Boivin et al. (1996), however, since the two light conditions of the Mann & Sanders study were not reported in lux. One would also presume that eye closure that is required for hypnotic induction using the standard hypnotic susceptibility scales would also impact on the lighting conditions in an as yet not understood manner. That it would be appropriate to replicate the Mann & Sanders study under more carefully specified experimental conditions is suggested by the next study documenting the resetting of the circadian clock by Pavlovian conditioned stimuli that apparently accessed the level of gene expression.

This next research report is particularly interesting because it relates to our fundamental idea that the chronobiological rhythms associated with the "mind-gene connection" are potentially associated with stress and healing in psychotherapy as well as everyday life. Amir and Stewart (1996, p. 542) abstract their research as follows.

Environmental light is the dominant temporal cue for the entrainment of circadian rhythms. In mammals, light entrains circadian rhythms by daily resetting a pacemaker located in hypothalamic suprachiasmatic nucleus (SCN). Although it is widely held that the phase resetting by light involves cellular elements within the SCN that are uniquely responsive to photic cues, we now report that non-photic cues that reliably precede to the onset of light can, through associative learning, come to activate these elements. In rats, a neutral non-photic stimulus paired with light in Pavlovian conditioning trials was capable of eliciting cellular and behavioral effects characteristic of phase-dependent resetting of the pacemaker by light, the expression of the transcription factors *Fos* in SCN cells, and phase shifts in free-running activity and temperature rhythms. Thus an associative learning process, Pavlovian conditioning, provides a means whereby environmental cues that predict light onset can come to mimic the effects of light on the SCN pacemaker and thereby bring about entrainment of circadian rhythms.

It would be difficult to over estimate the significance of this research for understanding the mind-gene connection. This research implies that Pavlovian conditioning, one of the foundations of modern learning theory and adaptive behavior, is now related to the cellular-genetic level since it is able to modulate the expression of the genetic transcription factor *Fos* in the superchiasmatic nucleus of the brain. That is, the process of associative learning, here considered an experience of mind and behavior, turns on the expression of certain genes in the brain; this is the essence of what I call the mind-gene connection or communication. This is what I would regard as the bottom line of any form of psychotherapy that purports to facilitate healing. Healing usually involves the activation of certain gene systems that can produce the proteins and enzymes that facilitate the organic healing of the body as discussed above.

On a broader philosophical level we can regard this research documenting the mind-gene connection as establishing the experimental foundation for a practical approach to the so-called *mindbody problem:* the Cartesian split between mind and body. It was Descartes who said centuries ago that mind and body were two separate realms. The next question was, Do mind and body somehow run parallel together by a pre-established harmony or do mind and body interact to coordinate their activity together? Research such as that of Glaser and now Amir & Stewart support the interactional view of mindbody dynamics and, further, provide evidence for the actual molecular-genetic mechanisms that are involved.

It requires another level of scientific documentation to now prove that mind-gene communication is in fact the actual mechanism of healing in many of the holistic methods in general and hypnotherapeutic work in particular. The actual evidence we have at hand at this time is by implication only. To even begin the process of conceptualizing how such research on mind-gene communication takes place in hypnosis, however, we need to gain a broader perspective on the psychophysiological domain of hypnotherapy. As is often the case with important paradigm shifts, clues to the new path are provided by the paradoxes that block the further advance of the old paradigm. Let us therefore continue to explore the paradoxes and impasse of current theory and research in hypnosis with which we began our search for new foundations in chapter one.

The Activity-Passivity Paradox in Hypnosis

The relatively primitive state of our understanding psychophysiology during the first century of research in hypnosis meant that it could only conceptualized as some sort of reflex or pathology. Bernheim (1886/1957), the leader of the Nancy school in France, for example, described hypnosis as the "exaltation of the ideo-motor reflex excitability, which effects the unconscious transformation of the thought into movement, unknown to the will ... The mechanism of suggestion in general, may then be summed up in the following formula: increase of the reflex ideo-motor, ideo-sensitivity, and ideo-excitability." The idea that hypnosis involved an *increase in "sensitivity" and "excitability"* for "transforming the idea received into an act" is in striking contrast to the view of the Salpêtrière school in Paris led by Charcot who maintained, to the contrary, that hypnosis was a *pathological condition of passivity* that progressed from "lethargy" and "catalepsy" to "somnambulism."

This apparent paradox in our fundamental understanding of the nature of hypnosis — *Is hypnosis heightened activity or passivity?* — continued into the next generation of leading researchers. The great Russian physiologist, Ivan Pavlov, for example, believed hypnosis was a cerebral state of inhibition, a kind of *"partial sleep"* while the American learning theorist, Clark Hull, maintained the opposite view that hypnosis is a state of *arousal* characterized by "hypersuggestibility." Hull summarizes his pioneering research as follows "In concluding this discussion we seem forced to the view *that hypnosis is not sleep...*Thus the extreme *lethargic* state is not hypnosis, but true sleep: *only the alert stage is hypnotic.* Lastly, evidence has been presented which indicates not only that conditioned reflexes may be set up during hypnosis, but that this may perhaps be accomplished with even greater ease than in the waking state. This probably disproves Pavlov's hypothesis that hypnosis is a state of *partial sleep* in the sense of a partial irradiation of *inhibition."* (Hull, (1933/1986, p 221, italics is ours).

Is it not surprising, then, that when the hypnotic susceptibility scales of Hull's generation and the next were developed, they once again reverted to the one-sided passive conception of hypnosis as "relaxation, comfort, drowsiness" and eye closure (Hilgard & Hilgard, 1965)? The patient or subject is told, "In a sense the hypnotized person is like a sleepwalker..." (Shor & Orne, 1962, p 5). Even when a more active method of hypnotic induction such as hand levitation is used, the suggestions are "Your eyes are very heavy and closing...closing...getting so heavy...soon they will be tightly closed while your hand continues to rise... " (Weitzenhoffer & Hilgard, 1967, p 7). How can it be that the entire edifice of the past two generations of academic research has been based on hypnotic susceptibility scales constructed with great scientific acumen but with such profoundly flawed premises? This flawed idea, of course, was supported by the behaviorist school that believed hypnosis was nothing but relaxation. Such has been the power of the misconception that can be traced all the way back to the 1784 report that hypnosis was nothing but imagination, faith, hope, and suggestion.

Milton Erickson, who was also a student of Clark Hull, did not make the same mistake of identifying hypnosis with passivity. What made Erickson so innovative was that he recognized both *intense activity* as well as *passivity* as valid dimensions of hypnotic experience. Erickson developed new methods of hypnotherapeutic induction that could utilize either the passive, relaxed and sleep-like tendencies of his patients ("You don't even have to listen to my voice.") or their more active, compulsive and even "acting out" behavior (the hand levitation approach to hypnotic induction). The form of hypnotic induction Erickson chose to use on any particular occasion was a function of his patient's mood, attitudes and presenting pattern of behavior in the therapy session. Erickson described the great variety of his induction approaches that made use of the full range of the patient's ongoing behavior as the "naturalistic" (Erickson, 1958/1980) or the "utilization" approach (Erickson, 1959, 1980).

The first modern effort to integrate Milton H. Erickson's views of hypnosis with the psychophysiology of healing was undertaken by his early colleague, Bernard Gorton. The main focus of Gorton's two initial papers on "The Physiology of Hypnosis" (1957, 1958) was on how the autonomic nervous system with its two main branches, the sympathetic system (arousal) and the parasympathetic system (relaxation) may be the major avenue through which therapeutic suggestion achieved its psychophysiological effects on the body. These two review papers that emphasized how hypnosis could be used to optimize peak performance associated with an arousal of the sympathetic branch of the autonomic system as well as relaxation associated with the parasympathetic branch was a challenge to the then dominating but erroneous view of behaviorism that hypnosis was nothing more than relaxation. More recent research supports the essential view that there is "A positive correlation between hypnotic susceptibility and autonomic responsiveness during hypnosis..." (DeBenedittis et al., 1994, p 140) and the nature of the "physiological responsiveness [arousal or relaxation] is dependent on the type of suggestions during hypnosis..." (Sturgis & Coe, 1990, p 205).

I propose that this current view of how hypnosis (as well as a variety of other psychosocial cues) can modulate the active (sympathetic) as well as the relaxation (parasympathetic) branches of the autonomic nervous system can help us resolve centuries of debate about the fundamental nature of hypnosis that goes back to Bernheim and Charcot. As is typical of many such great debates in science, both sides had small parts of the truth that could only come together when a broader conception finally emerged that could embrace both. Even today the implications of this basic psychobiological capacity of hypnotic suggestion to influence both branches of the autonomic system is not well understood by researchers who report on the apparently "paradoxical" nature of their experimental work.

In one of the all too rare efforts to measure molecular variables during therapeutic hypnosis, for example, Weinstein and Au (1991) reported that norepinephrine levels were significantly higher in the hypnotized group of patients undergoing angioplasty than in the control group. They report that this was *"unexpected and seemed paradoxical* (p 29) ... *One would expect that if hypnosis does cause relaxation, then those patients who were hypnotized would have a lower arterial catecholamine level than their controls. This was not the case. Just the opposite occurred and is hard to explain"* (p 35).

A pair of research reports by Hautkappe & Bongartz (1992) and Unterweger, Lamas & Bongartz (1992) supports the idea that hypnosis can involve and improve a significant *"work function"* rather than simple relaxation or passivity. They found that heart rate variability was a useful physiological parameter for discriminating high and low hypnotic susceptibility subjects. High susceptible hypnotic subjects compared with low susceptibles have less heart rate variability (particularly in the 0.1 Hertz band) under a *cognitive workload* (posthypnotic amnesia). They describe their interesting results that imply that high hypnotic susceptibles are more effective at both the high performance (arousal) and relaxation sides of the active-passive polarity of hypnosis as follows. "High susceptible subjects do not have to "work" as hard on passing a suggestion as do low susceptibles. As soon as they pass the suggestion, they are no longer asked by the experimenter to be mentally active and can stop the effort-demanding cognitive process. They do not need as much mental load for the complete period of suggestion as the low susceptibles do." (Unterweger et al., 1992, pp. 87).

High hypnotic susceptibility is apparently associated with a more efficient use of information and/or energy in psychophysiological responsiveness. In Ericksonian terms we would say they have higher "response attentiveness." In terms of the basic idea of this chapter we would say that they are more efficient in turning on and off the activating (sympathetic branch) and relaxation (parasympathetic branch) of their autonomic system (and thus the wave nature of their consciousness and being). This could be the psychophysiological basis of Erickson's view that in hypnosis people are more "literal" (Erickson, Rossi & Rossi, 1976; Erickson & Rossi, 1979). That is, the high hypnotic susceptibility subjects literally worked when they were asked to (even on a psychophysiological level) and by implication they literally did not work any longer when they did not have to.

This new concept of the hypnotherapeutic work function as the essence of the efficacy of hypnosis is supported by a more recent series of clinical studies summarized by Amigo (1994) who presents evidence for "self-regulation therapy" as a "cognitive-behavioral approach to hypnosis" that involves the "voluntary reproduction of the stimulant effects of epinephrine." An indication of the complexity of the relationship is provided by Harris et al., (1992) who report that "approximately 40% of the individual difference variance of hypnotic susceptibility was accounted for by baseline cardiac vegal tone and heart rate reactivity during mood state." Their research design yielded unexpectedly complex results when they found "both branches of the autonomic nervous system may contribute to hypnotic susceptibility. The vagal component of the parasympathetic system [relaxation] and the sympathetic nervous [arousal] system may have greater influences in individuals susceptible to hypnosis. (pp. 22)"

These recent results on the hypnotherapeutic work function are hard to explain only from the limited behaviorist conception of hypnosis as simple relaxation. Under the stressful (life threatening) situation of undergoing an operation for angioplasty and emotional arousal our integrated mindbody theory of hypnotherapeutic work would certainly predict that stress messenger molecules such as nore-pinephrine would be released and interact in a complex manner with relaxation as found by these three independent research reports with very different experimental designs. Understanding the natural psychobiology of the two branches of the autonomic system whereby arousal (sympathetic branch) is normally followed by relaxation (parasympathetic branch) greatly clarifies the apparently contradictory or paradoxical responses to hypnosis and brings us closer to understanding the mystery of the efficacy of hypnosis in problem solving and healing.

In an unrelated paper Lazarus and Mayne (1991) report a similar "paradoxical" finding on the behavioral level when they attempt to assess the effectiveness of relaxation techniques without the use of any formal process of hypnotic induction. They summarize their findings. "Deep-muscle relaxation has been widely regarded as anxiety inhibiting, and the relaxation response an antidote to tension and stress. However, some relaxation techniques have been shown to have negative effects. *These include relaxation-induced anxiety and panic, paradoxical increases in tension and parasympathetic rebound.*" (p 261).

Again I would emphasize that these results are paradoxical only if one maintains the erroneous view of the fundamental nature of hypnosis as a method of relaxation and suggestion. An understanding of hypnotherapeutic suggestion as capable of entraining both the activating as well as the relaxing branches of the autonomic nervous system easily resolves the apparent "paradox." With or without the use of a technique labeled as "hypnosis" therapeutic suggestions for relaxation will naturally (not paradoxically) increase sympathetic arousal before relaxation as is typical of any situation that involves new learning.

Even an apparently innocuous process of learning a new technique of "relaxation" involves novelty and the challenge of learning something new. Being confronted with an unusual or novel situation evokes attention and exploratory behavior that demands some sort of *performance or inner work* to manage the situation. This involves the essential processes of *complex adaptation and continual self-organization (autopoiesis)* that is the characteristic work function of life itself. As such we would expect that the sympathetic system would be aroused (and even spill over into "panic" in some subjects who may have had negative experience with new learning in the past) before the parasympathetic systems relaxation response would become engaged.

As is typical of the current psychological approach to resolving such paradoxes, Lazarus and Mayne (1991) propose further research to determine the psychological profiles or psychobiological "traits" of the subjects that experience such paradoxical responses to suggestions for relaxation. Such research may be worthwhile, indeed. It will be better informed and directed, however, if it is realized that this so-called paradoxical response may be a manifestation of the *sensitivity to initial conditions and perturbations* that is so typical of all naturally chaotic psychobiological rhythms. In the second half of this volume we will explore an interesting variety of ideo-dynamic approaches to the practical utilization of this so-called paradoxical response of activation to the introduction of novelty in the symmetry breaking approaches to hypnotic induction and hypnotherapeutic work.

We may also note here a potential psychoanalytic misconception of such paradoxical behavior as "resistance." Whenever the patient does not respond in a manner judged "appropriate" by the therapist it may be labeled as "resistance." It would be very interesting to determine what proportion of so-called "resistances" are actually entirely natural shifts or bifurcations of attention leading to different basins of attraction (meaning) in the minds of patient and therapist. Resistances from this point of view could be understood as *critical phase transitions* when the patient's and therapist's points of view diverge. They could be clues where therapist and patient both have important "inner work" to do on themselves as well as with each other.

From the Chronobiological to the Chaotobiological View of Hypnotherapeutic Work

The theoretical and practical significance of the chronobiological theory of hypnotherapeutic suggestion was that for the first time we could reconcile the apparently contradictory views of the fundamental nature of hypnosis over the past two hundred years as well as the "paradoxes" of current research (Rossi, 1982, 1986/1993, 1994). When we now look more deeply into the way in which all the self-regulatory systems of the mindbody operate (e.g. the autonomic nervous, endocrine and immune systems) we discover a fundamental fact about nature that was unknown in the early history of hypnosis and is still unappreciated by most current workers. *There are entirely natural albeit chaotic cycles, rhythms and periods of greater and lesser amplitude (the apparent active-passive paradox of hypnosis) in virtually all psychophysical (Gregson, 1992) and psychobiological processes involving active attention, high performance and work that have been carefully measured over time* (Brown, 1982; Guastello, 1995; Lloyd & Rossi, 1992 a & b, 1993; Rossi, 1986; Rossi, 1986/1993; Tschacher et al., 1992).

Memory, learning, sensation, emotions, dreaming and all forms of psychological work in health and illness evoke the arousal phase of what has been called the 90-120 minute Basic Rest-Activity Cycle (Kleitman, 1970; Kleitman & Rossi, 1992). They all evoke and entrain the sympathetic or active branch of our autonomic system for an optimal period of at least 20 minutes. After that the more relaxing parasympathetic branch begins to take over to move us to the lower, quiet or apparent "rest" level of the Basic Rest-Activity Cycle (BRAC). The body is not really resting during these quiet periods, of course; it is actually engaged in intense inner activity building up energy and resources on the cellular-genetic level in preparation for a peak of outer performance in the next BRAC.

As we have seen, it is very important to understand that these psychobiological rhythms are not fixed and regular in their operation like some sort of mechanical clock of the Newtonian Universe. They are *complex adaptive systems* of self-regulation; they are usually quasi-periodic and chaotic in their actual manifestation (Glass & Mackey, 1988). Robert May (1976, 1986), whose 1976 paper on "Simple Mathematical Models with Very Complicated Dynamics" did so much to initiate the current revolution in the application of chaos theory in biology and ecology, calls all such psychobiological periodicity "The chaotic rhythms of life" (May, 1991).

These chaotic (that is, highly deterministic but difficult to predict) rhythms are a highly flexible system of mindbody adaptation that are exquisitely sensitive and responsive to external cues; particularly psychosocial cues. As we have seen in previous chapters, a defining characteristic of chaotic systems is that they are *sensitive to initial conditions.* It is precisely this sensitivity to initial conditions that makes psychobiological systems so responsive to psychosocial cues. Demands for high performance during emergencies or novel situations such as war time conditions, a physical accident or even an important business meeting, and the need to work overtime to complete a project, for example, can lead to the emotional states of stress that can greatly shift the amplitude and duration of these rhythms (Kupfer et al., 1988).

I hypothesize that hypnotherapeutic suggestions are at least as powerful as these everyday examples of *significant work* in modulating ("shifting", "influencing," "controlling" or "entraining" are loosely used as synonymous terms with "modulating" in this chapter) our natural rhythms of activity (arousal) and rest (relaxation). As such, these chaotic psychobiological rhythms are at the core of the great historical debate about the fundamental nature of hypnosis as activity or passivity; *we now know that hypnosis can influence both the passive (low) and active (high) poles of our mindbody rhythms that are responsive to psychosocial cues.*

Here we now come to the great conceptual divide. There are still those who want to maintain that psychology in general and hypnotherapy in particular are either social or personal subjective experience existing somehow in an ethereal suggestion space with no relationship to the body and biology. For these, the chronobiological or, as we would now prefer to call it *"The Chaotobiological Theory of Hypnotherapeutic Work"* will make no sense at all; or, at best, it will seem to be a rather irrelevant issue. As we have seen in Chapter One, what is today called "traditional hypnosis" has become more or less synonymous with programming, suggestion and relaxation. Most traditional research that is published in journals of hypnosis has to do with how suggestion, programming and psychosocial cues can manipulate the subject's attitudes, beliefs and emotions.

There has always been great controversy in the traditional research literature of hypnosis about whether such manipulations can really facilitate mindbody healing of behavioral problems, psychosomatic and organic dysfunctions. This traditional research rarely focuses on the psychobiological processes that are involved. When they do, they fall into the contradictions and paradoxes described in the previous section. By recognizing the very real psychobiological foundations of hypnotherapeutic *work,* however, we have been able to resolve the paradoxes of hypnotherapeutic *suggestion.* The substitution of the word *work* for *suggestion* is a fundamental implication of the recognition of the normative psychobiological basis of hypnotherapy. When biology is involved we are engaging the dynamics of energy, entropy and the essentially dissipative systems that make up all the self-organizing processes of life. All dissipative systems do constructive work by utilizing actively available forms of matter, energy and information to maintain life processes at the expense of raising the total entropy of the universe.

For those who are willing to acknowledge the relevance of biology in human destiny, it is now important to understand that *all effective hypnotherapeutic "suggestion" actually involves active psychobiological work.* This work invariably evokes and utilizes the naturally chaotic dynamics of the Basic Rest-Activity Cycle every 90-120 minutes or so throughout the day that have been called *"ultradian rhythms"* (ultra- generally meaning more often than the daily *circadian* rhythm). The significance of this shift in emphasis from hypnotherapeutic *suggestion* to hypnotherapeutic *work* is that we are resolving the traditional split between mind and body. We are now clarifying how we can learn to recognize and utilize the natural chaotobiological transformations of matter, energy and information on all levels from the psychosocial and the behavioral to the neuroendocrinological and cellular-genetic levels.

This shift from the traditional focus on hypnotherapeutic *suggestion* to hypnothrapeutic *work* means that we can now greatly expand and legitimatize what we may call the "Domain of Hypnotherapeutic Work" (Rossi and Lippincott, 1992). Here the experimental assessment of the chaotobiological theory of hypotherapeutic work will be outlined to facilitate future research and as a preparation to help us appreciate the new ideo-dynamic approaches presented in the second half of this book.

Assessing the Chaotobiological Theory of Hypnotherapeutic Work

1. Matching the Phenomena of Classical Hypnosis and Chaotobiological Rhythms

The current ideal of unification in science is to integrate apparently different phenomena into a general theory of nature. The more widely divergent the phenomena that we can bring together in a meaningful way, the greater the beauty and potential utility of the theory. Chaotic chronobiological rhythms, one branch of the new science of Chaotology, may be viewed as coordinators of information transduction between environmental cues and signals such as temperature, food and psychosocial variables and the expression of genes in the process of complex adaptive homeostasis (Lloyd & Rossi, 1993). Failures in this process of adaptive homeostasis are reflected in what is commonly called "stress," "behavioral maladjustment" and "psychosomatic problems." Extensive matching of the clinical-experimental data of the two previously separate fields of chronobiology and hypnosis have been presented previously (Rossi, 1986, 1986/1993; Rossi & Lippincott, 1992).

These matchings indicate that over the past century chronobiology and hypnosis have shared the same areas of concern in attempting to understand the factors that modulate the central and autonomic nervous systems, the endocrine and the immune system as well as their relationships to the psychobiological processes of memory, learning, emotions, behavior, sensation and perception, appetites and psychosomatic problems. Box 4.3 provides more detail about the dynamics and terminology of this proposed unification of the literature in chronobiology and hypnotherapy (Rossi, 1994, b & c). The basic implication of the associations in Box 4.3 is that what has been traditionally called "clinical hypnosis" or "therapeutic suggestion" may be, in essence, the accessing, entrainment and utilization of the natural chaotic variability of ultradian and circadian processes that respond to psychosocial cues. Within this framework, the classical phenomena of hypnosis may be conceptualized as extreme manifestations and/or perseverations of time-dependent chaotic psychobiological processes that are responsive to psychosocial cues. What the biologist calls the *"entrainment* of ultradian and circadian rhythms by physical and psychosocial stimuli" is the psychobiological basis of what psychotherapists call *"hypnotherapeutic suggestion* to facilitate mindbody healing."

Box 4.3   Toward a Mathematical Model of Hypnotherapeutic Work

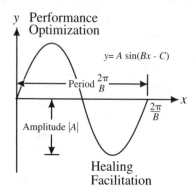

An illustration of the parameters of a mathematical model of how hypnotherapeutic work may entrain and utilize psychobiological rhythms.

Amplitude refers to the absolute value of the height or depth of a cycle or rhythm of responsible behavior: it measures how far rhythm deviates from its mean level. The amplitude may correspond to a "hypnotic constant" that refers to the hypnotizability of a subject or the degree to which hypnotherapeutic work may optimize performance variables or healing parameters.

Period is the time required for one complete cycle of a rhythm; the length of time after which one cycle recurs. The period is frequently a highly variable parameter of psychobiological rhythms that may be contracted or stretched by hypnotherapeutic work. The *frequency* is the reciprocal of the period.

Phase is that part of the cycle that is associated with behaviors of interest; it is the instantaneous state of a cycle within its period. The crest or peak phase of chronobiological behavior is often associated with activation (sympathetic system) while the low or trough phase is often associated with relaxation (parasympathetic system) behaviors. The number C/B, called the *phase shift*, is a measure of the degree to which certain portions of chronobiological behavior can be modulated or entrained with hypnotic work.

Entrainment or synchronization refers to the interaction of psychobiological rhythms (*x* and *y* below) with a psychsocial que such as hypnotherapeutic work (H below) that leads to the phase resetting (phase preservation, locking or trapping) of certain parts of a chronobiological cycle. Many hypnotherapeutic responses may be conceptualized as phase locked portions of the Basic Rest-Activity Cycle (BRAC) that are utilized for enhancing performance or facilitating healing. A mathematical model of the hypnotherapeutic entrainment of a Van der Pol oscillation of psychobiological rhythms (adapted from Kronauer, 1984) is illustrated below where H is the "influence coefficient;" ω_x and ω_y are the natural frequencies of individual or systems of psychobiological rhythms x and y; k may be a constant associated with the intrinsic entrainability of a particular psychological rhythm by psychosocial cues.

$$k^2\ddot{x} + k\mu_x\,(-1 + x^2)\dot{x} + \omega^2_x\,x + F_{yx}k\dot{y} = 0$$

$$(k = \pi/12)$$

$$k^2\ddot{y} + k\mu_y\,(-1 + y^2)\dot{y} + \omega^2_y\,y + F_{xy}k\dot{x} = F_y$$

$$H = F_{zy}\cos(k\omega_z + \theta_z)$$

This matching of the domains of chaotic chronobiological and hypnotherapeutic phenomena leads to an important test of the chaotobiological theory of hypnotherapeutic work. This is the so-called "falsifiability" criterion of Karl Popper (1966). In brief, if you can find a single chaotic chronobiological phenomena (any aspect of memory, learning and behavior, for example) that can be *entrained* by psychosocial cues (work, study, real world performance demands of all sorts) that is not responsive to *hypnotherapeutic suggestion* then you will have disproved the chaotobiological theory of hypnotherapeutic work. The reverse is also true. If you can find a single psychobiological process that you can influence through hypnotic suggestion that does not have a naturally chaotic rhythmicity then you will have disproven the chaotobiological theory of hypnotherapeutic work.

2. The Paradoxes of Event-Related P300 Brain Wave

A dramatic though unintended and previously unrecognized example of this falsifiability test of what we shall now call the chaotobiological theory of hypnotherapeutic work has taken place over the past generation in assessing the effects of hypnosis on cognition measured by the event-related brain potentials of the P300 wave. In one study Barabasz and Lonsdale (1983) measured an *increase* in the P300 wave amplitude in response to the hypnotic suggestion for a negative hallucination: "You can no longer smell anything at all." Then Spiegel et al., (1985) measured a *decrease* in the P300 amplitude in response to the hypnotic suggestion for a positive visual hallucination to see a box obstructing a visual stimulus. Subsequently Spiegel and Barabasz (1988) published a joint chapter explaining their contradictory findings in terms of the differences in the hypnotic instructions that were administered to the subjects. Whatever their *ad hoc* explanation might be, however, the fact remains that, as is the case in much psychological research, they did have contradictory experimental results.

As we learned in our earlier discussion of the active-passive paradox of hypnosis, whenever we have apparently contradictory findings we might well look to the Chaotology Theory that predicts that hypnotherapeutic work can entrain and modulate the high as well as the low end of any psychobiological process that is sensitive to psychosocial cues. Since hypnosis by Spiegel (and many others before him) found a decrease in the P300 wave while Barabasz found the reverse, the chaotobiological theory would predict that the P300 wave must have an inherent rhythmicity — some sort of circadian (one rhythm every 24 hours) or ultradian (many rhythms every 24 hours) rhythm. For a number of years I speculated aloud in many of my teaching workshops around the world that this could be an excellent falsifiability test for the chronobiological theory: if the P300 wave did not have a natural ultradian or circadian rhythmicity, then this simple fact alone would be sufficient to disprove the chronobiological theory.

No one, as far as I knew, however, had ever tested whether the P300 wave did have its own inherent chronobiological rhythm. You can imagine my surprise when a colleague in Italy recently informed me that this was the exact subject of a doctoral dissertation in Spain that was eventually published as "Ultradian rhythms in cognitive operations: evidence from the P300 component of the event-related potentials" (Escera et al., 1992). Thus, while no one actually set up a formal falsifiability test of the chronobiological theory, the experimental series of Spiegel, Barabasz and Escera are, in fact, a test that is even more impressive because none of these researchers were aware of the implications of their work for the chaotobiological theory of hypnosis. Therefore they could not have an "unconscious" experimental bias to shift the results one way or another.

3. The Chaotic Chronobiology of Hypnotic Susceptibility: The Ultradian Rhythms

There was a six year gap between my first speculations about the chronobiological theory of hypnosis based upon my observations of the way Milton H. Erickson apparently utilized behavioral cues of the ultradian rest phase of the Basic Rest-Activity Cycle in his routine use of hypnotherapy (Rossi, 1981,1982) and the first experimental testing of the theory (Aldrich and Bernstein, 1987). There was a ten year gap between this initial experimental support of the chronobiological theory and my current realization of the *chaotic nature of all chronobiological rhythms and hypnosis.* The story of this conceptual trail is marked by a number of twists, turns, misconceptions and corrections so that we now, hopefully, have a clearer vision of the psychobiology of the hypnotherapeutic work to guide future research and clinical practice.

The initial assessment of the chronobiological theory of hypnotic suggestion was carried out by Aldrich and Bernstein (1987) who found that "time of day" was a statistically significant factor in hypnotic susceptibility. They reported a bi-modal distribution of scores on The Harvard Group Scale of Hypnotic Susceptibility (HGSHS) in college students with a sharp major peak at 12 noon and a secondary, broader plateau around 5 to 6 p.m. The limitations of this study were that the subjects were tested in groups at hourly intervals during regular daytime class periods. The authors reported that "Research with individuals would also be a better test of Rossi's contention that an ultradian rhythm exists in hypnotizability These differences would have been canceled out when the individual rhythms were averaged together when analyzing the data in the present study" (Aldrich and Bernstein, 1987, p 144).

I therefore designed a pilot study whereby individual subjects could keep diaries that might identify periodicity in their daily patterns of self-hypnosis and ultradian rest (Rossi, 1992). A *Hypnosis Diary Group* were individuals who had expressed an interest in learning self-hypnosis and were led through at least one classical hypnotic induction involving eye fixation, imagery and relaxation to facilitate "mindbody healing." They were then encouraged to keep a "Self-Hypnosis Diary" for two weeks in which they daily recorded three items: (1) the time of day when they did self-hypnosis; (2) how much time they spent in self-hypnosis; and, (3) anything about their healing experience of self-hypnosis that they found interesting.

The *Ultradian Diary Group* consisted of people who attended one of the author's lectures on "The Ultradian Healing Response" (Rossi and Cheek, 1988) as an approach to optimizing mindbody healing. To facilitate this new approach to mindbody healing they were to record the same items as the self-hypnosis group. Both groups were given the same purposely vague and non-directive instruction about when and how often they should do their "inner healing work" and diary recording.

Figure 4.7 presents an overview of the data for the total group of 16 subjects used in this pilot study. The jagged line with dark filled circles represents the original data of 292 diary reports by the total group. The symmetrical curve of hollow circles is the results of the analysis on the original data with the computer technique of Multiple Complex Demodulation (MCD) carried out by Helen Sing of the Behavioral Biology Department of Walter Reed Army Institute of Research. This symmetrical curve represents a very prominent circadian rhythm with a peak between noon and 1 p.m. in the "number of incidents" of self-hypnosis and the ultradian healing response in the total group. This result is consistent with Aldrich and Berstein's finding of a peak in hypnotic susceptibility at noon but the secondary plateau they reported around 5 and 6 p.m. is only marginally evident by inspection of the jagged original data. The contrast between the smoothed computer generated circadian curve and the jagged original data which is more suggestive of an ultradian periodicity (with peaks at 9 a.m., noon, and perhaps at 2, 4 and 6 p.m.) provides some empirical support for the view that the circadian cycle is a composite of many ultradian rhythms (Lloyd & Rossi, 1992).

While I originally hypothesized there would be a 90-120 BRAC rhythm in the data, figures 4.8a and 4.8b illustrate a 180 minute rhythm that was a more prominent for both groups. I can only guess that the reason for this is that it is usually not convenient in normal everyday life to take a significant break. While the small number of observations of this pilot study do not permit us to make any statement about the significance of the differences between the two groups in the shape of the curves, it is evident that there are ultradian rhythms in the proclivities of these subjects to do "inner healing" whether it is identified as "self-hypnosis" or an "ultradian healing response." More carefully controlled replications of this type of study are now needed to identify the quasi-periodic or fully chaotic nature of these ultradian rhythms.

Fig. 4.7. An overview of the circadian rhythm in the "ultradian healing response" and "self-hypnosis" in 292 dairy recordings of 16 subjects over a one week period (Rossi, 1992).

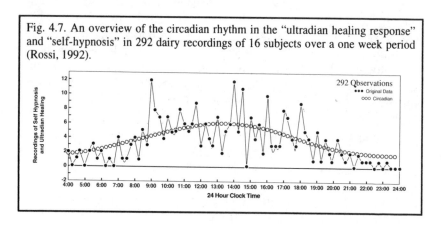

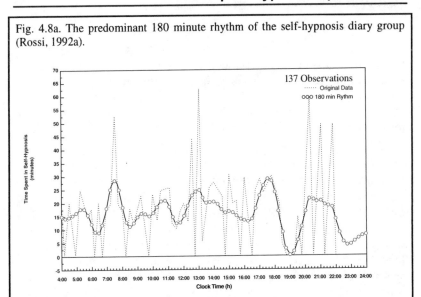

Fig. 4.8a. The predominant 180 minute rhythm of the self-hypnosis diary group (Rossi, 1992a).

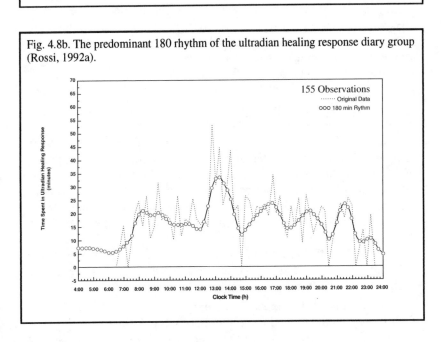

Fig. 4.8b. The predominant 180 rhythm of the ultradian healing response diary group (Rossi, 1992a).

4. The Naturalistic 20 Minute "Common Everyday Trance"

Another observation of significance in figures 4.8a and 4.8b is that both groups of subjects tended to remain in inner work for about 15 or 20 minutes just as ultradian theory predicted. I hypothesize that these results support Erickson's concept of "the common everyday trance" which he believed everyone experienced at different times throughout the day (Erickson and Rossi, 1979).

The striking confirmations of the predictions of the ultradian theory of hypnotherapeutic work in this pilot study led to another experimental design with two independent replications. I developed a variety of "naturalistic," permissive and non-directive approaches to therapeutic hypnosis (Rossi, 1986/1993) where individuals were encouraged to remain in a "naturalistic hypnosis" for as long as they wished with the following words: "You will remain in hypnosis as long as necessary to resolve the issue you have been dealing with in as satisfactory a manner as is possible at this time. Your unconscious (or 'inner mind') will then allow you to awaken entirely on your own feeling refreshed and alert." Notice how these "patient-centered" instructions are very different from the typical style of hypnotherapy. In traditional hypnotherapy the locus of control of the problem solving process remains within the therapist who directs each stage with suggestions. The patient-centered suggestions that I formulated allows the locus of control over entire problem solving process to remain within the patient. The patient even decides when the inner hypnotherapeutic work is finished and when to "wake up."

No further cues or statements were made while the patient remained in this self-guided state of naturalistic hypnotherapeutic work. After they indicated they had spontaneously awakened by opening their eyes, talking and moving normally, the therapist non-directively encouraged them to report something about their trance experience with questions such as: "What was that experience like? What did you actually experience? Can you tell me more about it?" As a check on the reliability of the amount of time spent on this "natural therapeutic trance" the entire procedure was repeated with each person usually within a week or two.

The results of this experiment supported the prediction of ultradian theory: patients tend to remain in a naturalistic state of hypnotherapeutic work for about twenty minutes. This naturalistic trance time was reliable in the sense that the correlation of 0.49 between time spent in the first and second trance was significant at the .02

level (df = 28). The large standard deviations and wide range of naturalistic trance times (between 2 and 67 minutes), however, does not recommend it as a useful predictor in practical therapeutic work. From our current perspective of the inherently chaotic nature of such self-organized "hypnotherapeutic work," we can more deeply appreciate the wide range of standard deviations as something more than "error variance."

This wide variability is highly characteristic of many chaotic ultradian behaviors because they are *highly sensitive to initial conditions* and instantly adaptive to changing environmental circumstances. Kleitman (1970) and Wever (1988,1989), have emphasized that most ultradian-circadian behaviors are easily modifiable by psychosocial stimuli. *It is precisely this sensitivity to initial conditions and responsiveness to ongoing psychosocial stimuli that supports the view that hypnotherapeutic work (certainly a class of psychosocial stimuli) may achieve its mindbody effects by relative entrainment or synchronization of the naturally wide variability of chaotic ultradian behavior in the process of complex adaptive homeostasis.* Kelso (1995) has clarified how it is the *relative entrainment* and the *relative coordination* rather than the absolute (phase-locked entrainment) of behavior on all levels that permits the flexibility for the very rapid adjustments of most *complex adaptive systems.*

Carol Sommer (1993) and Brian Lippincott (1990, 1992 a & b) each reported independent replications of the above study with (1) minor modifications of procedure, (2) subjects assessed in different age ranges and parts of the country and (3) scales for measuring hypnotic susceptibility. They both found essentially similar results: Sommer reported the mean naturalistic trance time for her 32 subjects to be 18.02 minutes (standard deviation, 9.62) when she controlled for a variety of variables such as sex (half her subjects were male and half were female) and amount of previous trance experience. Lippincott reported a mean naturalistic trance time of 18.55 minutes (standard deviation, 14.11). Sommer and Lippincott each carefully documented that while there were the typically wide variations in the nature of what each subject reported about the subjective aspects of their naturalistic trance experience, within their total groups virtually all the classical phenomena of hypnosis were experienced by implication even though they were not directly suggested.

A recent review of the literature of experimental hypnosis prompted by these findings turned up a number of earlier studies that could be interpreted as providing further support for a naturalistic 20 minute trance time. In an early methodological study Dorcus, Brintnall and Case (1941) compared the amount of time a group of 20 deeply hypnotizable subjects remained in trance after the hypnotist left the room with a control group who were told to simply lie down and relax. In both groups the majority of the subjects got up and left the room within 20 minutes. In two studies using control group subjects simulating hypnosis it was found that highly hypnotizable subjects remained in trance when they believed they were left unobserved for 10.7 and 16.5 minutes (Orne and Evans, 1966; Evans and Orne, 1971) while the simulating low hypnotizable subjects acted as if they were in trance for 25.2 minutes. In a more clinically oriented recent survey Sanders (In Press) mailed a self-hypnosis questionnaire to 1000 members of the American Society of Clinical Hypnosis. In the 233 responses she received it was found that a 15-20 minute period was most typical in the use of self-hypnosis. It is interesting that while none of these researchers set out to test the ultradian prediction that there is a naturalistic 20 minute trance time, all their data supports it.

5. Classical Hypnotic Phenomena Without Suggestion

An important implication of the chaotic chronobiological theory of hypnotic suggestion is that all the classical phenomena of hypnosis can be experienced in the normal course of everyday life without direct hypnotic suggestion. Rossi & Lippincott (1993) explored the use of Erickson's naturalistic approach on the experiencing of the classical phenomena of hypnosis without direction. Another interesting result of this study was that apparently all the classical phenomena of hypnosis were experienced without being directly suggested. When the self descriptions of their inner experiences written in the diaries of the hypnotic and ultradian diary groups were examined, it was found that while there were wide variations in what each individual reported, attenuated forms of all the classical hypnotic phenomena were described to some degree or other in the total group even though the therapist did not suggest them. That is while no single individual experienced all the classical phenomena of hypnosis, there were traces of evidence in the written diaries that the group as a whole experienced the classical phenomenology of hypnosis without direct suggestion.

When a subject wrote, for example, "A lot was going on during the trance but now I don't remember any of it," it implies that *hypnotic amnesia* was experienced. When a subject commented, "I felt I was outside my body," it implies that a *hypnotic dissociation* took place. When a subject wrote, "At one point I felt I was a baby screaming," it was taken to imply that at least a partial *hypnotic age regression* was experienced even though it was not in any way suggested by the experimenter. This aspect of the study was limited to the qualitative level because we have no standardized scales for quantifying such spontaneous hypnotic phenomena. While these observations are still qualitative, they are consistent with the basic hypothesis that the classical forms of hypnotic experience are all expressions of natural ultradian variations of a variety of the chaotic psychobiological processes of complex adaptive homeostasis. More carefully controlled and quantified studies are now needed to validate these tentative findings by identifying their chaotic parameters such as the locations of their bifurcations, the size of their Lypunov exponents, their basins of attraction etc. . The issues here are central to any post-modern theory of hypnosis: Are the classical phenomena of hypnosis the result of simple suggestion and imagination (as the King's 1784 commission concluded), or is there a deeper psychobiological connection, as proposed by the chaotobiological theory of hypnotherapeutic work?

6. Owls, Larks and Ultradian Hypnotic Susceptibility

The peak in hypnotic susceptibility found in the morning (noon) and evening by Aldrich and Bernstein (1987) led me to hypothesize that it could be a reflection of the differential performance of a mixed population of larks (people who claim to be more alert in the morning) and owls (people who claim to be more alert in the evening). Lippincott (1992a) then designed a study wherein he found evidence to support the hypothesis that (1) larks have higher hypnotic susceptibility in the late afternoon (4 p.m. to 6 p.m.), (2) owls have a higher susceptibility in the morning (8 a.m. to 10 a.m.) and (3) there were no difference in hypnotizability between midnight and 2 am when both groups would normally be asleep. These results were immediately challenged by Wallace (Wallace, 1993; Wallace & Kokoszka, 1995) who found the exact reverse: larks exhibited peak susceptibility at 10 a.m. and 2 p.m. while owls had their peaks around 1 p.m. and between 6 p.m. and 9 p.m. More recently Mann & Sanders (1995) obtained results more similar to those of Wallace than Lippincott by using different measures (hypnotic *depth* rather than hypnotic *susceptibility*).

So once again the fat is in the fire! Contradictory results! How can it be explained? Does it mean that everyone is wrong? Mann & Sanders explain their results, that were essentially the opposite of Lippincott's, in terms of the different ways their experimental variables were measured etc. This reminds us of our earlier description of how Spiegel and Barabasz attempted to reconcile their apparently contradictory finding that hypnotic suggestion could both increase and decrease the ultradian P300 wave. Psychological research has a long history of attempting to explain such contradictory results with such *post hoc* dissections of methodology. The outstanding fact remains, however, that statistically significant results are consistently found in the way psychosocial variables can modulate either the high or low end of many chaotic chronobiological processes of human experience. The fact that these statistically significant correlations are low rather than high has usually discouraged researchers and clinicians alike about the relevance of these psychosocial variables for real life application. As we have seen in Kelso's work (1995), however, these low correlation's may be reflecting how *relative coordination* rather than absolute correlation has important adaptive significance in all the complex systems of life and behavior.

The rise of the new chaos theory in modern mathematical dynamics is making us aware of the adaptive significance of nonlinearity and *sensitivity to initial conditions and even minor perturbations* in the measurement of all complex systems. *Practically speaking it is virtually impossible to replicate any psychological experiment exactly.* Even the inevitable small differences in initial conditions and apparently minor differences in procedure could be enough to lead to statistically significant but contradictory results whenever we are dealing with chronobiological variables that can be shifted into opposite directions in response to psychosocial cues.

What is most significant about the Lippincott and Wallace studies of hypnotic susceptibility is that, if the owls and larks had not been separated, there apparently would have been no significant differences in hypnotic susceptibility over time because the inverse periodic patterns of owls and larks may have canceled each other out. That is, we would have made a "Type II error": concluding there were no differences when in fact there were. If future studies confirm such chaotic ultradian and circadian performance shifts in owls and larks it will require a profound reevaluation of many previous studies on psychobiological variables in general, as well as hypnosis in particular. These results challenge previous conceptions of hypnotic susceptibility as a relatively fixed, unvarying trait of the individual (Hilgard, 1982) and suggest new studies to assess the hypothesis that chaotic psychobiological rhythms are a significant aspect of the mindbody processes of complex adaptive homeostasis that are accessed and utilized by hypnotherapeutic work and other approaches to holistic medicine in general (e.g., self-hypnosis meditation, imagery, the relaxation response, the ultradian healing response, autogenic training etc.).

7. Cross Cultural Studies of the Chaotobiological Theory of Hypnotherapeutic Work

From Japan comes a recent experimental study on "The diurnal fluctuation of hypnotic susceptibility" (Saito and Kano, 1992). They tested 40 subjects (20 males and 20 female university students) with the Harvard Group Scale of Hypnotic Susceptibility, Form A at three times of day (10 a.m., 1 p.m. and 4 p.m.). They analyzed their results in terms of four different types of response curves, relating hypnotic susceptibility to ultradian time, and found statistically significant results in three of the groups. They modestly "concluded that the present evidence simply confirmed the diurnal fluctuations of hypnotic susceptibility. And it also allowed an evaluation for the possibility of Rossi's ultradian hypothesis." In a personal communication with these authors they demurred on whether the rhythms were truly periodic. This was before any of us understood that from the current perspective of chaos theory they could not, of course, be truly periodic. Like all psychobiological rhythms it is actually more a question of whether they are quasi-periodic or chaotic. Another type of study with profound cross-cultural implications was done by Osowiec and others to which we will now turn our attention.

8. The Brain-Breath Link in Yoga and Hypnotherapeutic Work

One of the most intriguing areas of recent research exploring the association between hypnosis and psychobiological rhythms is the so-called nasal breath-brain connection. It has been known for one hundred years that there are widely varying ultradian shifts in the degree to which air is inhaled in the left or right chamber of the nose. In humans the left and right chambers of the nose alternate in their size and shape to change the degree of air flow through each side every few hours. Recently Debra Werntz (1981) reported a contralateral relationship between cerebral hemispheric activity (EEG) and the ultradian rhythm of the nasal cycle. She found that relatively greater integrated EEG values in the right hemisphere are positively correlated with a predominant airflow in the left nostril and vice versa.

In a wide ranging series of studies Werntz et al (1982a & b) found that subjects could voluntarily shift their nasal dominance by forced uninostril breathing through the closed nostril. Further, this shift in nasal dominance was associated with an accompanying shift in cerebral dominance to the contralateral hemisphere and autonomic nervous system balance throughout the body. The ultradian nasal cycle is not only a marker for cerebral hemispheric activity, but it also can be used to voluntarily change the loci of activity in the highest centers of the brain and autonomic system that are involved in cybernetic loops of communication with most organ systems, tissues and cells of the body. Some of these investigators hypothesize that this nasal-brain-mind link may be the essential path by which the ancient practice of breath regulation in yoga led to the voluntary control of many autonomic nervous system functions for which the Eastern adepts are noted (Brown, 1991 a & b; Rossi, 1990c &d, 1991 a & b).

These relationships inspired a recent Ph.D. dissertation by Darlene Osowiec (1992) who assessed hypothesized associations between the nasal ultradian rhythm, anxiety, symptoms of stress and the personality process of self-actualization. She found that: "(1) there is a significant positive correlation between self-actualizing individuals having low trait anxiety and stress related symptoms and a regular nasal cycle... and (2) non-self-actualizing individuals with high levels of trait anxiety and stress-related symptoms exhibiting significantly greater irregularity in the nasal cycle..." These results are reminiscent of the ancient texts that emphasize that an irregular nasal cycle, particularly one in which the person remains dominant in one nostril or the other for an excessively long period of time are associated with illness and mental disorder (Rama, Ballentine and Ajaya, 1976).

In a more recent 12-week follow up study Osowiec (personal communication) has found that highly hypnotizable subjects appeared to experience more regularity in their ultradian nasal rhythms when they practice self-hypnosis but low hypnotizable subjects do not. This study was conducted before our current awareness of the chaotic aspects of all psychobiological rhythms, however, and needs to be replicated with some of the newer approaches to the quantification of chaotobiological variables (Abraham & Gilgen, 1995; Robertson, & Combs, 1995). Osowiec tentatively concludes that her findings with the ultradian nasal rhythm are similar to the general types of association that are found between stress, symptoms, personality and responsiveness to therapeutic hypnosis.

More recently a number of researchers have explored the nostril cycle from the perspective of chaos theory. Combs & Winkler (1995) contrasted the traditional research approach of academic psychology with their findings of two dimensional attractors in the nasal cycles of individual subjects. They found that the fractal dimension estimates for their six subjects ranged from 1.661 to 1.811. In a follow up study Brown & Combs (1995) explored the use of newer algorhythms for their data and described the current flux of research attitudes. The consistent current findings of chaos in most psychobiological processes (where it has been looked for) has important implications for future research in psychology in general as well as the eight areas reviewed above. Most of the reported studies before those of Combs et al., were done within the older paradigm of simply seeking periodicity in hypnotherapeutic processes. As such most previous research on the periodicity of hypnosis now needs to be replicated from the new chaotobiological perspective to fully appreciate their nonlinear dynamics.

Reformulating the Psychobiological Foundations of Hypnotherapy

We now have some of the necessary concepts and research data required to help us reformulate the psychobiological foundations of hypnotherapy as was promised back in Chapter One. We will first briefly summarize how the activity-passivity paradox of historical hypnosis, reviewed earlier in this chapter, has become manifest in the most recent efforts to conceptualize the nature of hypnotic responsiveness. We will then illustrate how the chaotobiological theory of hypnotherapeutic work proposed in this chapter can resolve the current impasse that is being puzzled over by current workers. Woody, Bowers & Oakman (1992, p. 9-10) have contrasted the impasse between the two major schools of theory and research in hypnosis today as follows.

> The neodissociation and social-psychological models of hypnosis have decidedly different views of how reports of nonvolition and reports of various cognitive events (e.g., images and reported coping strategies) relate to the suggested target behavior. People working within the neodissociation model of

hypnosis, as proposed and elaborated by E. R. Hilgard (1973, 1977), tend to view reports of nonvolition as prima facie evidence that high-level executive initiative and effort are minimally involved in the production of hypnotically suggested behavior. Instead, they assume that hypnotic suggestions more or less indirectly activate subsystems of control. Insofar as the experience of volition is closely linked with executive initiative and ongoing effort, and insofar as the production of hypnotic responses tends to circumvent the need for such initiative and effort, it is not surprising that hypnotically suggested effects are often experienced and reported as occurring nonvolitionally...

In contrast to the neodissociation model, the socio-psychological model of hypnosis regards a host of person and demand variables as entirely sufficient to account for hypnotic responding. The person variables include a variety of factors (i.e., not just imagery or goal directed fantasy), such as expectations, positive attitudes toward hypnosis, motivations to please the hypnotist, the tendency to view hypnotic suggestions as something to be actively achieved, and so on (Spanos, 1986). What is *not* required — indeed, is specifically proscribed as an important variable in the production of hypnotic responses — is the "special process" of dissociation.

Given that the socio-psychological model views hypnotic responses as actively and purposively achieved, there has to be some way for it to handle the commonplace observation that subjects often report hypnotically suggested effects to be experienced as nonvolitional. As we have already seen, the socio-psychological model views these nonvolitional reports as mis-attributions — as errors in interpreting one's own behavior as nonvolitional when in fact it is strategically enacted, goal-directed behavior...

Stam and Spanos (1980, p. 760) sharpen the contrast between the neodissociation (or "special-state") and socio-psychological models as follows.

Is hypnotic responding automatic and nonvolitional, or is it strategic and mediated by the subject's cognitive responses to treatment generated expectations? The answer is that hypnotic responding is often both strategic and automatic — as long as it is understood that terms such as automatic and nonvolitional refer not to a quality of behavior but to an attribution of causality made by subjects about their own behavior...

Here we see once again the activity-passivity paradox of historical hypnosis — now being played out on a modern stage of well documented theory and research. The approach to resolving this paradox by Woody, Bowers & Oakman (1992, p. 20) is presented with these words.

Having raised so many problems that complicate the task of explaining what underlies individual differences in hypnotic responsiveness we here wish to suggest two possible approaches for moving beyond what may presently seem to be an impasse. We do so by raising two new considerations: (1) The items of hypnosis scales may contain useful information about individual differences that is concealed by the overall score; and (2) it may be productive to put somewhat more reliance on what has been called a "result-centered" strategy of research...

These researchers use spectral analysis to explore the individual items of hypnotic susceptibility scales into a 2-dimensional continuum that is called the "spectrum of hypnotic performance." A major finding (Balthazard & Woody, 1992) is that this spectrum falls between two major classes of hypnotic responses: (1) *Easy Responses* (e.g. ideomotor items such as nonvolitional hand and head movements) that are achieved by a high percent of subjects — even those who are classified as *low hypnotizable* and (2) *Hard Responses* (e.g. hallucinations, amnesias, post-hypnotic suggestion) that are only achieved by a much smaller proportion of subjects — usually classified as the *highly hypnotizable*. The incisive analysis of the implications of research on the *correlations between these easy and hard responses with other variables associated with hypnosis* provides a valuable approach to resolving the apparent impasse between our currently contrasting models of hypnosis (Balthazard & Woody, 1992; Woody, Bowers & Oakman, 1992).

These authors caution, however, that "The present approach considers [hypnotic item] 'factors' as frames of reference rather than necessarily meaningful entities — that is, as mathematical rather than conceptual entities." (Balthazard & Woody, 1992, p. 23). We use mathematics in science, however, to model *something!* As we reviewed in Chapter One, the problem with modern hypnosis has been that it has lost any sense of what that something is (Naish, 1986). The integrative chaotobiological theory of hypnotherapeutic work outlined in this chapter states that this *something — the basic stuff of hypnotherapy is the entrainment and utilization of the natural psychobiological processes of mindbody communication on all levels from mind to gene that are responsive to psychosocial cues — this is the domain of a hypnotherapy of the future.* The abstract mathematical factors isolated by Balthazard & Woody and many others are taken to model the chaotobiological dynamics of *hypnotherapeutic work* that burn up energy and increases entropy just like all self-organizing complex adaptive systems characteristic of life do to develop and maintain themselves in the real world.

Figure 4.9 illustrates how the well researched spectrum of hypnotic performance may be integrated with the chaotobiological dynamics of hypnotherapeutic work. The top of the wave of the 90-120 minute ultradian rhythm is when subjects are most likely to respond chronobiologically with the more *actively outer focused compliant strategies* emphasized by the *social-psychological theorists* such as the desire to please the therapist, and the tendency to view hypnotic suggestions as something to be actively achieved with cognitive effort. We may call this "High Phase Hypnosis." This strategy for achieving adequate responses fits the popular as well as the scientific conception of *active work, a labor expending energy* to optimize information processing to achieve a goal conforming with outer world demands and expectations. This strategy is associated with adequate performance on the easier ideo-dynamic responses but a lower score on hypnotic susceptibility scales that are typical of the more *Apollonian personality style* (Spiegel & Spiegel, 1978) with its clear, cognitively oriented attitudes to problem solving.

The bottom or "healing facilitation phase" of the ultradian rhythm in figure 4.9, by contrast, is what we may call "Low Phase Hypnosis." This is the phase when subjects are more likely to respond chronobiologically with the more *passive, dissociative and absorption strategy* that many *neodissociation and special-state theorists* believe is the real essence of traditional hypnosis with its focus on relaxation and sleep (Hilgard, 1992; Tellegen & Atkinson, 1974). These are the subjects who do well with the harder to achieve items on hypnotic susceptibility scales such as hallucinations, amnesia and post-hypnotic suggestion and achieve a higher overall score. These subjects have a more typically *Dionysian personality tendencies* whose behavior coincides with the popular conception of hypnosis as an essentially passive and receptive state that responds to suggestions easily in everyday life as well as in hypnosis. These subjects often perceive their hypnotic experience as effortless and nonvolitional. They don't seem to be making any active cognitive effort to achieve anything; they are apparently able to rely on their natural unconscious responses to carry out *hypnotherapeutic work* on an autonomous or nonviolitional level that sometimes seems miraculous to themselves and others. From our deeply psychobiological perspective, however, this seemingly autonomous inner work is just that: *work on a biological level that creates informational networks (the flow of messenger molecules or hormones) and burns energy (Adenosine TriPhosphate — ATP — on the cellular level) in the dynamics of growth, development and healing.*

Fig. 4.9: The Domain of Hypnotherapeutic Work: High and Low Phase Hypnosis. An integrated view of the entire spectrum of hypnotherapeutic work that resolves the activity-passivity paradox of historical hypnosis and current research. The domain of therapeutic hypnosis ranges from the ultradian peaks of performance with (1) High Phase Hypnosis with its active focus on problem solving in a compliant response to the contextual demands of the outer world as described by social-psychological theorists to (2) the more passive periods of inner absorption at the low phase of ultradian healing with Low Phase Hypnosis characterized by deeper inner world focus and dissociative dynamics as described by special-state theorists.

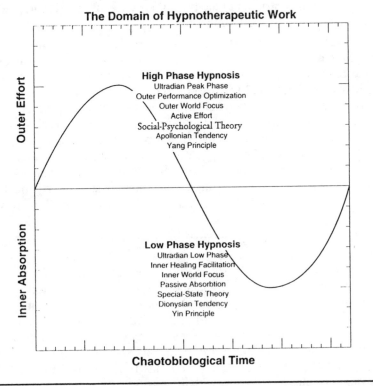

The Domain of Hypnotherapeutic Work

Outer Effort

High Phase Hypnosis
Ultradian Peak Phase
Outer Performance Optimization
Outer World Focus
Active Effort
Social-Psychological Theory
Apollonian Tendency
Yang Principle

Inner Absorption

Low Phase Hypnosis
Ultradian Low Phase
Inner Healing Facilitation
Inner World Focus
Passive Absorbtion
Special-State Theory
Dionysian Tendency
Yin Principle

Chaotobiological Time

Evidence currently available on the modulation of the immune system finds a role for both high and low phase hypnosis. Restricted Environmental Simulation Therapy (REST) has been shown to induce immune system enhancement as measured by its positive effects on salivary immunoglobulin (Turner, et al., 1993). Further research will be needed to determine whether such immune system enhancement of salivary immunoglobulin corresponds to what is here called low phase hypnosis. The study of Ruzyla-Smith, et al.,

(1995) cited above, by contrast, used a more active form of high phase hypnosis with instructions to (1) "Imagine your white blood cells attacking and destroying germ cells in your body" and (2) the "rapid alert self-hypnosis" the subjects were instructed to practice twice daily. This form of high phase hypnosis led to enhanced immune system functioning as measured by B-cells and helper T-cells. More detailed studies of the precise mindbody response to high and low phase hypnosis at the cellular-genetic level in psychoimmuniology will contribute to the type of specific information needed for hypnotherapeutic work of the future.

What would be the next step in exploring the concept of high and low phase hypnosis? What predictions could we make about changes in the brain and body during high and low phase hypnosis that we actually could measure? Predictions about changes in the body are relatively easy because so much work has already been done in this area as touched upon above (Hautkappe & Bongartz, 1992; Weinstein & Au, 1991). One challenge would be in designing a study that would clarify the apparently paradoxical post-surgical increases of adrenaline and cortisol, two of the bodies hormones associated with arousal (what we would call high phase hypnosis), when patients were given pre-surgical hypnotic suggestions for relaxation (low phase hypnosis).

Recent research on the neurobiology of consciousness could be adapted to assess changes in the brain during high and low phase hypnosis. Ommaya (1996), for example, has reported how there is a 10% overall increase in brain metabolism of oxygen measured with Positron Emission Tomography (PET) in human volunteers in two contrasting mental states: performing a complex visual task versus being at rest. We would predict that subjects in high phase hypnosis would have higher oxygen consumption than subjects in low phase hypnosis. Reiman (1996) used PET scans to investigate the neural substrates of human emotions with these results.

"Film- and recall-generated emotion were each associated with significant blood flow increases in the vicinity of the thalamus and prefrontal cortex (Brodmann's area 9). Film-generated emotion was distinguished from recall generated emotion by significantly greater symmetrical blood flow increases in the vicinity of occipito-temporal and tempopolar cortex, amygdala, hippocampal formation, hypothalamus, and lateral cerebellum."

We would predict that high and low phase hypnosis should be distinguished by blood flow increases to different areas of the brain.

High phase hypnosis, for example, might be characterized by blood flow increases to brain areas associated with emotional arousal.

We could go on and on exploring the psychobiological correlates associated with the ultradian polarity between *High and Low Phase Hypnosis* illustrated in Figure 4.9. From the original historical view of Franz Alton Mesmer, which we reviewed in Chapter One, for example, we can recognize that what he called the "intensification and remission" properties of life are what we now call high and low phase hypnosis respectively. From the cultural perspective of Chinese medicine we can recognize the fundamental polarity between their universal principles of *Yang and Yin* which alternate in chronobiological phases that are constant with our chaotobiological theory of hypnotherapeutic work. The massive research on the correlates of hypnosis with the left and right cerebral hemispheres, the nasal cycle and the state-dependent dynamics of emotional problems and psychosomatic symptoms reviewed in the previous chapter are all associated to varying degrees with the chaotobiological phases of our ultradian and circadian rhythms.

Figure 4.9 is therefore something of a heuristic compass pointing out directions for future research integrating a broad psychobiological domain of hypnotherapeutic work. Such research would be consistent with our goal of reformulating the foundation of hypnosis from first principles consistent with the leading edge of research in mathematics, physics, biology and the psychosocial sciences. In the first four chapters of this book our aim has been to rescue hypnosis from its rather narrow basin of attraction in psychiatry and abnormal psychology to intuit its fractal dynamics in optimal performance and healing on all levels in everyday life. In the next four chapters we will explore how we can learn to utilize these dynamics for facilitating the entire spectrum of hypnotherapeutic work in the process of self-organization, creativity and healing in clinical practice as well as normal living.

The Basic Ideas

1. *Two hundred years of the history of hypnotherapy (from its origins in Mesmerism to Charcot, Janet, Freud and Jung, to twentieth century methods of Milton Erickson and current research with hypnotic susceptibility scales) have recorded observations that we recognize today as consistent with the chaotobiological dynamics of complex adaptive rhythms of*

human experience on all psychological levels from the psycho-physical to the psychosocial.

2. *Current research supports the view that the source of these complex adaptive rhythms — that are expressed in the major self-regulating systems of mind and body (the central nervous system, the autonomic, endocrine and immune systems etc.) — is in chaotobiological dynamics at all levels from the molecular-genetic to the cognitive-behavioral. It is hypothesized that a major source of stress and psychosomatic illness may be found in the chronic abuse of our naturally alternating mindbody rhythms of performance and healing.*

3. *It is speculated that most of our current approaches to holistic healing (hypnosis, meditation, imagery, ritual, prayer, biofeedback, etc.) share a common denominator in facilitating the complex adaptive periodicity of our chatobiological rhythms of performance and healing — particularly the 20 minute ultradian healing response that apparently plays a role in coordinating the major systems of mindbody self regulation every 90-120 minutes throughout the day.*

4. *The chaotobiological approach to hypnotherapeutic work utilizes the entire spectrum of hypnotic performance. We call the high amplitude or arousal phase of ultradian experience "High Phase Hypnosis" in contrast to the low amplitude or relaxed phase of ultradian experience that we call "Low Phase Hypnosis." Current research implies that the classical phenomena of hypnosis are all manifestations of this broad range of chaotological psychobiological phenomena that are responsive to psychosocial cues.*

5. *The key to a genuine psychobiological therapy is to access the critical transition points of the mindbody communication systems that facilitate shifts to more desirable patterns of problem solving and behavior. This conjecture is a key dynamic of hypnotherapeutic work that points to new directions for future research reformulating the foundation of hypnosis from first principles consistent with the leading edge of research in mathematics, physics, biology and the psychosocial sciences.*

Part 2:
New Approaches
to Creative
Hypnotherapeutic Work

Chapter Five:
The Language of
Hypnotherapeutic Work

The word did not exist before the question came.

John Archibald Wheeler (1994)

The history of hypnosis and psychotherapy could be well written as the development of new approaches for accessing and facilitating healing and creativity. The evolution of our current approaches from Mesmerism to classical hypnosis and its transitions through Sigmund Freud, Carl Jung, Frederick Perls and Milton Erickson is well known. In this chapter we will only touch lightly upon this history of therapeutic technique to provide a broad context for introducing a new approach to the ideo-*dynamic* use of language and mindbody signaling to facilitate hypnotherapeutic work. As we shall see it is usually the subtle combinations and interactions of both verbal and non-verbal language that are most effective in the new ideo-*dynamic approaches* that use *psychological implication* to turn the tumblers of the patient's mind into problem solving combinations (Erickson, Rossi & Rossi, 1976).

The most basic approach to psychological implication is well illustrated by a recent development that I now call *"The Basic Accessing Questions"* which are the major focus of this chapter. The Basic Accessing Question is of special value in helping patients in the following ways.

(1) Recognizing what emotional problems are currently pressing for resolution within themselves.

(2) Creating a safe and supportive atmosphere that helps patients learn to resolve their own problems and facilitate their own healing in their own unique way.

(3) Initiating a naturalistic process of arousal, problem solving and relaxation that is characteristic of the natural phase transitions associated with ultradian rhythm of performance and healing in everyday life.

Freud's Free Association:
From Suggestion to Communication

While the history of hypnotherapy can be traced to ancient times, it was the transition from Mesmerism to hypnosis where scientific attention was focused on the nature of therapeutic suggestion (Ellenberger, 1970). Freud, for example, began his career with the hypnotherapeutic approaches he learned from Pierre Janet and Hippolyte Bernheim. He describes his use of the Bernheim model to access the unconscious and remove symptoms by direct suggestion as follows:

This astonishing and instructive experiment served as my model. I decided to start from the assumption that my patients knew everything that was of any pathogenic significance and that it was only a question of obliging them to *communicate* it.

Thus when I reached a point at which, after asking a patient some question such as: 'How long have you had this symptom?' or: 'What was its origin?', I was met with the answer: 'I really don't know.' I proceeded as follows:

I placed my hand on the patient's forehead or took her head between my hands and said: 'You will think of it under the pressure of my hand. At the moment at which I relax my pressure you will see something in front of you or something will come into your head. Catch hold of it. It will be what we are looking for, — Well, what have you seen or what has occurred to you?" (Breuer and Freud, 1895/1957, p 110).

Freud then goes on to explain his hand pressure method as a form of *"**communication**"* that *"could be replaced by any other signal or by some other exercise of physical influence on the patient... for a 'momentarily' intensified hypnosis"* as follows (italic bold face are my emphasis). Notice that Freud emphasizes communication rather than suggestion even in his early use of hypnosis. This emphasis on communication rather than suggestion, of course, is the main shift in the focus of this entire book from hypnotherapeutic suggestion to hypnotherapeutic work.

In these circumstances I make use in the first instance of a small technical device. I inform the patient that, a moment later, I shall apply pressure to his forehead and I assure him that, all the time the pressure lasts, he will see before him a recollection in the form of a picture or will have it in his thoughts in the form of an idea occurring to him; and I pledge him to *communicate* this picture or idea to me, whatever it may be.

He is not to keep it to himself because he may happen to think it is not what is wanted, not the right thing, or because it would be too disagreeable for him to say it.

There is to be no criticism of it, no reticence, either for emotional reasons or because it is judged unimportant. Only in this manner can we find what we are in search of, but in this manner we shall find it infallibly.

Having said this, I press for a few seconds on the forehead of the patient as he lies in front of me; I then leave go and ask quietly, as though there were no question of a disappointment: "What did you see?' or 'What occurred to you?"

This procedure has taught me much and has also invariably achieved its aim. Today I can no longer do without it. I am of course aware that a pressure on the forehead like this could be replaced by *any other signal or by some other exercise of physical influence on the patient;* but since the patient is lying in front of me, pressure on his forehead, or taking his head between my two hands, seems to be the most convenient way of applying suggestion for the purpose I have in view. It would be possible for me to say by way of explaining the efficacy of this device that it corresponded to a 'momentarily intensified hypnosis'; but *the mechanism of hypnosis is so puzzling to me that I would rather not make use of it as an explanation.*

I am rather of opinion that the advantage of the procedure lies in the fact that by means of it I dissociate the patient's attention from his conscious searching and reflecting — from everything, in short, on which he can employ his will — in the same sort of way in which this is effected by staring into a crystal ball, and so on.

The conclusion which I draw from the fact that what I am looking for always appears under the pressure of my hand is as follows. The pathogenic idea which has ostensibly been forgotten is always lying ready 'close at hand' and can be reached by associations that are easily accessible.

It is merely a question of getting some obstacle out of the way. This obstacle seems once again to be the subject's will, and different people can learn with different degrees of ease to free themselves from their intentional thinking and to adopt an attitude of completely objective observation towards the psychical processes taking place in them. (Breuer and Freud, 1895/1957, p 270-271).

Freud soon gave up the use of hypnosis, or thought he did, because, as he clearly states above, *The mechanism of hypnosis is so puzzling to me that I would rather not make use of it as an explanation.*

Freud wanted to learn more about how the mind actually worked. What was actually going on during therapeutic trance? What were the sources of human problems and how were they resolved? How does healing actually take place? In Freud's time hypnosis was still a mysterious art with almost no scientific research and explanation.

He could have no understanding of the naturalistic foundation of hypnotherapy in the chaotological approach to chronobiology and ultradian theory as we are attempting to formulate it (Rossi, 1982, 1986/1993; Lloyd & Rossi, 1992). To explore his questions Freud experimented with various ways of working with his patients and eventually came up with what he called "Free Association." Simply ask a patient to lie down on a comfortable couch in a quiet, dimly lit room with the analyst sitting out of sight and freely express whatever comes up in the mind all by itself without criticizing oneself or attempting to direct oneself in any way.

We now recognize that these conditions are quite ideal for evoking and entraining the rest phase of our 90-120 minute Basic Rest Activity Cycle so that reverie, imagery and fantasy become more active (Wallace, 1993; Wallace et al., 1992) along with what Erickson would call the "The Common Everyday Trance" (Erickson & Rossi, 1981).

Freud apparently found that free associations under such conditions could sometimes *"dissociate the patient's attention from his conscious searching and reflecting"* just as well as the more formal induction by the laying on of hands. Such free association would often lead to states of emotional arousal and the recall of traumatic memories that turned out to represent the sources of the patient's problems. The emotional re-experiencing and therapeutic understanding of the sources of problems, generally called "catharsis," then led to their resolution. During Freud's early creative period of discovery this healing resolution sometimes took place entirely within the patient, *"As the climax of its achievement."* This climax of achievement points precisely to what we mean by "hypnotherapeutic work" in this book.

Sometimes, however, the psychoanalyst had to play detective by carefully following the quiet clues in a patient's associations that would lead the analyst to make an "interpretation" of what the source of the patient's problem must have been. As the students of Freud diverged further and further from the original source of his inspiration in the dynamics of hypnosis that allowed patients to find their own understanding and healing, psychoanalysis became more and more an art of interpretation by the therapist — now sometimes called, *The Difficult Art* (Carotenuto, 1992). The *"locus of control,"* understanding and healing shifted from being centered in the patient's personal inner process and emerging consciousness to the authority of the therapist's world view.

One therapist's carefully formulated interpretation in time, however, easily became another's myth or ideology. Even after generations of effort no generally agreed upon objective criteria for assessing the validity of a psychoanalytic interpretation has emerged. It was not for want of trying to find such generally valid criteria of interpretation. As a matter of fact, it was precisely because different analysts found so many different criteria for understanding the sources of human problems that the psychoanalytic movement soon split up into many different schools of thought about the essence of psychological and psychosomatic problems and their resolution.

Jung's Active Imagination:
From the Occult to the Numinosium

Carl Jung also began his career by using hypnosis and achieved some success in facilitating healing. He also developed a scientific explanation of many *"so-called occult phenomena"* as being early techniques for communicating with the unconscious. In his earliest writing about automatic writing and table turning, for example, Jung describes the dynamics of dissociation and what he called the *"partial hypnosis"* of motor areas of the mind and body, particularly the arms and hands, as follows:

> It was not a question here of total hypnosis, put of a partial one, limited entirely to the motor area of the arm, like the cerebral anesthesia produced by magnetic passes for a painful spot in the body (Jung 1902/1957, pg. 49) ... However, I have noticed in a few cases that the suggestion is realized despite its comparative boldness (it is after all directed to the waking consciousness of a so-called normal person!), but that it does so in a peculiar way, by putting only the purely motor part of the central nervous system under hypnosis and that the deeper hypnosis is then obtained from the motor phenomenon by auto-suggestion, as in the procedure for table-turning described above." (Jung, 1902/1957, pg. 54-55).

Jung's concept of a "partial" hypnosis of a motor area is what we would call today "mindbody communication." Jung's partial hypnosis was apparently rediscovered independently by Milton Erickson as "segmentalized hypnotic phenomenon." In a segmentalized hypnotic experience the patient apparently remained normally awake and communicative with the therapist while only a part of the body like the hand, fingers or head would move to signal dissociated responses from the unconscious (Erickson Rossi & Rossi, 1976). Erickson's student, David Cheek, then focused on the use of such partial, or seg-mentalized, hypnotic phenomena with fingers and combined it with LeCron's 20 questions method to develop the finger signaling approach to accessing information from the unconscious (Rossi & Cheek, 1988) to facilitate problem solving and healing. From our new nonlinear perspective this 20 question approach to accessing information can be reconceptuallized as a bifurcating form of iteration.

Like Freud, Jung had a scientific turn of mind and wanted to learn more about how the psyche actually worked. His recognition of the essentially informational or communicative nature of many occult and spiritual phenomena was an important step in the current evolution of The Basic Accessing Question and the Ideodynamic Accessing Scale (IDEAS-1) that utilizes hand signaling as a partial, or segmentalized, trance phenomenon that will be illustrated later in this chapter. Jung tried Freud's method of free association for a while, but found it unsatisfactory because it often led to patterns of associations that became too divergent and actually led away from the source of problems.

By degrees, Jung was led to develop another method that was very different from Freud's. Jung called his new method, "Active Imagination." Have the patient concentrate on a vivid or emotionally significant image from a dream or fantasy and encourage the patient to have a dialogue with the image. This inner dialogue was used to facilitate what Jung called, the "Transcendent Function," the bridge between the conscious and the unconscious in all forms of creativity and healing. Active imagination was to be carried out privately by patients on their own time rather than in therapy in the presence of the therapist.

The "numinous" (emotionally arousing, tremendous, mysterious) and sometimes spiritual images that came up spontaneously during active imagination led Jung to see the source of human problems in one's relation to the god or, rather, to the "image of god" (the Self) within. How different this was from Freud's finding that free associa-tions led to the view that it was the "vicissitudes of sexuality" that was the essential source of human problems.

From our current psychobiological perspective it is important to recognize that active imagination as Jung experienced (Jung, 1961) and as it is described by his closest followers (Hannah, 1981) usually begins with a quiet and deep reflective mood (sometimes recognizable as a clinically depressive state) that is suggestive of the natural rest phase of our ultradian rhythms. Some of the most interesting examples of the creative process of active imagination report how it may lead to ecstatic states of emotional arousal, heightened insight and consciousness for about fifteen to twenty minutes or more that are similar to those celebrated in the classical literature of mysticism (Rossi & Nimmons, 1991). This again suggests an association with our natural chronobiological shifts from the rest phase of the Basic Rest Activity Cycle to the peak phase of the arousal of consciousness.

Perls' Gestalt Dialogue: From Arousal to Insight

This problem of developing ever more effective methods of communication with the unconscious (or the "mindbody") with shifting states of emotion and consciousness continues to our day. Over and over again a pioneering therapist comes up with a new method of investigating the mind and a new set of interpretations about the source and means of resolving human problems.

Fritz Perls, for example, developed Gestalt Therapy by employing what could be seen as an extroverted variation of Jung's active imagination. Perls would have a volunteer in group therapy begin by sitting in the center of a circle on the *"hot seat."* The volunteer would then begin by telling a dream or describing a difficult life situation until Fritz understood just enough of the situation to encourage the volunteer to break through an emotional difficulty with an emotionally confronting psychodrama. The patient was encouraged to focus and imagine (hypnotically hallucinate?), for example, that their mother was present (or whoever else the patient had difficulties with) and telling their mother what needed to be said.

Fritz would then encourage a lively dialogue between the imagined mother and the suffering patient until an emotionally significant breakthrough in the form of important insights was experienced.

From my own personal experiences with Fritz Perls I can attest to the deeply arousing aspects of these emotional confrontations on the "hot seat" in the center of a circle of one's peers that were just as cathartic as Freud's descriptions of his early work and often as profoundly numinous as Jung's private epiphanies. What is profoundly different about the approach of Perls and his students is that what was an essentially private experience of communication with the unconscious in the methods of Freud and Jung became a public and confrontational approach to communication in the arousing experience of the hot seat. Like the public rituals of exorcism and healing from the middle ages to the present (Ellenberger, 1970), Perls discovered how much more potent communication with the self could be when it was carried out in public with a supportive and sympathetic audience.

In their classical volume on *Gestalt Therapy: Excitement and Growth in the Human Personality* (Perls et al., 1951, p 409) describe the role of emotional arousal during the peak periods of anxiety, conflict, confusion, breakthrough, insight and creative adjustment in psychotherapy as follows:

> Excitement persists and increases through the sequence of creative adjustment and is strongest at the final contact. This is so even if obstacles and lost conflicts prevent the finale; but in such a case the excitement becomes spectacularly disruptive of the organizing self itself.

> Rage turns into tantrum, there is grief and exhaustion, and perhaps hallucination (day-dream of victory, revenge, and gratification). These are emergency functions to release tension and enable one to start afresh the next time, for of course the physiological need and its excitation are still unfinished. This process, of total frustration and unlimited explosion, is not unhealthy but it is not, needless to say — despite the opinion of many parents — useful for learning anything... (Perls et al., 1951 p. 409).

From our chronobiological perspective, we would view such states of excitement in Gestalt therapy as obvious manifestations of the peak periods of the ultradian rhythms when the stress, or arousing hormones, are at their peaks for optimizing integration of the inner and outer realities of the therapy situation (Rossi, 1990b). Most therapists recognize that a "good session" usually involves some states of emotional arousal, communication and breakthrough, however mild they may seem, in contrast to the extremes reported in the literature of many emotion sensation and *"body-energy"* oriented therapies (Rossi, 1986/1993).

Let us now summarize these significant developments in the evolution of psychotherapy as a prelude in coming to grips with the subtlety of the late Milton H. Erickson's indirect approaches to mind-body communication in hypnotherapy. In general we witness a movement away from direct hypnotic induction techniques in Freud, Jung and Perls. We see each of their major innovations — free association, active imagination and Gestalt dialogue — as mild rituals of induction that evoke a special state of therapeutic communication and expectation that shifts the locus of control from the authority of the therapist to the inherent creativity of the patient. These newly named rituals of induction, however, all retain some of the tell-tail signs of naturalistic hypnosis. They all entrain and utilize our alternating ultradian rhythms of peaks of arousal and activity with our quieter periods of naturalistic rest and healing.

A special ritual of induction, emotional arousal and a mild therapeutic dissociation that facilitates communication with subjective realities and the expectation of accessing inner resources for healing are some of the common denominators between the classical direct hypnosis of the past and the innovations of Freud, Jung and Perls as well as a host of other current schools that do not acknowledge their historical sources in hypnosis (Rossi, 1986/1993).

Erickson's Naturalistic Hypnosis: From the Implied Directive to The Basic Accessing Questions

With this background we are now prepared to appreciate the essence of Milton H. Erickson's innovative contributions to therapeutic suggestion. The myth of classical hypnosis is that an authoritarian therapist induces a patient into a special state of receptivity wherein they are relaxed, sleepy or occasionally even in a somnambulistic-like state of sleep-walking. In this receptive state the patient is then to be programmed by the therapist with direct suggestions that are believed to be the *raison d'être* of hypnotherapy. There are varying degrees of authoritarian directness of suggestion. Patient's may be vigorously commanded, persuaded or gradually led through a series of inner experiences that enable them to give up their errant attitudes, bad habits or symptoms.

There can be no denying that Erickson believed in and used many varieties of direct suggestion throughout his career. Erickson carefully noted, however, that attempting to directly program people without understanding their individuality was *"A very uninformed way"* of doing therapy (Erickson & Rossi, 1979, p 288). An important aspect of Erickson's genius was to spell out the conditions for optimizing both direct and indirect suggestions by utilizing the patient's own belief system and inner resources (Erickson & Rossi, 1979, p 119).

A careful analysis of Erickson's innovative approaches to accessing and utilizing the patient's own inner resources for problem solving and healing led to what we called "indirect suggestion" in our first collaborative effort. Of these, what we originally called *"The Implied Directive"* has turned out to be the most useful in my current efforts to isolate the essence of hypnotherapeutic work (Erickson, Rossi & Rossi, 1976). Erickson and I regarded *"Implication"* as the essence of the dynamics of suggestion because it is not what the therapist says that is important as much as what the patient does with what the therapist says.

> It is important in formulating psychological implications to realize that the therapist only provides a stimulus; the hypnotic aspect of psychological implications is created on an unconscious level by the listener.

> The most effective aspect of any suggestion is that which stirs the listener's own associations and mental processes into automatic action. It is this autonomous activity of the listener's own associations and mental processes that creates hypnotic experience (Erickson, Rossi & Rossi, 1976, p 61).

In brief, *Psychological implication is a key that automatically turns the tumblers of a patient's associative processes into predictable patterns without awareness of how it happened* (ibid., p 59).

Twenty years after we formulated this concept, the fundamental role of implication for learning by the "cognitive unconscious" is being recognized and actively pursued in current research (Reber, 1993).

We originally described Erickson's use of the implied directive to facilitate a somnambulistic state of deep hypnotic rapport in the following:

The implied directive usually has three parts: (1) a time-binding introduction, (2) the implied (or assumed) suggestion, and (3) a behavioral response to signal when the implied suggestion has been accomplished.

(1) A time-binding introduction that focuses the patient on the suggestion to follow

As soon as you know...

(2) The implied (or assumed) suggestion

Only you or I, or only you and my voice are here...

(3) The behavioral response signaling that the suggestion has been accomplished."

Your right hand will descend to your thigh...

An implied directive frequently used by Rossi to end a hypnotherapeutic session is as follows:

(1) A time-binding introduction that facilitates dissociation and reliance on the unconscious

As soon as your unconscious knows...

(2) The implied suggestion for easy reentry to trance phrased in a therapeutically motivating manner.

It can again return to this state comfortably and easily to do constructive work the next time we are together...

(3) The behavioral response signaling that the above suggestion has been accomplished.

You will find yourself awakening feeling refreshed and alert...

When the behavioral response signaling the accomplishment is a response that *the patient wants to happen* (as in the above examples), we have a situation where the behavioral response obviously has *motivating* properties. The behavioral response signaling the accomplishment of the suggestion takes place on an involuntary or unconscious level. Thus the unconscious that carries out the suggestion also signals when it is accomplished.

The implied directive is thus a way of facilitating an intense state of internal learning or problem solving. We may suppose that all of a subject's available mental resources (e.g., stored memories, sensory and verbal associational patterns, various forms of previous learning, etc.) are marshaled toward a creative state of learning and problem solving.

Since recent experiments in the neurophysiology of learning suggest that new proteins are actually synthesized in the appropriate brain cells during learning (Rossi, 1973, 1986/1993), we may speculate that the implied directive facilitates the internal synthesis of new protein structures that could function as the biological basis of new behavior and phenomenological experience in the patient" (Erickson, Rossi and Rossi, 1976, pg. 188-189). The implied directive has become so important in the development of my current approaches that I have generalized it into a wide variety of forms that I now call "The Basic Accessing Question." The Basic Accessing Question utilizes the same three stage dynamics as the implied directive outlined above, except that the so-called "directive" is always turned into a question.

Figure 5.1 THE BASIC ACCESSING QUESTIONS

Stage 1

When your inner mind is ready to solve your problem will those hands move together all by themselves to signal yes?

Stage 2

When the inner you is able to experience all the sources, memories and emotions related to your problem will one hand drift down all by itself?

Stage 3

As soon as it is appropriate to review all the options for solving that problem in the best manner will that other hand go down?

Stage 4

When your unconscious knows it can continue that inner healing, and when your conscious mind knows it can cooperate by helping you recognize those periods during the day when you need to take a healing rest (a 15-20 minute break), will you find yourself awakening?

Figure 5.1: A simplified four stage outline of a complete pattern of hypnotherapy using the Ideodynamic Accessing Scale (IDEAS-1).

A three step Basic Accessing Question at each stage utilizes hand signaling to facilitate mindbody communication and healing. In the final step, awakening from trance becomes a behavioral signal that the patient's conscious and unconscious will cooperate in the posthypnotic suggestion to continue the inner work during nature's ultradian healing response throughout the day.

Reformulating the implied directive as a three step question adds an important degree of patient-centerdness as well as activation of the patient's inner resources. The question format also adds a permissive and "fail-safe" quality to the process of mindbody communication. The only way it can fail is when there is no answer or involuntary behavioral signal in response to the question. This is a safe situation because it can be taken to simply mean that the "unconscious" is not yet ready to respond. The implication is that more time is needed for the process of autonomous growth and communication to take place. This is very different from the obvious and grievous failure that occurs when a patient does not respond to the direct hypnotic suggestions by the therapist to be "Healed Now!"

The Basic Accessing Question thus relieves both the therapist and the patient of the stress of "fear of failure" in hypnotherapy. Even when nothing seems to happen, it focuses the patient's attention on the essential processes of self communication and buys time for continuing therapeutic developments in the future.

In Figure 5.1 I have outlined how an entire hypnotherapeutic session can be carried out by using the Basic Accessing Question with hand signaling to: (1) induce a permissive state of therapeutic hypnosis; (2) access the sources and history of an emotional problem or symptom; (3) explore the options for solving the problem and facilitating healing and; (4) reorienting from the inner focus of the therapeutic state to our normal generalized reality orientation with a new understanding of what patients can do to continue the therapeutic work on their own. Each of these four typical therapeutic uses of the Basic Accessing Question focuses the patient's inner resources on a specific therapeutic task in a manner that allows the psychodynamics of Freud's free association, Jung's active imagination and Perl's Gestalt dialogue to become operative in a patient-centered therapy that may or may not involve the manifestation of classical hypnotic phenomena.

Taken together, the four stage pattern using an appropriate form of the Basic Accessing Question at each stage is illustrated in Figure 5.1 and is currently being developed as a standardized approach to hypnotherapy called the Ideodynamic Exploratory Accessing Scale (IDEAS-1) that can be used with individuals or groups. Readers who are interested in obtaining a copy of the IDEAS-1 for research purposes may contact Brian Lippincott, Ph.D. (John F. Kennedy University, Graduate School of Professional Psychology, 1 West Campbell Ave., # 67, Campbell, CA., 95008, USA). The following cases illustrate the flexible use of this approach with three very different problems: (1) the recovery of the memory of lost tickets by an organically brain-damaged patient; (2) the recall and emotional catharsis of sexual molestation and; (3) a five year follow-up on facilitating the creative process in demonstration therapy. Each of these cases documents the far-reaching effects of a single hypnotherapeutic session using the dynamics of the Basic Accessing Question in the IDEAS-1 format.

Case One: Memory in Organic Brain Damage.

A woman telephones in a much agitated, confused state and requests hypnosis to help her find where she has hidden $ 2000.00 worth of tickets to a Michael Jackson Rock Concert.

In the interview her appearance is clean but oddly disheveled. Her speech is slurred and she is not able to give her name, address or telephone number with full clarity.

She reveals she is wearing a wig because her scalp still shows an ugly scar and evidence of many stitches she received when she had an auto accident several months ago. She is able to care for herself at home alone, but when a man delivered the already paid for concert tickets a few days ago she hid them someplace in the home where neither she nor any one else in the family could find them when they all returned from work that day.

I initially attempted to help facilitate her memory by having her carefully recall several times in serial order everything she did that day from the moment she woke up. Eventually she asked plaintively if I could not do the hypnosis that she really came for. A bit hastily I reassured her that I could and further, I was going to use a special form of effective hypnosis that was designed especially for memory problems because her mind would grow more alert rather than going into sleep.

I then proceeded with the IDEAS-1 approach illustrated in figure 5.1 with these modifications of the Basic Accessing Questions to suit her particular needs.

Stage 1: If your inner mind really knows where those tickets are will those hands move together all by themselves to signal yes?

After a few moments of slowly oscillating back and forth — together and apart for a few centimeters — her hands suddenly clapped loudly, stuck together and she looked up at me as if shocked.

Stage 2: Now, will one of those hands slowly move down all by itself to signal that you are again reviewing your whole day and this time remembering exactly where you hid those tickets?

Her right hand did begin moving down slowly as her head and other arm bobbed about uncertainly. After two or three minutes when her hand was just about to reach her lap she suddenly startled, sat straight up in the chair and stared at me in wide eyed wonderment.

I cautiously responded with,

Stage 3: And now you really do know where you hid those tickets, do you not?

She slowly nodded her head yes and spontaneously closed her eyes again. It is not uncommon for some patients to occasionally open their eyes at some critical phase transition or other during the ongoing hypnotherapeutic work. I simply acknowledge the meaningfulness of their experience with a kindly nod of my head if they are looking at me. I fully expect they will close their eyes again when they are ready to continue their inner focused work.

Stage 4: Now will that other hand begin to drift down all by itself as you review over and over again just where those tickets are and how happy your family is going to be when they see them?

With a broadening smile on her face the other hand went slowly down to her lap whereupon she opened her eyes with a grin and told me the tickets were safe in the linen closet. No one in her humble home would dare look in the linen closet because it was absolutely forbidden to go there except when special company came to the house for a special occasion that deserved the family's best linen.

I then wrote down on a slip of paper the location of the tickets in the linen closet and gave it to her so that she and her family would be sure to find them. When a family member called the next day to thank me for helping find the tickets we were both so enthused that I forgot that I never did get the name, address and telephone number clear enough to bill them. For some reason or other I was quite satisfied not being paid for this memorable single session of therapy.

Box 5.1: Creative Variations of The Basic Accessing Question

Here are a few creative variations in the Basic Accessing Question that use different forms of body, head, hand, finger, foot, speech, breathing or eye signaling to facilitate the essence of hypnotherapeutic healing in three steps:

(1) A time-binding introduction;

(2) An implied suggestion for problem solving or healing to be carried out by the unconscious — a more or less autonomous response by the mindbody — and

(3) An involuntary, observable behavioral signal that the suggestion is being carried out.

1. When your UCS knows

2. It can allow you to experience a comfortable therapeutic trance

3. Will those eyes finally close all by themselves?

1. And when

2. You find yourself reviewing important emotional issues

3. Will your breathing change all by itself to facilitate healing?

1. As you experience yourself

2. Going more deeply into the best state to explore your issues

3. Will that head nod yes when everything is going well?

And will that head shake no to everything you do not want?

1. When you feel

2. The emotional truth someplace within

3. Will you find yourself expressing a sentence or two,

Only what I really need to hear to help you further?

1. As you review all the sources of these problems,

2. Memories, dreams and reflections

3. Will your fingers signal yes or no by moving one way or another?

1. At some time within the next few minutes

2. Will you experience only enough of your symptoms so that your

3. Body makes a deep adjustment for comfort and healing?

1. When your inner self (inner guide, etc.) knows

2. You have completed enough inner work for today

3. Will you find your feet moving first or will your arms stretch first

as you awaken ready to discuss whatever is necessary?

Case Two: Memory and Sexual Molestation

A rather conservative corporate executive officer presented himself for hypnotherapy to help him remember if he had really sexually molested his son and daughter more than twenty-five years ago as they were now accusing him in court of law.

He insisted with some indignation he had no memories of molesting his very own children. After discussing with him the ambiguous legal status of hypnosis, as evidence in legal cases, he then made it clear that he wanted hypnosis for his own benefit and curiosity. He decided he would not make use of his hypnotic experience in the law suit he was faced with.

Because of his sense of urgency and my surmise that this might be a single session case I proceeded immediately with the IDEAS-1 as follows:

Stage 1: If your unconscious has some valid information regarding this urgent question about sexual molestation of your children will those hands signal yes by moving together all by themselves as if a magnet were pulling them together?

After five long minutes of staring at his apparently fixed and unmoving hands I suspected we might have an inconclusive fail-safe outcome wherein nothing much happens.

Out of habit, I attempted to turn the situation into a therapeutic double-bind (Rossi & Ryan, 1992) by adding,

Or will those hands be pushed apart to signal that there is no reliable information available to answer your question?

Paradoxically, he responded to this by slowly closing his eyes as his hands hesitantly moved together with that very fine and slight but rapid vibratory movement that is so characteristic of involuntary finger and hand signaling (Rossi & Cheek, 1988). As soon as the hands touched together, I continued with stage two.

Stage 2. When your unconscious knows it can make available privately [pause] to you alone [pause] the simple truth and only the truth, will one of those hands slowly drift down all by itself?

Tears slowly welled up as one hand began drifting down. When his hand finally reached his lap after a few minutes he gave a deep sigh with much quiet weeping. I had no way of knowing the details of what he was really going through but I suspected that his continuing privacy was necessary to obviate "resistance" that could easily rupture his experience. So I proceeded methodically to stage three.

Stage 3. And when your unconscious is ready to explore how you can now proceed with the situation [pause] will that other hand now drift down more or less by itself to signal that you are sorting through options for dealing fairly and appropriately with your personal issues?

As the other hand drifted down he gradually composed himself so that he apparently recovered his acumen by the time it reached his lap. After a moment or two, I continued with stage four.

Stage 4. And when you become aware that you can awaken with a full memory of all you need to know about your situation, will your eyes open as you come fully alert with a comfortable stretch?

After another moment or two he shuffled his feet, stretched, opened his eyes and casually touched himself a bit about his lap, arms, face and head as is highly characteristic of patients reorienting themselves to their fully awakened state after a trance experience. Without any prompting, he reported how he had recovered long forgotten memories of playing and romping about naked on a bed and running about the house with his children when they were about three, or at the most four years old. He thought it was play but not sexual molestation.

Would his children believe his version of what really happened? He asked if he could bring his son and daughter to a family therapy session with me to discuss it all. I assured him that I thought that was an excellent idea. I never heard from him again, however.

Case Three: Facilitating Creativity: A Five Year Follow Up

The following report written by a volunteer after a single session of therapy in one of my training workshops is self explanatory.

I wanted to know how I stopped myself from being creative, particularly in painting. I wanted to paint in an abstract way, while I continued to paint realistically.

As I recall we worked with my arms outstretched in front of me, fingers apart. We questioned the willingness of my unconscious to work on this issue and my right hand rose to at least shoulder level and seemed to have a life of its own.

My arm and hand moved without volition and I knew that an inner process was taking place. I expected it to be accomplished by words, symbols, memories, color — (something!) but there was a total blank.

I remember expressing disappointment at this state of affairs. As I recall, you also wondered if the unconscious process of creativity might not also, or instead of painting, find expression in other ways.

At your wondering if the unconscious would be willing to continue to work on the problem and report to you in seven days. I expressed a willingness to do so (and an inner certainty that I would get information during that time).

The following morning about 5 a.m., while in a waking-dreaming state I had a fantasy-vision of a garden with tender green shoots just coming up.

When I bent down to weed this garden a voice said, No, at this point you don't know what is a weed and what is a flower. Wait. This was followed by a vision of a canvas-like sheet pulling tight over me, as though I was lying down with room to breathe but not to move. I, or someone, rolled back this canvas and exposed light and air.

I was enchanted with both visions and knew the unconscious was at work. This was followed by a dream exploration during our workshop practicum, another dream the following night (Saturday). Synchronicity also has seemed to be at work, with affirmations by friends and acquaintances and reading I have done.

The outcome has been abstract sand sculpture at the beach with feelings of delight and acceptance on my part, with my first abstract collage-painting last night — with also a sense of delight and acceptance.

The acceptance and allowing part of me seems really activated and I am living life with delight and wonder and joy.

In a 5 year follow up she writes.

I paint sporadically, still primarily in a realistic way. The times I have made collages to express an emotion or an idea I have done well, though my real appreciation of the work doesn't come until at least a year later, when I think That's good — did I do that? These are abstract.

The most significant changes have been in the way I view creativity and how I use it in my life. My recall of our session was that you implanted a suggestion that creativity could take many forms. I have felt I used it in my work as a psychotherapist in the use of insights, metaphors, images. I often pictured myself as an artist with images and words.

I have claimed creativity in an attitude toward life of excitement, curiosity, openness, a willingness to experiment, a belief of 'I can do it,' whatever the task. Much of this is new for me — or perhaps new in my willingness to claim it. I have written poetry, become more creative in my dress, in my entertaining...I also took the bull by the horn and decided to conduct a class at our local art center entitled Awakening Creativity, which I co-led with a colleague.

This subject's self-described sense of how her "arm and hand moved without volition" and her sense of "a total blank" instead of her expectation of "words, symbols, memories, colors — something!" is indicative of the surprising and counter intuitive aspect of much of the autonomous creative inner processing that takes place all by itself in genuine hypnotherapy versus the conscious and ego driven mental processes that are characteristic of much cognitive-behavioral therapy that is so popular today.

The acceptance of this autonomous process as an important aspect of the natural dynamics of the creative process is supported by her statement, *"The acceptance and allowing part of me seems really activated and I am living a life with delight, wonder and joy."* The late Carl Rogers in personal communications with me agreed that the activation patients experienced in what he called, "Demonstration Therapy" where he illustrated his "client-centered" approach in front of large groups of professionals in training was at least in part responsible for the effectiveness of single session psychotherapy. Other therapists have wondered why single session therapy, particularly when demonstrated in front of a large group, is so effective that we may ask whether such therapy illustrates the dynamics of "Miracle Cures" (Barber, 1990).

From the perspective of the ultradian dynamics of psychotherapy we would say that presenting one's self for essentially private work in public is inherently exciting and activating. Certainly most of the subjects I have questioned when they first came up in front of a group to experience hypnotherapy immediately admit they are in an excited state with a rapid heart beat, perspiration, breathing changes, etc., all indicative of an arousal of their sympathetic nervous system. This cannot but help remind us of how in the early days Mesmerism and hypnosis were usually carried out in front of a group to demonstrate its "miraculous" potentials for healing.

Demonstrating in front of a group turns out to be an ideal way of evoking and entraining the peak phase of our psychobiological rhythms when the arousing hormones (messenger molecules) of the mindbody are able to activate the same state-dependent memory, learning and behavior systems that originally encoded the problem the patient wants to resolve.

These considerations present us with another increment of evidence that the essence of effective hypnotherapy may be in the accessing and arousal of the same psychobiological dynamics that encoded the problem in the first place.

While the three cases presented here all illustrate how the Basic Accessing Question can be used to facilitate problem solving in a single session, particularly when combined in the four stage IDEAS-1 format, they may be regarded as the exception rather than the rule.

Psychotherapy usually requires many roles for the therapist: counselor, confessor, guide, advisor, good parent and so forth. The typical course of psychotherapy requires time and many sessions to correct tragic histories and life styles.

In its essence, however, the Basic Accessing Question in its many disguises and variations, can be regarded as the sine qua non of psychotherapy in general and hypnotherapy in particular. Every school of psychotherapy, whatever its theoretical orientation, usually requires the patient to go through the four stages of the IDEAS-1 in some form or other. As illustrated in this chapter, the Basic Accessing Question in the IDEAS-1 format is simply a compact way of carefully focusing and optimizing the usually serpentine paths of communication in psychotherapy.

In the next chapter we will explore in greater detail how this compact approach can be expanded to facilitate each of the four stages of the creative process in the ultradian dynamics of psycho-therapy as well as everyday life. We will focus on the types of language and methods the therapist uses to facilitate each stage:

(1) Identifying and focusing on the presenting problem;

(2) Accessing the sources, emotions and dynamics of problems and symptoms;

(3) Exploring options for problem solving and healing and;

(4) Recognizing the important insights and the practical pathways for taking a new step toward therapeutic change as the conclusion of every session.

**Box 5.2   Symptom Scaling: The Problem Ruler and Psychotherapy
With Children**

In a recent doctoral dissertation, Mary Pratt (1993), developed the image of a
"Problem Ruler" so that children could rate the intensity of the problem they were
experiencing at the beginning and end of a counseling or therapy session. This
imagery approach to *symptom scaling*, of course, is useful for adults as well.

In the beginning of a therapy session, children or adults will typically report a high
number on the Problem Ruler corresponding to the frowning or crying face that
mirrors a high degree of suffering. When the session goes well patients will typically
report a low number on the Problem Ruler corresponding to the smiling face.

One particularly poignant case was a four year old who complained, "I just can't get
my beauty rest." Her parents believed that her troubled sleep and constant
awakening at night was related to the family's sorrow over the recent death of a
grandparent.

After an initial interview where the little girl articulated her thoughts well about her
grandfather's death without any apparent emotional problems, the counselor asked
her if she would like to use her hands to help her solve her sleeping problem. When
the little girl immediately agreed the counselor demonstrated the beginning hand
positions and asked if the little girl's hands would "move together all by themselves"
to say they would help her solve her problem. The little girl then asked if it would be
"like clapping?" When the counselor agreed that it would, the little girl began to
stare at her hands that soon began to move together while vibrating slightly as is
quite characteristic of the first stage of the process.

The counselor then went on to Stage Two by asking, "I wonder if your inner mind
would explore everything about this problem so it can plan how to solve it? As it
does that...I wonder if one of those hands will begin to fall down to that lap?" As the
child's left hand began to slowly move downward the counselor said, "Please tell me
anything that pops into your mind as your hand is falling." When the hand was about
half way down the child said, "I have a dog." With the help of the counselor's
appropriate questions the little girl soon acknowledged that the dog would startle her
awake at night when the dog scratched herself.

By that time the left hand had reached her lap and the counselor went on to Stage
Three by wondering whether the other hand would soon begin to fall down all by
itself along with a plan for solving the problem. After a few moments the right hand
fell to her lap and the child immediately began to talk about the bear puppet in the
chair next to her. The counselor joined in with this conversation naturally and the
problem of sleeplessness was not mentioned again.

The family agreed that the dog should have her own place to sleep separately from
the child and the problem was immediately solved. A month follow up indicated that
the child was now sleeping well at night and she rated her old problem as zero on the
Pratt Problem Ruler. What is most noteworthy about this simple approach is how
quickly and easily the problem was solved by helping the child access her own
understanding of the problem with the three step Basic Accessing Questions and
hand signaling. The parent's initial hunch that the sleeplessness was related to the
grandparent's death was apparently not the immediate source of the child's problem
and its simple solution.

Box 5.3   Creative Iteration and the Pregnant Pause

From the new perspective of nonlinear dynamics we now recognize that any process of internal review, iteration or feedback can facilitate *inner work* whereby the patient's mind attempts to search, compute and solve problems. We could reconceptualize the entire history of holistic healing methods from the ancient sleep and dream temples of the ancients to hypnotic suggestion and all its variants in Freud's free association, Jung's active imagination, Gestalt dialogue, Cheek's 20 questions and the indirect approaches of Erickson as methods of facilitating an aroused state of creative iteration and problem solving.

The general public and patients, in particular, often have a pejorative view of creative iteration, they call it *worrying* or *obsessing about something*. In the following examples the *casual* use of the word(s) in bold face tends to facilitate the ideo-dynamics of iterative inner search that leads to problem solving and healing. A **pregnant pause** (indicated with ellipsis in bold face **...**) is used to imply that something is incomplete; the subject must do some inner work to carry out the therapeutic implications of the therapist's words. At the ellipsis *the therapist's voice loops slightly upward* as if a question is being asked rather than downward as we usually do at the end of a declarative statement.

You can **wonder about** the nature of your problem...

It can be **interesting to review** the backround of that issue...

Sometimes it's worthwhile to **simply experience** what you're feeling...

It does require **courage** to **explore** what is really happening...

You **can go over** that **as often as you need to...**

What you call **worrying** can be a way to **...** **review** everything you need to...

Obsessing...as you call it, may be a way of **exploring your growing edge...**

Going over something again and again can be the mind's way of **problem solving...**

Box 5.4   Ideo-dynamic Questions Motivating Hypnotherapeutic Work

Ideodynamic questions evoke inner dynamics to facilitate the self-exploration of the person's own phenomenological world as a prelude to problem solving. Ideodynamic questions are open-ended and have no right or wrong answer. They are evocative of curiosity, wonder, emotional arousal, sensing and inner search. They usually are asked with the implication that they may be reviewed privately within; they do not require an answer that needs to be spoken aloud to the therapist. They are most useful in initiating a *non-directive inner search* that may initiate hypnotherapeutic work. They may be so non-directive that they may be nothing more than "psychological noise" — the type of *stochastic resonance* described in chapter three that may evoke arousal and problem solving in an almost random way. A series of ideodynamic questions such as the following may initiate motivation for hypnotherapeutic work.

Would you like to do some important inner work now or later?

What are you experiencing within yourself right now that requires attention?

Have a hunch (intuition, feeling etc.) you can explore that within yourself right now?

What is really most curious about what you're privately feeling at this moment?

Where is the you that considers the most important things?

Wonder how your unconscious (inner mind, guide, spirit, body etc.) could deal with that issue right now?

Does that make you wonder (curious)?

Do you feel okay about exploring that within yourself right now?

How do you experience that symptom (problem)?

Where is that problem (issue, symptom, worry etc.) taking you?

Where do you experience that tension (anxiety, concern etc.) within yourself?

Do you realize that confusion (depression, anxiety, headaches or whatever symptom) sometimes is an invitation to learn something new?

Ever wonder what kind of inner work you would need to do to solve that problem?

Sense some other part of you calling?

Have a secret sense of sympathy for the part of you that does that (whatever troublesome behavior)?

How do you experience the hidden part of you that needs aid and support?

Could you have a living dream about that right now?

Box 5.5 The Therapeutic Double Bind

The therapeutic use of the double bind in hypnotherapy has been carefully distinguished from the original schizogenic double bind in human dynamics (Erickson and Rossi, 1975). Here I will further illustrate how the double bind can be used to facilitate creative choice in hypnotic induction and hypnotherapeutic work (Rossi and Jichaku, 1992).

Basic Accessing Questions are easily turned into therapeutic double binds by adding creative alternatives usually introduced with the word **"or"** and/or **"until"** as illustrated in steps three and four in the following examples.

(1) If your inner mind is ready to deal with that issue...

(2) Will those hands move together all by themselves to signal yes...

(3) Or will they move apart all by themselves to signal no...

(4) Until a more significant question comes up privately in your mind?

(1) If your hidden self wants to explore that problem privately...

(2) Will those eyes close all by themselves to signal yes...

(3) Or will they remain open...

(4) Until a deeper problem comes up that you need to deal with first?

(1) If your symptoms [pain, anxiety, depression or whatever] are really related to the personal problem(s) you associate it with...

(2) Will those symptoms momentarily get better...

(3) Or worse for just for a moment or two as a signal that something is changing...

(4) Will those eyes close more or less all by themselves so you can explore the source and solution of that whole problem more deeply within yourself?

How shall we conceptualize the dynamics of such double binds? It is easy to recognize how the double bind may be a way of setting *boundary conditions* on human experience just as boundary conditions may be set on mathematical equations. The boundary conditions are a way of focusing hypnotherapeutic work on a particular problem area. *Focusing attention*, of course, has been a traditional way of conceptualizing what hypnosis actually is.

In terms of *nonlinear dynamics* notice how the double bind may facilitate *critical phase transitions* and inner work between two or three (and possibly more) *basins of attraction*. That is, the double bind gives the mindbody the freedom to explore a few alternative areas that the therapist hypothesizes as being of relevance for the patient's problem solving and healing. The therapist, of course, can only hypothesize about what may help the patient. The therapist can never really know because a human being is too complex and inherently chaotic a system to predict and control.

The double bind allows the therapist to safely test hypotheses and offer the patient possible paths for creative inner work. In a sense, then, the double bind is a fail-safe way of doing therapy. If the therapist's hypotheses are wrong then the worst that can happen is that nothing happens. Nothing happens because the double binding alternatives that the therapist offered did not engage the patient's motivation and inner process sufficiently because they were apparently non relevant. In this sense, the double bind may serve as a constant corrective to the therapist. It imposes a *reality check* as well as discipline on the therapist's speculations!

Workshop Questions and Answers

Q: In terms of your ultradian model of hypnotherapeutic work would you say that the Basic Accessing Questions usually facilitate "High Phase Hypnosis" where patients experience initially experience arousal rather than relaxation and comfort ("Low Phase Hypnosis") as is more typical of traditional hypnotherapy?

A: Yes, usually, but not always! I like to believe that I am using Erickson's naturalistic or utilization approach wherein the therapist recognizes and facilitates whatever states of consciousness and being the patient is experiencing at the moment. This is very different from many of the body approaches, for example, that push for arousal and loud expressiveness of anger and affect where the idea is that catharsis in itself is therapeutic. The Basic Accessing Questions do, however, tend to evoke states of arousal because they require the patient to do some sort of important inner work. Even though the traditional hypnotherapeutic approach begins with suggests for relaxation, comfort and even sleep, most therapists have in mind that they will soon focus the patient's attention on the inner work of psychotherapeutic change that needs to take place. The active phases of most forms of psychotherapy usually require some form of arousal or other to facilitate the critical phase transitions the patient needs to go through. This is particularly true of the current trend to brief therapy (Zeig, 1990) which was pioneered by Erickson (Zeig and Gilligan, 1994).

Q: What is the difference between your approach and cognitive-behavioral therapy?

A: Cognitive-behavioral is such a broad classification that I would have to say that my current developments are certainly consistent with this framework but not limited to it. The common denominator between most cognitive-behavioral approaches is a focus on information processing (Beck, 1976, 1987; Pekala, 1991; Shapiro, 1995). I prefer to focus on, *information transduction:* how information changes its forms of expression on all levels of complex cybernetic communication from mind (cognitions, emotions, imagery etc.) to molecule. What is really exciting today is the phenomenal advances of research on the molecular-genetic basis of life; essentially, our new understanding of the critical phase trans*formations* between consciousness, information and energy as discussed earlier in chapter's two and three. Information *transduction* rather than information *processing* is the fascinating but little understood alchemy of our age. I seek to broaden the typical cognitive-behavioral approach to include all these many levels of information transduction and healing that take place on deeper psychobiological levels of neuroscience all the way to the molecular-genetic level. In my most interesting work I usually see the four stages of the creative process and their associated psychobiological states of arousal and relaxation that seems missing in the literature of cognitive-behavioral therapy. This is the subject of our next chapter.

Chapter Six:
Creative Choice in
Hypnotherapeutic Work

What I cannot create, I do not understand.
Richard Feyman

As we view the history of hypnosis and its many hidden derivatives in hundreds of schools of psychotherapy and healing that exist today, we find ourselves asking the same fundamental questions. Do all these apparently different forms of psychotherapy have anything in common? More specifically, is there any common denominator between the psychobiological basis of hypnosis and the process of creative change that most psychotherapies attempt to facilitate? We will explore the idea that our natural 90-120 minute ultradian rhythm of activity and healing rest is the chronobiological foundation of the creative process of evolving consciousness in everyday life as well as permissive hypnotherapy and the many schools of psychotherapy in general. In this patient-centered approach, Basic Accessing Questions are used to focus the locus of control and problem solving within the patient rather than the therapist as the agent of healing, as is characteristic of traditional hypnotherapy.

The idea that our typical 90-120 minute ultradian rhythms of activity and healing rest are the natural psychobiological units of creativity in everyday life, as well as psychotherapy, may seem surprising at first. We usually associate creativity with the apparently rare breakthroughs of exceptionally talented artists and scientists. Current research, however, explores the role of creativity in everyday life of the average individual who frequently must find novel solutions to the constantly changing circumstances of daily life (Boden,

1991). The most diverse schools of psychotherapy today, ranging from Heinz Kohut's psychoanalysis, Carl Rogers' client centered counseling and to Milton Erickson's hypnotherapy, all utilize the creative as is emphasized in this quotation (Rogers, 1987, p. 180).

"Erickson used the term 'unconscious' to represent the core of the person. For him, the therapeutic task was to *arrange the conditions* that would encourage and facilitate the emergence of the unconscious as a positive force. He said, 'Unconscious processes can operate in an intelligent, autonomous and creative fashion, ... People have stored in their unconscious all the resources necessary to transform their experience' (Gilligan, 1982, p. 87-103).

"This similarity of views — seeing the human organism as essentially positive in nature — is profoundly radical. It flies in the face of traditional psychoanalysis, runs counter to the Christian tradition, and is opposed to the philosophy of most institutions, including our educational institutions [where] our core is seen as untamed, wild, destructive. ... Persons must be guided, corrected, disciplined [and] punished, so that they will not follow the pathway set by their inherent natures."

I have previously presented many cases of creativity in dreams and normal everyday life as the essence of psychological development throughout life, as well as in psychotherapy (Rossi, 1972/1986/1998). I now regard the typical everyday failures in the optimal utilization of our ultradian rhythms of creative work and healing as an important source of psychological problems and psychosomatic symptoms. This leads to the view that the essence of creative psychotherapy in general, and permissive patient-centered hypnotherapy in particular, is to *"arrange the conditions"* that will help people learn how to recognize and utilize their normal ultradian rhythms of activity and rest for optimal performance and healing in everyday life.

We may best understand this new view by extending our initial explorations of how we may utilize and enhance our natural ultradian rhythms of creative work and healing in everyday life with permissive hypnotherapy (Rossi, 1995a & b). Figure 6.1 illustrates the four stages of the creative process (Rossi, 1968, 1972/1986/1998) superimposed on one of the typical ultradian waves of optimal performance and healing in everyday life. The basic hypothesis of this chapter is that the normal ultradian 90-120 minute basic activity and rest rhythms that we all experience throughout day and night are the natural psychobiological basis of the well known four stage creative cycle of human experience. This means that in a 24 hour period, a person who is awake for 16 hours has between 8 to 10 ultradian periods for facilitating their own optimal performance and healing. The typical person who is asleep for 8 hours ideally experiences 4 or 5 natural ultradian cycles of deep healing (stages 3 and 4 of sleep) that alternate with 4 or 5 periods of dreaming (Rapid Eye Movement Sleep) during which memory, learning and behavior are optimized as illustrated in Figure 6.1.

There is a broad range of research that supports the idea that the 90-120 minute Basic Rest-Activity Cycle is a fundamental characteristic of all life processes from the cellular-genetic and neuroendocrinological levels. These are involved with our major concerns with mind, memory, learning emotions and behavior (Lloyd & Rossi, 1992). The most recent research that is of vital interest for the psychotherapist is the basic process of learning at the cellular level within the neurons of our brain called "long-term potentiation" requires about 90 minutes or precisely one ultradian Basic Rest-Activity Cycle.

Researchers emphasize that there are two types of learning in humans: short-term memory where learning lasts for seconds, minutes or hours and long-term learning that can persist for days, weeks and even a lifetime. Short term memory depends only on the modification of proteins and connections that already exist within and between neurons of the brain. Nothing new needs to be synthesized for short term memory. Long-term memory and learning that can last for a lifetime, by contrast, requires certain genes to turn on ("gene expression") leading to the manufacture of new proteins that creates new connections between the neurons of the brain. It is this long-term learning that requires the process called, naturally enough, "long-term potentiation" (Bailey & Kandel, 1995). This process of long-term potentiation requires appropriate stimulation for about 90 minutes that we hope to facilitate in the ultradian dynamics of creative psychotherapy.

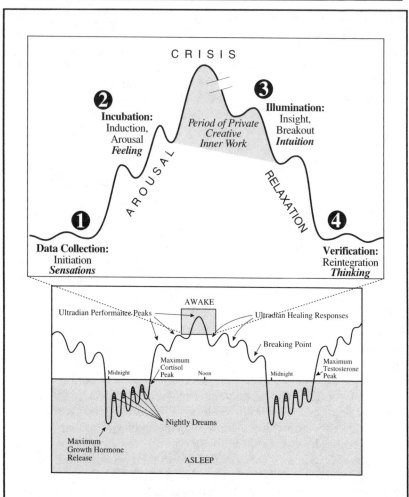

Fig. 6.1: The four stages of the creative process illustrated in the upper part of the diagram are an approximation of one idealized 90-120 minute ultradian rhythm of optimal performance and healing in therapy as well as everyday life. The role of the therapist in patient-centered hypnotherapy is to "arrange the conditions" so the patient has an opportunity to recognize and learn to utilize the four stages of this creative process half a dozen or so times a day.

Note from the lower diagram of a typical 24 hour day, that there are at least 6 "Ultradian Performance Peaks" alternating with an equal number of "Ultradian Healing Responses" when we are awake. It is an important function of consciousness to learn to recognize and utilize these opportunities for optimizing outer performance as well as inner healing during the daytime. Notice that when we are asleep there are about 4 or 5 natural ultradian rhythms of dreaming (nature doing inner work to optimize memory, learning and behavior) that alternate with the deeper stages of sleep (nature doing deeper healing by facilitating the production and flow of hormones, the immune system etc.). The overall curve in the lower diagram is the author's hypothetical illustration summarizing the concepts and data from Kleitman's Basic Rest Activity Cycle (BRAC), Wever's human isolation studies and the ultradian chronobiology of all the major systems of self-regulation from the genetic to the socio-cultural as discussed in chapter four.

The shaded upper portion of the upper diagram is the most important period of the patient's private inner creative work that typically contains much uncertainty, self exploration and original psychological experience wherein long-term potentiation is becoming manifest. Therapists can disturb or actually abort this period of the patient's creative inner work when they prematurely introduce interpretations and attempt to discuss the patient's private original experience before the patient fully experiences it. I have mapped Jung's four psychological functions: Sensations, Feeling, Intuition and Thinking on to this creative process. Notice how Thinking (or cognitive) processing comes in most appropriately only at the end to simply reinforce the validity, significance and applications of the creative process for the patient's inner and outer life.

Other researchers, such as Johnston & Miao-sin Wu (1995), emphasize different stages in this 90 minute process of long-term potentiation. There is an early induction phase that may last from a few minutes (up to about 30 minutes) that is called short-term potentiation. Following this induction phase is what they call the "maintenance phase" wherein sufficient stimulation is required for about an hour during which the new proteins and connections between brain cells are expressed. Although the correspondence is not exact, the induction and maintenance phases of long-term potentiation documented on the cellular-genetic level by current researchers sounds remarkably similar to the induction, deepening and maintenance stages of most traditional hypnotherapy.

Milton H. Erickson, for example, reported that for careful experimental work in hypnosis he would take approximately 20 minutes to develop "a deep trance state," another 20 minutes to achieve "a stuporous trance state" and finally another 15 minutes to develop "a somnambulistic state" (Erickson, 1954/1980, p. 53). It is here subjects could act as if they were awake even though they were in deep hypnosis. It was only after about two hours of the induction and maintenance of such deep hypnotic states (Erickson, 1938/1980, p. 82) that he would do the type of hypnotherapeutic work that would last for months, years or a lifetime just as current researches do with long-term potentiation.

Current research on long-term potentiation thus supports our view that effective hypnotherapy and psychotherapy is essentially a process of arousal and activation on all levels from the cellular-genetic to the behavioral (Rossi, 1993). Researchers investigating long-term potentiation emphasize that it is intensely interesting and novel stimuli and emotional situations that are most effective in initiating long-term memory and learning. This reminds us of the early classical view of hypnosis as essentially a process of fascination, as well as the current idea that hypnosis is especially useful because it helps people access their emotionally based State Dependent Memory and Learning systems particularly when they were encoded by highly stressful or traumatic situations (Rossi, 1986, 1993). Likewise, much of the success of the creative approaches we will present in this chapter requires a certain novelty in the initial stage of induction as well as the natural accessing of emotional states during the following stages.

Facilitating The Creative Process in Permissive Hypnotherapy

Facilitating the creative process in permissive hypnotherapy by utilizing our natural ultradian dynamics is very different from the traditional authoritarian view of hypnotherapy. In a traditional approach the hypnotherapist maintains the locus of control (Bowers, 1994). The hypnotherapist is supposed to induce the patient into a special state of receptivity during which the therapist can prescribe and somehow program therapeutic suggestions into the patient's mind. In this traditional authoritarian method the hypnotherapist's words are regarded as the agency of problem solving and healing.

The permissive patient-centered hypnotherapeutic approach to be discussed here, by contrast, utilizes the patient's own natural ultradian dynamics to help them access their own creative resources to do their own problem solving and healing in their own way. The locus of hypnotherapeutic control remains within the patient at all times. The therapist's major role is to *"arrange the conditions"* so that the patient has an opportunity to learn how to recognize and facilitate their own natural ultradian creative processes as the agency

216

of problem solving and healing. Psychotherapy becomes an experiential education wherein the patient learns how to optimize their own natural rhythms of performance and healing.

In discussing each of the four stages of the creative process illustrated in Figure 6.1 I will outline and contrast the important work that must be done by therapist and patient. I will focus on the key questions the therapist may ask to facilitate each phase of the patient's ultradian dynamics and the typical experiences of patients during each stage. I will occasionally note the type of errors the beginning therapist may make. These errors usually involve an unfortunate shifting of the locus of control from the patient to the therapist. I will then answer some of the more common questions that are asked by students and professionals in my teaching workshops about this novel approach to permissive hypnotherapy.

Stage One: Initiating a Wave of Creative Ultradian Dynamics

The typical therapeutic session ideally begins with patient and therapist cooperating in a search for the problems and issues that the patient hopes to resolve. The therapist's role in this initial stage is to facilitate this search with open ended questions such as the following.

Key Questions to Initiate Stage One:

What's most important on your mind today?

What issue is absorbing your attention today?

What is most interesting to you right now?

What is the most important emotional problem right now?

Focusing the patient's attention on the most important issue of the moment is an effective approach to utilizing the patient's own mental preoccupations for trance induction and problem solving. Asking such open-ended questions tends to access the relevant state dependent memories at the source of a patient's problems.

Such questions may initiate enough motivation and emotional arousal to evoke and/or heighten the patient's natural 90 - 120 minute ultradian psychobiological cascade from mind to gene that are typically involved in problem solving in everyday life as well as in emotional emergencies, trauma and stress. That is, the therapist's task in this first phase is to facilitate a creative wave of ultradian

217

dynamics wherein the patient's attention is focused on the source of their problems which will tend to evoke the state dependent memory, learning and behavior associated with the original emotional encoding of their problem (see the Neuropeptide hypothesis of consciousness and catharsis in Rossi, 1990b). In terms of currently evolving chaos theory in psychotherapy, we would say that the state dependent encoding of emotional problems acts as a strange attractor that pulls the patient's attention inward with a sense of fascination that has always been a hallmark of hypnotherapeutic states (Rossi, 1989; Abraham & Gilgen, 1995).

Patient's Experiences in Stage One:

Curiosity, confusion, uncertainty, hope, expectancy and an exploratory attitude are typical experiences at this initial stage when the patient's major task is to identify what issues or problems are most pressing in the here and now. Some patients may express stress, anxiety, anger hopelessness, frustration and a variety of negative attitudes about themselves and the therapeutic process.

While it is certainly important to establish as much of a positive sense of emotional rapport and ego support with the patient as is necessary to initiate and maintain the therapeutic encounter, it is not the task of the therapist at this early stage to try to reduce the patient's anxiety and stress. Anxiety, stress are often cues of the patient's emotional arousal and readiness to embark on Stage Two of the therapeutic process.

Stage Two: The Inner Journey: Incubation & Arousal

Is there any fundamental difference between shaman, priest and the modern psychotherapist who initiates an inner process of problem solving and healing with a ritual of hypnotic induction? When we witness hundreds — better yet, thousands of people — flocking to charismatic church services for faith healing with music and singing, do we recognize any kinship between them and psychotherapeutic science today?

While the belief systems and the style of initiating the healing process may certainly appear to be different, many researchers would agree that faith, hope and expectancy of healing alone evokes a therapeutic state of emotional arousal that are common denominators of therapy by whatever name. One of Erickson's major contributions to the art of hypnotherapeutic induction was the invention of the so-called "Naturalistic or Utilization Techniques" (Erickson, 1958/1980,

1959/1980). Rather than initiating a ritual of hypnotic induction by having the patient focus on a candle flame, a swinging pendulum or the sound and rhythm of a drum beat, Erickson focused the patient's attention inward on their own behavior, moods, anxieties, emotions, stresses, thoughts or whatever else was uppermost in the patient's ongoing experience at that moment.

I have previously outlined dozens of relatively simple three step approaches to facilitating permissive hypnotherapeutic trance induction that allow the patient to maintain their own internal locus of control (Rossi, 1986/1993; Rossi & Cheek, 1988). Most of these are variations of The Basic Accessing Question that simply ask the patients about their current inner state and provide them with an opportunity to give a more or less involuntary behavioral signal about whether they are able to carry out a bit of inner self-guided therapeutic activity.

I now regard Basic Accessing Questions such as the following as the essence of Erickson's indirect approach to naturalistic suggestion that evokes and utilizes the patient's own inner resources for problem solving in a permissive manner.

1: If the

2: Healing (problem solving or whatever) can now take place

3: Will those eyes close all by themselves?

The typical error of the beginning therapist is to change this question into a direct statement so that part three becomes *"Those eyes will close by themselves."* However subtle this shift from the question to the direct imperative mode may be, it effects a profound shift in the locus of control from the patient's internal dynamics (facilitated by the question mode) to the locus of control maintained by the therapist who uses the authoritarian imperative *"Those eyes will close all by themselves!"* The authoritarian stereotype of direct suggestion accumulated over 200 years of hypnotherapeutic practice is difficult to break. Directly telling patients to close their eyes, however, throws away valuable information. Asking their unconscious to give an involuntary signal of eye closure in response to an important Basic Accessing Question, by contrast, empowers autonomous creative processes within patients.

Erickson frequently used the direct imperative mode of suggestion at critical points in the therapeutic process when the patient seemed to be hopelessly caught in ambivalence or with children where the inner locus of control was undeveloped. I would certainly use the direct imperative during emergencies when the patient's ego was obviously damaged as when there has been a physical accident or the patient is under the influence of drugs. At the scene of an accident, for example, one might say to the semi-conscious victim: *"You have been in an accident, but help is on the way so that excess bleeding can stop now!"* By contrast, however, the more typical patients who self-refer themselves for therapy on an outpatient basis *do* have sufficient internal controls so that they can make optimal use of The Basic Accessing Question.

Eyelid Behavior and Vibrations in Hypnotherapeutic Induction

In hypnotherapeutic work the most obvious manifestation of *critical slowing down* (discussed previously in Chapter Two) may be the general slowing of the psychomotor behavior that is observed during hypnotic induction. Is this phenomenon of what the hypnotherapist calls *"relaxation"* an example of dynamical *critical slowing down* during the moment of *psychological phase transition* to the so-called hypnotic state? Is it related to the quiescent state of immobility that has traditionally been called "catalepsy" in the historical literature? The typical phase transition from normal waking consciousness to hypnotherapeutic work is particularly obvious if one studies the spontaneous eyelid behavior of subjects in the critical moment just before the eyelids shut and stay shut. This eye closure is usually taken as the official beginning of trance particularly when the closing of the eyes has not been suggested by the therapist. While there are many individual variations in this critical transition phase of hypnotic induction the typical pattern usually involves four steps:

(1) The eyelids initially blink quickly two or three times (what nonlinear dynamics calls *critical fluctuations?*)

(2) then more slowly for a few times (what nonlinear dynamics calls *critical slowing down?*)

(3) until the eyes close momentarily and then open again once or twice until

(4) the eyes finally close for the duration of the hypnotherapeutic work that follows.

The closed eyelids then manifest a rich variety of behavior ranging from momentary bursts of very rapid and fine vibrations seemingly similar to rapid eye movement sleep (REM), to slower vibrations mixed in with side-to-side shifts of the eyes as if the subject was watching a scene on their internal landscape, to much slower inward movements of the eyeball. While some investigators have attempted to describe and categorize this eyelid behavior (Weitzenhoffer, 1971) and even relate it to changing physiological conditions during hypnosis, these efforts have not been replicated or studied systematically. They certainly represent a rich area for future research into the quantifiable dynamics of trance induction and behavior. One could easily imagine that the laser detectors of body movement could be used to great advantage in such research.

Another particularly prominent area of observable behavioral phase transitions in hypnosis is the spontaneous (definitely not suggested by the therapist) vibrations of fingers, hands and arms that are especially evident with the new ideodynamic approaches to hypnotherapeutic induction that the author has developed over the past twenty years. I now regard these spontaneous and involuntary vibrations as a reliable behavioral signal that confirms the presence of a critical phase transition to hypnothrapeutic work. When these vibrations first appear I frequently ask the subject if they are really involuntary.

Subjects are sometimes surprised by this query because they are not even aware that their hands or fingers are vibrating! This simple query about the involuntary nature of their movements, however, often seems to enhance the intensity and amplitude of the vibrations. This is somewhat reminiscent of the fact that the apparently related involuntary ideodynamic movements of the Chevreul pendulum are also enhanced when the subject is allowed to watch its movements (Rossi & Cheek, 1988). Since the Chevreul pendulum's amplitude is so easily measurable it would be another convenient approach to quantifying the characteristics of the involuntary vibrations during various phase transitions of the hypnotherapeutic process.

Is there another manifestation of critical fluctuations and critical slowing down of the entire mindbody as the hypnotherapeutic process flows from the large fluctuations of sympathetic system arousal so characteristic of the emotional catharsis and crisis of Stage Two toward the kind of quiet inner focusing of Stage Three that culminates in the transition to new insights? Is this a clearly observable pattern of behavior on the edge of chaos that is relatively coordinated to phase transitions on the internal phenomenological landscape so characteristic of "creativity?" Only research will tell!

Notice that we are pointing out the possibility of measuring the relative coordination of four levels simultaneously: (1) the observable involuntary vibrations of the limbs, (2) measurable sympathetic system arousal (cortisol, epinephrine etc.), (3) quasi-measurable behavior of emotional catharsis and (4) subjective scaling (from 1 to 10) of "new insights."

Key Accessing Questions to Facilitate Stage Two

The most important role of the therapist in Stage Two is to encourage and support the patients' inner journey where state-dependent sources of their problems and symptoms often evoke negative memories and emotions. It is precisely here that we witness the main difference between the typical failures of problem solving in everyday life and the therapeutic situation.

In everyday life the patient typically retreats, quits or in some way blocks the natural process of ultradian arousal that normally takes place whenever people are engaged in learning or problem solving of any sort. Because problem solving situations involving states of arousal have frequently been associated with stress, failure and negative feelings, the patient tends to "turn off" to them in everyday life as well as in psychotherapy.

To solve a problem, however, the mindbody needs to arouse itself to do some active work. Just before we awaken in the morning, for example, we automatically experience the highest level of the cortisol secretion (a hormonal messenger molecule) which has the effect of stimulating the cells of the body to prepare for activity (See Figure 6.1). Each of the subsequent ultradian peaks of psychobiological arousal that then take place every few hours throughout the day have a similar peak of cortisol (as well as many other hormones such as insulin) that optimizes the possibility for creative problem solving.

When such hormonal arousal leads the patient to access and experience past painful states they may experience varying degrees of *emotional catharsis*. A spontaneous catharsis is a signal that they probably are successfully accessing and releasing the important state dependent memories and emotions that are encoding their problem. The therapist's role is to support this inner accessing so the patient does not break it off prematurely before the all important process problem solving and symptom resolution has a chance to take place in Stage Three. The following are some of the key questions the therapist may ask to facilitate a safe locus of control within the patient during this phase of arousal.

Key Questions Facilitating Stage Two

Can you let yourself continue to experience that for another moment or two in a <u>private</u> manner — only long enough to experience what it leads to next?

Good, can you stay with that only long enough to learn what it is all about?

Will it be okay to allow yourself to continue experiencing that <u>privately</u> for a while, difficult though it may be, so you can learn what you need for healing (problem solving or whatever)?

And will it be all right to keep most of that a <u>secret</u> that you don't have to share with anyone?

Private Experience: Bypassing Resistance in Hypnotherapeutic Work

Allowing the patient to explore privately, or secretly, is one of the major innovations of this approach. Permitting private experience is a direct and most effective approach to reducing the so-called "resistance." Privacy greatly enhances the patient's ability to access inner emotional issues without having to be concerned about how to verbalize them for the therapist. This allows the personal material to remain closer to its original state and sources within the patient's inner dynamics that may involve emotions, imagery, intuitions and sensations in ways that cannot be easily verbalized. Patients are able to remain within their own unique creative matrix to solve their own problems in their own way. An appropriate period of privacy during inner work empowers patients to do their own problem solving with the locus of control safely within themselves.

Box 6.1   Private Inner Creation

Inner creative work done in privacy — in secret even — is an effective way of facilitating rapid resolutions that tend to (1) bypass resistance to telling the therapist embarrassing material, (2) bypass the difficulties of translating essentially holistic, emotional right hemispheric dynamics into the verbal rational left hemispheric processing and (3) plant secret seeds for future developments that are not yet ready for the critical light of day. Here are a few accessing phrases that may facilitate private inner work.

Within the privacy of a person's mind anything is possible...

And knowing you can quietly review all that privately...

The whispers of things that have been...

Shameful though it may be, you can review what is known only to yourself...

Private possibilities to come in surprising ways...

Secrets can be important when something new is coming up...

Sacred promises of what can be...

Wisdom whispers...

Patient Experiences in Stage Two:

Sympathetic system arousal accompanied by psychobiological responses with an increase in sweating, heart rate, pulse and breathing, together with a feeling of heat "as if burning up" are highly characteristic of patient experiences in Stage Two.

When the ideodynamic hand approaches to hypnotic induction are used (Rossi & Cheek, 1988; Rossi, 1995a) patients may ask, "Why am I experiencing this shaking, vibrating and pulsing!" Patients are surprised and sometimes a bit disturbed by these signs of arousal because they have frequently been associated with stress, discomfort or failure in the past. As discussed earlier, many patients have learned to block their own natural patterns of psychobiological arousal that are important for problem solving. This may be why they cannot solve their problems — they have learned to shut off their natural ultradian problem solving process to the point where they need a therapist to help them relearn how to experience the normal tension of arousal in problem solving in everyday life. They can be facilitated in this relearning with *therapeutically reframing questions.*

Yes, breathing like that often means your mind and body are getting ready to deal with important issues — Will you allow it to continue for another moment or two until you recognize what it is?

Can you actually enjoy your experience of energy (sweat, shaking, trembling, nervousness, confusion, uncertainty or whatever) coming up for a moment or two as a sign that you are on you way to dealing with whatever you need to?

Have you ever let yourself have a good shakeup (or whatever) like this before so you could really reorganize yourself?

Reframing Negativity and Confusion

Sometimes patients will emphasize the negative: *"This won't work with me. This is stupid! I don't know how to do this. I am blocked! I can't do this. I can't think. I don't feel anything. Cannot remember anything!"* Other patients will complain of confusion, not knowing, and doubts with feelings of being dizzy, foggy, or misty. The therapist can recognize and reframe such experiences as important transition signs of the creative process.

Are you aware of how your feelings of being stupid (inadequate or whatever) are telling you that you're ready for something better?

Have you ever experienced confusion before you learned something new?

Yes, will your confusion be the first step toward wisdom?

The Therapeutic Dissociation: Creative Bifurcations of Consciousness

Sometimes patients experience anxiety, tension, stress and fear to the point where therapists fear that patients will lose control when they say things like, *"I feel crazy-like! What is happening to me?"* While patients rarely lose control in private practice, it is still the greatest fear of students and professionals when they first use this patient-centered approach where the locus of control remains within the patient.

The therapeutic dissociation is very useful at this point to facilitate the patient's control over their own experience. The therapeutic dissociation divides the patient's experience into one part, that is obviously going through important emotions, and into other parts that can watch safely from the sidelines, so to speak, to guide the patient's emotional process with care, control and wisdom. The therapeutic dissociation that focuses the locus of control within the patient can be facilitated with the following types of questions.

Can one part of you feel that as fully as you need to, while another part of you carefully guides you safely?

Will it be OK to continue experiencing that as much as necessary for another moment or so, while a wise healer within you helps you maintain control?

Can you continue to experience those tears [or whatever] as intensely as some part of you wants to while another part of you observes calmly and learns what it needs to help you?

There are also many wrong ways of attempting to facilitate this arousal phase of Stage Two. Out of habit from previous models of training in the counseling process (where such questions may be entirely appropriate) the beginning hypnotherapist's most common error at this point is to ask questions such as these.

What can I do to help you?
Would you like an handkerchief?
Do you need help?

Well, of course the patient needs help, who doesn't! This kind of an open ended offer to help tends to stop the patient's ongoing personal process, however. It shifts the patients' attention from their own experience to the therapist. Patients tend to immediately turn off their uncomfortable state of arousal in hopes that the therapist will have an easier solution. That is, such questions tend to shift the locus of control and healing to the therapist instead of allowing it to continue cooking within the patient where the creative dynamics of healing need to take place. It implies that the patient is weak and must fall back on the therapist's skill rather than the patient continuing to explore his own inner resources for creative problem solving.

Sometimes the beginning therapist is uncomfortable not knowing what is happening, particularly if the patient with eyes closed is frowning, crying or evidently caught in negative affect. The art at this stage is in how to ask a question without stopping the patient's inner process. Such open ended questions as the following place no interfering demands upon patients yet allow them to speak if necessary.

Will it be all right for you to share a sentence or two with me in a moment if you need to — only what I need to hear to help you?

Will you have the courage to let that continue until you really experience everything necessary — sharing only a word or two if you need to?

On the other hand, if the patient directly asks for help the therapist should immediately provide it with an appropriate guiding question. Now the basic question becomes: How should the therapist provide help? What can any therapist really know about what is going on in the patient on so many levels simultaneously (from imagery, emotion and thinking all the way down to the hormonal and genetic levels)? With six trillion cells in the human body, each with hundreds of thousands of receptors on their surfaces mediating one form of communication or another, who is the therapist who feels wise enough to take control, direct and program the patient?

What can the therapist do? The therapist can wisely respond to the request for help by focusing the problem area with more specific questions.

Yes, I really want to help you! Can you let yourself continue with those feelings just for another moment or so until you find yourself expressing a sentence or two — only what I need to hear to help you further?

Notice how much is being accomplished with this seemingly simple question.

First, the therapist is responding positively and supportively to the patient's request for help.

Second, the therapist is reinforcing the patient's ongoing experience, but with a safe time limitation: *"Just for another moment or so."*

Third, there is a mild therapeutic dissociation implied in the words *"let yourself continue with those feelings."* If you *"let yourself"* that implies there is another stronger part of the patient that is allowing their hurt, crying side to express itself. Since you are *"letting yourself"* it means that the patient is no longer lost in emotions. The patient is essentially maintaining an internal locus of control by allowing the experience of a good healthy cry to take place.

Fourth, the therapist is permissively, by implication, asking the patient to do a major piece of therapeutic work: *"Find yourself sharing a sentence or two"* presumes that the patient is able to sum up the entire inner situation and give an adequate report on it. The therapist responds to whatever the patient says by feeding it back to the patient to facilitate accessing inner resources for problem solving. Suppose the patient says something like:

I feel blocked just like I have all my life when I feel hopeless about my feeling. Can't you help me break through this block?

The Affect Bridge: Facilitating Phase Transitions

Of course the therapist wants to do something with this plaintiff call for help. What therapist does not feel instant despair about trying to help a patient break through a lifetime block all within the limits of a fifty minute therapeutic session or less? The well-trained therapist can now respond by accessing potential critical phase transitions with the state-dependent dynamics of the affect bridge (Rossi, 1986/1993; Watkins, 1978).

Yes, I really want to help you break through that block in the best possible way by asking you, "Can you experience another time in your life when you had these kinds of feelings?"

The therapist guides the patient backward in time, step by step, on this state-dependent affect bridge so the patient can re-experience past problems, stress and traumas within the safe context of therapy. This further fuels the arousal phase and prepares the patient to move on to the third stage of the creative process: the moment of illumination wherein the patient gets a new insight or sense of meaning about their experience so they feel as if they are breaking out of some of their previous limitations.

Stage Three: The Illumination: Surprise and Emergent Insights

During the period of inner exploration and emotional release, the patient's overt behavior manifests many subtle shifts that are observable to the therapist. There may be sudden increases or reductions in tension that are evident in the movements of the patient's closed eyes throughout Stages Two and Three, for example. While such eye behavior has been studied for centuries there is no general agreement about its significance during hypnotherapy (Edmonston, 1986). When I notice periodic or momentary bursts of rapid eyelid vibration or a shifting of the eyeballs from side to side as if the patient is following an inner moving scene I will occasionally support it with these questions.

Yes, noticing interesting things there?

Umm, something important to recognize about that?

Sometimes, there seems to be an inward pulling within the eye ball and the patient's whole head may even pull backward slightly — occasionally with a slight expression of surprise or a momentary frown.

Umm, Surprising?

Yes! The courage to receive that as well?

Experiencing that too, can you not?

Slow and sideward rolling motions of various types during hypnosis have been described as "strongly indicative of a shift in the balance of neural control from cortical to subcortical structures" (Weitzenhoffer, 1971, p 120). I usually reinforce such apparently deeper states with quiet questions that are not meant to be answered.

Umm — good allowing that to go on a bit deeper?

Yes, okay for that deeper experiencing all by itself?

Nice to experience that deeper place?

Sometimes there is a moment of absolute stillness as if the patient is receiving something from within with bated breath. This may be the moment of insight that has been described as the "*Ah-hah*" experience in humanistic and scientific literature on the creative process (Rossi, 1972/1986). There may a slight smile and the head may slowly nod "*yes*" with minimal repetitive movement. I'll softly support this behavior with these questions.

Umm — receiving something you like?

Worth receiving?

Yes — and more?

It is not always easy to recognize the transition from the arousal phases of Stage Two to the moments of significant insight in Stage Three. Some patients shift uncertainly for a while back and forth between Stages Two and Three several times before a settling into Stage Three and a movement toward resolution in Stage Four is confirmed. Confirmation that a *unit of the inner work* may be completed for the session often comes from larger postural adjustments of the head, neck, arms or legs as if an opening, loosening or relaxation is taking place. Previous muscle constrictions and tensions evident in the jaws, hands and arms seem to *"let go"* and patients may actually shake themselves out. The patient shifts from the metaphorical postures and movements of defensiveness, anger, frustration, sorrow or depression so characteristic of Stage Two to expressions of lifting, lightness and well being in Stages Three and Four.

Oddly enough, many patients are not entirely aware of the significance of this profound *critical phase transition*. They often need help to recognize the value of the spontaneous creative breakthroughs they are experiencing in Stage Three. They often don't know that this creative experience is the essence of their therapy. They are still looking for the answer or some magic of healing to come from the therapist. The task of the therapist is to help such patients recognize the value of their own spontaneous therapeutic transitions at this critical moment — and above all helping patients recognize that the locus of creativity and therapy is within themselves during these moments of creative insight and seemingly spontaneous symptom relief. *In essence the therapist often need to help people learn how to recognize their own personal experiences of creativity!*

Patients sometimes suspect that their insights and good feelings during these therapeutic breakthrough moments are only temporary delusions or a placebo response. They are all too ready to criticize their critical phase transitions, the essence of their creative experience, as something immature or pathetic somehow. Indeed, that is how most of their creative moments may have been put down since childhood when parents and teachers did not recognize and support the patient's mini-breakthroughs and developing awareness in everyday life because creative experience is so often accompanied by what seems to be confusion, rebellion and emotional chaos (Rossi, 1968, 1972/1985/1998).

The therapist's key questions at this point are not really meant to be answered — they are simply gentle supportive remarks that help the patients recognize and stabilize their still nascent creative state and emergent insights.

> ### Key Questions Stabilizing Stage Three:
> *Interesting?*
> **Curious isn't it?**
> **A little surprise?**
> *Umm — rather unexpected somehow?*
> *Yes, are you experiencing something a little different now?*
> *My goodness, is something really changing now?*
> *Mmm — really appreciating what continues all by itself?*

Therapist errors at this stage usually consist of irrelevant and premature efforts to document or interpret the process with rather dull questions such as the following:

Where did the pain go?
What's happening now?
Tell me why you feel better now.
What do you understand about yourself now?

Such questions at this stage tend to interrupt and block the flow of the patients ongoing creative experience. They place an undue demand on the patient to prematurely shift from the ordinarily non-cognitive mode of their creative moment to cognitive explanations of dynamics for the benefit of the therapist. Again, the error involves a shift in the locus of control from the delicate experiencing patient to the pragmatic therapist who presumes to be an arbitrator of what's going on.

Patient Experiences in Stage Three:

The profoundly significant shift from crisis and catharsis to the moment of insight and the release of tension in Stage Three is often accompanied by a sense of relief, surprise and laughter. Patients may softly whisper, "*It's strange, weird, odd!*" The usage of such words means that they are experiencing something new. They may even mention, "*Something really new, something I was never aware of before suddenly popped into my mind.*" In the classical descriptions of the creative process, i.e., a sense of light, illumination, colors or fascinating and meaningful visual imagery, are frequently mentioned during these moments. I speculate that these creative moments are precisely the point at which the new proteins and connections synthesized at the cellular-genetic level in long-term potentiation actually make their effects known on a conscious level as a new and original psychological experience. Patients are usually full of questions about these moments of creative experiencing and have a need to ratify and stabilize their reality.

Darwinian Selection of Evolving States of Consciousness

There is a profound evolutionary significance to the patient's questions at these creative moments. These questions imply that patients are experiencing a creative moment in the Darwinian natural selection of their own states of consciousness. These are at critical choice points in selecting the emotional qualities, as well as the contents, of their present and future states of consciousness. To recognize, reinforce and utilize these precious moments of self-reflection and experiencing the "new" may be the most important function of consciousness. This may be the basic reason why consciousness evolved in the first place.

It is a tragic error, indeed, a heinous crime against the evolution of human consciousness for the therapist to jump in and attempt to analyze or interpret the patient's creative experience at this point! Any interpretation the therapist can make is only a reflection of the past — probably something the therapist has read in a book written a generation or two ago. There is nothing new in that! The therapist's appropriate role at these delicate creative moments is simply to acknowledge and support the value of the patient's experiencing and evolving self-awareness with these types of questions.

Okay, simply receiving that privately for a while?

Yes, recognizing whatever is interesting about that?

Wonderful, exploring this experience as much as you need to?

Really appreciating the value of this kind of experience!

The patients' need to evaluate and utilize the "new" brings them to Stage Four and the important work of making the creative real in their lives.

Stage Four: Ratifying the Reality of the New

After a few moments of savoring the "new" in Stage Three the patient may now make bigger postural adjustments that are signaling that the evaluative period of their current creative experience is at hand. Sometimes patients will spontaneously stretch and open their eyes entirely on their own. The therapist never told them to close their eyes in the first place so this spontaneous eye opening is an excellent validation that the locus of control is really within the patient who is now ready to come back to outer consensual reality to discuss whatever is necessary with the therapist. When patients do not open their eyes and awaken spontaneously they may be under the impression that the therapist is supposed to tell them to wake up or give a signal to end the process. I will usually satisfy this need with the following Basic Accessing Question with a *"posthypnotic suggestion"* that once again emphasizes that patients really have the locus of control within themselves.

1. *When*

2. *Something within you knows it can continue this creative healing entirely on its own at appropriate times throughout the day when you need to take a break — and when your conscious mind knows it can simply cooperate in helping you recognize when it is the right time to tune inward —*

3. *Will that give you a feeling, a signal that its time for you to stretch, open your eyes and come fully alert so you can discuss whatever is necessary for now?*

Here, at last, in Stage Four the traditionally trained therapist can indulge in some of the talk, analysis and behavioral prescriptions that are supposed to be the vehicle of therapeutic change. I personally prefer to maintain an attitude of restraint even here, however, and continue to facilitate the locus of control within patients so that they can now interpret, synthesize and rationalize their own internal experiences in their own way.

Key Questions to Ratify Stage Four:

Something you would like to share about that?

Yes, can you say more about it?

How much of this is new to you?

What is most significant about this for you?

Have you ever understood this before?

What does this lead you to now?

How will this experience help you to make changes in your life?

What will you actually do in your life that is different this week?

Patient Experiences in Stage Four:

Patients invariably feel good in Stage Four with a sense of relief and well being. Symptom scaling was introduced in Stage One. Now, in Stage Four it is the time to ask them to re-scale their symptom once more. The fact that their symptom is usually less intense validates the therapeutic experience they have just gone through. If the symptom has disappeared completely this is the time to plan how the patient can learn to do this type of inner healing for themselves in everyday life. I usually remind patients that it is precisely when they are in their ultradian rest periods that they may have best access to this type of inner healing (Rossi & Nimmons, 1991).

If the symptom scaling has dropped only a few points, it can be taken as a partial success that can be built upon in future sessions. To prepare for that further improvement the patient is encouraged to explore the ultradian healing response in everyday life and even keep a written record of their experiences, if they are so disposed, that can provide hints of the next step that is needed to facilitate further creative phase transitions in healing and problem solving.

Patients have a positive outlook and genuine sense of self-empowerment as they learn to recognize their personal periods for optimal healing and problem solving. The essence of therapy becomes the process of learning to optimize their own skills in facilitating the evolution of their own skills at self-relatedness. They may sometimes acknowledge that their insights and healing experiences were not entirely new. They had thought of some of these things before and had stumbled upon their own ultradian healing responses before but they thought it was just a happy accident. Now, however, they can develop a conviction of what options and possibilities are truly possible for them to facilitate their own development in a practical and realistic way. They are usually able to give themselves their own behavioral prescriptions. They are also usually able to tell the therapist how they will change their behavior and try to do things differently.

Workshop Questions and Answers

Q: Will the patient ever get out of control or be re-traumatized in reviewing traumatic memories in Stage Two? How long does this period of arousal or catharsis usually last?

A: This common fear of emotional arousal and a loss of control of the "therapeutic catharsis" is due to our profession's previous lack of understanding about the natural psychobiological foundation of such emotional experiences. Ultradian theory and preliminary research indicate that the arousal phase rarely goes on for more than about 20 minutes when the locus of control is within the patient (Rossi & Lippincott, 1992). This psychobiologically natural *High Phase of Hypnotherapeutic Work* can go on much longer, however, if the patient believes the therapist is in control and wants the patient to go on experiencing ever greater heights of pain and catharsis. How long does it take to have a good cry with a friend and then dry one's tears with a better feeling about life's possibilities? Remember, we are doing nothing more than facilitating such natural ultradian processes of problem solving and healing in everyday life with the patient-centered creative approach outlined here.

In my experience, patients are not re-traumatized when they re-experience their state dependent memories. This may be because I am always carefully watching and therapeutically utilizing minimal cues revealed in the patient's face and body language. When signs of anger, pain or negative emotions of any sort become evident, I always make supportive remarks within the context of a *therapeutic reframe* that evokes the patient's own inner resources of self-control, problem solving and healing. Review the kinds of key questions I recommend in Stage Two.

Note how patients are always encouraged to maintain an internal locus of control that enables them to carefully monitor and guide their own emotional progress. At no time do I ever provoke or incite the patient on to higher states of arousal. I only help them recognize and facilitate their own natural ultradian states of arousal that are experience spontaneously whenever they become engaged with truly motivating inner unfinished business. If they experience their natural arousal as painful, I always help them cope with it by careful time-limiting suggestions to *"allow it to continue only for another moment or so until it is transformed"* into whatever they need to experience for therapeutic progress. That is, I am only interested in facilitating whatever *critical phase transition* they need to experience. I am not interested in arousal, pain or catharsis for its own sake! Negative emotional states are only brief transitions in the process of communication between mind and the molecular-genetic level that are the essence of all therapeutic processes (Rossi 1986/1993, 1995).

Q: What if the therapy process is interrupted before it's over? What if you come to the end of the therapy hour and the patient is still in a painful catharsis?

A: In the real world it is not always possible to complete a psychotherapeutic process in the way we would like. To avoid running out of time, I usually try to initiate the inner work within the first quarter of a 50 minute therapy session. I try to leave the last quarter of the session (at least 10 minutes) for a wide-awake discussion of what was learned during the inner experience.

If a patient seems to need more time, I will usually arrange a double session to go for 90 -120 minutes. The ultradian theory proposes that this is really the optimal time period for therapy or any other task in everyday life. A patient may not always be ready to come to a satisfactory solution even within these time limits, however. That is, more preparatory inner work on many levels of mind-gene communication may be needed before consciousness can recognize a new life possibility. That is why most forms of psychotherapy require many sessions over weeks, months or even years.

Q: Since most patients are usually pleased with their insights and sense of progress with this creative approach, does it really mean they have found the correct insight, the real truth about the nature and resolution of their problems? Isn't it supposed to be the therapist's job to correct the patient's misconceptions, analyze and interpret things for them?

A: It would be naive to believe that there really is some ultimate truth, analysis or interpretation that can solve all problems for all time. Insight, meaning and a sense of the value of one's therapeutic experiences are usually a highly personal and a subjective construction of what is significant for one's self at this particular moment in time. Hypnosis and psychotherapy are not vehicles for establishing the truth or validity of human experience. What therapist has the wisdom to interpret, correct or program the six trillion cells of the human body each with hundreds of thousands of communication devices (cell receptors) between mind and gene that are constantly changing from second to second?

Pioneers such as Freud and Jung always warned their students to beware of over-enthusiasm in their interpretive efforts and their "therapeutic zeal." Carl Rogers, for the most part, gave up interpretation altogether. Even with these warnings, how tragic it is that a new generation of therapists are over-interpreting and generating what is now called "The False Memory Syndrome." Scientific research does not support the use of hypnosis and psychotherapy to establish the validity of delayed recall (See special issues of *The International Journal of Clinical and Experimental Hypnosis*, October, 1994 and April 1995 on hypnosis and delayed recall).

With the permissive patient-centered approach to hypnotherapy outlined here problems may be resolved, symptoms may disappear and a new life plan may be created which is meaningful for the patient only here and now. Hopefully these benefits will last for a while, but life is a moving stream forever flowing through fresh channels that are perpetually changing. The main task of the therapist is to help patients learn to recognize and utilize their own natural ultradian psychobiological process of problem solving and healing that comes up every hour and a half, or so, throughout the day. Yes, I am saying that a Darwinian process of natural selection in problem solving and healing has evolved in humans that cycles every hour and a half or so to help us cope with ever-changing life circumstances. The cycle runs even more quickly in lower animals and bacteria so they are even more adaptive than we are.

Q: Aren't you really overemphasizing the permissive patient-centered aspect of this approach wherein the locus of control is supposed to remain in the client? Although the Basic Accessing Questions do focus the patient inward to access their own resources for problem solving, the therapist is still maintaining control by observing the patient carefully and asking the right questions at the right time.

A: You do have a point there, but it is very important to emphasize how different this patient-centered psychobiological approach is from the traditional idea that hypnosis puts people into a sort of blank state wherein they are to be programmed like robots by the therapist. This authoritarian approach to what we would now call "low phase hypnosis" is still a fundamental misconception perpetuated in the popular media as well as in some granting agencies where research funds are allocated. The new vision about the nature of healing in hypnosis is to recognize that *creative uncertainty* is a natural part of the uniquely individual *critical phase transitions* that are experienced by the therapist as well as the patient. Hypnotherapeutic work is an inherently creative process wherein both therapist and cooperate in a process but neither really knows exactly how it will turn out. Instead of saying "the therapist *is still maintaining control...*" I would rather say "the therapist *facilitates a relationship* by observing the patient carefully and asking some open ended questions at the right time."

Q: What are the counter-indications of this approach?

A: The usual counter-indications for any form of psychotherapy apply. One must be careful with paranoids, character disorders or patients with secondary gain issues (e.g., insurance money) who may be more interested in exploiting the psychotherapeutic situation than in problem solving and healing. One difficulty with a highly permissive patient-centered approach is that some patients may not have an adequate understanding of what they really need from hypnotherapy. The classical example would be the workaholic who wants to use hypnosis to increase their work capacity and skills even more. It is precisely here, however, that the rather neutral stance that the Basic Accessing Questions allows the therapist to take, is most valuable. The patient's own ideodynamic hand signaling, may give persistently negative responses to their consciously stated wish to do more work. Often the basic enlightenment such patients get is they need to "work smarter, not harder!" They learn how to use appropriate ultradian healing breaks (low phase hypnosis) throughout their work day so they can be refreshed sufficiently to put forth a more highly efficient and creative effort (high phase hypnosis) during their next 90 minute work period.

Research is now needed to determine how our new psychobiological distinction between high and low phase hypnotherapeutic work can facilitate healing with the various kinds of psychosomatic problems, dysfunctional personality problems, borderline and hospitalized patients. One would intuitively expect, for example, that low phase hypnosis with an emphasis on learning to use the ultradian healing response to facilitate relaxation, comfort and healing half a dozen times throughout the day would be best for psychosomatic problems. High phase hypnotherapeutic work would seem especially appropriate with personality problems where the patient needs to learn how to access and utilize their capacity to optimize their relationship skills and do constructive work in the world. It seems likely, however, that any well integrated hypnothrapeutic session will have an appropriate balance of low and high phase hypnosis. Each psychobiological phase has its own unique contribution to make.

Chapter Seven:
Self-Organization In
Hypnotherapeutic Work

So is anything ever new? I would answer "most definitely,"
and so reject Parmenidean changelessness in favor of
novelty emerging, according to Heraclitus, from an
"attunement of opposite tensions."
James Crutchfield, 1994

We facilitate self-organization in hypnotherapeutic work by focusing patients' attention inward, on their own natural dynamics of experiencing, to facilitate their own original pathways of healing and psychological transformation. A new class of permissive hypnotherapeutic approaches that immediately engages patients' interest and fascination with their own inner creative dynamics of change is outlined and discussed in this chapter. These new *symmetry breaking, duality* or *polarity* approaches involve patients in experiencing *critical phase transitions* in semi-autonomous movements and sensations in their hands, arms, fingers, feet, eyes or other parts of their bodies as "signaling systems." These mindbody signals facilitate the resolution of emotional conflicts and the evolution of consciousness by optimizing the flow of information transduction in the natural dynamics of psychobiological self-organization.

The idea of symmetry breaking and critical phase transitions as an approach to hypnotherapeutic work comes from the recognition of the critical role of bifurcation in the new nonlinear dynamics of self-organization theory. The idea of duality or polarity comes from many deep sources in mythology, art and literature that have been discussed in the psychoanalytic literature, particularly the pioneering

239

ideas of Carl G. Jung (Edinger, 1996; Jung, 1953). Ancient as well as modern scholarship recognize the characteristic presence of "twoness," the double or duality that appears when something new is experienced. The source of creativity as well as conflict is typically signaled by the bifurcation or splitting of a former unity into two in nature as well as psychological processes: In creation myths the earth and sky are separated from a single undifferentiated pleroma; the godhead splits into heaven and hell; from a single cell comes two in all forms of life; a single political group typically splits in two over a critical issue; good versus bad; strong versus weak. We could go on and on. In this chapter terms and phrases like *bifurcation, critical phase transitions, duality, doubling, and polarity symmetry breaking* will be used with slightly varying connotations to describe the dynamics of the creation of something new in psychological experience and consciousness. Such creations are obviously related to the transformations of matter, energy and information described earlier in Chapter Three in ways that are of fundamental significance but not yet well understood. Here is a typical effort to explain some of these transformations.

> To begin with, *symmetry breaking* is the manifestation of an *intrinsic differentiation* between different parts of a system, or between the system and its environment. In this respect, it is one of the prerequisites of *complex behavior* and must have been at work during such events as the condensation of primordial matter to form galaxies, or the appearances of the first living cells. Second, once such a differentiation is ensured, further processes that would be impossible in an undifferentiated medium may be switched on... the appearance of spatial inhomogenates in a biological medium may enable undifferentiated cells in a population to recognize their environment and differentiate in specialized cells, thus allowing the genetic material to manifest its *potentialities*. In this respect, symmetry breaking appears to also be a prerequisite to *information*. (Nicolis & Prigogine, 1989, p. 74, italics mostly added here.)

These symmetry breaking or polarity approaches are thus fundamental to the process of information transduction that we now regard as of essence in hypnotherapeutic work. These approaches to facilitating creative experience in psychotherapy evolved gradually over the past twenty-five years through exploratory demonstrations of Ericksonian hypnotherapy in my training workshops for mental health professionals. In this chapter I will describe some of the most interesting practical approaches to utilizing the naturally motivating emotional conflicts or polarities of human experience in facilitating symmetry breaking and critical phase transitions in hypnotherapeutic work (Barnier & McConkey, 1995). The surprising effectiveness and subtlety of these approaches leads us on a new quest exploring the fundamental nature and dynamics of hypnotherapeutic work.

This quest was motivated by failure — my previous failure to understand why some subjects became irritated during professional demonstrations when I apparently bothered them by offering therapeutic suggestions. Some of the demonstration subjects were so rapt in inner concentration on their own personal, private experiencing that they responded to my suggestions and inquiries as if they were an irritating outside interference. This reminded me of Milton H. Erickson's early observation that one needed to deal *"very gingerly with deeply hypnotized subjects to avoid losing their cooperation."* Erickson discussed these observations in his very first professional paper on hypnosis titled, *"Possible Detrimental Effects of Experimental Hypnosis,"* published in 1932 (when he was thirty-one years old) as follows.

> The first of these theories of possible detrimental effects centers around the question of the development of hyper-suggestibility. The literature is barren of information in this regard. However, there is carefully planned and controlled work under way in a well known psychological laboratory, and results so far, though not yet complete, are negative. In the writer's own experience, upon which it unfortunately will be necessary to a large extent to base the elaboration of these various questions, *hyper-suggestibility was not noticed,* although the list of individual subjects totals approximately 300 and the number of trances several thousand. Further, a considerable number were hypnotized from 300 to 500 times each over a period of years. Also, several of the subjects were immediate relatives with consequent intimate daily contact, and they were trained to respond, in experimentation, quickly and readily to the slightest suggestion. *Far from making them hyper-suggestible, it was found necessary to deal very gingerly with them to keep from losing their cooperation, and it was often felt that they developed a compensatory negativism toward the hypnotist to offset any increased suggestibility.* Subjects trained to go into a deep trance instantly at the snap of a finger would successfully resist when unwilling or more interested in other projects. Even when persuaded to give their consent against their original wishes, the induction of a trance was impossible. Nor were those subjects more suggestible to other people, since, when their services were "loaned" to the author's colleagues, the production of hypnosis in them, despite their extensive training, was just as hard as it had been originally for the author. And the same thing was found true when the author "borrowed" subjects. In brief, it seems probable that *if there is a development of increased suggestibility, it is negligible in extent. (*Erickson, 1932/1980, p. 495, Italics added here.)

What is going on here? Is it really possible that the man who was to reawaken and revolutionize the modern course of hypnotherapy began his career by reporting that during trance *"hyper-suggestibility was not noticed"* and *"it seems probable that if there is a develop-ment of increased suggestibility, it is negligible in extent."* How could the "Master of Hypnosis" say that *"hyper-suggestibility"* and *"increased suggestibility"* are *"negligible in extent"*? Isn't suggesti-bility supposed to be the essence of hypnosis? Perhaps we are mis-reading Erickson. Maybe the above words were a youthful indis-cretion that he later gave up as he became more of a "Master." Let's check the record again when he is at the height of his career sixteen years later. Surely a man should know his own mind by then. In a profoundly important paper on *"Hypnotic Psychotherapy"* the more mature Erickson at the age of forty-seven summarizes his observa-tions on the *"Role of Suggestion in Hypnosis"* as follows.

The next consideration concerns the general role of suggestion in hypnosis. *Too often the unwarranted and unsound assumption is made that, since a trance state is induced and maintained by suggestion, and since hypnotic manifestations can be elicited by suggestion, whatever develops from hypnosis must necessarily be completely a result of suggestion and primarily an expression of it.*

Contrary to such misconceptions, the hypnotized person remains the same person. His or her behavior only is altered by the trance state, but even so that altered behavior derives from the life experience of the patient and not from the therapist. At the most the therapist can influence only the manner of self-expression. *The induction and maintenance of a trance serve to provide a special psychological state in which patients can re-associate and reorganize their inner psychological complexities and utilize their own capacities in a manner in accord with their own experiential life.* Hypnosis does not change people nor does it alter their past experiential life. It serves to permit them to learn more about themselves and to express themselves more adequately.

Direct suggestion is based primarily, if unwittingly, upon the assumption that whatever develops in hypnosis derives from the suggestions given. It implies that the therapist has the miraculous power of effecting therapeutic changes in the patient, and disregards the fact that *therapy results from an inner re-synthesis of the patient's behavior achieved by the patient himself.* It is true that direct suggestion can effect an alteration in the patient's behavior and result in a symptomatic cure, at least temporarily. However, such a "cure" is simply a response to the suggestion and does not entail that re-association and reorganization of ideas, understandings, and memories so essential for an actual cure. *It is this experience of re-associating and reorganizing his own experi-ential life that eventuates in a cure, not the manifestation of responsive behavior which can, at best, satisfy only the observer.* (Erickson, 1948/1980, pp. 38, italics added here.)

Startling, isn't it? Not at all what the popular media and many enthusiastic but misinformed professionals believe about the role of direct suggestion as the essence of hypnotherapy. Erickson is saying that *"It is this experience of re-associating and reorganizing his own experiential life that eventuates in a cure, not the manifestation of responsive behavior* [that is, behavior suggested by the therapist] *which can, at best, satisfy only the observer."* Erickson does not believe *"that the therapist has the miraculous power of effecting therapeutic changes in the patient."*

This was the most important lesson I had to learn during the intense period of training I had with Erickson during the last eight years of his life: suggestion in the popular sense of direct programming, manipulation or putting something into a person's mind is not the essence of healing in hypnosis. While Erickson did experiment extensively in his early career with "therapeutic implants" and the induction of "experimental neuroses" in the 1930s and 1940s (republished in Erickson, 1980, pp. 287-355; Erickson & Rossi, 1989), by the 1970s he had concluded that programming, *"It is a very uninformed way."* (Erickson and Rossi, 1979, p. 288).

Toward the end of his career his focus was on the *"indirect forms of suggestion"* that were designed to evoke and utilize the patients' own inner resources so they could create their own cure. As we stated at the end of our first book, *"The invention and systematic use of a variety of these* [indirect] *hypnotic forms for the study and utilization of a patient's own associative structure and mental skills in ways that are outside his usual range of conscious ego control to effect therapeutic goals."* However, it does appear to be one of Erickson's original contributions to the theory and practice of "suggestion" (Erickson, Rossi & Rossi, 1976, pp. 311).

The New Dynamics of Hypnotherapeutic Work

One leading edge of current hypnotherapeutic practice is how we can continue to develop Erickson's innovative approaches to facilitate patients learning how to utilize their own inner resources for problem solving and healing in their own unique ways. Recently I summarized ten tutorials designed to teach therapists how to facilitate such processes of self-healing or *"autocatalytic healing"* within the patient as follows.

People have conflicts because of the natural, but peculiar, psychological property of spontaneously dissociating different sides of their personality so they are expressed at different times. It is apparently difficult for most people to experience their loving and hateful feelings at the same moment. It is usually "fight or flight" but rarely both at the same time. Such conflicts can be resolved with insight by structuring a mindbody psychodrama that allows the patient to experience both sides together in a therapeutic encounter (Lightfoot, 1992). The therapists initial task is to formulate an appropriate basic accessing question that facilitates a simultaneous experience of both sides of the contending forces of the personality so they may be engaged in autocatalytic healing. (Rossi, 1986/1993, p 127).

I typically initiate the self-organizational dynamics of integrating dissociated parts of the personality and resolving conflicts with a series of accessing questions as follows.

If you are ready to do some important inner work on that problem, will you place your hands with your palms up as when you are ready to receive something [Therapist demonstrates with his or her own hands as illustrated in Figure 7.1]?

Focus on those hands in a sensitive manner and I wonder if you will begin by letting me know which hand seems to experience or express that fear (or whatever the negative side of the patient's conflict may be) more than the other? [Pause]

As soon as the patient acknowledges that one hand, arm or side of the body seems to express the negative aspect of their conflict it is a sign that the previously unconscious and, more-or-less, hidden dynamics of their conflict are becoming engaged and open to expression in observable behavior. The patient has, in effect, given up their usual outer reality orientation and are now engaging and responding to their inner realities as they might in a dream or fantasy. The therapist then continues by evoking a contrasting, opposite and usually the more positive side of the conflict.

Wonderful, now at the same time I wonder what you experience in your other hand by contrast?

When the patient responds by labeling or describing a contrasting experience in the other hand, the therapist then continues to engage the dynamics of the patient's conflict as follows.

Figure 7.1: HANDS POLARITY: Four stages of the creative process with the typical hand movements. Converting a problem into a resource.

Stage 1: Initiation — Sensations

If you are ready to do some important inner work on that problem will you place your hands with your palms up as when you are ready to receive something?

As you focus on those hands in a sensitive manner, I wonder if you can begin by letting me know which hand seems to experience or express that fear (or whatever the negative side of the patient's conflict may be) more than the other?

Stage 2: Incubation, Arousal — Feeling

Wonderful, now I wonder what you experience in your other hand by contrast at the same time?

Good, as you continue experiencing both sides of that conflict will it be okay to let me know what begins to happen?

Stage 3: Insight, Breakout — Intuition

Interesting?

Something changing?

And is that going well?

Is it really possible?

Stage 4: Reintegration — Thinking

What does all that mean to you?

How will your life be different now?

How will your behavior change now?

What will you do that is different now?

Good, now let yourself continue to experience both sides of yourself in those hands at the same time... and will it be okay to let me know what begins to happen between them?

Patients typically respond with a series of uncertain hand movements and begin to verbalize experiences wherein their emotions, symptoms and inner conflicts become engaged and somehow transformed. It sometimes seems as if patients are "acting out" their conflicts in a self-directed mythopoetic adventure within the safe boundaries of the experimental theater of their own mindbody. It becomes interesting for the therapist to simply observe how patients seem to become *entranced* with their own spontaneous and semi-autonomous experience of *transforming* their inner conflicts into more or less involuntary observable behavior. Patients will often go through a mildly cathartic process wherein they may express anguish and pain along with the relevant *psychodynamics* of their problems. Their head, eyes, hands, arms and fingers sometimes seem to move in an involuntary manner, characteristic of automatic handwriting or finger signaling, that is well described in the hypnotic literature (Rossi & Cheek,1988).

Patients usually function on many psychological levels at the same time. On one level they are experiencing and moving in a more or less involuntary manner. On another level they are simultaneously observing themselves and responding to spontaneously generated inner forces and fantasies. On yet another level they are apparently directing their own psychotherapeutic inner work and describing it to the therapist. Here are a few examples illustrating the types of problems that are easily accessed and resolved with the polarity approach.

Dynamics of Hands Polarity: Converting a Problem into a Resource

Stage One: Data Collection, Initiation. A scholarly looking young man complains of feeling weak and being a failure. I direct him to the initial palms up hand position illustrated in Figure 7.1 and ask, *Can you tell me which hand feels weaker and more of a failure at this moment?* After a moment of self-reflection he hesitantly acknowledges that his right hand feels a bit weaker.

I then ask, *And what do you experience in your other hand by contrast?* He takes a slow deep breath and admits the other side seems lost in daydreams of heroic adventures.

I then proceed with, *Wonderful how you can experience both sides of yourself at the same time! Now I wonder if you can let yourself continue to experience both sides together and explore what begins to happen between them?*

The "weaker" right hand begins to tremble and after a few moments I solicitously ask, *My goodness is that hand really trembling all by itself?* Blushing somewhat the young man admits that the right hand is shaking all by itself because it is so nervous about a fantasy that the left hand is experiencing.

Stage Two: Incubation, Arousal. *I deeply respect his privacy by not asking him to tell me what his fantasy is.* Instead, I quietly support his obvious struggle by asking, *I wonder if you have the courage to allow that to continue privately within yourself for another moment or two so you can experience what takes place next?* His eyes close at this point and many private emotions cross his face as his hands slowly approach each other and then retreat just before they touch. Finally the hands do touch in a seemingly accidental manner and as they do so his entire body goes through a slight startle response.

I quietly question, *Quite a surprise?* He merely nods his head slowly a few times as the hands now touch each other again and again in a tentative, exploratory manner.

Stage Three: Illumination, Insight. Finally the left "fantasy" hand covers the fearful and still trembling right hand. After a few moments the trembling stops and the anxious expression on his face is replaced by calm and perhaps even the slightest of smiles. After a few more moments when his apparently calm and satisfactory state seems stabilized I quietly ask, *And is that now going well?* After about thirty seconds of delay he silently nods his head yes and asks, *I wonder if that is really possible?*

After a few more minutes of silent inner contemplation he finally opens his eyes, stares at the floor and slowly stretches and touches himself on the arms, head, sides and legs that is very characteristic of people coming out of a hypnotherapeutic state.

To my silent look of inquiry he describes how he had been reading recently that humans are essentially "herd animals" who take comfort in each other's presence and touch. In his apparently spontaneous hypnotic inner work he explored an inner drama of how it might be possible to touch a young woman he had met recently "without acting like a creep and offending her." He explains how he finally imagined going on a hike with her and as they moved through more and more difficult terrain their hands might reach out to each other and then finally touch to support each other.

Stage Four: Verification, Reintegration. The final stage of this therapeutic session was to engage the young man in a discussion about the possibility that he could in fact ask his woman friend out for just such a hike in reality. He acknowledged that he could and would. At the same time, his left fantasy hand kept grasping his formerly trembling but now calm right hand. After a few moments of such absentminded *"hand play"* he looked up at me sheepishly and said, *Such stuff as dreams are made of.* We both smiled, stretched, looked at the clock and realized it was time for the session to end.

We spent the next few sessions discussing how his occasional feelings of being weak and lost in fantasy were actually indications that he was going into a creative state of introversion wherein he needed to experience and recognize how he needed to take new steps to move forward in his life. His previous *"symptoms"* of being a weak failure lost in fantasy was thereby reframed into a creative resource.

What are the actual dynamics of exploring and resolving problems by externalizing conflicts into observable behavior in this manner? In what way are these polarity or bifurcation dynamics similar to Sigmund Freud's *free association,* Carl Jung's *active imagination,* Fritz Perl's *Gestalt dialogue,* Carl Roger's *reflecting* what the client says, and Milton Erickson's *indirect suggestion*?

Careful study indicates that the main line in the evolution of psychotherapeutic technique from Freud to Erickson over the past one hundred years has been away from the direct suggestion and programming of traditional hypnosis and toward the facilitation of mindbody communication within the patient. All the therapeutic innovations of this century were designed to avoid outside influence as much as possible so that patients could have an opportunity to explore the *critical phase transitions* of their own evolving personality and consciousness. Polarity dynamics are similar in taking another step in moving away from direct suggestion to facilitating mindbody communication and transductions within patients so they can learn to optimize their own healing and consciousness in their own way. Polarity dynamics are different, however, in at least two ways:

1. Polarity approaches entrain the natural psychobiological rhythms of ultradian arousal and relaxation to:

2. Facilitate the four stages of the creative process that in the best circumstances are a normal component of these rhythms.

There seems to be a wide range of applications for polarity dynamics to psychological problems and symptoms of all sorts. In training workshops it has been demonstrated successfully on videotape with a variety of emotions and states such as anger, anxiety, depression, stress, panic, phobia, post-traumatic stress syndromes, dissociative states and psychosomatic symptoms.

There are at least three keys to its successful application:

1. The therapist recognizing and utilizing the creative moment when the patient is already in a state of ultradian arousal complaining about an ongoing experience of a problem or symptom.

2. The therapist immediately offering a polarity question that can embody the patient's arousal and complaint in one hand and simultaneously another aspect of themselves in the other hand (usually a more constructive or healing aspect of the personality).

3. The patient's suspension of the usual everyday reality orientation in order to experience a numinous mythopoetic encounter with themselves.

Here are a few more examples of polarity accessing questions usually verbalized slowly and quietly by the therapist but with a certain sense of drama and determination while demonstrating the initial palms up hand position illustrated in Figure 7.1.

To what extent can you actually experience your anger in one hand more than the other? [Pause until the patient acknowledges one hand or the other] *Wonderful! And now at the same time what do you experience in the other hand by contrast?*

Can you tell me which hand seems to sense [whatever psychosomatic symptom or pain the patient complains of] *the most?* [Pause] *And now what does the other hand experience that is different?*

As you let yourself continue with that stress [post-traumatic symptoms or whatever] *for another moment or two I wonder if you can tell me which hand or part of your body feels it most strongly?* [Pause] *Good! At the same time tell me what the other hand feels by way of contrast?*

Tell me which hand is the one that reaches for a cigarette [alcohol, drugs or whatever the addiction or habit problem] *and which represents the side of you that wants to quit?*

As soon as the patient acknowledges experiencing two or more sides of their symptom, problem or personality in different hands or parts of the body, the therapist can assume that the process of hypnotic induction has been successfully engaged. The patient's inner dynamics have been primed for a self-therapeutic engagement that now is ready to take place. The therapist then merely wonders aloud what will happen next between the different forces or parts that are being experienced and encourages whatever autonomous psychodynamic process that evolves, more or less all by itself.

Remarkably enough, after about ten to twenty minutes of inner self-encounter many patients spontaneously remark, with either a sense of satisfaction or disappointment, that the inner process is now over. They feel satisfied when they feel they have received an important insight. They feel wistfully disappointed when they feel they have received something of value but they intuit that there is much more that needs to come. I tend to warmly support the reality of such evaluations when they appear to be objective. Some patients really do solve a significant problem. Others may make some progress in their inner experience, but their inner world needs more time to synthesize the new realities of their evolving relationship to themselves. The most important learning for the patient is how to recognize the reality of their creative experience rather than any particular problem they may have solved. It is often helpful to talk about the four stages of the creative process (presented previously in Chapter Six) so patients learn how to appreciate the ongoing evolution that is taking place within themselves.

Sometime patients report that their creative inner process, which was as engrossing as a dream for about 10 or 20 minutes, seems to vanish like a puff of smoke or a bubble popping. They are often puzzled about why it ended just when it did. It is precisely the patient's sense of reality and semi-autonomous nature of their inner process that comes and goes, more-or-less by itself, that leads me to believe that it is a psychobiologically distinct state of consciousness like the REM state. It is something like a fantasy or daydream that validates its psychobiological reality as an altered state of consciousness. I fully expect that we will eventually find some measurable ultradian psychobiological correlates of this private creative inner process.

Dynamics of Arm Polarity: Pain and the Addictions — Changing a Symptom into a Signal

Case One: Heroin Addiction

Stage One: Data Collection, Initiation.

A local resident of Needle Park finally stumbled into a community rehabilitation center and after a drying out period is being seen for a private session by an addiction counselor, who was a former addict himself, and wise in the ways of withdrawal. The addict complains of withdrawal symptoms: pain, negative emotions and flashbacks. He feels too sick to talk.

The counselor holds his arm straight out in front of himself as illustrated in Figure 7.2 and says, *Lets work with that right now! Can you hold your arm out as if it is a lever that can tell us how strongly you are experiencing those feelings? [Pause] And can you let me know how bad they are on a scale of one to ten where ten is the worst?*

The recovering addict holds his arm out, fixes his attention on it and tentatively says it feels like six.

Stage Two: Incubation, Arousal.

The counselor slowly lowers his own hand while saying in a low voice, *As you continue watching your arm can you let yourself be so sensitive that your arm goes up if the feelings get worse and your arm goes down when you feel better?"*

The counselor notices that his subject's arm quivers a bit, his face flushes, his breathing becomes more shallow and a fine sheen of sweat makes his forehead and nose slightly shinny. The arm quivers up a bit and the subject begins to frown and grimace in obvious discomfort.

The counselor continues, *That's right, the courage to allow that to continue all by itself for another moment or two until...?*

After a full minute the arm is still going up very slowly and the subject gasps, *Until what, man?!*

Cool as a cucumber the counselor replies, *Until you experience a little surprise. [Pause] And what number are you experiencing now?*

251

Figure 7.2: Arm Polarity: Four stages of the creative process for assessing and facilitating the resolution of symptoms, addictions and habits.

Stage One: Initiation Symptom Scaling

Can you hold your arm out as if it is a lever that can tell us how strongly you are experiencing those feelings? [Pause] And will you let me know how bad they are on a scale of one to ten where ten is the worst?

Stage Two: Incubation, Arousal.

As you continue watching your arm can you let yourself be so sensitive that your arm goes up if the feelings get worse and your arm goes down when you feel better?

That's right, the *courage* to allow that to continue all by itself for another moment or two until? [Pause] Until you experience a little surprise? What number are you experiencing?

Stage Three: Transformation, Insight.

Um-mmm!?

Surprising?

Learning everything you need?

And what number is it at now?

Stage Four: Verification, Reintegration

Any of that make sense to you?

Will you be able to do this for yourself? How can this help you from now on?

What changes will you now make?

What will you do differently this week?

Stage Three: Illumination, Insight.

The arm suddenly bobs downward momentarily about an inch or two and the counselor immediately responds with, *Um-mmm!?*

The subject in slight surprise looks at his now drooping arm and says, *"Hey it's getting tired, you know, I got problems man, I really don't need this."*

The counselor persists with, *What number is it at now?*

The recovering addict with a tight gasp says, *"It's up to eight and getting worse all the time!"*

After another moment the counselor offers, *And I wonder just how bad its going to get before...?*

The subject's face turns red, his fist clinches and he sputters, *"No use even talking to you, you ain't saying nothing!"*

The counselor persists with, *What number is it at now?* He hears the subject grumble that it's now down to five.

The counselor with mock gravity now wonders aloud whether it will get worse again before it gets better. The arm tentatively makes another effort to bob up a bit perhaps to a level six and then sags rather quickly down to a level three or four. The subject now takes a giant step toward recovery by willfully dropping his arm all the way down to his lap and says, *"Enough of this shit man, I got problems I got to talk about, you know?"* The traditional view might be to regard his impatient breaking off of the arm signaling as resistance. It is only resistance, however, to going on to the mere formalities of the therapist's approach to arm signaling. The patient's impatience to now speak about his problems actually means that the therapist's arm signaling approach has succeeded, since the patient is now ready to go on with his therapy by talking about his problems.

Stage Four: Verification, Reintegration.

The now obviously relieved subject pours out his story and current concerns with a modicum of insight here and there to which the counselor responds affirmatively in his best non-directive manner. And so it goes. Toward the end of the session the counselor inquires again about what number describes how the subject now feels. The recovering addict ruefully rubs his arm and grumbles how he is sick-and-tired of feeling bad and doing this numbers game but, *"I feel a lot better now and I will let you know when I need another shot in the arm."*

What are the dynamics of this therapeutic interaction? Erickson frequently explored *"polarities"* in his patient's experience although he never used this word to describe it. Erickson called this process a *"yo-yoing of consciousness"* or a *"yo-yoing of symptoms"* so that they would be experienced as alternately getting worse and better.

The paradox, Erickson believed, is that patients do not realize that as they allow symptoms or pains to get worse for a moment and then better they are actually gaining control over them. I have speculated that this is not a paradox but rather the best way for patients to engage their own state-dependent memory and learning systems through alternating states of ultradian arousal and relaxation. These alternations are associated with the release of hormones and messenger molecules on all levels of mindbody communication to mediate psychotherapy (Rossi, 1986/1993).

It is now well known that all addicting drugs achieve their effects by mimicking the molecular structure and functions of the mindbody's natural hormones, messenger molecules (neurotransmitters and neuromodulators). Many of these are the same messenger molecules that encode stress and traumatic experiences in a state-dependent manner that are responsible for the amnesias, dissociated states and general symptomatology of the addictions (Rossi, 1987, 1986/1993).

Symptom Scaling Polarity:
Mind-body Communication in Life Crisis

Case Two: Vaginal Herpes

Stage One: Data Collection, Initiation.

A patient in her thirties going through a period of great emotional stress in personal relationships suddenly begins to experience unusual and uncomfortable sensations of heat in her vagina and, upon medical examination, is diagnosed as having an outbreak of vaginal herpes for the first time in her life. She claims she has had no new sexual partners for over three years and her current partner has apparently been faithful. How come herpes now?

I initiate her into a state of inner search by introducing her to symptom scaling. *On a scale of one to ten where ten is the worst you have ever experienced that heat and five is average, just how strong is your sense of heat in your vagina right now?*

She replies that the heat is *"Seven right now,"* and crosses her legs with a facial grimace of distaste.

I ask her, *Do you have the courage to really receive honestly just what you are feeling right now so you can fully experience what it leads to next?*

Stage Two: Incubation, Arousal.

She responds with her feeling that the herpes is the source of the heat she is feeling and it seems to be getting worse by the moment as she focuses on it.

I slowly and quietly murmur an incomplete sentence, *I wonder if you can stay with it until...?*

Her eyes close as she apparently focuses inward. Her body tenses and she leans forward slightly over the next few minutes as she hesitantly whispers the following series of apparently spontaneous symptomatic transformations and free associations with many pauses. *"Now the heat is shifting around a little to my butt on the left cheek. ... now heat is moving through my body everywhere ... it's like a burning allergy ... my head hurts ... feels like an outbreak of psoriasis on my scalp ... I feel like I should confess it all to my mother like I did as a kid ... my right shoulder aches ... Why is my right side trembling?... Why am I starting to cry? ... Why do I still try to get approval from my mother even when she never gave it but only punished me instead?... I'm burning up with heat all over!"*

Stage Three: Illumination, Insight.

For a few tense minutes she continues with, *"Burning! Burning! I know.....I know I have to leave* [her current boyfriend*]. I always knew it was only temporary, really, but now I really do have to leave.....He punishes me too, even when he doesn't know it.....my left knee is twitching uncontrollably.....Can't you make it stop?.....Oh, I'm tired of all this.....I will leave.....I'm getting sleepy.....I feel warm.....just warm now.....I really have to leave* [boyfriend]." Her body sags back and she remains silent for about three or four minutes as her face gradually becomes calm, smooth and apparently relaxed.

Stage Four: Verification, Reintegration.

I look at the clock and with a mild sense of concern notice there are only ten minutes left to the session. I clear my throat and murmur, Y*es, and is that still going well?*

After a moment she shifts her feet, nods her head yes, adjusts her posture to a more normal sitting position, blinks a bit and finally opens her eyes.

I then ask, *And I wonder what number describes what your level of comfort is now?*

Somewhat surprised she acknowledges that she is at one or two or maybe zero. It's no longer a feeling of heat in her vagina, but rather a feeling of warmth, or is it a slight pressure, or an awareness somehow?

I ask her if she now knows what she has to do and she nods yes. She makes a few remarks about how she experiences it as a sense of relief to know that she can make up her own mind. She will leave her boyfriend and later she will tell others about it. By the next session a week later she reports that she has navigated the separation well. The herpes and burning sensations are apparently gone.

The Merry Symptom Chase:
From Symptoms to Enlightenment

What was the major polarity or bifurcation is this case? We could think of symptom scaling as introducing the subtle dynamics of polarity on a scale from one to ten rather than the simple duality of the left and right hand, or arm polarity, as described in the previous cases. We could hypothesize that the symptom scaling then spontaneously generalizes all over the body. It is the apparently *involuntary* aspect of these spontaneous sensory-motor transformations that Bernheim recognized as the essence of hypnosis in what he called the "*ideo-dynamic*" a century ago.

The entire process of spontaneous symptom transformations with constantly changing qualities and locations throughout her body is very characteristic of the polarity dynamics of the mindbody whenever we explore the free play of somatic symptoms in hypnotherapy. It was this same spontaneous transformation and shifting of symptoms that was used by the French neurologist Charcot over 150 years ago as a criterion to distinguish between psychogenic (so-*called* "*hysterical symptoms*") and true organic pathology.

The dynamics of *the merry symptom chase* begins when the therapist notices that the patient is apparently going through a spontaneous process of symptom transformation and/or substitution (as this patient did in Stages Two and Three). That is, as soon as patients are asked to scale their symptom intensity or level of awareness in the initial stage of hypnotherapeutic work, they begin a litany of other somatic complaints. The older literature of historical hypnosis and psychiatry regarded this as hysterical behavior or malingering. Today we recognize it as evidence of the meta or multi-stability of mental, sensory-perceptual, and emotional nonlinear dynamics. The therapist does not attempt to initiate this process, we are definitely not trying to teach patients how to experience symptom substitution. We simply recognize it when it is taking place and utilize it for therapeutic purposes as illustrated in this case.

It will require the use of modern brain imaging methods such as the PET (positron emission tomography) scans and MRIs (magnetic resonance images) to document the reality of these mindbody transformation dynamics in the healing process of hypnotherapy. An excellent beginning has been made by Decety et al., (1994) whose research on *"Mapping motor representations with Positron Emission Tomography"* provides the strongest evidence thus far of how our hand polarity approaches could access deep psychobiological sources of problems and their resolution. While their experiments have not related to therapy yet, the following abstract of their research certainly has important implications for polarity dynamics and creative phase transitions in healing.

> Brain activity was mapped in normal subjects during passive observation of the movements of an 'alien' hand and while imagining grasping objects with their own hand. None of the tasks required actual movement. Shifting from one mental task to the other greatly changed the pattern of brain activation. During observation of hand movements, activation was mainly found in visual cortical areas, but also in subcortical areas involved in motor behavior, such as the basal ganglia and the cerebellum. During motor imagery, cortical and subcortical areas related to motor preparation and programming were strongly activated. These data support the notion that motor learning during observation of movements and mental practice involves rehearsal of neural pathways related to cognitive stages of motor control (Decety et al., 1994, p 600).

Such experimental findings suggest that the semi-autonomous polarity dynamics that are engaged in this approach to hypnotherapy are more than hysteria or "mere figments of the imagination." Our fundamental conjecture is that patients engaged in such apparently chaotic inner experiencing are actually involved in an initial phase of recreating and re-synthesizing themselves on deeply organic levels of the mind-brain (Rossi, 1986/1993). They usually are not aware of the positive potentials in this experience, however. Our western culture labels these spontaneous transformations as a kind of neurotic sickness or malingering so patients feel badly about themselves and do

257

not go on to the next phase of the transformative process of insight and healing. The therapist's task is to (1) recognize that potentially healing chaotological dynamics are being initiated (2) encourage the patient to allow the process to continue (3) recognize when potentially valuable insights and healing are being achieved and (4) verify and support these dynamics for future healing. That is, we note once again how the therapist simply supports the patient's natural healing dynamics through Poincaré's four stage creative process.

The Dynamics of Bifurcation:
Polarity, Conflict and Self Transformation

There are many other possible ways of conceptualizing the dynamics of these bifurcating polarity approaches. Carl Jung, for example, described polarity as an essence of the dynamics of psychological processes of self transformations:

> Everything human is relative, because everything rests on an inner polarity; for everything is a phenomenon of energy. Energy necessarily depends on a pre-existing polarity, without which there could be no energy. There must always be a high and low, hot and cold, etc., so that the equilibrating process — which is energy — can take place. Therefore the tendency to deny all previous values in favor of their opposites is just as much of an exaggeration as the earlier one-sidedness....

> The point is not conversion into the opposite but conservation of previous values together with the recognition of their opposites. Naturally this means conflict and self-division. It is understandable enough that one should shrink from it, philosophically as well as morally; hence the alternative sought, more often than conversion into the opposite, is a compulsive stiffening of the previous attitude." (Jung, 1966, Vol. 7, pp. 75-76)

> The shuttling to and fro of arguments and affects represents the transcendent functions of opposites. The confrontation of the two positions generates a tension charged with energy and creates a living, third thing — not a logical still birth in accordance with the principle *tertium non datur* but a movement out of the suspension between opposites, a living birth that leads to a new level of being, a new situation. The transcendent function manifests itself as a quality of conjoined opposites. So long as they are kept apart — naturally for the purpose of avoiding conflict — they do not function and remain inert.... (Jung, 1960, Vol. 8, 90-91)

From a Jungian perspective the polarity approaches described in this chapter could be conceptualized as a way of facilitating the transcendent function. The polarity approaches tend to energize the patient's psychodynamics and initiate a process of inner dialogue and self discovery that usually emerges out of a confrontation between different parts or voices of the personality; however, they may be projected into the hands, arms or any other part of the body.

An attitude of wonder and an openness to surprise and the unexpected is the best way for both the patient and therapist to receive the bifurcation dynamics of evolving consciousness activated by the polarity approaches. Above all, the idea is to let nature speak with as little bias as possible from the patient and the therapist's habitual conscious preoccupations.

Jung's *Commentary on "The Secret of the Golden Flower,"* an ancient Taoist text concerned with Chinese yoga subtitled as *"A Chinese Book of Life,"* provides us with a very deep and comprehensive approach to understanding the dynamics of facilitating the evolution of consciousness with the polarity methods.

Now and then it happened in my practice that a patient grew beyond himself because of the unknown potentialities, and this became an experience of prime importance to me. In the meantime, I had learned that all the greatest and most important problems of life are fundamentally insoluble. They must be so, for they express the necessary polarity inherent in every self-regulating system. They can never be solved, but only outgrown. I therefore asked myself whether this outgrowing, this possibility of further psychic development, was not the normal thing, and whether getting stuck in a conflict was pathological. Everyone must possess that higher level, at least in embryonic form, and must under favorable circumstances be able to develop this potentiality. When I examined the course of development in patients who quietly, and as if unconsciously, outgrew themselves, I saw that their fates had something in common. The new thing came to them from obscure possibilities either outside or inside themselves; they accepted it and grew with its help....

What did these people do in order to bring about the development that set them free? As far as I could see they did nothing (wu wei) but let things happen. As Master Lü-tsu teaches in our text, the light circulates according to its own law if one does not give up ones ordinary occupation. The art of letting things happen, action through non-action, letting go of oneself as taught by Meister Eckhart, became for me the key that opens the door to the way. We must be able to let things happen in the psyche. For us, this is an art of which most people know nothing. Consciousness is forever interfering, helping, correcting, and negating, never leaving the psychic processes in peace. It would be simple enough, if only simplicity was not the most difficult of all things. To begin with, the tasks consist solely in observing objectively how a fragment of fantasy develops. Nothing could be simpler, and yet right here the difficulties begin. Apparently no one has fantasy fragments — or yes, there is one, but it is too stupid! Dozens of good reasons are brought against it. One cannot concentrate on it — it is too boring — what would come of it anyway? It is "Nothing but" this or that, and so on. The conscious mind raises innumerable objections, in fact it often seems bent on blotting out the spontaneous fantasy activity in spite of real insight and in spite of firm determination to allow the psychic process to go forward without interference. Occasionally there is a veritable cramp of consciousness.(Jung, 1967, Vol. 13, 15-17)

We witness in these words Jung's intuitive understanding of something more than the typical problem self derogation that depresses the creative life of so many people. As we learned back in Chapter Two, there is a natural tendency, indeed, it is a major function of the conscious, rational mind to linearize and thus constrain or even oppose the fancy-free nonlinear dynamics of the unconscious. Polarity dynamics facilitate a creative dialogue between the conscious mind's need to linearize and predict the nonlinear nature of the unconscious.

Jung's careful observations of the creative process of self-transformation have much to say to psychotherapists who view themselves as experts who are supposed to analyze, interpret and direct the patient's behavior. To the contrary, the dynamics of natural phase transitions require that the wise therapist remains as silent as possible during Stages Two and Three of the patient's inner self-engagement. *Direct suggestions or interpretations are usually not required during Stages Two and Three when the patient is engaged in self discovery.* Indeed, they are counter-indicated in these stages of the patient's creative process.

What therapist is wise enough to know what is really going on so that they could presume to interpret or direct the creative process? When the patient is successfully launched in Stage Two, the therapist's premature interpretations or suggestions could actually abort the patients' inner experience and rob them of their own creative process. The interfering therapist robs the patient of the significant peak parts of Stage Two and Three of the *"Period of Private Creative Inner Work"* as illustrated in Figure 7.1. Rather than attempting to interpret or suggest during these stages, the therapist has the more important role of facilitating the patient's ongoing experience with a series of basic accessing questions as described in the previous chapter.

In order to emphasize how patient and therapist have different tasks at different stages of this inner process of self engagement, I have mapped Jung's four psychological functions onto the four stages of creative psychotherapeutic process in Figure 7.1. In Stage One, Data Collection, when the patient is searching for the problem, Jung's *Sensation function* is most appropriately engaged. As the patient moves successfully on to the second stage of Incubation, or emotional arousal, Jung's *Feeling function* obviously becomes more prominent.

Box 7.1:   Imagery Facilitating Ultradian Performance and Healing

It is well established that there are significant relationships between visual imagery and psychophysiological responses (Kunzendorf & Sheikh, 1990). I am not aware, however, of any scientific data on the question of whether visual imagery can be combined with the natural periodicity of our 90-120 minute ultradian cycle to optimize performance and/or healing. Here are a few approaches that I have explored using the general four stage paradigm of the creative process in clinical practice. They now await experimental documentation, particularly with the brain imagery methods such as *Positron Emission Tomography* touched upon previously in Chapter Four. On a more modest level it would be fascinating to gather normative data on the types of imagery and the differential responses of children, adults and seniors at different times of day and night to the following Basic Accessing Questions that offer bifurcating polarities of ultradian psychobiological response.

1. Initiation: Begin with a series of Basic Accessing Questions that may evoke inner exploratory sets within the patient. The patient is usually not expected to respond to these questions with a verbal answer. The Basic Accessing Question simple set the stage for the hypnotherapeutic work that is about to take place.

Would you like to explore what your mindbody needs to do right now?
How can we allow your inner nature to guide you on an inner path?
Wonder how to improve your performance or healing at this time?

2. Induction: Offer a series of bifurcating possibilities to explore whether the patient's mindbody is moving or needs to move in the direction of psychobiological arousal to optimize some aspect of performance (*high phase hypnosis*) or ultradian rest, recovery and inner healing (*low phase hypnosis*).

Wonder whether your mindbody will take you on a path in nature where you will experience yourself *moving upward... or downward?*
***See yourself m*oving upward with *energy and exhilaration* on a mountain trail...or downward toward a *pleasant and restful* valley?**
Wonder whether your inner nature takes you *flying upward and away to an high energy adventure...*or *relaxing in a comfortable* and beautiful setting?

3. Creative Inner Work: Support the patient's self-selected psychobiological movement toward ultradian arousal and performance optimization or ultradian rest and healing facilitation.

Yes, curious how that continues all by itself...for a while?
Umm-m, allowing your inner nature to experience what it needs?
Appreciating and really going along with that...as it continues?

4. Reintegration: Verify the patient's therapeutic inner work and discuss how the patient can continue to use the patterns of performance and/or healing in real life as their personal approach to self-hypnosis or the ultradian healing response.

What was of most value for you in this experience?
How will you allow yourself to continue this kind of inner work?
What, When and Where will you to explore this again by yourself?

Ideally in the third stage of Insight we would expect that Jung's *Intuitive function* would come into play. Finally, only in the fourth stage of Verification does Jung's *Thinking function* have its best role. It is somewhat surprising for most therapists to recognize that conscious cognition, meaning and understanding usually comes last, at the end of the creative experience. Consciousness is usually the last to know! The body with its sensations, perceptions and feelings usually come first as has been documented previously (Rossi & Cheek, 1988). The novel mapping of Jung's psychological functions on the four stages of the creative process is, of course, artificial and only approximate. It can be taken only as a heuristic guide for the therapist rather than another procrustean bed to fit the patient into. Usually all psychological functions are operative at some level or other at all times (Hall, 1989).

Workshop Questions and Answers

Q: I have been a practicing psychotherapist for almost twenty years but in your training workshops I find it very difficult to remain silent during Stage Two and Three of the creative process. What's my problem?

A: This is the most typical problem that most well trained psychotherapists have. We have been trained to believe we really have the answers to our patient's problems. My approach deeply challenges that belief. We need to better respect and understand the wisdom of *wu wei* — letting things happen and allow nature to do it as Jung describes above. *Wu wei* is the essence of the dynamical view of nature that operates all by itself as we outlined earlier in chapters two and three of this book. Do we really have to try to tell people in therapy what to do? Or is our task essentially one of helping them learn to explore the natural dynamics of their own creative process?

My approach recognizes the value of the *creative uncertainty* of the psychotherapist. The therapist is giving up the illusion of being able to predict and control the patient's behavior. What patients gain is a more direct access to their own creative dynamics of self evolution. But remember, I am not recommending that the therapist simply remain passive and silent during Stages Two and Three. You are actually engaged in the very important work of learning to observe the patient's natural mindbody language and you must be ever alert as to how to facilitate creative dynamics at those critical phase transitions when the patient may need the support of a Basic Accessing Question or two.

Q: What if the patient does not respond to the therapist's Basic Accessing Questions with emotional arousal, creative self engagement and so forth? What if they are resistant?

A: In my training workshops most therapists are surprised to witness that about 90% of patients do respond in an essentially creative manner with natural arousal and ideodynamic hand movements when their motivating dynamics are accessed. Yet, there is that remaining 10% who will hold their hands out and nothing seems to happen. Rather than call this *"resistance"* I hypothesize that such patients simply do not understand what is expected of them. Some sort of *ignition* or emotional engagement does not take place right in the beginning to motivate the patient's inner ideodynamic process.

A good demonstration of a successful ignition and ideodynamic engagement is my 1992 videotape of "A Sensitive Fail-Safe Approach to Hypnosis" with a young woman with arthritis (Video # E297-V9, available from the Milton H. Erickson Foundation, 3606 N. 24th St., Phoenix, AZ, 85016-6500). A typical failure in *ideodynamic ignition* was demonstrated in my 1995 videotape "The Basic Accessing Question to Facilitate Creative Hypnotherapy" (Video # H260-CPV5, also available from the Erickson Foundation). Although I tried several ideodynamic approaches in this demonstration, ignition did not take place. The subject simply did not become engaged in a period of creative inner hypnotherapeutic work. I was able to save the situation somewhat in the end by offering her a creative reframe for her anxieties which she thanked me for, but I suspect there was some initial lack of understanding or rapport between us that left the subject with the expectation that the answer to her problem was going to come from me rather than her own inner work.

The Basic Accessing Question is not some sort of magical approach that does all the work. The basic accessing questions simply provide an opportunity for motivated patients to express their ongoing state of arousal and confusion about some issue, problem or symptom in a potentially therapeutic manner. The therapist's initial task is to recognize what Erickson called the patient's *"response readiness."* The patient is eager to respond but does not know how to engage their own inner resources. The basic accessing questions are a permissive approach to opening a channel of information transduction in the fascinating borderland between voluntary and involuntary experience and behavior. They mediate what Jung called the *"transcendent function"* between conscious and unconscious processes.

Sometimes it is best to introduce new patients to this type of creative ideodynamic work by having them attend group psychotherapy where they can first witness how others experience it. Another approach is to do some preliminary facilitation of the patient's sensory and perceptual sensitivity to their own natural polarity dynamics with questions such as:

And will you let me know what you begin to experience in your hands, fingers and arms?

Ideally, patients respond with remarks about their sensations, feelings or attitudes about their hands or whatever they are experiencing. Otherwise, the therapist continues to offer such questions until the patient gets the idea and begins to notice their sensations and mindbody experiences with greater sensitivity so they finally learn to recognize and engage their own natural patterns of mindbody communication and healing.

Another approach is to explore and enhance sensitivity with the magnet metaphor. Magnets and the sensation of magnetic force has been used as a suggestive metaphor for psychological dynamics for centuries (Edinger, 1996). Recall that the ideo-dynamic experience of *hand lowering* (81% passed) and *moving hands* (70% passed) are the items that are most easily experienced on the Stanford Hypnotic Susceptibility Scale (Hilgard, 1965). My experience is that an even higher percentage of people can experience these ideo-dynamic movements in a involuntary or semi-involuntary manner when the magnetic metaphor and the double bind are added. Some subjects who are initially unsuccessful in experiencing ideo-dynamic hand movements with Basic Accessing Questions that focus on their personal dynamics, as illustrated earlier in Chapter Five, are able to experience movements of hands and fingers more easily with the magnetic metaphor used purely as a training exercise without any attempt to engage their personal dynamics.

This entire area of ideodynamical movements remains open for clinical-experimental research. In view of the potential clinical value of these dynamical approaches, it is truly amazing that they have been so little investigated (Rossi & Cheek, 1988). It seems that when it was found that the ideo-dynamical signaling with the Chevrule pendulum and the Oiji board were due to involuntary movements the subject was making without being aware of it, rather than real magic, the scientific community lost interest in it. Conventional scientific wisdom interpreted such findings as having established that ideo-dynamic signaling was a "fake." Yes, ideodynamic signaling is a fake if you thought it was some sort of mystical magic that had access to some sort of ultimate truth. Rather, I think of ideodynamic signaling as an observable behavioral expression of usually hidden personality dynamics. Ideodynamic signaling is a kind of projective technique revealing ongoing critical phase transitions of creative problem solving and healing.

There is no evidence, however, that these involuntary ideo-dynamic movements give access to any special "truth of the uncon-scious." We now fully accept there is no eternal truth in the uncon-scious (Sheehan, 1995). The unconscious is an ongoing, *complex adaptive*, and *multi-stable dynamical psychobiological system* that is the source of creativity and conflict as well as symptomatic behavior. Libet (1993) has established through a lifetime of exhaustive, well replicated research that brain processes determine behavior on an unconscious level about half a second before we become aware of our thoughts, feelings and what we are going to do. It is the *critical phase transitions* in the dynamics of this unconscious matrix of psychobiological processes that we seek to access and facilitate with the ideo-dynamic Basic Accessing Questions and the various approaches to the creative we have illustrated with hypnothrapeutic work in this book.

I hypothesize that hypnotherapeutic work is the little understood essential dynamic that gives rise to the vast literature of historical hypnosis that reports the so-called amazing but unreliable "miracles" of healing. These accounts are unreliable and difficult to replicate because we have misunderstood the dynamics of hypnotherapeutic healing. The basic misunderstanding is that hypnotherapeutic healing is due to the therapist's suggestions somehow becoming imprinted on the so-called blank and receptive mind of the patient experiencing a special state of trance. The entire thrust of modern scientific research in hypnosis has established that this conventional view is wrong (Barber, 1984; Eysenck, 1991; Hilgard, 1992; Sarbin & Coe, 1972; Spanos and Chaves, 1989). We now desperately need research on an alternative view of therapeutic hypnosis that I call *hypnothera-peutic work*. The dynamics of real *work* is a concept that has replaced the idea of magic in the scientific world view and other

,jor fields such as physics and biology. Why should *work* not replace magic in psychology as well? The concept of hypnotherapeutic work rather than the "magic of suggestion" is entirely consistent with the broad scientific dynamics of entropy and information in physics, biology and mathematics. The nonlinear psychobiological dynamics of problem solving and healing, as presented in the first half of this volume point to some possible directions that future research in hypnotherapeutic work may take.

Ideo-dynamic Signaling with the Magnetic Metaphor

It is sometimes best to begin the process of learning how to experience ideo-dynamic signaling in a rather neutral manner without loading it initially with the patient's ongoing psychological problems. The therapist sets the general context by helping the patient develop the following point of view and understanding.

1. Basic Attitudes and Expectations

We will begin by exploring and enhancing your mindbody sensitivity and communication skills...

The basic idea is that you can solve your problems by learning to recognize your own natural mindbody signals...

Many problems can be solved and symptoms relieved in hypnosis simply by letting your mind and body do its own thing...

It could be fascinating to let yourself experience some of the natural forces that are taking care of you...

2. Facilitating Any Ideo-Dynamic Sensation or Movement

As you hold those hands, palms facing each other about six inches apart...

you can simply watch them and wonder to what extent you can begin to experience a magnetic force beginning to pull them together...or push them apart...

This is really an exercise in imagination...

Some people feel it like a wind or puff of air pushing or pulling those hands together or apart...

Some feel as if they are lightly holding an expanding balloon...

Um-mm... yes...surprising isn't it...wow, are those hands really moving all by themselves...

Wonderful, allowing that to continue in any way it wants to...

3. Practicing Voluntary Control and "Involuntary" Movements

Oh, yes, of course, you can control it in any way you want to...

You can stop it or start it any time you want to...

You always have control over this learning process...You are really the boss...

Its just like focusing your eyes or unfocusing them if you want to...Or voluntarily clenching your fist or relaxing it when you want to...

Yes, why don't you experiment with it a little right now...First stop it altogether...that's right...Now practice letting it go all by itself again for a moment or two...

And when you feel safe with it you can wonder what it feels like to let it go all by itself for a while so you don't have to control it...

4. Beginning to Experience Ideo-Dynamic Signaling

You seem to be experiencing that very well...wonder if you can begin to experience whether those hands come together or go apart more or less all by themselves when you think about something privately...

Explore that privately within yourself for a while...Do the hands move in any special way when you think about something that pleases you...

Yes, just explore pleasant thoughts and notice if the hands or fingers or whatever seem to signal yes by coming together or pushing apart...

How is it going...do you get a consistent signal for yes...

Now explore how your hands move more or less by themselves to signal no...maybe simply by thinking or remembering something not so pleasant...

Fine, you are really beginning to experience some interesting stuff...in a sense you are learning to talk or communicate with your natural mindbody...wonder what it can help you understand...

5. Private Ideo-dynamic Signaling and Problem Solving

Many detailed protocols for series of questions to explore psychological problems and stress symptoms via ideo-motor hand, finger and head signaling have been presented previously (Rossi & Cheek, 1988). Here are just a few ways of initiating the process.

Sometimes the arms, hands or fingers initially will move with slight quivering motions. The therapist supports this beginning as follows.

That's right! Are those fingers really moving slightly all by them selves...

Once such minimal movements are experienced it then becomes something of a playful game to explore how to extend the ideo-dynamic movements in further directions.

And you can now wonder if the hands (fingers, arms) can now shift direction all by themselves and move apart (or together) as if a magnetic force or a wind were pushing them apart...

You can privately continue to explore these movements and learn whether they can respond more or less all by themselves to your inner feelings or questions...

For example, do the hands move together or apart or however they wish as you think about some particular problem...perhaps an inner issue you have not even told me about...something you would rather keep private for now...

Would you like to explore privately whether you get a yes response (usually the hands moving together) or a no response (usually the hands moving apart) when you ask yourself a question...

I don't know whether being left- or right-handed makes any difference...maybe you can explore just how it works for you...

When patients begin to experience such positive and negative signaling to private questions they give themselves, they are usually ready to engage the therapeutically motivating ideo-dynamic Basic Accessing Questions offered by the therapist. In addition to ideo-dynamic movements, of course, some people may experience valuable ideo-dynamic sensations such as warmth, coolness, numbness, itchiness, goose-bumps etc.. All such sensations can be explored for their signaling value (Rossi & Cheek, 1988).

6. Therapeutic Attitudes Toward Ideo-Dynamic Signaling

Some people may want to make more of ideo-dynamic signaling than it is. It is not a royal road to the unconscious or the truth in any ultimate sense. It is simply a step toward accessing and perhaps facilitating the normal nexus of the *critical phase transitions* that make up our experiential life.

No, there is no evidence that this is a way to learn the real truth about yourself...that is an old-fashioned way of thinking about it...

This is more like an exploratory inner theater...an inner drama just like a daydream that is interesting to wonder about...

Sometimes it gives you ideas...sometimes you stumble on what you're really feeling in your heart...sometimes it helps you realize something important...

But it can also be wrong...it may signal an inner wish...but you have to check it with reality just as you would with any other wish you may have...

We all have to be practical and figure out how to survive and have a creative relationship with our inner world as well as the outer world...

It is really best to simply ask questions...No, I don't think this is a good way to try to tell your unconscious what to do...

No, this is not a way to suggest or program yourself...It is the exact opposite... it's just a way of exploring...asking your inner nature questions...sometimes it works...but sometimes it doesn't...it's best just to respect your inner self...there is no way of telling it what to do...

You wonder if this is spiritual? Well, I suppose some people may experience this as spiritual...in what sense is it spiritual for you?

It could be consistent with some spiritual beliefs...that is something you may like to explore with a spiritual guide...

We may get a spiritual intuition from within but you must always use your best conscious moral sense to evaluate the worth of anything that comes to you intutively...

No, I certainly would not believe an inner voice, inner signal or intuition of any sort without checking it out carefully with my conscious moral sense...Some scientists have even hypothesized that this is precisely the role of consciousness — to check out whatever comes to us from within as well as the outside world so we have an opportunity to decide what to do with it...an essential role of consciousness is to say "No!" to what is inappropriate (Libet, 1993).

No, you are not to blame nor even entirely responsible for what comes up within you...you are indeed responsible for what you do with what comes up within yourself.

You don't go around trying to kill people in the outside world...so what makes you think you can kill those things you don't like in yourself...

Rather than naively believing you can get rid of your problem why not wonder what it is trying to tell you about what creative changes may be needed...

The real question is how you develop a moral and creative relationship toward the negative things that come up within...

Yes, that's right, your so-called problems and symptoms may really be a signaling system...the way nature is trying to get your conscious attention...you don't want to kill the messenger...you want to explore how to develop a "response-able" way of relating to it so healing can take place...

I really don't know if stress symptoms can always lead to enlightenment but maybe they can at least give us some hints in that direction...

I would rather explore this with you in the natural realm...it can be very fascinating, highly numinous and spiritual in some sort of natural sense but it's really not magic...just something interesting to explore and test like anything else in life.

Symptom Scaling and the Ultradian Path to Enlightenment

Polarity dynamics are universal in the sense that they can utilize any dimension of experience that the subject can recognize (sensations, images, emotions, symptoms, thoughts etc.) to facilitate hypnotherapeutic work. In terms of nonlinear dynamics or Chaos Theory, we could say that the human experience of polarity or duality is a kind of highly motivated bifurcation, catastrophe cusp or symmetry breaking during critical phase transitions in behavior. The advantage of using a behavioral response such as head, hand, arm or finger signaling to catalyze polarity is that the therapist and patient both have an observable index of what may be happening on a more-or-less involuntary level that is closer to their creative matrix of self-organization.

The essence of Erickson's hypnotherapeutic genius, however, was in his utilization of whatever behavior the patient was experiencing as the starting point for hypnotherapeutic work (Erickson 1958/1980, 1959/1980). What I call the symptom path to enlightenment utilizes the patient's sense of their own level of awareness or the intensity of a symptom or problem to facilitate hypnotherapeutic work. From the basic chronobiological facts presented in Chapter Four we know that our levels of awareness and symptom intensity are continually changing. We utilize these entirely natural changes (rather than suggestion) to facilitate whatever *critical phase transition* is required for the healing or problem solving to take place.

At all times throughout this protocol the therapist notes with approval whatever changes the patient notices in the natural ongoing flow of their experiencing. The therapist continually encourages the patient's further expectation of naturally changing experiential states — gradually facilitating the patient's shifting phase transitions toward a critical therapeutic cusp in Thom's catastrophe model.

(1) Scaling Level of Awareness. When the patient complains of a problem or symptom they are *experiencing right now in the current moment* we take it as a mindbody signal that needs attention — that is, a signal to start inner work that may lead to problem solving and/or healing. We initiate this inner work by asking the patient where he/she is right now on a *Subjective Scale of Awareness or Intensity of the Symptom* from one to ten where ten is most intense, five is average and one is little or no problem. If one is simply scaling levels of awareness this is similar to the Stanford Sleepiness Scale developed by Hoddes et. al. (1973). Symptom scaling is a way of focusing and accessing the state dependent dynamics in the here and now for problem resolution.

What are you experiencing right now, at this moment, on a subjective scale of your awareness of [whatever symptom] from one to ten: where ten is most, five is average and one is very little and zero is none?

The therapist accepts with positive regard whatever subjective scaling the patient offers of their level of awareness or symptom intensity and continues with Stage Two as follows.

(2) Initiating Inner Work.

Good! And as you continue sensing your problem (symptoms, pain etc.) let me know whatever changes you begin to notice...

How are you experiencing yourself...

Notice whether you becoming more intense or less...

Are you becoming more aroused or relaxed...

It does not matter what the patient's initial state may be. We are only interested in what is changing. (From the mathematical point of view we are not as interested in the value of a variable as much as we are interested in its *derivative*). *Any change may mean that potentially therapeutic dynamics are being engaged!* After about three or four minutes of inner experiencing the patient is again asked to subjectively scale the level of awareness that is being experienced.

Um-hmm... what number are you experiencing at this moment?

The therapist, of course, accepts whatever the patient presents. There are only three possible options.

Option 1: A higher subjective scaling number. Some patients may become more aroused initially, sometimes with a temporary increased awareness of symptoms, emotionality, catharsis etc. That is, the initial movement of their level of awareness shifts upward to what we would call "High Phase Hypnosis." The therapist, of course, immediately accepts and facilitates this.

Fine...Nice to notice how you can become more aware of [whatever symptom] for a moment or two as you get in contact with it so the therapeutic process can begin...

Courage to continue experiencing and wondering what changes take place all by themselves at first...

If the patient continues to move toward High Phase Hypnosis with increasing arousal, symptom substitution and/or catharsis the therapist facilitates these natural dynamics by picking up with Stage Two (the arousal phase) of the four stage creative process illustrated above. A particularly interesting therapeutic opportunity comes up when the patient with a negative attitude complains about other *symptoms* or *negative thoughts* coming into their experience. The patient's spontaneous experience of *symptom substitution* can be utilized to facilitate healing by what I call *"The Merry Symptom Chase."*

Option 2: A lower subjective scaling number. There may be an immediate or slow drop in the awareness of the symptom — typically with the patient moving toward a natural relaxation. That is, the initial movement of their awareness is downward to what we would call "Low Phase Hypnosis." The therapist immediately accepts this and facilitates with the following.

Good, allowing yourself to appreciate your good fortune (wonderful blessing etc.) in experiencing that natural therapeutic movement...

Toward greater relaxation and comfort...

Rather amazing how that [whatever symptom or problem] seems to take care of [heal] it self when you allow it...

And simply allowing that healing to continue all by itself...

Occasionally telling me what number you are experiencing...

Nice to know you can continue to explore this way of cooperating with your natural healing response...

It is a fortunate situation, indeed, when the patient goes into a spontaneous remission or natural healing. We really don't know, of course, whether the good experience will last for how long. *We really don't know if a genuine path to healing has been experienced or a placebo response or outright denial.* We can, however, support whatever positive possibility the patient may have discovered through the process.

Continuing to deeply appreciate learning how this healing can continue all by itself...

And will it be possible for you to let yourself continue learning how to experience this natural ultradian healing response a few times throughout the day when you need to?

Option 3: No change in subjective scaling number. With no change in subjective scaling number after a few minutes (at most five minutes with no subjective or objectively observable behavior change) the therapist accepts that something may not be working. For whatever reason the patient's inner dynamics have not become engaged. A seed may have been planted for future work but for now a fresh approach is needed. Interpretations or any subtle implication that the patient is resisting are to be avoided! The patient needs support for learning how to do this kind of inner work.

Ummm... it is possible that something within yourself is not ready to express itself yet...

It sometimes requires a little practice — a kind of sensitivity training — learning just what you are naturally experiencing...

Would you like to let that continue for another moment or two...

You may experience whatever comes up all by itself that you feel you would like to talk about next.

Okay, perhaps that is enough for now...what else is coming up within you at this point?

(3) A Path to Enlightenment. Patients may gradually shift into the dynamics of stage three of the creative process with a cognitive insight or natural ultradian shifts in awareness, emotions and/or symptomatic experience. The therapist's task is to facilitate a recognition of the possible utility of their changing experiences and developing awareness as *A Path to Enlightenment* about whatever meaning or wisdom comes up about themselves.

Um-mm, rather profound possibilities in what you say...

Yes, it is well known that an illness [or whatever problem] sometimes can lead to a new level of meaning and wisdom...

Curious what lessons you can learn from your [whatever]...

A rather surprising path to enlightenment for you...

Is this the first time you realized that about yourself...

Wonder what else comes to you about your new understanding...

And how will you continue cultivating this new awareness?

(4) Verification, Reintegration. Most patients are pleasantly surprised by going through an experience of the valley of shadow and doubt to find themselves in a better place after a shorter (five or ten minutes) or longer period (up to about ninety minutes). They often wonder aloud about what the therapist did to make them feel better. Of course, the therapist did nothing but facilitate their natural ultradian dynamics of healing and problem solving. The therapist can be very frank about just what her/his role was with the clear implication that the patient can now learn to do just as well with a little practice on their own. It is only in this final reality-orientations phase of the creative process that I ever demur about the attitude some patients may have about controlling or programming themselves.

Really, I only encouraged you to stay with whatever natural [symptom or problem] your inner self really needed the time to deal with...

I wonder if you will find that when you do this on your own you typically go through an initial period of doubt and self-criticism as you did here today...or perhaps the doubt was only a first-time experience in facing the unknown and not how you naturally work...

Notice how I simply encouraged you to experience the honesty of those negative feelings [or whatever]...

And how they somehow were transformed...even in ways we do not understand...

Surprising, isn't it, how it comes to its own natural ending even before you expect it sometimes...I know you would like to extend that nice inner state a while longer...but nature is saying she has finished her inner work for now and she is eager to get on with outer living...

Yes, I know you want to be able to control this healing process...yes, yes, you again ask how you can learn to program this even better...I am telling you that you do not control it, you have just had a wonderful experience of symptom relief by simply relating to yourself in a sympathetic manner...

No, you do not program yourself as is claimed in the pop psychology books and the movies ...You simply learn to recognize when the natural phase of inner healing wants to take place all by itself and you let it ...

Um-hum, yes, you let It ... some say you "Let God ..."

No, I'm not teaching you how to control your symptoms! I prefer to say I am helping you learn how to have a deeply sympathetic and creative relationship with your inner self ... so it will not need to make symptoms to get your attention.

Can you learn to have a secret sympathy for your natural self that really wants to relate to you when it calls with your so-called [whatever symptom or problem] ...

Yes, you are learning how to have a healing relationship with yourself ... you are learning how to cooperate in a natural way with what your own mindbody wisdom is trying to tell you ...

Yes, this is what I call the Symptom Path to Enlightenment ...

What was your high point of wisdom — enlightenment today?

Um-hmm ... yes, now that is a good question, indeed! ... how do you get in your own way?

How do you usually interfere with your own mindbody signals that
healing?
level of awareness as we
natural end ...
riate to explore this kind of
wn?
feel fatigued, when your
ou know your inner nature
aling.

and Counterwill

ideo-dynamic signaling via
al, *spontaneous* or *autono-*
vements is the *subjective*
l. We are not referring here
ce ideo-dynamic signaling.
re eager and willing to ex-
eed, often have a consider-
ideo-dynamic signaling.
These people are sometimes so sensitive to the shifting currents

within themselves that they will experience surprising, unexpected and subtle shifts in the direction and ease of their ideo-dynamic signaling movements. Sometimes they expect or want to experience a "yes" signal and are disappointed to find their hands signaling "no." Their hands, for example, may be moving slowly together as if a magnetic force was signaling "yes" and at some point they unexpectedly experience what some have called "a wall...a block...a cushion of air stopping my hands...a magnetic field just reversed itself and is now pushing the hands apart..."

It is just such surprising and nonvolitional shifts and often unwanted changes in ideo-dynamic signaling that gives the clinician grounds for speculating about the shifting psychodynamics — that is, the bifurcations or critical phase transitions that are currently unfolding within the patient. Are we here making visible in observable behavior the usually hidden dynamics of the so-called *unconscious*? It would be interesting to assess this hypothesis by means of Libet's (1993) interesting neurophysiological approach to exploring the relationship between conscious and voluntary actions and the involuntary, unconscious brain processes that precede them by about half a second.

Sometimes patients will label such behavior as *resistance*. Of course, some therapists are all too eager to agree with this pejorative diagnosis. But is it really resistance or evidence of a counterwill or important change taking place within their psychodynamics. Are we here observing a bifurcation, a critical phase transition to new and original psychological experience that the patient never experienced before. This is the hope and possibility we are trying to facilitate with the new ideo-dynamics of hypnotherapeutic work. Here are a few phrases that can be used to facilitate such surprising and potentially useful approaches to the essence of creative inner work. Since many patients have their eyes closed (even though I never tell patients to close their eyes), they may not even be aware of their own ideo-dynamic movements. Because of this *I am careful to never intrude with any of the following remarks; I only use them to confirm the patient's own perceptions or respond to their questions about what they are experiencing.*

Really...you say you are experiencing a glass wall there...your hands are momentarily blocked...I wonder how long that will continue?

How it will change...curious to know what will happen next...

Yes, it is surprising to experience these unexpected changes...

No, you do not program yourself as is claimed in the pop psychology books and the movies ...You simply learn to recognize when the natural phase of inner healing wants to take place all by itself and you let it ...

Um-hum, yes, you let It ... some say you "Let God ..."

No, I'm not teaching you how to control your symptoms! I prefer to say I am helping you learn how to have a deeply sympathetic and creative relationship with your inner self ... so it will not need to make symptoms to get your attention.

Can you learn to have a secret sympathy for your natural self that really wants to relate to you when it calls with your so-called [whatever symptom or problem] ...

Yes, you are learning how to have a healing relationship with yourself... you are learning how to cooperate in a natural way with what your own mindbody wisdom is trying to tell you ...

Yes, this is what I call the Symptom Path to Enlightenment ...

What was your high point of wisdom — enlightenment today?

Um-hmm ... yes, now that is a good question, indeed! ... how do you get in your own way?

How do you usually interfere with your own mindbody signals that you need in order to let nature do her own healing?

And what number describes your current level of awareness as we bring this unit of inner healing work to its natural end ...

And how will you know when it is appropriate to explore this kind of inner healing (problem solving) on your own?

Yes, that's right, it's precisely when you feel fatigued, when your symptoms seem to be getting worse that you know your inner nature may be calling you for a period of inner healing.

The Ideo-Dynamics of Surprise, Will and Counterwill

One of the most surprising aspects of ideo-dynamic signaling via *involuntary* (sometimes called *nonvolitional, spontaneous* or *autonomous*) eye, head, hand, arm or finger movements is the *subjective experience of resistance* some patients feel. We are not referring here to a conscious unwillingness to experience ideo-dynamic signaling. Rather we are referring to subjects who are eager and willing to explore themselves in this way and who, indeed, often have a considerable talent for apparently nonvolitional ideo-dynamic signaling. These people are sometimes so sensitive to the shifting currents within themselves that they will experience surprising, unexpected and subtle shifts in the direction and ease of their ideo-dynamic signaling movements. Sometimes they expect or want to experience a "yes" signal and are disappointed to find their hands signaling "no." Their hands, for example, may be moving slowly together as if a magnetic force was signaling "yes" and at some point they unexpectedly experience what some have called "a wall...a block...a cushion of air stopping my hands...a magnetic field just reversed itself and is now pushing the hands apart..."

It is just such surprising and nonvolitional shifts and often unwanted changes in ideo-dynamic signaling that gives the clinician grounds for speculating about the shifting psychodynamics — that is, the bifurcations or critical phase transitions that are currently unfolding within the patient. Are we here making visible in observable behavior the usually hidden dynamics of the so-called *unconscious*? It would be interesting to assess this hypothesis by means of Libet's (1993) interesting neurophysiological approach to exploring the relationship between conscious and voluntary actions and the involuntary, unconscious brain processes that precede them by about half a second.

Sometimes patients will label such behavior as *resistance*. Of course, some therapists are all too eager to agree with this pejorative diagnosis. But is it really resistance or evidence of a counterwill or important change taking place within their psychodynamics. Are we here observing a bifurcation, a critical phase transition to new and original psychological experience that the patient never experienced before. This is the hope and possibility we are trying to facilitate with the new ideo-dynamics of hypnotherapeutic work. Here are a few phrases that can be used to facilitate such surprising and potentially useful approaches to the essence of creative inner work. Since many patients have their eyes closed (even though I never tell patients to close their eyes), they may not even be aware of their own ideo-dynamic movements. Because of this *I am careful to never intrude with any of the following remarks; I only use them to confirm the patient's own perceptions or respond to their questions about what they are experiencing.*

Really...you say you are experiencing a glass wall there...your hands are momentarily blocked...I wonder how long that will continue?

How it will change...curious to know what will happen next...

Yes, it is surprising to experience these unexpected changes...

276

And do you have the courage to allow those fingers [or whatever] to continue all by themselves for a little while so you can experience what they are leading to...

Um-mm, you say those hands are really reversing direction all by themselves...nice little surprise you can wonder about...

And that may continue until...

Who knows what is coming up...

Nice to know you may be ready to experience something special...

Umm...in just such unexpected changes there comes some new...

Yes, that can be the best...to allow the inner mindbody the freedom to experience what it will...to say what it wants...

The nonvolitional (involuntary) experiences of will and counter-will that are so common and useful in hypnotherapeutic work have important implications for the deep philosophical questions about free will and the evolution of consciousness as well as the relationships between mind and body. Our approach to ideo-dynamic experiences, for example, appear to be observable manifestations of Spinoza's understanding of the will and its relationship to the body as expressed in his *Ethics* published in 1677.

> The act of will and the movement of the body are not two different things objectively known, which the bond of causality unites; they do not stand in the relation of cause and effect; they are one and the same, but they are given in entirely different ways,— immediately, and again in perception...The action of the body is nothing but the act of the will objectified. This is true of every movement of the body;...the whole body is nothing but objectified will...The parts of the body must therefore completely correspond to the principal desires through which the will manifests itself; they must be the visible expression of these desires. (This quotation from Spinoza's *Ethics* adapted from Durant, 1933, p.341.)

The modern experimental assessment of the phenomena of ideo-dynamic signaling and its relationship to conscious and unconscious will and idea will require the use of brain-imaging technology. It will be fascinating, for example, to learn about the differences in the locations and changing relationships between the brain fields that are activated during nonvolitional ideo-dynamic signaling versus similar voluntary movements (Decety et al., 1994). Here, at last, we will have an objective means of exploring the philosophical and clinical questions that will contribute to the new foundations of a genuine science of hypnotherapeutic work.

Chapter Eight:
The Symptom Path to Enlightenment: Ultradian Dynamics in Hypnotherapeutic Work

Nature cannot be ordered about, except by obeying her.

Francis Bacon

In this chapter we bring together the new creative dynamics of self-organization with the ultradian theory of hypnotherapeutic work. Dynamical approaches to psychosomatic problems are integrated with concepts from chronobiology to provide a broad rationale for accessing and facilitating the pathways of information transduction between mind, brain and body as the psychobiological basis for therapeutic hypnosis. It is hypothesized that interference with these pathways by trauma, acute and chronic psychodynamic issues and extended performance demands distort normal ultradian rest-rejuvenation rhythms and that this, in turn, leads to the experience of stress and psychosomatic problems. A series of case studies are used to illustrate utilization of the ultradian healing response as a common denominator between hypnosis and many forms of mindbody healing. While these cases are anecdotal, they do suggest new directions for future research on the psychobiological foundations of a naturalistic approach to therapeutic hypnosis.

The ultradian theory of hypnotherapeutic work proposes that Milton H. Erickson's unusually long hypnotherapeutic sessions utilized many natural processes of mindbody healing that take place periodically throughout the day (Erickson, Rossi and Rossi, 1976; Erickson and Rossi, 1979; Rossi, 1982, 1986a, 1990b) . As reviewed previously in Chapter Four, recent research that documents the significance of time and rhythms in hypnotic work provides the first phase of experimental support for the ultradian theory of hypnotherapeutic work that may be summarized as follows:

1. The classical phenomena of hypnosis appear to be natural non-linear chronobiological processes that can be experienced in an attenuated form during the 15-20 minute rest-rejuvenation phase of the Basic Rest Activity Cycle (BRAC) that usually takes place as an ultradian rhythm every 90-120 minutes throughout the day (Lippincott, 1990; Rossi, 1982, 1986, 1990c, Sommer, 1990).

2. The chronic overriding of this natural rest-rejuvenation period due to psychodynamic issues and extended performance demands can eventually lead to a de-synchrony of the ultradian rhythms and the consequent expression of the classical symptoms of stress and psychosomatic problems (Friedman, 1978; Friedman and Fischer, 1967; Kupfer, Monk and Barches, 1988; Rossi, 1986; Rossi and Cheek, 1988). This is called *The Ultradian Stress Response* (Rossi & Nimmons, 1991)

3. Because ultradian psychobiological processes of self regulation are so sensitive to psychosocial cues they can easily be accessed, entrained and therapeutically utilized by what has been tradi-tionally called "hypnotic suggestion," particularly during the 20 minute rest-rejuvenation phase of the BRAC. This systematic utilization of our natural 20 minute rest-rejuvenation period to optimize the resolution of psychological and psychosomatic prob-lems has been called *The Ultradian Healing Response* (Rossi, 1986, 1990b; Rossi and Cheek, 1988, Rossi & Nimmons, 1991).

4. The healing of stress and mindbody problems can be facilitated by utilizing the rest-rejuvenation phase of *The Ultradian Healing Response* as a "window of opportunity" for optimizing the resolution of interpersonal and psychodynamic problems. It can be easily incorporated by many traditional schools of psychotherapy as well as by many alternative forms of holistic therapy.

5. The *Ultradian Healing Response* is the psychobiological basis of self-hypnosis that may facilitate problem solving and healing on

many levels of the information transduction loop between mind and gene.

We hypothesize that *The Ultradian Healing Response* is the generally unrecognized common denominator of the chaotological periodicity found in many forms of mindbody therapy such as Jacobson's Progressive Relaxation (1924), Benson's Relaxation Response (1975), biofeedback and many forms of imagery (Green and Green, 1987) and meditation training (e.g. transcendental) that usually require about 20 minutes (West, 1987). It is interesting to note that many experimental studies of psychological and holistic healing typically report that 20 minutes was used for the treatment effect (Green and Green, 1987; Rider and Achterberg, 1989). Some researchers have already provided evidence that "entrainment mechanisms" are involved in pain reduction, potentiating the immune system and the treatment of chronic diseases via muscle relaxation and music-mediated imagery (Rider, 1985, 1987). These therapeutic effects have been attributed to the impact of the use of imagery and relaxation on adrenal corticosteroids and "the re-entrainment of circadian rhythms" (Rider, Floyd, & Kirkpatrick, 1985).

Evidence has been cited for the view that the 20 minute rest-rejuvenation phase of the BRAC is a period during which many cybernetic processes of mindbody rejuvenation and healing are taking place on many levels from the molecular-genetic to the psychodynamic (Rossi, 1990a). On the *mind-brain level* these include the encoding of state-dependent and long term memory (Freeman, 1995; Kandel, 1989; Rossi and Ryan 1986). On the *brain-body level* there is the ultradian release of many hormonal information molecules associated with stress, such as cortisol and B-endorphin (Iranmanesh et al., 1989); with sexuality, such as testosterone, luteinizing hormone and follicle-stimulating hormone (Veldhuis et al., 1987); and with growth, such as growth hormone, prolactin and insulin (Veldhuis and Johnson, 1988; Mejean et al, 1988). The ultimate effects of many of these hormones on the *cellular-genetic level* is to turn on, turn off or modulate gene transcription and translation. Recent research, for example, indicates that there is a 90-120 minute ultradian rhythm to cell division with a critical 20 minute window during which intracellular messenger molecules called "cyclins" can trigger genetic replication and mitosis (Murray, Solomon & Kirschner, 1989). There is much to suggest that circadian as well as ultradian rhythms have their source in the interaction of the so-called clock genes such as *per*(iod) and *tim*(eless) (Barinaga, 1995; Myers et al., 1995; Sehgal et al., 1995; Takahashi & Hoffman, 1995). These genes initiate the cascades of metabolism, energy and informational dynamics of cell division and healing. The healing of the stress response at the cellular-genetic level has a number of ultradian (less than an hour to within hours) as well as circadian components peaking at about 60 hours (Todorov, 1990).

How can we utilize this knowledge of the natural dynamics of stress and healing to facilitate the critical phase transitions of practical hypnotherapeutic work? The case studies of this chapter document how we can explore the use of ultradian healing dynamics with a variety of psychotherapeutic approaches to a variety of clinical problems. These cases were selected to illustrate the types of family processes, psychodynamic issues and performance demands that may lead to a disruption of normal functioning and consequent psychosomatic problems. While space limitations do not permit a detailed presentation of all the psychodynamic and interpersonal issues involved, these abbreviated case examples should not be taken to imply that the psychobiological aspects of ultradian rhythms replace or are more important than traditional psychodynamic and interpersonal theory. To the contrary, the ultradian healing response is hypothesized to be a period during which many traditional approaches to the resolution of clinical problems can be optimized. The *psychobiological* nature of ultradian processes is hypothesized to be a missing link between the social-psychological and the biological levels in many of the traditional approaches to hypnotherapy.

Because the relationships between family systems theory, psychodynamics, mindbody communication and ultradian rhythms as presented in this chapter are anecdotal, these case histories are of heuristic value only; they are of use primarily in suggesting further lines of clinical-experimental research to assess the hypothesis that ultradian/circadian dynamics may be used as a "window of opportunity" for accessing and resolving many mindbody problems. We freely speculate about the possible role of a variety of hormonal messenger molecules that may be involved at various critical phase transitions of the therapy process only as a heuristic for suggesting the type of mindbody research that needs to be done in the future. A number of these cases are composites designed to summarize experience with a number of typical clinical situations that apparently involve chaotological ultradian periodicity. The most obvious application of ultradian-circadian dynamics is in those syndromes where the presenting problem involves a clear de-synchronization of the patient's typical rhythms of activity and rest.

Case 1: Jane — Narcolepsy, Catalepsy, Insomnia and Depression

Presenting Problem:

Jane is a 36-year-old woman who was referred by her family physician because of depression, brought on in response to her current divorce. Jane also was suffering from narcolepsy and cataplexy and was receiving medical treatment for this from a nearby university sleep disorder clinic. She was prescribed a high daily dose of Ritalin to keep her awake while driving. For the first year of treatment at the clinic the focus was on the depression associated with her divorce. During the second year deep seated issues related to growing up in a dysfunctional alcoholic home was the focus of treatment. Jane's complete DSM-R diagnosis at the clinic was as follows:

Axis I: 296.23 Major Depression with Melancholia

Axis II: 301.81 Narcissistic Personality Disorder

Axis III: Narcolepsy and Cataplexy

Treatment:

After being referred by the clinic Jane was interested in exploring the thoughts and feelings of the past and present that seemed to be associated with her Narcolepsy and Cataplexy. Since she was interested in meditation to clear her mind, Jane was given an opportunity to practice "a comfortable, natural hypnotic meditative trance" during the first therapy session "while her inner mind reviewed and dealt with whatever issues came up all by themselves."

After a quiet period of apparently rapt inner focus for *about fifteen minutes,* Jane stirred a bit. This was taken as a natural behavioral indication that she would be awakening soon so she was asked, *Will your eyes open as you awaken when your inner mind knows you have done as much healing as is appropriate at this time?*

An evaluation of this initial trance experience with The Indirect Trance Assessment Scale (ITAS) suggested that Jane had easy access to a very rich inner life that could be used for exploring and utilizing her own inner resources for problem solving (Rossi, 1986). After she awakened, for example, she spontaneously reported feeling "refreshed, alive and energized...Even the colors in the room now seemed brighter." She wondered if this "energizing experience could be used to support the effects of Ritalin at those times of the day when the drug seems to wear out?"

Jane was encouraged to explore this speculation by reviewing whatever possible patterns might be evident in her symptomatology in the course of her typical day. In the context of this review we discussed "the normal ultradian variations in consciousness and energy level that most people experience throughout the day." She quickly developed an intuitive appreciation of how she was "pushing herself into further stress" when she did not let herself have these normal breaks because of her fears that any feeling of tiredness or depression meant that she was falling into narcolepsy. Jane's perceptive intelligence led her to wonder whether some of her tiredness, depression and even narcolepsy could be manifestations of her personal "ultradian stress syndrome." She was intrigued by the therapist's suggestion that it might be interesting to explore the possibility that her ultradian stress syndrome might be transformed into an "ultradian healing response" by letting herself experience "a comfortable meditative trance" several times a day when she felt her energy level waning (Rossi and Nimmons, 1991).

The following week Jane reported some success with potentiating her "consciousness and energy levels" by enjoying an ultradian healing response several times a day *when she felt herself getting tired.* Most important, she said, was the relief she felt now that she no longer had to fear that taking such breaks meant that she and her medicine were failing. After a month of continuing success, in co-operation with her medical doctor's advice, she was allowed to substitute a 20 minute ultradian healing response in the mid-afternoon for her usual 10 mg dose of Ritalin.

Two months later, with her medical doctor's permission, she substituted an ultradian healing period for another 10 mg dose of Ritalin after lunch. She reported that "This really works for me because I'm more productive now because my mind is clear and alert throughout the workday." When she was non-directively queried about what was clear in her mind she discussed a number of personal issues and relationships that she was handling better since she was *"taking time out to mull them over during her ultradian healing periods."*

The final stage of her therapy when she stopped taking any Ritalin came a few months later when she added another ultradian break at about 10:00 a.m. which "rejuvenates" her and allows her to keep her energy up until the after lunch ultradian. When she occasionally forgets to do an ultradian healing response she finds she can use the first mild signs of waning enthusiasm and tiredness to remind her that it is time for her ultradian healing response.

It is possible that a participating factor in Jane's depression, narcolepsy and cataplexy was the stressful overriding of her natural ultradian rhythms of rest and rejuvenation during the several years when she was unable to resolve the many familial and psychodynamic issues that she was trying to cover up with obsessive concern about her "productivity." This view is consistent with the current literature in this area as follows.

> Narcolepsy is a serious disorder that is marked by abnormal REM patterns, Cataplexy, sleep paralysis, and hypnagogic hallucinations. In the sleep laboratory the narcoleptic shows early REM periods within the first 15 minutes of sleep. Cataplexy is a brief, sudden loss of skeletal muscle tone that is often observed after the person has had an emotional reaction such as laughter, anger, or excitement. The narcoleptic remains aware of the surroundings during the attack, which differentiates the event from a seizure. About 60% of narcoleptics experience Cataplexy. . . .Generally, narcoleptics will begin to have periods of excessive daytime sleepiness in their early teens or twenties. . . .*This disorder is probably best conceptualized as an imbalance between the waking, REM, and NREM systems that can be experienced as anything from a slight nuisance to a severely incapacitating disease.* . . .Spouses, friends, and employers are likely to interpret the narcoleptic's frequent naps and sleepiness as lethargy, sloth, and lack of motivation. (Lacks, 1987, p. 43, Italics are ours)

Jane's clinical progress is consistent with the view that for some patients the practice of the ultradian healing response when they experience an ultradian stress syndrome may facilitate a therapeutic synchronization of waking and sleeping patterns of behavior (Dement & Kleitman, 1957; Kleitman, 1970). That the resolution of her clinical depression was at least in part related to this ultradian/circadian synchronization is consistent with the emerging research literature on biological rhythms and mental disorders (Kupfer, Monk, & Barchas, 1988).

At least two profound mindbody issues are raised by this case: (1) What are the psychobiological syndromes that can be ameliorated by using the ultradian healing response to support and even replace medication; and, (2) to what extent can the early, mild symptoms of stress disorders be used as a signal to initiate an ultradian healing response to thereby avoid the course of more severe ultradian stress syndrome (Rossi, 1990d; Rossi and Cheek, 1988; Rossi and Ryan, 1986)? An extensive scientific literature that documents how administering drugs at appropriate phases of ultradian and circadian rhythms can reduce dosage levels for many clinical conditions such as asthma, cancer and depression already exists (Klevecz et al., 1987; Klevecz and Braly, 1987). The case of Jane presented here, however, is the first report of the use of the ultradian healing response to completely replace the need for a drug.

We strongly suspect that Jane's personal belief system in the efficacy of meditation for mind healing, her extraordinary sensitivity to her inner states and her lively interest in "converting her ultradian stress syndrome into an ultradian healing response" were contributing factors to her success. We speculate that the *utilization* of this interest in her inner states enabled her to go through a *critical phase transition in converting the symptoms of stress into signals* that she needed a period of rest and recovery. Jane was obviously using *Low Phase Hypnosis* since she practiced "when she felt herself getting tired." She was doing some very important inner work in relationship to herself and others during this period, however, as was indicated by her report of "taking time out to mull things over." Apparently useful therapeutic insights were more accessible to her during the ultradian healing response. The appropriateness of the ultradian approach with many different types of personality and life situations (even when psychodynamic insights are not easily available) is illustrated in a number of the following cases.

Case 2: Millie — Insomnia

Presenting Problem:

Millie is a 68-year-old woman who was referred by her internist for treatment of persistent insomnia. Millie had a sleep onset latency of 60-90 minutes almost every night. For the past nine months, she had slept for less than 4 1/2 hours per night, and the experience of daytime fatigue had led to depression and irritability. This mood disturbance had become so severe that it was affecting her marriage of 38 years and there was potential for divorce.

While it became apparent during the initial stages of her psychotherapy that there was a connection between Millie's mood disturbance and her marriage problems, her husband was unresponsive to insight therapy and just kept telling her to "try harder to relax" and "it's all in the mind." It got so bad that he accused her of getting more sleep than she claimed, and he began to sleep in another bedroom. She had used the Benzodiazepine, Dalmane, the antidepressant, Desyrel and the barbiturate, Seconal, but did not like the side effects of these medicines.

Now that both she and her husband were retired Millie felt she "had nothing important to do since the kids are gone." She began lying in bed until late morning. She also stopped eating, meeting friends, shopping and walking which she had formerly enjoyed. During the first session, Millie talked about anxieties she was having, including her husband having a heart attack, their home being burglarized, or dying in a fire.

Treatment:

Our first impression is that Millie is facing a crisis, an obvious *critical phase transition* in her life having to do with retirement and a new relationship that was now required with her husband. To facilitate an initial phase of rapport in therapy and to reassure Millie that her world view was fully accepted, we had her contact workmen, the police and fire inspectors to check the locks and smoke detectors in her home. She was taught a progressive approach to relaxation to help reduce anxiety during the day, but it did not help with her insomnia. Millie was told of the sleep research that documented how older individuals sleep less due to a decrease in delta stage sleep (deep sleep) and an increase in light sleep, which makes them easier to awaken.

Millie was taught to go into a natural ultradian healing response in an early therapy session with these words:

When your eyes close all by themselves in a moment or two, will it be a signal that your inner mind is ready to help solve your sleep problem? I wonder if you can recall a time when you slept very well? And will your unconscious help you go comfortably to sleep before you even realize it? When you feel like waking up and stretching, will it be a signal that your inner mind has learned something useful to help you find comfort and healing when you lay down to rest?

After 13 minutes, Millie spontaneously opened her eyes, stretched and talked of her inner experiences of vague fragmented thoughts about her husband, seeing colors with no form, and being very relaxed.

Millie was assured that everyone experiences a natural 90-minute Basic Rest Activity Cycle. She was told to continue her usual schedule but to do an ultradian healing response when she felt a need to. It was emphasized that her inner mind and body could use this time to solve their own problems in their own way. Problems with marriage and family, for example, sometimes could be "sorted out" in ways that were surprising or even unknown to the conscious mind.

The next week she reported much less irritability and "a lot more energy throughout the day, but I only slept a little better." She said her ultradian healing periods took 20-30 minutes and she noticed that she seemed to have "a lot going on inside during these times." She was encouraged to discuss whatever ideas and fantasies were going on during her ultradian rest-rejuvenation periods that might be related to her mood problems. She reviewed a number of family problems and summarized them by saying it was important to "live and let live in order to get along in this world." The depth of this insight certainly was not profound from a traditional psychodynamic point of view, but it apparently was enough so that she could recover her emotional equilibrium and sense of well being.

For the next week she was instructed to keep her bedtime the same but to get up at 8:00 a.m. instead of later in the morning and to keep up the ultradian healing when it felt right. She reported that this gave her energy during the day so she was not irritable but she still had trouble getting to sleep. She stated: "The energy is so good I have my husband doing ultradian healing too. It helps pace our day, and we have been eating regular meals and bike riding together." This was a hint that while her husband still remained refractory to psychological insight, there was at least a synchronization of their activities that led to some improvement in their relationship. She reports that her husband now feels rested enough so they can both enjoy being together baby-sitting their grandchildren in the evenings two nights per week while their son and daughter-in-law attend night-school courses. That is, by enjoying more comfortable, guilt-free low phase ultradian healing responses throughout the day, they were both able to enjoy better high ultradian phases of peak activities and family relatedness as well. It is very important that senior citizens in retirement have adequate rest so they can more fully participate in the 20 minute peaks of the Basic Rest Activity Cycle. Getting optimal exercise in the daytime, such as bicycle riding for this couple, will in turn help them sleep better at night. Hopefully they will get enough exercise so they will sleep more deeply so that the release of growth hormone may be facilitated in the first 90 minutes of sleep that will in turn tend to optimize the immune system and a host of other natural healing functions during sleep (See Figure 6.1).

One of the more significant unresolved issues of this case involves the patient's communication problems with her husband which had become acute due to their being together more after retirement. There is at least a hint in this case, however, that their *learning how to synchronize their mindbody states by eating, resting, bike riding and baby-sitting together may lead to further rapport on an emotional-cognitive level.* This view is supported by empirical studies that document the importance of the synchronization of ultradian and circadian rhythms for harmonious interaction between couples (Chiba et al., 1977; Rossi and Nimmons, 1991) and the social process in general (Hayes and Cobb, 1978; Moore-Ede et al., 1982).

Addictions: Alcohol, Sugar, Cocaine, Marijuana, Caffeine, Nicotine

The relationship between stress and addiction (Gottheil et al., 1987) has led us to explore the utilization of ultradian dynamics with a variety of chemical dependencies and their associated behavioral and psychosomatic dysfunctions. It has been proposed (Rossi, 1990b; Rossi and Nimmons, 1991) that when stress-related disruptions of ultradian rhythms lead to an experience of excessive fatigue many people will attempt to override their need for rest by taking an "upper" (caffeine, nicotine, cocaine etc.). When over-stimulated by the mindbody's own natural messenger molecules for heightened activation (the stress associated hormones such as ACTH, cortisol, epinephrine) people will attempt self-medication with "downers" (alcohol, marijuana, opiates etc.). Such artificial methods of chemical self-regulation ultimately fail; however, they leave a tell-tale trail of many associated habit, behavioral and psychosomatic disorders. The following cases illustrate how a variety of ultradian approaches can facilitate recovery.

Case 3: James — Smoking

Presenting Problem:

James was self-referred because he wanted to use hypnosis to quit smoking. James felt he was constantly under stress working as a high school teacher in a school where violence, drug abuse, and suicide were almost daily occurrences. His wife was pregnant with their first child, and he wanted to quit smoking before the baby was born.

Treatment:

James was administered Speigels' *Hypnotic Induction Profile* where he scored in the highly hypnotizable zone. Even in his first session he appeared to experience a deep trance that was ratified with arm levitation, amnesia and other behavioral cues. *Direct suggestions that utilized his desire to be a healthy role model* for his child were enough to motivate him to stop smoking in one session. By utilizing his desire to be a healthy role model for his child the therapist recognized how the anticipated birth of his child was a *critical phase transition* in his life that could lead to either problems of adjustment or a creative adaptive response. Utilizing his desire to be (1) a good role model for his child by (2) stopping smoking solved two problems at the same time.

Three weeks later James called stating he had not smoked but that *"several times a day"* he noted having an intense craving for a cigarette; he had resisted, but he didn't know how long he could hold out. An immediate follow-up appointment was made. During the session we first talked for half-an-hour about the smoking problem. Then James yawned, his eyes teared, and he stated, "I really need a cigarette, I really want one right now...I have a lot of stress and need to smoke." This association of typical behavioral cues of a need for ultradian rest-rejuvenation (yawning, tearing) with the experience of stress and the symptomatic need to smoke was recognized by the therapist as *an opportunity to convert what may be called an "ultradian stress syndrome" into an "ultradian healing response"* (Rossi and Nimmons, 1991).

From an Ericksonian perspective, his yawning suggested that he was beginning to experience what Erickson called "the common everyday trance" (Erickson, Rossi & Rossi, 1976; Erickson and Rossi, 1979). Jame's ongoing experience was utilized to facilitate a permissive naturalistic trance induction with the following words: *That's okay, just let yourself take a comfortable break right now ... that's right ... just allow yourself to sit back and be with the craving and enjoy not having to do anything right now about your stress ... when your inner mind is ready to let the relaxation deepen so that it can relieve the stress and craving while you rest, will you notice your eyes closing naturally all by themselves?*

James' eyes closed immediately and remained closed for about 12 minutes while he appeared to be in rapt inner focus while his body remained absolutely still. When he finally stirred a bit with a little sigh he was told: *When your conscious and unconscious minds know they can continue to allow you to enjoy periods of rest and comfort like this several times a day so you don't have to experience stress and smoking, will you find yourself awakening refreshed and alert?* About three to four minutes later, James' eyes opened and he stretched. He reported visualizing himself holding his baby and feeling proud that he did not smoke. He stated that his craving for smoking was gone.

James was instructed to let the craving to smoke become a signal that he needed an ultradian break *several times a day*; whenever he felt a craving he was to take the next available break at school to sit down and explore the deeper and more satisfying comfort of an ultradian healing rest. Two weeks later James reported that the urge to smoke had been converted into comfortable ultradian breaks *"several times a day"* when he enjoyed positive fantasies. The school brunch break was between 10:20 and 10:40 and he had developed a new habit of using it to enjoy an ultradian healing break. This also prevented him from eating the two or three doughnuts and drinking the cup of coffee he usually had during brunch. This helped him avoid the weight gain that is feared when one stops smoking.

Direct hypnotic suggestion was not enough to stop James' smoking initially because the stress he continued to experience threatened a relapse. By reframing his need to smoke into a need to do an ultradian healing response, he was able to reduce stress and give up his smoking addiction. An important clue to the appropriateness of this ultradian reframe was his exact way of phrasing how he needed to smoke *"several times a day."* While this phrase can be understood as being merely a simple cliché from a linguistic point of view, it acquires deeper significance from a chronobiological perspective where it often serves to identify an ultradian rhythm of behavior. This brief example illustrates the integration of at least four of Erickson's approaches with the ultradian psychobiological model proposed in this chapter: (1) the utilization of the patient's exact words, behavior and world view (Erickson, 1958/1980); (2) the casual and permissive utilization of the patient's ongoing behavior to initiate an indirect, permissive, naturalistic hypnotic induction (Erickson, 1959/1980; Erickson and

Rossi, 1979); (3) the reframing of symptoms of stress and converting them into signals for therapeutic self-care (Erickson and Rossi, 1989); and, (4) associating a post-hypnotic suggestion with a future behavioral inevitability (Erickson and Erickson, 1941/1980; Erickson and Rossi, 1976; Rossi, 1982). The post-hypnotic suggestion to enjoy a comforting ultradian healing response several times a day instead of smoking was associated with the behavioral inevitability that he would experience periods of stress several times a day. Taken together these four technical approaches work particularly well as a mini-model for facilitating many types of critical phase transitions in life associated with addiction problems.

Cerebral Hemisphere Dominance and Ultradian Rhythms

One of the most interesting mindbody ultradian relationships is the contralateral shift that takes place between cerebral hemispheric dominance and nasal breathing every 90-120 minutes (Gilbert and Rosenwasser, 1987; Rossi, 1986; Werntz et al., 1981). In general when the right nostril is more open (right nasal dominance) so that air enters the nose primarily on that side, the left cerebral hemispheric functions manifest more dominance; when the left nostril is more open the right hemispheric functions appear to be more evident (Klein and Armitage, 1979; Klein et al., 1986). A number of researchers are now accumulating experimental data that supports the view that this may be the psychobiological process that has been used for centuries as a yoga method of breath-brain-autonomic nervous system regulation (Funk & Clark, 1980; Kennedy et al., 1986; Rama, 1980).

It is possible to shift the nostril through which more air is entering the nose by either blocking one nostril manually or simply by lying down on one side or another (Rao and Potdar, 1970; Werntz et al., 1987). Lying down on the right side, for example, will within a few minutes open the left nostril for most individuals and will reflexively activate right hemispheric functions and sympathetic system dominance on that side of the body. In this way it is possible to gain some control over the autonomic nervous system and associated mental states (Adler, 1990; Rama et al., 1976; Werntz et al., 1981, 1983b). The associations found between hypnosis and laterality of cerebral hemispheric dominance (Frumkin et al., 1978; Levine et al., 1984; Sackeim, 1982) suggest that naturalistic hypnotic states may be facilitated by allowing patients to explore their personal experiences of this "brain-breath-autonomic nervous system link" (Rossi, 1986; Rossi and Cheek, 1988).

Case 4: Rex — Alcoholism

Presenting Problem:

Rex is a 44-year-old construction worker who has been involved in long-term treatment for alcoholism. After going through a traditional 30-day inpatient treatment program, he was referred for ongoing alcoholism counseling with the present therapist. From the beginning, he complained of cravings for alcohol *throughout the day but especially after work.*" Rex's psychodynamically-oriented therapy has been very complicated, so only the specific ultradian intervention for alcohol cravings will be presented here.

Treatment:

Rex was first taught traditional craving control techniques. He was taught to achieve a state of general relaxation using a progressive relaxation method. Along with this, he received training in developing "alcohol refusal skills" and self-assertiveness. Rex was taught the *decision delay technique* where he would delay any decision for 20 minutes before deciding to drink or not. These techniques eventually failed and Rex relapsed after work one day when his "buddies" asked him if he wanted a beer. Rex intellectually understood the techniques but "at certain times of the day the craving was just too much."

Rex's association of drinking with "certain times of the day" suggested that there may have been an ultradian component to his alcoholism. Because of this the therapist decided to help Rex explore "a possible ultradian brain-breath link" in his cravings for alcohol (Rossi, 1990b; Rossi and Cheek, 1988). During the next session while he was discussing his craving for alcohol, he found that his right nostril was open suggesting he was experiencing left hemispheric dominance at that moment. Therefore Rex was instructed to lie on his right side to "turn on his right brain hemisphere" to explore whether his feelings and cravings changed. A permissive hypnotic induction was facilitated with these words: *It's curious how just lying down on one side or the other can allow us to feel differently...if your unconscious is really ready to see pictures, have ideas, thoughts or feelings about how to handle your problem with greater comfort and ease [pause], will your eyes close comfortably all by themselves?*

Rex's eyes closed after a few moments and the therapist followed up with a *Basic Accessing Question: When your inner mind has learned some interesting ways of dealing with those problems, will you awaken feeling refreshed and alert?*

Fourteen minutes later, Rex's body moved a little in what seemed to be a prelude to awakening. The therapist then administered a posthypnotic suggestion: *When you feel like moving and opening your eyes, will that be a signal that your inner mind will continue to help you deal comfortably with your problems throughout the day but especially after work?*

Three minutes later he opened his eyes and sat up. He reported visualizing some friends from A. A. saying, "One day at a time, one minute at a time." Rex was instructed to continue using the ultradian healing response to explore shifts in his cerebral hemispheric dominance at appropriate times throughout the day. After work was chosen as a consistent time to do the exercise, since this was the time when he usually began drinking. When he checked which nostril was open at that time he found it was usually the right. This suggested that he was still in a "work mode" when his left cerebral hemisphere was more dominant. We speculated that this may be one reason why he felt a need to drink after work; perhaps the alcohol was facilitating a shift to a right hemispheric mode of relaxation. He therefore was encouraged to continue experimenting with doing an ultradian healing response by lying down on his right side to reflexively shift his hemispheric dominance to the right after work.

This therapeutic approach seemed to be just what he felt he needed to navigate safely through the dangerous time of temptation after work. In association with his continuing attendance at Alcoholics Anonymous and further insight-oriented therapy, he has been able to stop drinking completely for over a year.

It is not known whether the purported cerebral hemispheric shift during an after work ultradian healing period was a real mindbody dynamic in this case or whether it was simply just another clever suggestion with a pseudo-rationale of the type sometimes used by Erickson (1966/1980). Current research indicates that the right hemisphere is actually associated with a particular style of "the vigilance aspects of normal human attention to sensory stimuli" (Pardo et al., 1991, p. 61) rather than with simple relaxation and imagery. Further controlled research studies are required to determine whether the focus on internal sensory stimuli emphasized in the self exploratory brain-breath shift can actually enhance certain psychobiological aspects of brain laterality.

The use of a comforting ultradian approach to relaxation and self hypnosis as a therapeutic substitute for alcohol in this case, however, does appear to be an effective therapeutic strategy that has much in common with many of the other cases of addiction reported in this chapter.

Case 5: Mary — Headaches and Nausea

Presenting Problem:

Mary was referred by the County Health Department because she was experiencing extreme headaches and nausea with no explainable physical cause. She was a 17-year-old, high school senior, who had been addicted to cocaine for one year (from age 15 to 16) and had gone through a hospital treatment program. During the time she was using drugs, however, she had several older boyfriends who abused her sexually.

She had received more than a year of weekly psychotherapy with a psychiatrist who prescribed antidepressant medication. In this period of psychotherapy she worked through many of her past problems and eventually was taken off the medication, but the headaches and nausea continued. Hypnosis was considered as a last resort. Mary's present life situation was that she was working 30 hours per week while attending high school. She was almost constantly on the move and says *I never seem to have a moment to take a breather.*

Treatment:

During the first session Mary was given the *Hypnotic Induction Profile* developed by Herbert Spiegel which suggested that she was not a good subject for hypnosis. Nonetheless she appeared responsive to a traditional eye closure to hypnotic induction, and an arm levitation was used to ratify trance. Mary was given several different suggestions using auditory (relaxing music), kinesthetic (warmth) and visual (breathing in light) modalities. Prior to trance she reported her headache at 70 on a 1 - 100 subjective scale; after the trance it was 68 even though she said, "I did have some relief while I was under." During the next 8 sessions several more indirect hypnotic approaches were used including progressive relaxation, age regression, autogenic training, and metaphor. All were without much success.

On the 9th session Mary reported a severe headache (90 on a 1 to 100 subjective scale). She reported that she was in a "terrible state of tension right now because I'm so much on the go today." We wondered together whether her current feelings were typical of the way she habitually forced herself into too much activity. When she was asked to check, she found that her right nostril was open which suggested that her left cerebral hemisphere was dominant at this moment when she had a headache. Mary was instructed to lie comfortably on her right side to allow gravity to clear her left nostril and to induce a shift in cerebral hemispheric dominance to "the right emotional hemisphere." She was told that "even though your conscious mind may not know what is happening your unconscious can help find the source of your current stress and symptoms."

As Mary focused inward in apparently deep concentration, her eyelids began to flutter occasionally with a slight but high frequency as expressions of frowning, fear and discomfort crossed her face. In a few moments the facial cues of distress and restlessness became more and more pronounced. She was encouraged to explore these negative feelings with, *That's right, you can have the courage right now to continue receiving all those feelings of distress that tell the real story of your troubling symptoms.* She began to whimper softly with a few tears and then cry loudly with much restless tossing about on the couch. Since it was now evident that she was going into a strong cathartic reaction that threatened to get out of control she was supported with a *therapeutic dissociation* as follows, *That's right, as one part of you really feels that fully another part of you can watch comfortably and calmly from the sidelines so you can give an accurate report about the source of your problems later.* From the new perspective of nonlinear dynamics theory, this type of *hypnotherapeutic dissociation* would be called a *bifurcation of consciousness* that facilitated the patient's path to self-organization.

Mary then went through what appeared to be a series of emotional "flashbacks" with occasionally shouted words and phrases suggesting that she was reliving some of the negative sexual encounters she experienced while under drugs. After about twenty minutes of couch pounding and kicking off imaginary assailants Mary appeared exhausted and began to calm down. She then apparently dozed for about five minutes with a calm face. She coughed and seemed about to awaken. Taking this cue the therapist facilitated awakening with a therapeutically double-binding posthypnotic suggestion as follows: *When your unconscious mind knows it can continue this healing work all by itself whenever it's entirely appropriate [pause], and when your conscious mind knows it can cooperate by helping you recognize those moments throughout the day when it is right to take a breather [pause] will you find yourself awakening feeling refreshed, alert and as aware as you need to be of the meaning of your experience here today?*

In this way awakening from trance was made contingent on the inner healing continuing on an unconscious level while the conscious mind focused on cooperating by recognizing those ultradian mind-body cues that she needed to enjoy an ultradian healing response to break the stress cycle. When she awakened she reviewed some of the negative memories she had just re-experienced with an attitude that is rather characteristic of many young patients dealing with flash-backs to traumatic drug experiences: a part of her always seemed to know this was the source of her continuing distress, but she was not able to help herself with it in any way other than by denial and being over busy all the time in order to avoid really thinking about it.

The hypnotherapeutic work allowed both parts of her to come together: (1) the side that experienced the painful emotionally-laden memories and (2) the more rational side that needed time and support in a safe therapeutic milieu to assimilate the traumatic experience in a meaningful manner. The next few sessions were spent exploring her deepening appreciation of psychodynamic issues associated with her traumatic drug experiences, being *"too much on the go"* and helping her recognize how they were related to her symptoms of headache and nausea. During a few of her ultradian rest-rejuvenation periods she became aware that even before she had a bad headache she felt a heat in her stomach and a tension around the eyes as the first symptoms that she was under too much stress. She was instruc-ted that whenever she felt these initial *"signaling symptoms"* she was to check which nostril was open and to lie down on that side so that her "inner mind could work through whatever it needed to in a safe way." The school nurse was contacted so she would be allowed to go to her office to do this therapeutic exercise.

During the next 3 weeks Mary was able to prevent all but one headache and nausea attack and that one only reached a 40 on her 1 to 100 subjective scale. Mary reported needing to use the ultradian healing response two or three times per day. It has developed into a positive part of her lifestyle of dealing with inner issues, coping with

297

outer sources of tension before they become full-blown physical symptoms.

This case of Mary is a composite containing elements from a number of typical cases seen by the authors wherein catharsis and insight therapy were facilitated by the purported "brain-breath link to access another side of the personality." Again we stress that these cases do not prove that such a link really is responsible for the therapeutic result. The so-called "brain-breath link" may be merely a new metaphor for utilizing the current belief system in "the other side of the brain" that has been popularized in the press. Current research on the chaotobiological dynamics of the brain-breath link would be a appropriate approach to research in this area (Brown & Combs, 1995; Combs & Winkler, 1995).

Case 6: Lucy — Anxiety over Breast Feeding

Presenting Problem:

Lucy was a 21-year-old patient in marriage counseling when her first child was born. Shortly after the birth she phoned the therapist at 11 p.m. and reported severe anxiety that she could not breast feed her daughter. She had become depressed and felt guilty that her marriage problems had affected her ability to bond with the baby. At night, Lucy would lie down while facing her daughter and attempt to breast feed her and sometimes the "milk would just not come." Then the baby would cry and a vicious cycle of guilt, anxiety and further upset would take place between husband and wife.

Treatment:

During a previous session with the couple they were both taught to recognize which nostril was open. Then they were taught to lie on the side of the open nostril to "change cerebral hemispheric dominance and mood" when they were having a bad time together. This was initially used to provide a strategic intervention to disrupt the pattern of escalating argument and mutual recrimination that had developed between them about their issues and the breast feeding problem.

On the phone the therapist asked Lucy to check which nostril was open and she reported that the right nostril was. She also reported that she had been lying on her left side trying to sleep and feed the baby. The therapist instructed Lucy to lie down on her right side and take 15 minutes "to allow her inner mindbody to make the necessary changes that would enable her to nurture the baby." Then her husband was to bring her the baby to feed while she was still lying on the right side.

The next morning a follow-up call determined that this intervention had indeed helped Lucy's milk to resume flowing. She was instructed that whenever she had problems feeding her daughter, she was to check which nostril was open and lie on that side until she could "feel her cerebral hemispheric dominance change" and then to feed the baby lying on that same side. She reported that this was very effective and greatly reduced her guilt and self-derogation.

This clinical presentation does not enable us to distinguish whether the purported nasal-cerebral hemispheric dominance shift associated with a change in body position was the real therapeutic mechanism. It could, for example, simply be another illustration of a strategic family intervention facilitated by the *stochastic resonance* of the type of Ericksonian suggestions that are laden with "false contingencies and false relationships" (as discussed previously in Chapter Three). Suggestions containing false relationships and contingencies could have been effective simply because the patient and her husband believed in them. While we do not recommend the intentional use of suggestions with false relationships and contingencies, human history is rich in documentation of their effectiveness when they are believed in.

This case does provide a model, however, of a new class of ultradian approaches that could be used in controlled clinical research to explore the possibility of a complex cybernetic loop of mind-molecular communication. It is now well known, for example that prolactin is a peptide messenger molecule (hormone) released from the pituitary in typical ultradian rhythms (Veldhuis and Johnson, 1988) to mediate lactation at the cellular-genetic level (Bolander, 1989). Recent reports have documented how a 20 minute relaxation/imagery tape can increase milk flow for premature infants (Feher et al., 1989). Research now is needed to assess the hypothesis that many methods of relaxation, imagery, hypnosis and holistic healing in general may be effective because they can facilitate a shift in the cerebral hemispheric brain-breath link that may, in turn, entrain our natural ultradian rhythms of mindbody communication at the molecular-genetic level.

Eating and Gastrointestinal Disorders

Eating and gastrointestinal disorders are another group of mindbody problems that have many ultradian components. There are well documented 90-120 minute ultradian rhythms in eating (Hiatt and Kripke, 1975), insulin and glucose levels (Mejean et al., 1988; Van Cauter et al., 1989) and urination (Lavie and Kripke, 1977). Friedman has outlined a psychophysiological model of psychosomatic illness based on the relationships between stress, psychodynamic factors and the de-synchronization of ultradian/circadian rhythms (Friedman, 1972, 1978; Friedman and Fischer, 1967).

Case 7: Jennifer — Diabetes

Presenting problem:

This 37-year-old client requested help with her "addiction for sugar." She is a severe diabetic (diagnosed at age eleven) and is currently taking 65 units of insulin daily. Her father died in 1969 from diabetes. She had a long history of denying seriousness of her condition and routinely binged on sugar and sweets. She had a particular weakness for the icing on birthday and wedding cakes and was hospitalized once for such sugar bingeing.

The younger of 2 children, having a half-sister 5 years her senior, the client grew up in turmoil. Her father was physically abusive and both mother and sister had history of alcoholism and suicide attempts. She attempted suicide at age 15 and then became pregnant and married at age 15 in order, "to get away from home." She was divorced 4 years later and raised her son on her own.

She was seen a total of 7 times over a 2 month period. She routinely took "20 minute naps" during her lunch break. Therefore, the therapist talked to her about the ultradian healing response and suggested that she increase the number to 4-6 times daily. She never was able to do that but she did average at least one or two extra healing periods daily. Since she apparently had an ability to do lucid dreaming, we utilized that skill during the ultradian healing response to enhance her feeling of comfort and well being. Her ability to relate creatively to her dreams was continually linked with her growing ability to cope with her sugar addiction.

She reports that she has not eaten any sugar for the past 4 1/2 months. She described how a friend had her over for a visit this week and offered her a piece of pie with coffee. She casually refused by saying, "I don't do pie!" During a 4 1/2 month period, she has been to three birthday parties and has been "exposed" to the type of cake she formerly found irresistible. She ate none of it. She is still aware of her psychological/emotional desire for sugar, but she now feels she can continue to control it. She describes herself as being "inner-motivated by the deep comfort" she can experience during her ultradians which is a new experience for her. She still takes her one or two rest breaks daily, and describes them by saying: "They take the cake! Really, they relieve the anxiety that in the past would have caused me to eat cake or sweets. They replace the cake!" When asked if it was difficult to find time for the ultradian breaks each day, she laughingly replied, "Are you kidding? It's a piece of cake!"

While there was no reported increase in traditional psycho-dynamic insight in this case, the humorous word play she used to describe her experience is reminiscent of Erickson's emphasis on humor as a significant dynamic in the healing process (Erickson and Rossi, 1989). Her spontaneous remarks equating her ultradian comfort with the anxiety relief that she formerly received from cake ("They replace the cake...It's a piece of cake!") sound like what Erickson might describe as the "literal and concrete" crossover or overlapping of two essentially different types of experience (rest and eating) to facilitate the healing process (Erickson and Rossi, 1976, p. 21). She was able to access the comfort of the ultradian rest-rejuvenation state and utilize it rather than cake to cope with anxiety.

We can only speculate about the actual psychobiological mechanisms involved in this type of situation. We do know that many messenger molecules with similar relaxing and comforting effects (e.g. the endorphin family) are released by eating and rest (Tache et al., 1989). That may be the reason why eating and rest feel so right together. Further research will be needed to assess the hypothesis that there is an actual overlap in the release of similar messenger molecules by such crossover experiences in the ultradian approaches to facilitating psychotherapy. This would provide a psychobiological communication link at the molecular level for the cybernetic process whereby the inner resources of one type of life experience (e.g. the ultradian healing response) are used to facilitate healing of another life experience (e.g. anxiety problems and sugar addiction).

Case 8: Fred — Obesity

Presenting problem:

After a year of rather unsuccessful conventional hypnotic approaches to diet control (and a lifetime of unsuccessful dieting by most advertised methods) a 67-year-old lawyer had success for the first time with what the senior author has dubbed "The Ultradian

Diet." The Ultradian Diet consists of six small meals of 200 to 300 well balanced calories spaced throughout the day to coincide with our natural 90-120 minute ultradian hunger rhythm (Rossi and Nimmons, 1991). The cholesterol lowering, the reduced need for insulin, and the generally health-promoting aspects of such an ultradian eating pattern are now well documented (Jenkins, 1989 et al.,). The patient is usually advised to enjoy the meal and then "reward yourself with a 20 minute Ultradian Healing Response during which your body will make an efficient beginning in digesting the food to the point where you will feel completely satisfied." This process is carried out first in a hypnotherapy session wherein the patient actually eats his 200-300 calories and then experiences a natural ultradian therapeutic trance under the direction of the therapist. Posthypnotic suggestions are given to support the same type of ultradian eating-rest rejuvenation experience every few hours in daily life.

Treatment:

The 67-year-old lawyer was able to use these natural ultradian healing periods after each meal for what he called "deep meditations" on the course and meaning of his life. He "spontaneously" received insights into the early life sources of his hunger in a series of remarkable "flashbacks" wherein he felt himself to be a baby who continually had to spit out food because he was overfed by his mother. During a naturalistic and permissively oriented hypnotherapy he would spontaneously (with no suggestions from the therapist) lay down on the couch and go through an apparent age regression wherein he made sucking and eating movements as if he was an infant. He believed that this forced overeating as an infant accounted for the fact that even now when he overeats he really does not feel hungry and does not want to eat.

He was able to use this insight to relate to his compulsion to overeat by following the post-hypnotic suggestion to have a small meal every two or three hours followed by what he called his "deep ultradian meditation." The effectiveness of this post-hypnotic suggestion in helping him steadily lose 30 pounds over a two year period may be accounted for by Erickson's method of reinforcing post-hypnotic suggestions by "associating them with behavioral inevitabilities" (Erickson and Erickson, 1941/1980; Erickson and Rossi, 1979). It is a normal behavioral inevitability that (1) most people will experience hunger every few hours throughout the day (Freidman and Fischer, 1967; Hiatt, 1975) and (2) people need to experience rest, relaxation and sometimes sleep after eating. Associating post-hypnotic suggestions for small meals with both of these behavioral inevitabilities thus provides the meals with a double reinforcement.

Case 9: Gary — Encopresis.

Presenting Problem:

The family was referred by the school counselor because the oldest son, Andy, had developed a severe behavior problem, was cutting school and had been suspended for smoking marijuana at a night football game. The 14-year-old was placed in a drug and alcohol intervention group. In the group sessions he discussed some of the problems in his family that were associated with both parents being "high powered executives" under terrible stress. These parents apparently had very high expectations that both Andy and his little brother Gary, age 10, did not feel they could live up to.

Family therapy was indicated and the family complied probably because of the guilt the parents had about their overworking. The group therapy and family therapy improved Andy's self esteem and his school behavior after about nine months of hard work. During that time the therapist developed a deep level of trust with the whole family. At one point, about three months into the treatment (as treatment began to truly focus on the family system) as the focus started to come off Andy as the identified patient, the issue of Gary's soiling came up. Gary had been potty trained by the age of four but occasionally soiled his pants until age six when his mother went back to work.

For the past three years, one to two times per week, while Gary was playing during the day, he would have an "accident" and pass feces. He would then call his mother to come and take care of him. This could be very shaming for him at the school, day care, or even at home if he was playing with friends. Sometimes his mother could not get off work so the father would have to bring Gary some clean clothes. The family dynamics showed an overly strong coalition between Gary and his mother with Gary's father being distant and aloof from him. The father enjoyed Andy more because, "he's more into sports and cars like I am." This structure indicated that more bonding was needed between Gary and his father. An adequate presentation of the psychodynamics of this entire family therapy is beyond the scope of this chapter; therefore the focus will be on the utilization of the Ultradian Healing Response as a strategic maneuver to cope with the encopresis.

Treatment:

A few sessions were conducted with Gary and his father to help them relate together. In one of these sessions Gary's father brought up the soiling issue, and while we were discussing it Gary's eyes teared up, his breathing deepened, and he began staring out the window. The therapist believed this withdrawal behavior was at least in part related to his need to turn inward to cope with the shame he was experiencing. Since some of these withdrawal behaviors were similar to those that are naturally experienced when entering a natural ultradian rest-rejuvenation period, however, the therapist reframed his obvious state of discomfort into an ultradian healing response by saying, *I notice you seem to be getting quieter in the last few minutes and you're not saying much while you're looking out the window. I wonder if that means you would really like to just rest a bit and be comfortable with your father. Just continue as you are Gary and see if it feels good to take a rest or maybe nap with your dad.* Gary eyes fluttered for a few minutes and then closed. I motioned the father to put his arms around Gary as he snuggled close to his father.

The father then closed his eyes as the therapist stated, *I wonder just how aware you are that you're both doing just what you need to do to feel good together and solve your problems...take some time to enjoy it.* After about twenty minutes they stirred, so the therapist said, *Continue your good feelings together and know that it can continue in the whole family when you enjoy being together. When something within you feels it has dealt with your problems as much as possible right now, will you find yourselves waking up refreshed and alert with a good stretch?*

After a while they both opened their eyes and stretched. They commented how they had not really rested together like that since before Gary started school. Gary said, "Even though it seemed kind of kooky I really feel good now." A few minutes later Gary asked if he could use the bathroom, as he "could now feel his tummy moving." He successfully passed stools under complete voluntary control and was obviously pleased with himself as he came out of the rest room and faced his father and the therapist with a broad smile.

Gary and his father were told to rest comfortably together this way once or twice a day when it "felt right." They agreed to this and the school nurse was notified to let Gary lie down in her office during recess or lunch time when he asked. His teacher was also instructed to let him go to the nurse's office when he needed to. Gary later reported that the "napping" helped him feel what was "going on" inside him. He has not had an accidental bowl movement for the past six months.

Recognizing the optimal therapeutic moment when the young boy's shameful behavior overlapped the typical withdrawal aspects of the normal rest-rejuvenation phase of ultradian behavior was the key to the critical transition in a deeply healing naturalistic trance that brought Gary and his father together in a comfortable mindbody state of non-verbal synchrony. This was clearly an example of how "Low Phase Hypnosis" (discussed in Chapter Four) can be used in parent-child relationships (Rossi & Nimmons, 1991). The use of appropriate touch and non-verbal communication for indirect trance induction via "the common everyday trance" has been a central theme in much of Erickson's work (Erickson, 1964/1980; Erickson and Rossi, 1976). The ultradian theory of hypnotherapeutic work simply makes clear that there are particularly auspicious periods throughout the day when mindbody synchrony and emotional rapport can be facilitated in an optimal manner.

Ultradian Sensitivity and Psychological Insight

One of the most significant aspects of experiencing the Ultradian Healing Response from a clinical point of view is the heightened sensitivity many people develop for their usually unnoticed mindbody sensations during these subtle shifts in consciousness throughout the day (Broughton, 1975; Dinges and Broughton, 1989). This is particularly true of women undergoing the hormonal shifts in many mindbody messenger molecules associated with their monthly cycles. This case, quoted verbatim from a patient's ultradian diary, was contributed by Donna Spencer of St. Louis (Rossi and Cheek, 1988).

Case 10: Barbara — Ovulation, Sensation and Insight

Barbara writes the following in her diary:

I was very intent on finishing the final chapter of the book I had been reading for the past few hours when my eyes began to droop and my concentration waned. I forced myself to keep reading, yet realized an ultradian was coming on — so maybe I'd best let my eyes close for just a moment. Just as I sighed and closed my eyes I was aware of the feeling of a module-like substance in my fallopian tube with accompanying familiar feeling of sensitivity and receptivity. I thought, "Oh, I must be ovulating..." As I relaxed more I became aware of an immense feeling of warmth and lubrication in my genital area. I decided to feel down there. Sure enough — a warm, lubricated and pulsating vagina — all ready to make a baby — if only I were 26 years old instead of being 47 years old — and didn't already have all the beautiful children I could handle! Yet, how wonderfully and simply this body responds and communicates with consciousness moment by moment. We need only to "tune in" to the rhythm by paying attention to the natural ultradian moments throughout normal everyday life. If I were 26, this would be the exact time to become impregnated.

This unusually perceptive ultradian diary report supports the view that the ultradian healing response can be used as "a window of heightened inner awareness for accessing subtle mindbody signals and inner resources for dealing with problems" (Rossi and Nimmons, 1991). The following case reports another set of quotations from a patient's ultradian diary in which she apparently receives "spontaneous insights" into psychological as well as dietary sources of her sinus condition.

Case 11: Andrea — Sinus Congestion

Andrea writes the following in her diary.

I laid down but my mind seemed resistant to taking an ultradian break. I listen to sounds around me (birds, children, classical music). Thoughts were of things I 'have to do' or 'should be doing.' I just let these thoughts be, but also chanted a mantra silently to myself. Breathing became more shallow and I worried about falling asleep. *One thought kept recurring that seemed significant. Sinus congestion occurs more frequently when I have something to say that might not be agreeable to my partner.*

Next day: Lots of long, luxurious stretching. But, would you believe it, also feelings of guilt for tuning into quiet ultradian time (my partner would call this "the Catholic-girl syndrome"). After a while these guilt feelings/thoughts went away and I felt extremely relaxed. *Another thought that came to mind regarding my sinus congestion is wine. I've noticed that if I have wine with my dinner, I am much more congested the following morning.*

These spontaneous insights into the possible interpersonal (difficulty talking with her partner) and dietary sources of her sinus condition certainly are not in themselves evidence of real causation in a scientific sense. They do, however, provide her with hints about what changes she might explore to cope with the sinus symptoms. Further research will be needed to determine the similarities and differences between perceptions received during the ultradian healing response, classical psychoanalytic free association and what has been traditionally called "hypnogogic" and "hypnopompic" states on the border of going to sleep and waking up (Rossi, 1972/1985/1988), Rossi, 1990d).

Shock and Insight in the Resolution of Psychosomatic Problems

One of the most dramatic examples of how the ultradian healing response can facilitate psychological insight and the resolution of traumatically induced psychosomatic problems is presented in the following diary record of a psychotherapist in his sixties who had previously tried many forms of psychotherapy and hypnosis with no success in resolving a chronic problem of "throat constriction" that had bothered him for about thirty years. This person attended a professional presentation on "The Ultradian Healing Response" by the senior author and a few months later mailed him an ultradian diary that included the following entries from the third and fourth day of exploring his personal experiences.

Case 12: John — Throat Constriction, Electric Shock and Memory

John writes in his ultradian diary:

> Relaxed almost immediately, letting go of thoughts, trying not to concentrate on anything. Memory of an electrical shock in 1954 (one phase 220V of a 440V circuit), the sulfuric taste in my throat again just as it was then. Strange, I haven't thought of that in years. Throat relaxes, taste fades, no sense of constriction. As I arose from rest, my legs tingled with the increased flow of blood to them as I stood up.

> *Next day*: Relaxed almost immediately, become aware of my body, tension in my throat. Throat begins to relax, all feeling of stricture leaves throat. Thoughts of the afternoon's plans and activities. Up relaxed and refreshed.

Follow up calls six months and a year after these journal entries indicate that he is still using the ultradian healing response about once a day to maintain a satisfactory resolution of his throat constriction.

This apparently "spontaneous" resolution of a significant, traumatically induced psychosomatic symptom during the ultradian healing response reminds us of the discovery of the role of trauma and stress in the early history of psychopathology and psychoanalysis (Ellenbeger, 1970; Zilboorg and Henry, 1941). Breuer and Freud (1985/1957) reported how their work led from a gradual replacement of an authoritative approach, to hypnotic induction, to the use of "free association" to access and trace the sources of traumatically induced psychological problems and psychosomatic symptoms.

Freud believed he had given up the use of hypnosis. From our point of view he had only given up a direct and obvious form of hypnotic induction; his procedure of allowing patients to lie on a couch and free associate is actually an indirect form of hypnotic induction that has much in common with what we now call the "ultradian healing response." We speculate that in the ordinary course of everyday life most people have an "ultradian rest-rejuvenation deficit": they have skipped one or more of the natural 20 minute rest-rejuvenation phases of the Basic Rest Activity Cycle (BRAC) we typically experience every few hours throughout the day (Kleitman, 1970). Because of this ultradian deficit most people will immediately and automatically experience an ultradian healing response whenever they are given an opportunity to sit or lie down and rest a bit.

We hypothesize that the mild stress of lying down and "free associating" about one's problems can occasionally reactivate the state-dependent encoding of trauma/stress induced psychosomatic problems that lead to a recovery of memories about their sources (Rossi, 1986; Rossi and Cheek, 1988; Rossi 1990c & d; Rossi, 1996a). The senior author has outlined research supporting *The Neuropeptide Hypothesis Of Consciousness And Catharsis* that accounts for the arousal and relaxation phases of cathartic psychotherapy by the time-linked release of ACTH and B-endorphin from their mother molecule, POMC (proopiomelanocortin) over a 20-30 minute period. Carefully controlled research monitoring the real time release of these informational messenger molecules during psychotherapy will be required to assess this hypothesis and our proposed use of the 20 minute ultradian rest-rejuvenation period as a "window of opportunity" for accessing and facilitating many natural mindbody healing processes.

The following report contributed by Jeffrey Auerbach, Ph.D., a psychotherapist in Los Angeles, documents a vivid experience of our hypothesized relationship between shock, trauma, stress, symptom formation and the ultradian healing response. It also illustrates how a spontaneous "hypnotic phenomenon" like catalepsy (italicized below) can occur in response to a shock in everyday life (Erickson and Rossi, 1981).

Case 13: William — Shock, Trauma and Ultradian Dynamics

"Does a shock to the body trigger an ultradian rest state?" One morning at the office, I fell off a chair and crashed to the ground on my right hip. Stunned, I lay there without moving and thought that I had badly injured myself.

The secretary rushed in, asked if I was all right, and said, *You can put that chair down. Without realizing it, I was holding a chair that I bumped into, up in the air with one hand.* I found that I had no injuries. After a few moments I stood up and prepared to see patients. I felt unfocused, a lack of ability to concentrate, tired, and in general, "spacey." I realized that I felt as if I was in the "rest" phase of an ultradian cycle — which I normally did not feel at that time of the day. I wanted very much to just lay down and close my eyes, which I did. Twenty minutes later I felt alert and I returned to work.

"It was as if the significant shock to my body produced an alteration in consciousness very similar to the feeling of being in the rest phase of the ultradian cycle. Cheek reports that often a sudden movement to the body of a hospitalized patient produces a hypnotic state (Rossi & Cheek, 1988). Then, after twenty minutes, which approximates my usual ultradian healing response period, I felt rejuvenated and alert."

Discussion

Taken together these cases suggest how the chaotobiological dynamics of hypnotherapeutic work can utilize ultradian dynamics to facilitate a variety of naturalistic approaches to mindbody healing. Ultradian dynamics open up the possibility of breaking hypnosis out of the rather one-sided overemphasis on psychological causation proposed since the Benjamin Franklin Commission of 1784, which reported that the essential nature of hypnosis was nothing but imagination, faith, hope and suggestion. Two hundred years of therapeutic experience with hypnosis indicates that something more than imagination, suggestion and metaphor is involved. Mental experience can modulate body processes, and vice versa, in cybernetic patterns of information transduction.

There has been no comprehensive theory of therapeutic hypnosis that could account for the source of the psychobiological phenomena of hypnosis or its healing effects on the body. The ultradian theory of hypnotherapeutic work proposes a systematic approach to exploring this gap in our understanding by providing a new window of opportunity for accessing and resolving mindbody problems at many levels — from the social-psychological to the molecular-genetic. The case studies of this chapter suggest a number of new ways of utilizing ultradian\circadian psychobiological dynamics for facilitating a number of naturalistic approaches to psychotherapy as follows.

1. *How to recognize ultradian/circadian related problems.*

Therapists can recognize a possible ultradian\circadian etiology whenever patients describe the periodic occurrence of their symptoms and problems with such commonly-used phrases as: "These symptoms keep coming up *several times a day*...every once in a while throughout the day...when I get tired... when I get stressed...a few times in the afternoon and evening...when I get hungry...usually after eating...when I need to go to the rest room...when I start to fall behind in my work...every few hours throughout the night." These phrases are such commonly used clichés that their significance as signals of the ultradian, periodic nature of the reported symptoms are usually not recognized by patients or therapists.

The circadian periodicity of problems can be recognized by the patient's statements about the *daily* occurrence of a symptom at a particular time of the day: "It usually feels worse in the morning... afternoon ... evening ... night." A very common form of circadian problem periodicity takes place in the middle or late afternoon. This has been called "Breaking Point" (Tsuji and Kobayashi, 1988) which is precisely the time when the *per* gene turns on to eventually initiate another circadian cycle at the cellular level (Takahashi & Hoffman, 1995). By this time of the day many people have already skipped two or three natural ultradian rest periods so that an accumulated ultradian deficit and stress syndrome is expressed with these common complaints: "I'm exhausted by mid-afternoon...I get stressed, tense and irritable toward the end of the workday...I need a drink after work ... My addiction gets worse later in the day when I have to have something ... I get sleepy in the afternoon...the worst time is when I have to go home after school and I'm too tired to do homework...just before dinner everybody is irritable and that's when arguments start." Many of these acute and chronic periodic problems man be ameliorated by taking one or two ultradian breaks earlier in the day or taking a nap after lunch or early in the afternoon.

Other periodic psychobiological problems with a longer rhythms such as the monthly menstrual cycle and the yearly seasonal affect disorders (SAD), have been omitted in this chapter but they have been dealt with in detail elsewhere (Kupfer et al., 1988; Rossi and Nimmons, 1991; Rosenthal, 1989).

2. *Utilizing minimal cues and heightened sensitivity to mindbody signaling.*

Our hypothesized association between the normal behaviors of the rest phase of the ultradian Basic Rest Activity Cycle and Erickson's common everyday trance and "Indicators of Trance Development" (Erickson and Rossi, 1976) can help therapists become more aware of the significance of many minimal cues of patient's changing states of consciousness for facilitating hypnotherapy and "creative moments" of inner work utilizing imagery, free association, meditative and emotional re-experiencing. This approach was documented in most of the cases in this chapter where patients learned to become more aware of the first subtle mindbody signals of their need to take ultradian rest-rejuvenation breaks to avoid the type of excess stress that could exacerbate their symptomatology.

Symptom scaling is a very useful approach for heightening patients' sensitivity to their symptoms so that they can better appreciate those periods throughout the day when symptoms threaten to get worse as well as the "just noticeable therapeutic improvements" that can motivate and reinforce their progress. The associated therapeutic approach of *symptom prescription* to help patients learn to recognize "how to turn on their symptoms to make them momentarily worse" is useful for accessing the state dependent encoding of mindbody problems so they can more readily learn "how to make the symptom better (Rossi, 1986/1993)."

3. *The entrainment and synchronization of inner resources for problem solving.*

While Erickson and his students have extensively documented how to help patients access their personal repertoire of social and psychological life experiences as "inner resources" for problem solving (Erickson, 1980; Lankton and Lankton, 1983; Lankton and Zeig, 1989; Yapko, 1989, 1990; Zeig, 1994), there has been relatively little updating of what Erickson called the "psychoneurophysiological" basis of hypnotherapy (Erickson, 1980b; Rossi & Cheek, 1988; Rossi & Ryan, 1989). A variety of the cases presented in this chapter document how it is precisely those mindbody processes that have an ultradian or circadian periodicity that are sensitive to distortion by the types of psychosocial stimuli that may lead to psychosomatic symptoms.

Just as acute and chronic aversive psychosocial stimuli can desynchronize our normal rhythms of psychobiological health so too can the constructive use of psychosocial stimuli in hypnotherapeutic work be used to entrain and synchronize a return to optimal chaotological dynamics of mindbody communication for healing within the individual patient (cases 1, 3, 4, 5, 7, 8, 12 and 13) as well as healing between people (cases 2, 6, 9, 11).

4. *Converting symptoms into signals, problems into resources.*

The psychobiological perspective presented in this chapter interprets many mindbody problems as symptoms of the *ultradian stress response*: many psychosomatic symptoms are a response to the stress engendered when patients chronically ignore and override their natural need to have a rest-rejuvenation period every few hours throughout the day (Rossi and Nimmons, 1991). A useful therapeutic approach in such cases frequently involves the utilization of patients' current feelings of distress and experiences of psychosomatic symptoms in the therapy session to access the sources of their mindbody problems and motivate appropriate changes in their lives.

This may involve utilizing and reframing many stress symptoms of resistance in psychotherapy into an ultradian healing experience. This was demonstrated in case nine when Gary's feelings of shame and withdrawal were converted into an ultradian healing response wherein he could experience a warm non-verbal emotional bonding with his father. A careful review of Erickson's methods of "utilizing the patient's resistance" from this perspective documents how he frequently channeled the patient's withdrawal behavior into an inner experience of therapeutic trance (Erickson, 1958\1980, 1959/1980.)

5. *Evolving Consciousness in Psychotherapy and Everyday life.*

From the broadest point of view the ultradian healing response may be understood as a window for accessing and facilitating "creative moments" in everyday life as well as in psychotherapy (Broughton, 1975; Rossi, 1972/1985/1998). Erickson demonstrated how hypnotherapy can facilitate profound shifts and broadening of an individual's consciousness during "The common every day trance" (Erickson, 1980; Erickson and Rossi, 1989; Rossi and Ryan, 1991). In this chapter we have seen how this can take place during the ultradian healing response in a variety of ways as formal self-hypnosis without participation by the therapist (Cases 5, 8, 10, 11, 12 and 13).

The Basic Ideas

1. *Hypnotherapeutic work with psychosomatic disorders may be regarded as a process of facilitating information transduction between mind, brain and body. The case presentations of this chapter document how a variety of naturalistic approaches can be used to help patients enhance their sensitivity and awareness of their personal patterns of mindbody coding and signaling to access and resolve their problems.*

2. *The ultradian healing response is the psychobiological basis of self-hypnosis: a natural 15-20 minute window of opportunity for accessing mindbody problems that come up every 90-120 minutes or so throughout the day (at night we dream for about 20-30 minutes every 90-120 minutes). This means that there are about six periods during our waking ours in which naturalistic ultradian approaches to hypnosis can be optimized. Since hypnotherapeutic work can be encoded in a state-dependent manner during these ultradian periods this may provide a new psychobiological basis for facilitating posthypnotic suggestion. Once a suggestion has been encoded in an ultradian healing period, it will be more easily accessed and expressed to some degree in subsequent ultradian periods.*

3. *The concept of hypnotherapeutic work as a process of entraining the natural chaotobiological variations of our ultradian rhythms of self-regulation provides a systematic approach to exploring new hypnotherapeutic approaches in the consulting room as well as in everyday life. We hypothesize that any rhythmic psychobiological process that is entrained and synchronized by psychosocial cues will be responsive to hypnotherapeutic work and visa versa.*

Epilogue:
Future Prospects For
Mind-body Healing

This book had its earliest roots in my journeyman days 25 years ago when I observed and studied the hypnotherapeutic work of Milton H. Erickson. Right from the beginning my observations and understanding were mostly wrong. Erickson's first lesson was for me to stop watching him during hypnotherapy. He taught me how to focus my attention entirely on the patient. It was an error to believe that Erickson was doing things *to* people — that he was putting them into trance — that *he* was the active therapeutic agent while the patient was the passive receiver.

Erickson explained that his approach was *naturalistic* in the sense that he very carefully observed his patients natural behavior and continually *utilized* their own language, world view and inner resources to help them solve their own problems in their own way. This is easier said than done! How does one learn to do this? What are the critical observations that need be made? How does one utilize these observations to facilitate the patient's own problem solving and healing?

My eight years of intensive study with Erickson during the last years of his life gradually led me to observe certain regularities within the continually original, humorous and endless creativity of his hypnotherapeutic work. People usually would come into his office and tell their story in their own way without interruption. After about 20 minutes, a half hour, or at most an hour or so, the patient might pause with a look of inquiry at Erickson. The Golden Moment! Erickson called it a moment of *response attentiveness*: the patient was fully focused on Erickson with an attitude of expectation and an apparent readiness to receive and respond to what Erickson now said or did.

In normal everyday life Erickson made related observations that suggested how most people will *pause spontaneously* and experience what he called *"The Common Everyday Trance"* at various times throughout the day in a natural sort of way all by themselves. Most of us are aware of this in ourselves and others but we usually do not pay too much attention to it. Our usual perception is that we were tired, daydreaming, sleepy or just a little hungry and we needed to pause and take-a-break for a little while. We need to catch up with ourselves, recover from our efforts to cope with the stresses of life and prepare for the next task that is facing us. Humble as it may seem, this simple, common everyday observation is the foundation of what this book is all about.

As I explored the question of why people might be more receptive to therapeutic suggestion, recovery and healing during these natural rest periods, I stumbled upon a vast landscape of chronobiological research stretching back about 200 years — approximately the same age as the field of hypnotherapy! What is the purpose and meaning of the recurring time periods, rhythms and synchronies of behavior ranging from the seasons of one's life to the monthly, daily, hourly and even minute by minute cycles we all experience? Is it really just a coincidence that Anton Mesmer, a major source of what we today call "hypnotherapy," believed that all healing was related to these natural rhythms of *"the intensification and the remission"* of all life processes? Is this related to the paradoxical finding of current theory and research that hypnosis apparently can be a state of *active arousal* as well as *passive relaxation*?

Until recently, the rhythms and wave nature of consciousness and behavior have been a little appreciated leitmotif of research in all the life sciences. We now know that memory, learning and behavior are related to the natural rhythms in the circadian (daily) and ultradian (90-120 minute) pulsate flow of hormonal messenger molecules that are the major communication channel between brain and body. Yes, these messenger molecules were the original form of communication when life first evolved on the single cell level. These messenger molecules modulate the activity of all our nerves and every cell of our brain. Further, these messenger molecules modulate the rhythmical expression of genes within every cell of the body, which in turn leads to the production of other messenger molecules that flow through the blood stream back to the brain to modulate the state-dependent experiences of cognition, imagery and emotion that we loosely call "mind."

The basic hypothesis of this book is that this complex loop of "mind-gene" communication is expressed in our everyday experience of the alternating rhythms of waking and sleeping, active work, play and relaxation, problem solving and healing. I view Erickson's "Common Everyday Trance" and "response readiness" as a window through which we may observe, communicate and interact with these naturally alternating phases of arousal and relaxation that take place on all levels from mind and behavior to gene. The basic idea is that hypnotherapy may "entrain" (synchronize or optimize) the arousal phase ("High Phase Hypnosis") to facilitate performance in learning, work and play as well as the relaxation phase ("Low Phase Hypnosis") to support our natural psychobiological processes of healing and recovery. Chronobiology provides a window into the psychobiology of hypnotherapy

The unexpected implication of this new point of view is that we do not have to analyze, suggest or program behavior in hypnotherapeutic work. People undergo entirely natural phase transitions in the chronobiological flux of mindbody communication that is the basic dynamic of problem solving and healing. The new ideo-dynamic approaches presented in this book, such as the Basic Accessing Question, help people access these naturally adaptive capacities and inner resources to facilitate creativity in a permissive manner that respects their individuality. We find, to our surprise, that psychological problems and symptoms are actually mindbody signals of potentially creative phase transitions taking place in our lives. With a bit of wisdom we can learn how to use our so-called problems as The Symptom Path to Enlightenment.

But is all this really true? Aye, there's the rub! A handful of researchers over the past decade have done about a dozen pilot studies to document that there is some sort of relationship between hypnotic susceptibility, healing, psychoimmunology and chronobiology. But what, precisely, is the relationship? We still see it only through a window darkly. The first interpretation of the data was that hypnotic susceptibility was periodic on a circadian (daily) and ultradian (approximately every few hours or so) basis. Further research to confirm this early interpretation immediately ran into difficulties, however. The relationship is not a simple linear, one-to-one association between hypnosis and time of day; it involves a host of variables involving personality, stress, and psychobiological factors such as whether one is an owl or lark (more alert in the evening or early morning). This is exactly what we should have expected, yet it leaves the chronobiological theory of hypnotherapeutic mindbody healing on shaky scientific ground. How do we cope with this?

Welcome to the brave new world of nonlinear dynamics and Chaos Theory in psychology and the life sciences. If current research methods establish that there is some sort of relationship between complex and constantly changing variables that is difficult to measure and confirm because it is not linear then, *ipso facto*, it must be nonlinear! We now enter the world of mathematical dynamics as it evolved over the past few centuries from its classical beginning in the calculus of Newton and Leibniz to the development of nonlinear dynamics in the work of Poincaré about 100 years ago. It is only now, about 100 years later, that we suddenly notice that the nonlinear dynamics of Poincaré and the psychodynamics of Freud and Jung developed simultaneously within the same *zeitgeist*. Are they related? Have we found, at last, the mathematical language for a truly scientific depth psychology and hypnotherapy?

We began this book with the quixotic quest of bringing together the psycho*dynamics* of hypnosis with the nonlinear *dynamics* of modern Chaos Theory. We are under no illusion of having completed in this quest. We honestly acknowledge that we are still in a preparatory stage where we sometimes appear to be tilting at windmills. We have seen how similarities in the language of psychodynamics and nonlinear dynamics are intuitively compelling. We do not yet have a generally accepted scientific methodology, however, to explore their apparent association either empirically or by formal proof. The first half of this book has only begun the assembly of the types of theory, data and research that are needed to reformulate the foundations of hypnotherapy from the first principles it shares with the current mainstream of mathematics, physics and biology. Even this beginning, however, is sufficient to clarify how hypnotherapy may move from mystery and magic to genuine understanding.

Our new understanding is that the so-called "magic" of hypnotherapeutic suggestion operates just as many other psychosocial variables that can influence (that is, modulate, entrain, synchronize, orchestrate, optimize or disrupt, desynchronize and suppress) our natural psychobiological rhythms of performance and healing on all levels from the cognitive-behavioral to the molecular biology of genetic expression. Hypnosis was a mystery only because we did not understand the "Mindbody Problem": how are all the different levels of mind and behavior related to brain, body and gene? The big news is that they communicate! The "messenger molecules" of mind and body speak the same language! The currently emerging fields of neurobehavioral science such as psychoneuroimmunology and psychoendocrinology are providing the linguistic psychobiological data base for a hypnotherapy of the future.

The communicational and informational aspects of these emerging sciences, however, still remains hidden from the psychotherapist behind the scientific verbiage of neuroscience that models itself after physiology rather than psychology. There is actually very little *psycho* in the emerging field of *psycho*neuroimmunology, for example. The messenger molecules that mediate mindbody communication are rarely described as such. Rather, they are called "hormones, peptides, cytokines, tumor necrosis factor, macrophage colony-stimulating factor" and so on. These are all meaningful labels for the physiologist and molecular biologist but they leave the psychologist out in the cold with no hint of the essentially informational and communicational nature of these "physiological" messenger molecules. Neuroscience today is acknowledged to be a branch of information theory, yet its speech is still garbed in the world-view of early physiology that originally had no place for mind and psychology.

What hopes can we have, then, for a deeper understanding of the *Symptom Path to Enlightenment* that facilitates the resolution of psychological problems and the healing of stress related body symptoms by facilitating optimal mindbody communication? *We must rescue the informational and communication function of messenger molecules from physiological reductionism!* How can we do this? In a word, technology! We already have brain imaging devices that document how conscious thought, planning, problem solving, imagery, emotions and music appreciation as well as dreams can modulate the flow of fuel (e.g., glucose) and the consumption of energy in the brain. They are not yet of practical use in psychotherapy, of course, because they cost millions and only take brief snapshots.

Who can doubt that in the future we will be able to develop inexpensive versions of such imaging technology that will enable us to watch the actual flow of messenger molecules throughout the brain and body of the moving, struggling, and sweating human being in psychotherapy projected on a screen bigger than life? We will no longer be limited to merely hypothesizing how stress, symptoms and problems are associated with "physiological factors." The psychological path to problem solving and healing will not be confined to the various schools of analysis and interpretation or our current approaches to suggestion and conditioning. We will actually see the flow of messenger molecules throughout the brain and body during hypnotherapeutic work. Patients and therapists will watch how certain cognitions and emotional complexes do vastly more than merely modulate muscle tension, blood pressure, heart rate and brain waves. They will actually witness how mind and meditation can move messenger molecules throughout the brain and body during the healing process. Surely by then *The Symptom Path to Enlightenment* will be universally recognized as being more than a metaphor.

Glossary

This glossary focuses primarily on some of the key new terms from *Nonlinear Dynamics* as they are related to the classical *Psychodynamics* of hypnosis and depth psychology.

Attractor is a new concept from self-organization theory that corresponds to the essence of what traditional hypnosis and depth psychology have always been concerned with: What is the hidden pattern or **Archetypal** source of those repetitive but puzzling aspects of mind and behavior that seem to have no rational meaning? **Attractors** describe the long-term behavior of dynamically changing systems such as the life of a person, a nation or a culture. A person's life, for example, may be stuck at **fixed point attractor** (e.g. depression or other apparently fixed symptom). One may be caught up in a **periodic attractor** such as a bipolar mood disorder, or one may be going around in repetitive circles getting nowhere that are called **limit-cycle attractors**. The most interesting life is one that manifests **chaotic or strange attractors** which involve continually changing, novel experiences within a creative framework. We want to know, for example, what is the **unconscious attractor** that drives some creative people to explore and make new discoveries that seem to have a similar theme in art, music and drama? From a traditional psychoanalytic point of view **attractors** correspond to **unconscious complexes.**

Basic Rest Activity Cycle (BRAC) is the fundamental 90-120 **ultradian rhythm** originally described by Nathaniel Kleitman to characterize the most important periodicity of human experience: social activities and human performance efficiency, memory and learning as well as hunger, hormonal flow, cellular growth, reproduction and healing are apparently all related by a common BRAC or multiple BRAC synchronizers. Kleitman's BRAC may be viewed as a kind of window on the most fundamental psychobiological processes of human experience that can be **accessed or entrained** by **hypnotherapeutic work** facilitate mindbody communication and healing.

Basin of Attraction is mathematical terminology for the common observation of water swirling down a drain in a water **basin**. We use mathematical modeling to illustrate how natural movements can be quantified to the basins they are attracted to on a map. A topographical map, for example, would illustrate the area over which water would flow to a low spot. Applying nonlinear dynamics to human psychology suggests we may be able to quantify the "basin of attraction" a mother and child have for each other as they move over the area of a room or a playground. More challenging would be the mapping of "brain fields" to represent the motivated flow of cognitions and behavior to the basins of attraction we call "ideals" or "obsessions and compulsions."

Bifurcation is a branching of one path or solution into two. Complex systems in math, physics, biology and psychology continually evolve by bifurcating (splitting) into more diverse patterns and pathways. Psychological phenomena such as **conflict, dissociation, duality, polarity** and **multiple personality**, for example, are all manifestations of bifurcations taking place outside one's perceived range conscious control. On the positive side, **creativity** also involves a **split, division** or **bifurcation** from one a more limited to a richer set of possibilities.

Chaos as in **Deterministic Chaos**. The concept used to characterize the evolution of certain mathematical equations, physical and biological systems that become so complex over time that they appear to be random and unpredictable to human perception even though they are fully lawful and deterministic.

Chaotological or chaotobiological processes are those in which the **nonlinear dynamics** of **deterministic chaos** make it difficult and usually impossible to predict behavior exactly over long periods of time. Most so-called periodic or rhythmical psychobiological processes of human nature and experience are actually chaotological. Human behavior and consciousness has a **wave nature** but with continually creative variations. Naturally we need a **chaotological theory of hypnotherapeutic work** to facilitate human problem solving and healing to deal with our inherently nonlinear dynamics.

Complex Adaptive Systems are those organizations in nature that are able to maintain their integrity and evolve over time by interacting in an adaptive matter with the environment. All living organisms are complex adaptive systems. The classical psychodynamics of psychoanalysis such as the mechanisms of defense, for example, are complex adaptive systems.

Critical Phase Transitions are broad generalizations of the changes that are called **bifurcations**. Adolescence is an obvious critical phase transition in the psychobiology of most people. Graduating from school, getting married, divorced or winning a million dollar lottery are obviously very important critical phase transitions in life. A new idea can initiate a critical phase transition in an entire society as well as the individual who creates it.

Cybernetic processes are those circular arrangements in nature wherein the outcome of a process is used as information to control the next output. The thermostat that regulates temperature in a home is the most common example. All biological, psychological, behavioral and socio-cultural processes are complex adaptive systems that utilize information in cybernetic loops between many levels for self-regulation. growth and healing.

Differential Equations express the **rate of change** of any process or dynamical system of nature. They are the mathematical essence of our models of nature on all levels from physical to living systems.

Dissipative Systems burn up and dissipate energy. The breaks on an auto, for example, are a dissipative system because they burn up energy and actually get hot from the friction needed to slow and stop the car. From an energy point of view all living systems are dissipative because they burn food as sources of energy to maintain themselves. You get hot and sweat when you do work and dissipate your energy. Some patients tremble and sweat from the emotional catharsis and the intensity of dissipating their energy in **hypnotherapeutic work.**

Dynamical Systems are those whose properties, positions and behavior change in time. They may be living or non-living. The **Classical Dynamics of Sir Isaac Newton** refer generally to deterministic and predictable phenomena of the physical universe such as the orbits of the planets that can be expressed with mathematical equations. This book explores the currently evolving view that the *psychodynamics of depth psychology and hypnosis* may be expressed in terms of the **Nonlinear Dynamics of the mathematician Poincaré** that describe most processes of change in living systems more adequately than the classical linear dynamics of Newton. It is interesting that the *nonlinear dynamics* of Poincaré, that is becoming known today as *Chaos Theory,* was originally developed around the same time that Freud, Jung and others formulated *psychodynamics*. This leads us to hypothesize that *the psychodynamics of human experience reflects the nonlinear dynamics of nature*. Studying the nonlinear dynamics of nature may therefore help us create a more adequate understanding of psychodynamics that can lead to better approaches to psychotherapy.

Entropy means almost the opposite of available energy and order to do work. Entropy is a measure of the disorganization or loss of information in a system. When a highly concentrated and well-organized form of energy is used up (i.e.. burned) it breaks down into a lower level of organization and lower energy levels that **increases the entropy** of the universe. A high level form of energy such as gasoline is burned in doing the work of moving your auto at the cost of producing disorganized waste products such as smog. The less organized molecules in smog have **more entropy and less information** than the highly organized molecules of gasoline. All living systems burn higher energy sources called "food" to drive their metabolism, build their organic structure and reproduce. They all do this at the cost of producing the lower energy products we call "waste" that increases the entropy of the universe. The great paradox is that living systems are continually evolving highly organized informational structures within themselves (that have less entropy) at the cost of increasing the general entropy or randomness of the universe. *The information created by life is negative entropy.* How long can this go on before all high level energy sources are used up resulting in a so-called "heat-death" of the universe?

Feedback refers to an arrangement whereby the outcome of a process is put back into the input of the process. In mathematics, for example, the answer to an equation is put back into the equation as the starting point for the next calculation. In different contexts this may be called **a process of iteration** or **recursion**. All living systems involve **feedback loops communicating** on many levels to guide processes of development, growth, self-regulation and healing. The **ultimate feedback loop** described in this book is that between the cognitive-behavioral level of mind and the expression of genes.

Fractal from the Latin *fractus,* "broken" is a new branch of geometry that is used to describe the apparently irregular patterns found in nature: clouds, fern leaves, the coast line of England etc. The fundamental characteristic of fractals is **self-similarity** on all scales of size and or time. Look at the parts of a cloud and you see similar cloud structures in smaller and smaller parts; look at a fern leaf under a microscope and you see smaller and smaller branches of the same leaf structure. Look at a chart of the price movement of the stock market over a century and you will see fractal patterns that repeat over time on shorter and shorter intervals of a decade, a year, a month, a day and even minute by minute. Thus, much of physical nature as well as mass psychology has a fractal structure. You can dream you are having a dream about a dream within a dream. You can think about your thinking about your thinking and so on.. From an ethical point of view a good deed may have unexpectedly harmful consequences — that later give rise to something else that is good — that in turn leads to something evil that in turn leads to something good again and so on. Politics anyone?

High Phase Hypnosis refers to the focusing of attention on of the high phase (or high amplitude end) of our natural 90-120 **Basic Rest Activity Cycle (BRAC)** in order to activate, utilize or entrain the arousal and facilitation of human performance. The **BRAC** is the fundamental **ultradian rhythm** that characterizes normal human experience on all levels from the (1) psychosocial (human conscious-ness, performance efficiency, memory and learning) to the (2) psy-chobiological (hormonal flow, dreaming (the rapid eye movement (REM), and hunger as well as responses to trauma and stress) to the (3) cellular-genetic level of psychoimmunology. An athletic couch exhorting a team to try harder on the playing field is attempting to entrain and enhance the high phase of the **BRAC** so they will play better; the couch is, in a sense trying to use what we call "high phase hypnosis." The psychotherapist who attempts to facilitate a patient's cognitive-emotional skills of attention, imagery and focusing on some aspect of their **outer-world experience in order to enhance performance** in athletics, work, academics, relationship skills etc. is attempting high phase hypnosis to optimize the high end of the patient's natural aptitude (high amplitude end of their BRAC).

Hypnotherapeutic Work refers to the creative effort involved in accessing and utilization of the various phases of our natural **Basic Rest Activity Cycle**. Hypnotherapeutic work may facilitate a wide range of behaviors ranging from the cognitive-emotional arousal usually required for optimal performance (**High Phase Hypnosis**) to the deep rest and relaxation more characteristic of recovery and healing (**Low Phase Hypnosis**).

Information Transduction is the process by which information is transformed or changes its forms in the realm of **psychobiology**. In this sense, information transduction is the essence of mindbody com-munication and provides a resolution of the mindbody problem. Mind and body are not separate realms; they have information as their common denominator. Exploration of the **transductions between matter, energy and information** within life is the leading edge of science and human understanding today. Information trans-duction is the essential process whereby **hypnotherapeutic work** may facilitate problem solving and healing on all levels from mind to gene.

Iteration is a method of solving a problem by performing the same set of steps repeatedly until one reaches a certain condition. In mathematics this usually involves putting an answer or solution to an equation back into the equation to get another solution for the next step. Life in general and psychology, in particular, could be considered a series or cyclic process of iteration by which we reach a certain goal by progressive approximations. In hypnotherapeutic work we ask a series of **basic accessing questions**, for example, to facilitate the creative resolution of problem solving and healing.

Life is most uniquely characterized as the only process within the universe that is able to mediate self-reflective transductions (transformations) between matter, energy and information. Yes, That's life!

Linear, from a mathematical point of view, refers to the Operations (Op) of **addition** [Op (f + g) = Op (f) + Op(g)] and **multiplication** [Op (c f) = c Op (f) where c is a constant. This is often referred to as the **superposition property** of linear operators. A **linear equation** frequently is illustrated as a relationship between two variables that produces a straight line when plotted on a graph. Such linear relationships make it is easy to predict from one point to another. A **nonlinear equation** by, contrast, produces a more complex curved line that makes it very difficult or even impossible to predict future behavior from any given set of initial conditions. Psychology is primarily about nonlinear relationships.

Low Phase Hypnosis in contrast to high phase hypnosis refers to the engagement of the low phase (or low end) of our natural 90-120 **Basic Rest Activity Cycle (BRAC)** in order to utilize or entrain the rest and relaxation side of human experience for the facilitation of **recovery and healing**. It is hypothesized that Kleitman's BRAC may be viewed as a kind of window on the most fundamental psychobiological processes of human experience that can be accessed and entrained by **hypnotherapeutic work** to facilitate mindbody communication and healing on all levels from the cognitive-behavioral to genetic expression. It is particularly noteworthy that the basic cell cycle of growth, replication (mitosis) and recovery from stress and trauma takes about 90-120 minutes. This cellular-genetic cycle may be the fundamental rhythm that underlies the chaotobiological periodicity of the autonomic nervous system, the neuroendocrine system and the immune system that are all related (synchronized) in human performance and healing.

Metastability or Multistability of Mind refers to our normal experience of many rapidly shifting states of cognition, emotionality and imagery *particularly when we are faced with ambiguous stimuli and situations.* The most common examples from psychology are the perceptual illusions where, for example, one can interpret a picture with an ambiguous figure-ground relationship as either a vase or the profile of two faces. These rapid perceptual shifts in perception are presumably reflecting *bifurcations* or *critical phase transitions* on a phenomenological level that match similar bifurcations of neural brain processes. In psychotherapy we are always utilizing this natural multistability of mind to help people "find a new point-of-view" or **reframe** their understanding of themselves or the world.

Mind is a chaotobiological process of self-reflective information transduction. That is, mind may be understood as a clearing house that mirrors (or self-reflects) the transformations and exchanges of mass, energy and information on all levels from the cognitive-behavioral to the physiological and genetic. Exactly why such a clearing house is needed is the "hard question" of trying to explain why consciousness evolved. Why do the **complex adaptive systems** of life need consciousness?

Nonlinear refers to all mathematical relationships that cannot meet the standard of addition and multiplication that define **Linear** operators (see definition of linear above). Nonlinear is descriptive of most physical, biological and psychosocial systems that behave in complex ways that are surprising (not easy to predict) since **the action of the whole is more than a simple sum of the parts.** A **linear system,** by contrast, is easy to predict since its behavior is a simple sum or proportion of its parts: one apple can be added to another apple for a linear sum of two apples. Put two people together, however, and you have a nonlinear psychosocial system because their complex interaction could produce anything from mutual inhibition to mutual enhancement.

Phase transitions are the important qualitative changes we recognize in nature such as the phase changes of water from ice to liquid to steam. Facilitating **Critical Phase Transitions** from symptomatic maladjustment to creativity, problem solving and healing is the most important task of **hypnotherapeutic work**.

Self-Organization describes the apparently spontaneous emergence of **adaptive complex systems** on a macroscopic level (a whole organism, for example) from the collective interactions between a large number of simpler, usually microscopic structures (the atoms and molecules that make up the organism).

Strange attractor means the same thing as a **chaotic attractor**: a pattern that continues to evolve within certain boundaries but it never repeats itself exactly. Your life is hopefully a strange attractor that has some recognizable framework (boundary conditions) that you know is "your life" yet you are continually experiencing creatively changing perceptions, cognition's, emotions etc. that are leading to... well, what: individuation, self-fulfillment? Or are you stuck in a fixed life situation or caught up in a boring limit cycle? If so you know you need to do some **creative hypnotherapeutic work** to help you go through a **critical phase transition** to breakout into a more meaningful chaotological existence!

Ultradian Rhythm is a term coined by the American chronobiologist, Franz Halberg, to correspond with the **ultra-violet** (higher frequency) end of the electromagnetic spectrum in contrast to the **infrared** (lower frequency) end. Ultradian rhythms are generally regarded as those that are 20 hours or less; they describe rhythms that are faster or more frequent than the **Circadian** (about a day) rhythm. **Infradian rhythms**, by contrast, are those that are longer than a day: the monthly menses cycle, for example. Heart rate, breathing and brain waves are all examples of **ultradian rhythms**. A basic hypothesis of this book is that ultradian rhythms are a window through which we may view the **chaotological patterns** of information and communication on all levels from mind to gene. This is the scientific basis for the common observation that "mind" can influence "body" and visa versa. Hypnotherapeutic work facilitates mindbody healing by optimizing the flow of **information transduction** or communication between the cognitive-behavioral level of mind to the hormonal messenger molecules and genes of the body.

Wave function is the most fundamental quantity in quantum theory; it is used to calculate the probability of an event occurring when an observation is made. Schrodinger's wave equation is a basic example. All phenomena of the universe, indeed, the universe itself can be expressed as a wave function. Waves seem to be the most universal common denominator by which the mathematics of human mind can conceptualize reality.

References

Abraham, F. (1995 a). Introduction to dynamics: A Basic language: a basic meta-modeling strategy. In Abraham, F. & Gilgen, A. (Eds.) (1995). *Chaos Theory in Psychology*. Westport, Connecticut: Greenwood Publishing Group, 31-49.

Abraham, F. (1995 b). Dynamics, bifurcation, self-organization, chaos, mind, conflict, insensitivity to initial conditions, time, unification, diversity, free will, and social responsibility. In Robertson, R. & Combs, A. (Eds.), *Chaos Theory in Psychology and the Life Sciences*. New Jersey, Lawrence Erlbaum Associates, 155-173.

Abraham, F., Abraham, R., & Shaw, C. (1992). *A Visual Introduction to Dynamical Systems Theory For Psychology*. Santa Cruz: Aerial Press.

Abraham, R. (1995a). *Chaos, Gaia, Eros*. San Francisco: Harper.

Abraham, R. (1995b). Ergodynamics and the dischaotic personality. In Abraham, F. & Gilgen, A. (Eds.) *Chaos Theory in Psychology*. Westport, Connecticut: Greenwood Publishing Group, 157-167.

Abraham F. & Gilgen, A. (Eds.) (1995). *Chaos Theory in Psychology*. Westport, Connecticut: Greenwood Publishing Group.

Ader, R. (1996). Historical Perspectives on Psychoneuroimmunology. In Friedman, H., Klein, T. & Friedman, A. (Eds.). *Psychoneuroimmunology, Stress, and Infection*. New York: CRC Press.

Adler, T. (1990). Breathing through nose may affect brain, mood. *APA Monitor*, 21, 6.

Albano, A., Mees, A., de Guzman, G, & Rapp, P. (1987). Data requirements for reliable estimation of correlated dimensions. p. 207-220. In: Degan, H., Holden, A. & Olsen, L. (eds.) *Chaos in Biological Systems*. New York: Plenum.

Aldrich, K., & Bernstein, D. (1987). The effect of time of day on hypnotizability. *International Journal of Clinical & Experimental Hypnosis, 35*(3), 141-145.

Amigo, S., (1994). Self-regulation therapy and the voluntary reproduction of stimulant effects of epinephrine: possible therapeutic applications. *Contemporary Hypnosis*, 11, 3, 108-120.

Amir, S., & Stewart, J. (1996). Resetting of the circadian clock by a conditioned stimulus. *Nature*, Vol. 379,(6565), February, pp. 542-545.

Bailey, C. & Kandel, E. (1995). Molecular and structural mechanisms underlying long-term memory. In Gazzaniga, M. (Ed.) *The Cognitive Sciences*. Cambridge: MIT Press, pp. 19-36.

Bak, P, & Chen, K., (1991). Self Organized Critically. *Scientific American*, Vol. 264,(1) January pp. 46-63.

Balthazard, C., & Woody, E. (1985). The "stuff" of hypnotic performance: A review of psychometric approaches. *Psychological Bulletin*, 98(2), 283-296.

Balthazard, C., & Woody, E. (1992). The spectral analysis of hypnotic performance with respect to "absorption." *The International Journal of Clinical and Experimental Hypnosis.* 40, 1, 21-43.

Barabasz, A., & Lonsdale, C. (1983). Effects of hypnosis on P300 olfactory-evoked potential amplitudes. *Journal of Abnormal Psychology.* 92, 520-523.

Barber, T. X. (1984). Changing unchangeable bodily processes by (hypnotic) suggestions: A new look at hypnosis cognitions, imagining, and the mindbody problem. *Advances, 1*(2), 7-40.

Barber, J. (1990). Miracle cures? Therapeutic consequences of clinical demonstrations. In Zeig, J. & Gilligan, S., *Brief Therapy: Myths, Methods, and Metaphors.* Brunner/Mazel, New York.

Barinaga, M. (1995). New Clock Gene Cloned. *Science*: 270 (3): 732-3.

Barnier, A. & McConkey, K. (1995). An experiential evaluation of conflict resolution in hypnosis In Burrows, G. & Stanley, R. (Eds.) *Contemporary International Hypnosis.* p. 89-96. New York: Wiley.

Beck, A., (1976). *Cognitive Therapy and the Emotional Disorders.* New York: International University Press.

Beck, A. , (1987). Cognitive Therapy. In Zeig, J. (Ed.). *The Evolution of Psychotherapy.* New York: Brunner-Mazel, 149-163.

Benson, H. (1975). *The Relaxation Response.* New York: Avon.

Benzer, S. (1971). From the gene to behavior. *Journal of the American Medical Association,* 218, 7, 1015-1022.

Bernheim, H. (1886/1957). *Suggestive Therapeutics: A Treatise on the Nature and Uses of Hypnotism.* Westport: Associated Booksellers.

Bezrukov, S. & and Vodyanoy, I. (1995). Noise-induced enhancement of signal transduction across voltage-dependent ion channels. *Nature,* 378, p. 362-364.

Bloom, P., (1990). The creative process in hypnotherapy. In Fass, M. & Brown, D. (Eds.) *Creative Mastery in Hypnosis and Hypnoanalysis.* Hillsdale, New Jersy, Earlbaum.

Boden, M. (1991). *The Creative Mind: Myths and Mechanisms.* New York: Basic Books.

Boivin, D., Duffy, J., Kronauer, R. & Czeisler, C., (1996). Dose-response relationships for resetting of human circadian clock by light. *Nature,* Vol. 379,(6565), February, pp. 540-542.

Bolander, F. (1989). *Molecular Endocrinology.* New York: Academic Press.

Bongartz, E. (Ed.), (1992) *Hypnosis: 175 Years after Mesmer: Recent Developments in Theory and Application.* Konstanz: Universitatsvergag.

Bongartz, W. (1995). *Einfluss von Hypnose und Stress auf das Blutbild.* [The Influence of Hypnosis and Stress on the Blood System]. Germany: Peter Langen Verlag.

References

Boole, G. (1854/1958). *An Investigation of the Laws of Thought*. Dover: New York.

Bowers, K. (1994). Hypnosis: Powerful or Innocuous? *Contemporary Hypnosis*, 11, 3, p 147-148.

Bowers, P., (1979). Hypnosis & Creativity: The Search for the Missing Link. *J Abnormal & Social Psychology* 88, 564-572.

Braid, J. (1855/1970). The Physiology of Fascination and the Critics Criticized. In Tinterow, M. (1970). *Foundations of Hypnosis*. Springfield, Ill: C. C. Thomas.

Braiman, Y., Linder, J. & Ditto, W. (1995). Taming spaitotemporal chaos with disorder. *Nature*, 378, 30, 465-467.

Brandenberger, G., (1992). Endocrine ultradian rhythms during sleep and wakefulness. In D. Lloyd & E. Rossi (Eds.), *Ultradian Rhythms in Life Processes: A Fundamental Inquiry into Chronobiology and Psychobiology*. New York: Springer-Verlag, 123-138.

Breuer, J., & Freud, S. (1895/1955). *Studies on Hysteria*. In J. Strachey (Ed. and Trans.), *The Standard Edition of the Complete Psychological Works of Sigmund Freud, Vol. II*. New York: W. W. Norton-Edmonston, W. (1986). *The Induction of Hypnosis*. New York: Wiley.

Brey, D. (1995). Protein molecules as computational elements in living cells. *Nature*, 376, 307-312.

Brodsky, V., (1992). Rhythms of protein synthesis and other circahoralian oscillations: The possible involvement of fractals. In D. Lloyd & E. Rossi (Eds.), *Ultra-dian Rhythms in Life Processes: A Fundamental Inquiry into Chronobiology and Psychobiology*. New York: Springer-Verlag, 23-40.

Broughton, R. (1975). Biorhythmic variations in consciousness and Psychological functions. *Canadian Psychological Review: Psychologie Canadienne*, 16 (4), 217-239.

Brown, P. (1991a). Ultradian rhythms of cerebral function and hypnosis. *Contemporary Hypnosis*, 8, 1, 17-24.

Brown, P. (1991b). *The Hypnotic Brain: Hypnotherapy and Social communication*. New Haven: Yale University Press.

Brown & R. Graeber (Eds.), (1982). *Rhythmic Aspects of Behavior*. Hillsdale, New Jersey: Lawrence Erlbaum.

Brown, T. & Combs, A. (1995). Constraint, complexity and chaos: A methodological follow-up on the nostril cycle. In Robertson, R. & Combs, A. (Eds.) *Chaos Theory in Psychology and the Life Sciences*. Mahwah, New Jersey: Lawrence Erlbaum.

Brush, F. R. & Levine, S. (1989). *Psychoendocrinology*. San Diego: Academic Press.

Buchanan, C., Eccles, J., & Becker, J. (1992). Are adolescents the victims of raging hormones: Evidence for activational effects of hormones on moods and behavior at adolescence. *Psychological Bulletin*, 111, 62-107.

Bucke, R., (1901). *Cosmic Consciousness: A Study in the Evolution of the Human Mind*. EP Dutton and Company, Inc., New York.

Cahill, L., Prins, B., Weber, M., & McGaugh, J. (1994). B-Adrenergic activation and memory for emotional events. *Nature*, 371, 20, 702-704.

Carotenuto, A. (1992) *The Difficult Art: A Critical Discourse on Psychotherapy.* Chiron, Wilmette, Illinois.

Casti, J., (1994). *Complexification: Explaining a Paradoxical World Through the Science of Surprise.* New York: Harper Collins.

Chambers, D., (1995). Facing up to the problem of consciousness. *J. Consciousness Studies,* 2,3, 200-219.

Changeux, J. & Connes, A., (1995). *Conversations on Mind, Matter, and Mathematics.* DeBevoise (Ed.). New Jersey, Princeton Univ. Press.

Cheek, D. (1994). *Hypnosis: The Application of Ideomotor Techniques.* Allyn & Bacon, Boston.

Chiba, Y., Chiba, K., Halberg, F., & Cutkomp, L. (1977). Longitudinal evaluation of circadian rhythm characteristics and their circaspetan modulation in an apparently healthy couple. In J. McGovern, J. Smolensky, & A. Reingerg (Eds.), *Chronobiology in allergy and Immunology* (pp. 17-35). Springfield, Illinois: Charles C. Thomas.

Combs, A. & Winkler, M. (1995). The nostril cycle: A study in the methodology of chaos science. In Robertson, R. & Combs, A. (Eds.) *Chaos Theory in Psychology and the Life Sciences.* Mahwah, New Jersey: Lawrence Erlbaum.

Coveney, P. & Highfield, R. (1995). *Frontiers of Complexity: The Search for Order in a Chaotic World.* Fawcett Columbine: New York.

Crabtree, G. (1989). Contingent Genetic Regulatory vents in T lymphocyte activation. *Science, 243,*(20), 355-361. Crutchfield, J. (1994). Is anything ever new? Considering emergence. In Cowan, G., Pines, D. & Meltzer, D. (Eds.) *Complexity: Metaphors, Models and Reality.* New York: Addison-Wesley.

Crasilneck, H., (1996). The use of the Crasilneck Bombardment Technique in problems of intractable organic pain. *Hypnos, 23,* 1, 19-29.

Crutchfield, J. & Young, K., (1990). Computation at the edge of chaos. In Zurek, W. (Ed.) (1990*). Complexity, Entropy and the Physics of Information.* New York: Addison-Wesley.

Dabic-Jeftic, M. & Barnes, G. (1993). Event-related potentials (P300) during cognitive processes of hypnotic and non-hypnotic conditions. *Psychiatria Danubina,* 5, 1-12.

Dafter, R. (1996). Why "Negative" emotions can sometimes be positive: The spectrum model of emotions and their role in Mind-Body healing. *Advances.* 12, 2, pp. 6-19.

Davis, L., & Husband, R. (1931). A study of hypnotic susceptibility in relation to personality traits. *J. Abnormal Social Psychology,* 26, 175-182.

Dawkins, R. (1989). *The Selfish Gene.* New York: Oxford University Press.

DeBenededittis, G., Cigada, E. & Gosi-Greguss, A. (1994). Autonomic changes during hypnosis, *American J. Clinical Hypnosis,* 42, 2, 140-152.

Decety, J., Perani, D., Jeannerod, M., Bettinardi, V., Tadary, B., Woods, R., Mazziotta, J. & Fazio, F. (1994). Mapping motor representations with positive emission tomography. *Nature.* vol. 371, Oct. 13, 600-602.

References

Dement, W., & Kleitman, N. (1957). Cyclic variations in EEG during sleep and their relation to eye movements, body motility, and dreaming. *Electroencephalography & Clinical Neurophysiology*, 9, 673-690.

Dinges, D. & Broughton, R., (1989). *Sleep and Alertness*. New York: Raven Press.

Dorcus, R., Britnall, A., & Case, H. (1941). Control experiments and their relation to theories of hypnotism. *J. Gen. Psychology*, 24, 217-221.

Dossey, L., (1982). *Space, Time and Medicine*. Boulder: Shambala.

Dossey, L., (1995). *Healing Words: The Power of Prayer and the Practice of Medicine*. New York: H & R.

Durant, W., (1933). *The Story of Philosophy.* Garden City Publishing. New York.

Edinger, E., (1996). *The Aion Lectures: Exploring the Self in C. G. Jung's Aion*. Toronto: Inner City Books.

Edmonston, W. (1986). *The Induction of Hypnosis*. New York: Wiley.

Eigen, M., (1971). Self-Organization of matter and the evolution of biological macro-molecules. *Naturwissenschaften* 58, pp. 465-523.

Eigen, M. & Schuster, P., (1977). The hypercycle: a principle of natural self-organization. Part A: The emergence of the hypercycle. *Naturwissenschaften* 64, pp. 541-565.

Eigen, M. & Winkler, R. (1981). *Laws of the Game: How the Principles of Nature Govern Chance*. NY: Harper & Row.

Eigen, M. & Winkler-Oswatitsch, R. (1992). *Steps Toward Life: A Perspective on Evolution*. Oxford: Oxford University Press.

Ellenberger, E. (1970), *The Discovery of the Unconscious*. Basic Books, New York.

Endo, Y., Mori, T., Kimura, M., Suzuki, H. & Endo, S. (1995). A study on the quantitative EEG during the hypnotic resting state. In Burrows, G. & Stanley, R. (Eds.) *Contemporary International Hypnosis*. p. 369-368. New York: Wiley.

Erickson, M., (1932/1980). Possible detrimental effects of experimental hypnosis. In E. Rossi (Ed.), *The Collected Papers of Milton H. Erickson on Hypnosis. I. The Nature of Hypnosis and Suggestion* (pp. 493-497). New York: Irvington.

Erickson, M. (1938/1980). A study of clinical and experimental findings on hypnotic deafness: I. Clinical experimentation and findings. In E. Rossi (Ed.), *The Collected Papers of Milton E. Erickson on Hypnosis. II. Hypnotic Alteration of Sensory, Perceptual, and Psychophysical Processes* (pp. 81-99). New York: Irvington.

Erickson, M., (1948/1980). Hypnotic Psychotherapy. In E. Rossi (Ed.), *The Collected Papers of Milton H. Erickson on Hypnosis. Vol. 4. Innovative Hypnotherapy* (pp. 35-48). New York: Irvington.

Erickson, M. (1954/1980). The development of an acute limited obsessional hysterical state in a normal hypnotic subject. In E. Rossi (Ed.), *The Collected Papers of Milton E. Erickson on Hypnosis. II. Hypnotic Alteration of Sensory, Perceptual, and Psychophysical Processes* (pp. 51-80). New York: Irvington.

Erickson, M. (1958/1980). Naturalistic techniques of hypnosis. E. Rossi (Eds.), *The Collected Papers of Milton H. Erickson on Hypnosis. Vol. I. The Nature of Hypnosis and Suggestion* (pp. 168-176). New York: Irvington.

Erickson, M. (1959/1980). Further clinical techniques of hypnosis: Utilization techniques. In E. Rossi (Eds.), *The Collected Papers of Milton H. Erickson on Hypnosis. Vol. I. The Nature of Hypnosis and Suggestion* (pp. 177-205). New York: Irvington.

Erickson, M. (1964/1980). Pantomime techniques in hypnosis and the implications. In E. Rossi (Eds.), *The Collected Papers of Milton H. Erickson on Hypnosis. I. The Nature of Hypnosis and Suggestion* (pp. 331-339). New York: Irvington.

Erickson, M. (1966/1980). The interspersal hypnotic technique for symptom correction and pain control. In E. Rossi (Ed.), *The Collected Papers of Milton H. Erickson on Hypnosis. I. The Nature of Hypnosis and Suggestion* (pp. 262-278). New York: Irvington.

Erickson, M. (1980a). Facilitating new identity. In E. Rossi (Ed.), *The Collected Papers of Milton H. Erickson on Hypnosis. IV. Innovative Hypnotherapy; Section nine.* (pp. 446-548). New York: Irvington.

Erickson, M. (1980b). An introduction to the study and application of hypnosis for pain control. In E. Rossi (Ed.), *The Collected Papers of Milton H. Erickson on Hypnosis. IV. Innovative Hypnotherapy; Section nine.* (pp. 237-245). New York: Irvington.

Erickson, M. (1980c). In E. Rossi (Ed.), *The Collected Papers of Milton E. Erickson on Hypnosis. II. Hypnotic Alteration of Sensory, Perceptual, and Psychophysical Processes* (pp. 51-80). New York: Irvington.

Erickson, M. and Erickson, E. (1941\1980). Concerning the nature and character of post-hypnotic behavior. In E. Rossi (Eds.), *The Collected Papers of Milton H. Erickson on Hypnosis. I. The Nature of Hypnosis and Suggestion* (pp. 360-365). New York: Irvington.

Erickson, M., & Rossi, E. (1975). Varieties of double bind. *The American Journal of Clinical Hypnosis, 17,* 3, 143-157.

Erickson, M., Rossi, E., & Rossi, S. (1976). *Hypnotic Realities.* New York: Irvington.

Erickson, M., & Rossi, E. (1979). *Hypnotherapy: An Exploratory Casebook.* New York: Irvington

Erickson, M., & Rossi, E. (1980). Indirect forms of suggestion in hand levitation. In E. Rossi (Ed.), *The Collected Papers of Milton H. Erickson on Hypnosis. I. The Nature of Hypnosis and Suggestion* (pp. 478-490). New York: Irvington.

Erickson, M., & Rossi, E. (1981). *Experiencing Hypnosis: Therapeutic Approaches to Altered States.* New York: Irvington.

Erickson, M., & Rossi, E. (1989). *The February Man: Evolving Consciousness and Identity in Hypnotherapy.* New York: Brunner/Mazel.

Erickson, M., Rossi, E., & Rossi, S. (1976). *Hypnotic Realities.* New York: Irvington.

Escera, C., Cilveti, R. & Grau, C., (1992). Ultradian rhythms in cognitive operations: Evidence from the P300 component of the event-related potentials. *Medical-Science-Research*, 20(4), 137-138.

Evans, F. (1972). Hypnosis and sleep: Techniques for exploring cognitive activity during sleep. In E. Fromm & R. Shor (Eds.), *Hypnosis: Research Developments and Perspectives* (pp. 43-83). Chicago: Aldine Publishing.

Evans, F. & Orne, M. (1971). The disappearing hypnotist: the use of simulating subjects to evaluate how subjects perceive experimental procedures. *The International Journal of Clinical and Experimental hypnosis, 19*, 277-296.

Eysenck, H., (1991). Is Suggestibility? In Schumaker, J. (Ed.) *Human Suggestibility: Advances in Theory, Research and Application.* New York: Routledge.

Feher, S., Berger, L., Johnson, J. & Wilde, J. (1989). Increasing breast milk production for premature infants with a relaxation/imagery audiotape. *Pediatrics, 83,* 57-60.

Feigenbaum, M., (1980). Universal behavior in nonlinear systems. *Los Alamos Science, 1,* 4-27.

Fischer, R. (1971a). Arousal-statebound recall of experience. *Diseases of the Nervous System,* 32, 373-382.

Fischer, R. (1971b). The "flashback": Arousal-statebound recall of experience. *Journal of Psychedelic Drugs,* 3, 31-39.

Fischer, R. (1971c). A cartography of ecstatic and meditative states. *Science,* 174, 897-904.

Fischer R. & Landon, G. M. (1972). On the arousal state-dependent recall of "subconscious" experience: stateboundedness. *British Journal of Psychiatry,* 120, 159-172.

Ford, J. (1986). Chaos: Solving the unsolvable, predicting the unpredictable! In M. Barnsley & S. Demko (Eds.), *Chaotic Dynamics and Fractals.* New York: Academic Press.

Ford, J. (1988). What is chaos, that we should be mindful if it? In S. Capelin and P. Davies (Eds.), *The New Physics* (pp. 248-372). Cambridge: Cambridge University Press.

Frederikson, R., McGaugh, J. & Felten, D., (eds.), (1991*) Peripheral Signaling of the Brain: Role in Neural-Immune Interactions, Learning and Memory.* New York: Hogrefe & Huber.

Freeman, W. (1995). *Societies of Brains.* New York: Lawrence Erlbaum.

Freud, A., (1946). *The Ego and the Mechanisms of Defense.* New York: International University Press.

Freidman, S. (1972). On the presence of a variant form of instinctual regression. *Psychoanalytic Quarterly,* 41, 364-383.

Friedman, S. (1978). A psychophysiological model for the chemotherapy of psychosomatic illness. *The Journal of Nervous & Mental Diseases,* 166, 110-116.

Friedman, S., & Fischer, C. (1967). On the presence of a rhythmic diurnal, oral instinctual drive cycle in man: A preliminary report. *Journal of the American Psychoanalytic Association,* 15, 317-343.

Fromm, E. (1992). An ego-psychological theory of hypnosis. In E. Fromm & M. Nash (Eds.), (pp. 131-148). New York: Guilford Press.

Frumkin, L., Ripley, H., & Cox, G. (1978). Changes in cerebral hemispheric lateralization with hypnosis. *Biological Psychiatry,* 13, 741-750.

Funk, F., & Clarke, J. (1980). The nasal cycle observations over prolonged periods of time. *Research Bulletin of the Himalayan International Institute,* Winter, 1-4.

Gekakis, N., Saez, L, Delahaye-Brown, A., Myers, M., Sehgal, A., Young, M., and Weitz, C. (1995), Isolation of timeless by PER Protein Interaction: Defective Interaction Between timeless Protein and Long-Period Mutant PER. *Science*: 270(3) p. 811-815.

Gheorghiu, V. & Kruse, P. (1991). *The Psychology of Suggestion: An Integrative Perspective.* in Schumaker, J. (1991). (Ed.) *Human Suggestibility: Advances in theory, research and application.* New York: Routledge.

Gilbert, A. & Rosenwasser, A. (1987). Biological rhythmicity of nasal airway patency: A re-examination of the 'nasal cycle." *Acta Otolaryngol*, 104, 180-186.

Gilligan, S., (1982,). *Ericksonian Approaches to Clinical Hypnosis.* p. 87-103, In Zeig, J., (ed.), (1982) *Ericksonian Approaches to Hypnosis and Psychotherapy.* New York: Brunner Mazel

Glass, L., & Mackey, M. (1988). *From Clocks to Chaos: The Rhythms of Life.* Princeton, New Jersey: Princeton University Press.

Glaser, J. & Glaser, R. (1988). Behavioral influences on immune function in humans. In Field, T., McCabe, P. & Schneiderman, N. (Eds.) Stress and Coping, Vol. 2. Hillsdale, N. J. : Lawrence Erlbaum. (p. 3-5).

Glaser, R., Kennedy, S., Lafuse, W., Bonneau, R., Speicher, C., Hillhouse, J. & Kiecolt-Glaser, J. (1990). Psychological stress-induced modulation of interleukin 2 receptor gene expression and interleukin 2 production in peripheral blood leukocytes. *Archives of General Psychiatry*, 47, 707-712.

Glaser, R., Lafuse, W., Bonneau, R., Atkinson, C., & Kiecolt-Glaser, J. (1993). Stress-associated modulation of proto-oncogene expression in human peripheral blood leukocytes. *Behavioral Neuroscience*, 107, 525-529.

Gleick, F., (1987). Chaos: Making a new science. New York: Viking.

Goerner, S., (1995). Chaos, Evolution and Deep Ecology. In Robertson, R. & Combs, A. (Eds.), (1995). *Chaos Theory in Psychology and the Life Sciences.* New Jersey, Lawrence Erlbaum Associates.

Goldbeter, A., (1996). *Biochemical Oscillations and Cellular Rhythms: The Molecular Basis of Periodic and Chaotic Behavior.* New York: Cambridge University Press.

Gorton, B. (1957). The physiology of hypnosis, I. *Journal of the Society of Psychosomatic Dentistry, 4*(3), 86-103.

Gorton, B. (1958). The physiology of hypnosis: Vasomotor activity in hypnosis. *Journal of the American Society of Psychosomatic Dentistry, 5*(1), 20-28.

Green, R. & Green, M. (1987) Relaxation increases salivary immunoglobulin A. *Psychological Reports,* 61, 623-629.

Gregson, R., (1992). *n-Dimensional nonlinear psychophysics.* Hillsdale, NJ: Lawrence Erlbaum.

Gruenewald, D., (1982). Problems of the Relevance in the Application of Laboratory Data to Clinical Situations, *The International Journal of Clinical and Experimental Hypnosis.* 30(4):345-353.

Güzeldere, G., (1995). Consciousness: What it is, how to study it, what to learn from its history. *J. of Consciousness Studies,* 2, 1, 30-51.

Guastello, S. (1995). *Chaos, Catastrophy, and Human Affairs.* Hillsdale, NJ: Lawrence Erlbaum.

Hadamard, J., (1954). *The Psychology of Invention in the Mathematical Field.* New York: Dover.

Haken, H., (1983). *Synergetics: An Introduction.* Springer-Verlag, New York.

Haken, H. & Koepchen, H. (Eds.), (1991). *Rhythms in Physiological Systems: Proceedings from the International Symposium at Schloss Elmau, Bavaria, October 22-25, 1990.* Springer-Verlag, New York.

Haken, H., (1992) *Synergetics in Psychology.* In Tschacher, W.; Schiepek, G., & Brunner, E., (1992). *Self-Organization and clinical Psychology: Empirical Approaches to Synergetics in Psychology.* Berlin, Springer-Verlag.

Hall, H. (1982-83). Hypnosis and the immune system: A review with implications for cancer and the psychology of healing. *The American Journal of Clinical Hypnosis, 25* (2-3), 92-103.

Hall, J. (1989). *Hypnosis: A Jungian Perspective.* New York: Guilford Press.

Hall, N. (ed.), (1991). *Exploring Chaos: A Guide to the New Science of Disorder.* New York: W. W. Norton.

Hannah, B., (1981). *Encounters with the Soul.* Sigo Press, Santa Monica, CA.

Harris, G. (1948). Neural control of the pituitary gland. *Physiological Review, 28,* 139-179.

Harris, R., Porges, S., Clemenson Carpenter, M. & Vincenz, L. (1993), Hypnotic Susceptibility, mood state, and cardiovascular reactivity, *American Journal of Clinical Hypnosis, 31,* 1, 15-25.

Hautkappe, H. & Bongartz, W., (1992). *Heart-Rate Variability as in Indicator for Post-Hypnotic Amnesia in Real and Simulating Subjects.* In Bongartz, E. (Ed.), (1992). *Hypnosis: 175 Years after Mesmer: Recent Developments in Theory and Application.* Konstanz: Universitatsvergag.

Havel, I., (1996). Remarks on Schrodinger's concept of Consciousness. *Consciousness at the Crossroads of Philosophy and Cognitive Science.* Maribor Conference, 1994. Thorverton, England: Imprint Academic, pp. 49-51.

Hayes, D. and Cobb, L., (1978). *Ultradian biorhythms in social interaction.* p.57-70.

Heisenberg, W., 1983. *Encounters with Einstein.* Princeton, NJ: Princeton University Press.

Hiatt, J., & Kripke, D. (1975). Ultradian rhythms in waking gastric activity. *Psychosomatic Medicine, 37,* 320-325.

Hilgard, E. (1965). *Hypnotic Susceptibility.* New York: Harcourt, Brace & World.

Hilgard, E., (1973), The domain of hypnosis: With some comments on alternative paradigms. *American Psychologist, 28,* 972-982.

Hilgard, E. (1977). *Divided Consciousness: Multiple Controls in Human Thought and Action.* New York: Wiley.

Hilgard, E., (1981). Hypnotic susceptibility scales under attack: An examination of Weitzenhoffer's criticisms. *The International Journal of Clinical and Experimental Hypnosis, 24,* 24-41.

Hilgard, E., (1982). Hypnotic susceptibility and implications for measurement. *Intern. J. Clinical. & Exp. Hypnosis.*, 30, 4, 394-403.

Hilgard, E., (1991). Suggestibility and Suggestions as Related to Hypnosis. In Schumaker, J. (Ed.) *Human Suggestibility: Advances in Theory, Research and Application.* New York: Routledge.

Hilgard, E., (1992). Dissociation and Theories of Hypnosis. In Fromm, E. & Nash, M. (Eds.). *Contemporary Hypnosis Research.* New York: Guilford.

Hilgard, E., & Hilgard, J. (1983). *Hypnosis in the relief of pain.* Los Altos, CA: William Kaufmann.

Hoddes, E., Zarcone, V., Smythe, H., Phillips, R. & Dement, W. (1973). Quantification of sleepiness: A new approach. *Psychophysiology,* 10, 4, 431-436.

Hoffman, S., (1994). *Whispers from Carnot: The origins of order and principles from adaptation in complex nonequilbrium systems.* In Cowan, G., Pines, D., & Melzer, D. (Eds.), *Complexity: Metaphors, Models and Reality. New York: Addison-Wesley*

Holland, J., (1995*). Hidden Order: How Adaptation Builds Complexity.* New York: Helix Books, Addison-Wesley Publishing.

Hoppenbrouwers, T., (1992). Ontogenesis of human ultradian rhythms. In Lloyd, D. & Rossi, E. (Eds.). *Ultradian Rhythms in Life Processes: A Fundamental Inquiry into Chronobiology and Psychobiology.* New York: Springer-Verlag, 173-196.

Hull, C. (1933/1968). *Hypnosis and Suggestibility.* New York: Appleton-Century-Crofts.

Iranmanesh, A., Veldhuis, J., Johnson, M., & Lizarralde, G. (1989). 24-hour pulsatile and circadian patterns of cortisol secretion in alcoholic men. *J. Androl.,* 10, 54-63.

Izquierdo, I., & Dias, R. (1984). Involvement of a-adrenergic receptors in the amnestic and anti-amnestic action of ACTH, B-endorphin and epinephrine. *Psychoneuroendocrinology, 9* (1), 77-81.

Izquierdo, I., Netto, C., Dalmaz, D., Chaves, M., Pereira, M., & Siegfried, B. (1988). Construction and reconstruction of memories. *Brazilian Journal of Medical and Biological Research, 21,* 9-25.

Jacobson, E. (1924). The technique of progressive relaxation. *Journal of Nervous and Mental Disorders,* 60, 568-78.

Jenkins, D., et al., (1989). Nibbling versus gorging: Metabolic advantages of increased meal frequency. *The New England Journal of Medicine,* 321(14), 929-935.

Jewett, J., Kronauer, R. & Czeisler, A. (1991). Light-induced suppression of endogenous circadian amplitude in humans. *Nature,* 350, 59-62.

Johnston, D. & Maio-sin Wu, S. (1995). *Foundations of Cellular Neurophysiology.* Cambridge: MIT Press.

Jung, C. (1902/1957). *Psychiatric Studies. Vol. 1, The Collected Works of C. G. Jung.* (R. F. C. Hull, Trans.). Bollingen Series XX. Princeton, New Jersey: Princeton University Press.

References

Jung, C. (1953). *Psychology and Alchemy, Vol. XII. The Collected Works of C. G. Jung.* (R. F. C. Hull, Trans.). Bollingen Series XX. Princeton, New Jersey: Princeton University Press.

Jung, C. (1954). *The Practice of Psychotherapy, Vol. XVI.* The Collected Works of C. G. Jung. (R. F. C. Hull, Trans.). Bollingen Series XX. Princeton, New Jersey: Princeton University Press.

Jung, C. (1959). *The Archetypes and the Collective Unconscious. Vol. IX (Part I). The Collected Works of C. G. Jung.* (R. F. C. Hull, Trans.). Bollingen Series XX. New York: Pantheon Books.

Jung, C. (1960). *The Structure and Dynamics of the Psyche. Vol. 8. The Collected Works of C. G. Jung.* (R. F. C. Hull, Trans.). Bollingen Series XX. Princeton, New Jersey: Princeton University Press.

Jung, C. J., (1961). *Memories, Dreams and Reflections.* Pantheon Books, New York.

Jung, C. (1966). *Two Essays on Analytical Psychology. Vol. VII. The Collected Works of C. G. Jung.* (R. F. C. Hull, Trans.). Bollingen Series XX. Princeton, New Jersey: Princeton University Press.

Jung, C. (1967). *Alchemical Studies. Vol. 13. The Collected Works of C. G. Jung.* (R. F. C. Hull, Trans.). Bollingen Series XX. Princeton, New Jersey: Princeton University Press.

Kandel, E. (1983). From metapsychology to molecular biology: Explorations into the nature of anxiety. *American Journal of Psychiatry, 140*(10), 1277-1293.

Kandel, E. (1989). Genes, nerve cells, and the remembrance of things past. *Journal of Neuropsychiatry 1*(2), 103-125.

Kaufmann, S. (1993). *Origins of Order: Self-Organization and Selection in Evolution.* Oxford: Oxford University Press.

Kaufmann, S. (1994). Whispers from Carnot: The origins or order and principles of adaptation in complex nonequilibrium systems. p. 83-160. In Cowan, G., Pines, D. & Meltzer, D. (Eds.) *Complexity: Metaphors, Models, and Reality.* New York: Addison-Wesley.

Kaufmann, S. (1995). At Home in the Universe: *The Search for the Laws of Self-Organization and Complexity.* Oxford: Oxford University Press.

Kelso, J.A.S., (1995). *Dynamic Patterns: The Self-Organization of Brain and Behavior.* MIT Press, Cambridge, Massachusetts.

Kennedy, B., Ziegler, M. & Shannahoff-Khalsa, D. (1986). Alternating lateralization of plasma catecholamines and nasal patency in humans. *Life Sciences*, 38, 1203-1214.

Kiecolt-Glaser, J. & Glaser, R. (1986). Psychological influences on immunity. *Psychosomatics,* 27, 9, 621-624.

Kihlstrom, J., (1980). Posthypnotic amnesia for recently learned material: Interactions with "episodic" and "semantic" memory. *Cognitive Psychology*, 12, 227-251.

Kirsch, I. (1993). Professional opinions about hypnosis: Results of the APA Division 30 survey. *Psychological Hypnosis*, 2(3), 4-5.

Kirsch, I & Lynn, S., (1995). The Altered State of Hypnosis: Changes in the Theoretical Landscape. *American Psychologist*, 50:10, pp. 846-858.

339

Klein, R., & Armitage, R. (1979). Rhythms in human performance: 1/2 hour oscillations in cognitive style. *Science*, 204, 1326-1328.

Klein, R., Pilon, D. & Prosser, S., Shannahoff-Khalsa, D. (1986). Nasal airflow asymmetries and human performance. *Biological Psychiatry*, 23, 127-137.

Kleitman, N. (1963). *Sleep and Wakefulness as Alternating Phases in the Cycle of Existence*. Chicago, Ill: University of Chicago.

Kleitman, N. (1969). Basic rest-activity cycle in relation to sleep and wakefulness. In A. Kales (Ed.), *Sleep: Physiology & Pathology* (pp. 33-38). Philadelphia: Lippincott.

Kleitman, N. (1970). Implications of the rest-activity cycle: Implications for organizing activity. In E. Hartmann (Ed.), *Sleep and Dreaming*. Boston: Little, Brown.

Kleitman, N. & Rossi, E. (1992). The basic rest-activity cycle — 32 years later: An interview with Nathaniel Kleitman at 96. Interviewed by E. Rossi. In D. Lloyd & E. Rossi (Eds.), *Ultradian Rhythms in Life Processes: A Fundamental Inquiry into Chronobiology and Psychobiology*. New York: Springer-Verlag, 303-306.

Klevecz, R., Shymko, R., Blumenfeld, D. & Braly, P. (1987). Circadian gating of S phase in human ovarian cancer, *Cancer Research*, 47, 6267-6271.

Klevecz, R., and Braly, P. (1987). Circadian and ultradian rhythms of proliferation in human ovarian cancer. *Chronologica International*, In Press.

Klevecz, R., (1992). A precise circadian clock from chaotic cell cycle oscillations. In D. Lloyd & E. Rossi (Eds.), *Ultradian Rhythms in Life Processes: A Fundamental Inquiry into Chronobiology and Psychobiology*. New York: Springer-Verlag, 41-70.

Knobil, E., & Hotchkiss, J. (1985). The circhoral gonadotropin releasing hormone (GnRH) pulse generator of the hypothalamus and its physiological significance. In H. Schulz & P. Lavie (Eds.), *Ultradian Rhythms in Physiology and Behavior* (pp. 32-40). New York: Springer-Verlag.

Koçak, H., (1989) *Differential and difference equations through computer experiments* (Phaser diskette included). New York: Springer-Verlag.

Konopka, R. & Benzer, (1971). Clock mutants of Drosophila melanogaster. *Proceedings of the National Academy of Sciences*. 68:2112-2116.

Kordon, C. (1993). *The Language of the Cell*. New York: McGraw-Hill.

Kronauer, R. (1984). Modeling principles for human circadian rhythms. In Moore-Ede, M. & Czeisler, C. (Eds.) *Mathematical Models of the Circadian Sleep-Wake Cycle* (pp. 105-128). New York: Raven Press.

Kupfer, D., Monk, T., & Barchas, J. (1988). *Biological Rhythms and Mental Disorders*. New York: Guilford.

Kruse, P. and Gheorghiyu, V., (1992) *Self-Organization Theory and Radical Constructivism: A New Concept for Understanding Hypnosis, Suggestion and Suggestibility*. in Bongartz, E. (Ed.), (1992). *Hypnosis: 175 Years after Mesmer: Recent Developments in Theory and Application*. Konstanz: Universitatsvergag.

Kruse, P., & Stadler, M. (1990). Stability and instability in cognitive systems: Multi-stability suggestion and psychosomatic Interaction. In: Haken, H., & Stadler, M. (Eds.), *Synergetics of Cognition*. Berlin: Springer-Verlag, pp. 201-215.

Kruse, P. & Stadler, M. (Eds.). (1994). *Multistability in Cognition*. Berlin: Springer-Verlag.

Kruse, P, & Stadler, M. (Eds.), (1995). *Ambiguity in Mind and Nature: Multistable Cognitive Phenomena*. New York: Springer Verlag.

Kruse, P, Stadler, M., Pavlekovic, B. & Gheorghiu, V. (1992). Instability and cognitive order formation: Self-Organization Principles, psychological experiments, and psychotherapeutic interventions. In Tschacher, W.; Schiepek, G., & Brunner, E., (1992). *Self-Organization and clinical Psychology: Empirical Approaches to Synergetics in Psychology*. Berlin, Springer-Verlag.

Kruse, P., Strüber, H. & Stadler, M. (1995). The Significance of Perceptual Multistability for Research on Cognitive Self-Organization. In Kruse, P. (Ed.) (1995) *Ambiguity in Mind and Nature. Springer Series in Synergetics, Vol. 64*. Berlin: Springer-Verlag.

Lacks, P. (1987). *Behavioral Treatment for Persistent Insomnia*. New York: Pergamon Press.

Langton, C., (1986). Studying artificial life with cellular automata. *Physica* 22D, 120-149.

Langton, C. (Ed.). (1989). *Artificial Life, Vol. VI*. Redwood City, CA: Addison-Wesley.

Langton, C., (1992). Life at the Edge of Chaos. In Langton, C., Taylor, C., Farmer, J., & Rasmussen, S. (Eds.) (1992). *Artificial Life II*. Redwood City, CA: Addison-Wesley.

Langton, C. (ed.), (1995). *Artificial Life: A Proceedings Volume in the Santa Fe Institute Studies in the Sciences of Complexity Vol. VI*. New York: Addison-Wesley.

Langton, C., Taylor, C., Farmer, J., & Rasmussen, S. (Eds.) (1992). *Artificial Life II*. Redwood City, CA: Addison-Wesley.

Lankton, S. & Lankton, C. (1983). *The Answer Within: A Clinical Framework of Ericksonian Hypnotherapy*. New York:

Lankton, S. & Zeig, J. (Eds.) (1989). *Extrapolations: Demonstrations of Ericksonian Therapy. Ericksonian Monographs*, 6. New York, Brunner/Mazel.

Lavie, P., & Kripke, D. (1977). Ultradian rhythms in urine flow in waking humans. *Nature*, 269, 142-144.

Levine, J., Kurtz, R. & Lauter, J. (1984). Hypnosis and itffects on left and right hemisphere activity. *Biological Psychiatry*, 19, 1461-1475.

Lazarus, A. & Mayne, T. (1991). Relaxation: Some limitations, side effects, and proposed solutions. *Psychotherapy*, 27, 261-266.

Leff, H. & Rex, (1990). *Maxwell's Demon; Entropy, Information, Computing*. New York: Princeton University Press.

LePage, K., Schafer, D. & Miller, A. (1992). Alternating Unilateral Lachrymation. *American Journal of Clinical Hypnosis*, 34, 255-260.

LePage, K. & Schafer, D. (1995). Unilateral lachrymation associated with somatic memory of pain. In Burrows, G. & Stanley, R. (Eds.) *Contemporary International Hypnosis*. p. 119-126. New York: Wiley.

Lewin, R. (1992). *Complexity: Life at the Edge of Chaos*. New York: Macmillan.

Libet, B., (1993). *Neurophysiology of Consciousness: Selected papers and New Essays*. Boston: Birkhäuser.

Lightfoot, J. J. (1992). The art of healing, the science of drama: How acting may affect the immune system. *Advances*, 8(4), 66-69.

Lippincott, B. (1990). Testing predictions of the ultradian theory of therapeutic hypnosis. Paper presented at 32nd Annual Scientific Meeting and Workshops on Clinical Hypnosis, March 24-28, 1990, Orlando, Florida. (Published in this issue of *Ericksonian Monographs*.)

Lippincott, B. (1992 a). Owls and Larks in Hypnosis: Individual differences in hypnotic susceptibility relating to biological rhythms. *American Journal of Clinical Hypnosis*, 34, 185-192.

Lippincott, B. (1992 b). Owls and larks in family therapy. *The California Therapist*, 4, pp. 35-38.

Lippincott, B., (1993). The temperature rhythm and hypnotizability: A brief report. *Contemporary Hypnosis*, 10,155-158.

Lloyd, D., & Edwards, S. (1984). Epigenetic oscillations during the cell cycles of lower eucaryotes are coupled to a clock: Life's slow dance to the music of time. In Edmunds, L. (ed.) *Cell Cycle Clocks*, NY, Dekker.

Lloyd, D. & Rossi, E. (1992a). *Ultradian Rhythms in Life Processes: A Fundamental Inquiry into Chronobiology and Psychobiology*. New York: Springer-Verlag.

Lloyd, D. & Rossi, E. (1992 b). Epilogue: the unification hypothesis of chrono-biology — psychobiology from molecule to mind. In Lloyd, D & Rossi, E. (Eds.) *Ultradian Rhythms in Life Processes: A Fundamental Inquiry into Chronobiology and Psychobiology*, (pp. 403-405). New York: Springer-Verlag.

Lloyd, D. & Rossi, E. (1993) Biological Rhythms as organization and information. *Biological Reviews*, 68, 563-577.

Locke, S., Kraus, L., Leserman, J., Hurst, M., Heisel, S., & Williams, R. (1984). Life change stress, psychiatric symptoms, and natural killer-cell activity. *Psychosomatic Medicine*, 46, 441-453.

Lorenz, E. (1963). Deterministic non-periodic flow. *Journal of Atmospheric Science*, 20, 130-141.

Lorenz, E. (1993). *The Essence of Chaos*. Seattle: Univ. Washington Press.

Mandelbrot, B. (1977). *The Fractal Geometry of Nature*. New York: Freeman.

Mann, B., & Sanders, S., (1995). The Effects of Light, Temperature, Trance Length, and Time of Day on Hypnotic Depth. *American Journal of Clinical Hypnosis*. 37(3) pp. 43-53.

Marijuan, P. (1995). Enzymes, artificial cells and the nature of biological information. *Biosystems*, 35, 167-170.

May, R. (1976). Simple Mathematical Models with very Complicated Dynamics. *Nature*. 261, 459-467.

References

McNamara, J. & Houston, A., (1996). State-dependent life histories. *Nature.* 380, 6571, 215-221.

Meier-Kroll, A., (1992). Ultradian behavior cycles in humans: Developmental and social aspects. In Lloyd, D. & Rossi, E. (Eds.). *Ultradian Rhythms in Life Processes: A Fundamental Inquiry into Chronobiology and Psychobiology.* New York: Springer-Verlag, 243-282.

Mejean, L., Bicakova-Rocher, A., Kolopp, M., Villaume, C., Levi, F., Debry, G., Reinberg, A., & Drouin, P. (1988). Circadian and ultradian rhythms in blood glucose and plasma insulin of healthy adults. *Chronobiology International,* 5(3), 227-236.

Merry, U. (1995). *Coping with Uncertainty: Insights from the New Sciences of Chaos, Self-Organization, and Complexity.* Westport, CN: Praeger.

Miller, G., (1956). The magic number seven, plus or minus two: Some limits on our capacity for processing information. *Psychological Review,* 63, 81-97.

Mishra, R. K., Maaß, D. & Zwierlein, E., (1994). *On Self-Organization: An Interdisciplinary Search for a Unifying Principle.* Springer-Verlag, New York.

Mitchell, M., Crutchfield, J. & Hraber, P., (1994). Dynamics, computation, and "The Edge of Chaos": A Re-Examination. In Cowan, G., Pines, D. & Meltzer, D. (Eds.) *Complexity, Metaphors, Models, and Reality.* New York: Addison-Wesley.

Moffitt, A. (1995). The creation of self: self reflections in dreaming and waking, *Psychological Perspectives*, 30, 42-69.

Moffitt, A., Kramer, M. & Hoffmann, R. (Eds.) (1993). The Functions of Dreaming. State University of New York Press, New York.

Moore-Ede, M., Sulzman, F. & Fuller, C. (1982). *The clocks that time us.* Cambridge: Harvard University Press.

Moss, F. (1994). *Stochastic Resonance: From the Ice Ages to the Monkey's Ear.* St. Louis: University of Missouri at Saint Louis.

Moss, F., Pierson, D. & O'gorman. (1994). Stochastic resonance: tutorial and update. *International Journal of Bifurcation and Chaos. 4, 6, 1383-1397.*

Murray, A., Solomon, M, & Kirschner, M. (1989). The role of cyclin synthesis and degradation in the control of maturation promoting factor activity. *Nature*, 339, 280-286.

Murray, A., & Kirschner, M. (1991) What controls the cell cycle? *Scientific American,* 266, 56-63. Myers, M. Wagner-Smith, K., Wesley, C., Young, M. & Sehgal, A. (1995). Positional Cloning and Sequence Analysis of the Drosophila Clock Gene, Timeless. Science: 270(3) p. 805-808.

Naish, P. (Ed.) (1986*). What is Hypnosis? Current Theories and Research.* Open University Press, Milton Keynes: Philadelphia.

Naliboff, B., Gilmore, S., Solomon, G. & Fahey, J., (1996). Psychophysiological and immune changes during an extended sixty minute laboratory stressor. Abstract A-13. Research Perspectives in Psychneuroimmunology. Santa Monica Meeting, California April 17-20, 1996.

Nash, M. (1991). Hypnosis as a special case of psychological regression. In S. J. Lynn & J. W. Rhue (Eds.), *Theories of hypnosis: Current Models and perspectives* (pp. 171-194). New York: Guilford Press.

Newtson, D. (1994). The perception and coupling of behavior waves. In Vallacher, R. & Nowak, J., (Eds.), *Dynamical Systems in Social Psychology*. New York: Academic Press.

Nicolis, G. & Prigogine, I, (1989*). Exploring complexity: An Introduction.* New York: W. H. Freeman and Company.

Neisser, U., (1967). *Cognitive Psychology*. New York: Appleton-Century-Crofts.

Nusse, H., and York, J. (1994). *Dynamics: Numerical Explorations*. New York: Springer-Verlag.

Ommaya, A., (1996). Emotions as consciousness: a thermodynamic approach. *Consciousness at the Crossroads of Philosophy and Science,* Thorverton, England, pp. 97.

Orne, M. (1972). On the simulating subject as a quasi-control group in hypnosis research: What, why, and how. In E. Fromm & R. Shor (Eds.), *Hypnosis: Research Developments and Perspectives* (pp. 399-443). Chicago: Aldine.

Orne, M. & Evans, F. (1966). Inadvertent termination of hypnosis with hypnotized and simulating subjects. *The International Journal of Clinical and Experimental Hypnosis, 14*, 61-78.

Orsucci, F., (1995). A nonlinear science perspective on psychosomatics. *Newsletter of the Society for Chaos Theory in Psychology and Life Sciences.* 3, 1, pp. 9-10.

Overton, D. (1978). Major theories of state-dependent learning. In B. Ho, D. Richards, & D. Chute (Eds.*), Drug Discrimination and State-Dependent Learning* (pp. 283-318). New York: Academic Press.

Osowiec, D. (1992). Ultradian rhythms in self-actualization, anxiety, and stress-related somatic symptoms. Ph.D. Dissertation, California Institute of Integral Studies.

Packard, N., (1988). Adaptation toward the edge of chaos. Technical Report, Center for Complex Systems Research, University of Illinois, CCSR-88-5.

Papez, J. (1937). A proposed mechanism of emotion. *Archives of Neurology & Psychiatry*, 38, 725-744.

Pardo, J., Fox, P. & Raichle, M. (1991). Localization of a human system for sustained attention by positron emission tomography. *Nature*, 349, 61-64.

Peak, D. & Frame, M., (1994). *Chaos Under Control: The Art and Science of Complexity.*

Peitgen, H., Jürgens, H. & Saupe D., (1992). *Chaos and Fractals: New Frontiers of Science.* New York: Springer-Verlag

Pekala, R., (1991). *Quantifying Consciousness: An Empirical Approach.* New York: Plenum.

Pekala, R., (1995 a). A short, unobtrusive hypnotic-assessment procedure for assessing hypnotizability level: I. Development and research. *American,. J. Clinical Hypnosis, 37*, 4, 271-283.

Pekala, R., (1995 b). A short, unobtrusive hypnotic-assessment procedure for assessing hypnotizability level: II. Clinical Case Reports. *American,. J. Clinical Hypnosis, 37*, 4, 284-293

Perls, F., Hefferline, R.F., Goodman, P., (1951). *Gestalt Therapy: Excitement and Growth in the Human personality*, Dell Publishing, New York.

References

Poincaré, H., (1905/1952). *Science and Hypothesis*. New York: Dover.

Popper, K. (1966). *The Logic of Scientific Discovery*. London: Hutchinson.

Pratt, M. (1993). The use of ideodynamic concepts with children for personal adjustment problem-solving in the counseling process. Doctoral Dissertation, Ann Arbor, MI: U.M.I.

Prechter, R. (1995). *At the Crest of the Title Wave: A Forecast for the Great Bear Market*. Gainesville, Georgia: New Classics Press.

Prigogine, I. (1980). *From Being to Becoming: Time and Complexity in the Physical Sciences*. San Francisco: Freeman.

Prigogine. I. & Stengers, I. (1984). *Order Out of Chaos*. New York: Bantam.

Rama, S. (1980). The science of Prana. *Research Bulletin of the Himalayan International Institute*. 2, 1-8.

Rama, S., Ballentine, R., & Ajaya, S. (1976). *Yoga and Psychotherapy: The Evolution of Consciousness*. Penn.: Himalayan International Institute of Yoga Science and Philosophy.

Rao, S., & Potdar, A. (1970). Nasal airflow with body in various positions. *Journal of Applied Psychology*, 28, 162-165.

Reiman, E., (1996). Positron Emission Tomography and the conscious experience of emotion. *Consciousness at the Crossroads of Philosophy and Science*, Thorverton, England, pp. 97.

Reber, A. (1993). *Implicit Learning and Tacit Knowledge: An Essay on the Cognitive Unconscious. Oxford University Press*, New York.

Revenstorf, D. (1992). *Hypnosis: A Therapy without Theory*. in Bongartz, E. (Ed.), (1992). *Hypnosis: 175 Years after Mesmer: Recent Developments in Theory and Application*. Konstanz: Universitatsvergag.

Rensing, L., Heiden, U. & Makey, M., (Eds.), (1987*). Temporal Disorder in Human Oscillatory Systems*. New York: Springer-Verlag.

Richardson, S., (1996). The end of the self. *Discover*. April, pp. 78-87.

Rider, M. (1985). Entrainment mechanisms are involved in pain reduction, muscle relaxation, and music-mediated imagery. *Journal of Music Therapy*, 22(4), 183-192.

Rider, M. (1987). Treating chronic disease and pain with music-Mediated Imagery. *Arts in Psychotherapy*, 14(2), 113-120.

Rider, M., & Achterberg, J. (1989). Effect of music-assisted imagery on neutrophils and lymphocytes. *Biofeedback and Self-Regulation*, 14(3), 247-257.

Rider, M., Floyd, J., & Kirkpatrick, J. (1985). The effect of music, imagery, and relaxation on adrenal corticosteroids and the re-entrainment of circadian rhythms. *Journal of Music Therapy,* 22(1), 46-58.

Ridge, J., Ephraim, F. & Matzinger, P. (1996). Neonatal tolerance revisited: turning on newborn T cells with dentritic cells. *Science, 271, 1723-1726.*

Robertson, R., (1995). *Jungian Archetypes: Jung, Gödel, and the History of Archetypes*. York Beach, Main: Nicholas-Hays.

Robertson, R. & Combs, A. (Eds.), (1995). *Chaos Theory in Psychology and the Life Sciences.* New Jersey, Lawrence Erlbaum Associates.

Rogers, C., (1980). *A Way of Being.* Boston: Houghton Mifflin.

Rogers, C. (1987). Rogers, Kohut, and Erickson: A personal perspective on some similarities and differences. In Zeig, J. (Ed.) *The Evolution of Psychotherapy,* New York: Brunner/Mazel.

Rose, F., (1989). *The Control of the Hypothalamo-Pituitary-Adrenocortical Axis,* New York: International Universities Press.

Rosenberg, S. & Barry, J. (1992). *The Transformed Cell: Unlocking the Mysteries of Cancer.* New York: Putnam/Chapmans.

Rosenthal, N. (1989). *Seasons of the Mind: Why You Get the Winter Blues.* New York: Bantam.

Rossi, E. (1968). The Breakout Heuristic: A Phenomenology of Growth Therapy with College Students. *Journal of Humanistic Psychology, 8,* 16-28.

Rossi, E., (1972/1985/1998). *Dreams and the Growth of Personality,* New York: Pergamon Press (1972); Brunner-Mazel (1986); Third Edition forthcoming in 1998 from Palisades Gateway Publishing, 505 Palisades Drive, Pacific Palisades, CA 90272 Phone/Fax: (310) 230-1067.

Rossi, E. (1973a). Psychological shocks and creative moments in psychotherapy. *The American Journal of Clinical Hypnosis, 16,* 9-22.

Rossi, E. (1973b). The dream-protein hypothesis, *American Journal of Psychiatry,* 130, 1094-1097.

Rossi, E. (1981). Hypnotist describes natural rhythm of trance readiness. *Brain Mind Bulletin,* 6, (7), 1.

Rossi, E. (1982). Hypnosis and ultradian cycles: A new state(s) theory of hypnosis? *The American Journal of Clinical Hypnosis,* 25 (1), 21-32.

Rossi, E. (1986/1993) *The Psychobiology of Mindbody Healing,* Revised Edition. New York: Norton.

Rossi, E. (1986). Altered states of consciousness in everyday life: The ultradian rhythms. In B. Wolman & M. Ullman (Eds.), *Handbook of Altered States of Consciousness* (pp. 97-132). New York: Van Nostrand.

Rossi, E. (1987). From mind to molecule: A state-dependent memory, learning, and behavior theory of mindbody healing. *Advances,* 4(2), 46-60.

Rossi, E. (1989a). Archetypes as strange attractors. *Psychological Perspectives,* 20, 4-14.

Rossi, E. (1989b). Mind-body healing, not suggestion, is the essence of hypnosis. *American Journal of Clinical Hypnosis,* 32, 14-15.

Rossi, E. (1990a). Mind-Molecular Communication: Can We Really Talk to Our Genes? *Hypnos,* 17(1), 3-14.

Rossi, E. (1990b). From mind to molecule: More than a metaphor. In Zeig, J. & Gilligan, S. (Eds.) *Brief Therapy: Myths, Methods and Metaphors,* (pp. 445-472). New York: Brunner/Mazel.

Rossi, E. (1990c). The new yoga of the west: Natural rhythms of mindbody healing. *Psychological Perspectives,* 22, 146-161.

Rossi, E. (1990d). The eternal quest: Hidden rhythms of stress and healing in everyday life. *Psychological Perspectives*, 22, 6-23.

Rossi, E. (1991a). A Clinical-Experimental Assessment of the Ultradian Theory of Therapeutic Suggestion. Paper presented at the 32nd Annual Scientific Meeting and Workshops on Clinical Hypnosis. March 24-28, 1990, Orlando, Florida. To be published in Ericksonian Monographs, 9.

Rossi, E., (1991b). The Wave Nature of Consciousness, *Psychological Perspectives*, 24, 1-10.

Rossi, E. (1992a). Periodicity in self-hypnosis and the ultradian healing response: A pilot study. *Hypnos*, 19. 4-13.

Rossi, E. (1992b). The wave nature of consciousness: A new direction for the evolution of psychotherapy. In Zeig, J. (Ed.) *The Evolution of Psychotherapy: The Second Conference*. New York: Brunner-Mazel, pp. 216-235.

Rossi, E. (1994a). Hypnose und die neue Homoostase: Auf der suche nach einem mathematischen modell fur Erickson's naturalistichen ansatz, *Hypnose und Kognition*, Band 11, Heft 1 und 2, 167-189.

Rossi, E. (1994b). Ericksonian Psychotherapy — Then and Now. In Zeig, J. (Ed.) *Ericksonian Methods: The Essence of the Story*, 46-76. New York: Brunner/Mazel.

Rossi, E. (1994c). The emergence of mind-gene communication. *European Journal of Clinical Hypnosis*, 3, 4-17.

Rossi, E. (1995a). The essence of hypnotherapeutic suggestion: Part One; The Basic Accessing Question and Ultradian Dynamics in Single Session Psychotherapy. *European Journal of Clinical Hypnosis*, 2, 6-17.

Rossi, E. (1995b) The Essence of Hypnotherapeutic Suggestion: Part Two: Ultradian dynamics of the creative process in psychotherapy. *The European Journal of Clinical Hypnosis*, 2, 4, pp. 4-16.

Rossi, E., (1995c). The chronobiological theory of therapeutic suggestion: Towards a mathematical model of Erickson's naturalistic approach. In Kleinhauz, M., Peter, B., Livnay, S., Delano, V., Fuchs, K. & Lost-Peter, A. (Eds.). *Jerusalem Lectures on Hypnosis and Hypnotherapy*. Munich: Hypnosis International Monographs, 1.

Rossi, E., (1995d). Accessing the creative process. Ernest Rossi interviewed by Barry Winbolt. *The Therapist*, 3,(1), 24-29.

Rossi, E. (1996a) The Essence of Hypnotherapeutic Suggestion: Part Three: Polarity and the creative dynamics of change. *The European Journal of Clinical Hypnosis*, 2, 3, pp. 2-17.

Rossi, E. (1996b). Research on process oriented psychobiological therapy: Mind-gene communication in psychobiologial work and healing. *Advances*, 12, 2, pp. 29-31.

Rossi, E., (1996c). The psychobiology of mindbody communication: The complex, self-organizing field of information transduction. *BioSystems*, (In Press).

Rossi, E., (1996d). The creative process in naturalistic ultradian hypnotherapy. *Hypnosis International Monographs*, 2, 1-15.

Rossi, E., & Cheek, D. (1988*). Mindbody Therapy: Ideodynamic Healing in Hypnosis*. New York: W. W. Norton.

Rossi, E., & Jichaku, P., (1992). Creative choice in therapeutic and transpersonal double binds. In Rossi, E. & Ryan, M. (Eds.) *Creative Choice in Hypnosis*, (pp. 225-253) New York: Irvington.

Rossi, E., & Jichaku, P., (1992). Creative choice in therapeutic and transpersonal double binds. In Rossi, E. & Ryan, M. (Eds.) *Creative Choice in Hypnosis*, (pp. 225-253) New York: Irvington.

Rossi, E. & Lippincott, B. (1992). The wave nature of being: Ultradian rhythms and mindbody communication. In Lloyd, D. & Rossi, E. (Eds.) *Ultradian Rhythms in Life Processes: A Fundamental Inquiry into Chronobiology and Psychobiology* (pp. 371-402). New York: Springer-Verlag.

Rossi, E., & Lippincott. B. (1993). A clinical-experimental exploration of Erickson's naturalistic approach: Ultradian time and trance phenomena. *Hypnos*, 20, 10-20.

Rossi, E., Lippincott, B., & Bessette, A. (1994). Ultradian Dynamics in Hypnotherapy: Part One. *The European Journal of Clinical Hypnosis, 2, 1, p. 10-20.*

Rossi, E., Lippencott, B. & Bessette, A. (1994b). The chronobiology of mindbody healing: Ultradian dynamics in hypnotherapy. Part one. *European Journal of Clinical Hypnosis*, 2, 1, 2-10.

Rossi, E., Lippincott, B., & Bessette, A. (1995). Ultradian Dynamics in Hypnotherapy: Part Two. *The European Journal of Clinical Hypnosis, 2, 2, p. 6-14.*

Rossi, E., & Nimmons, D. (1991). *The Twenty Minute Break: The Ultradian Healing Response.* New York: Jeremy Tarcher.

Rossi, E., & Ryan, M. (Eds.) (1986). *Mindbody Communication in Hypnosis. Vol. 3. The Seminars, Workshops, and Lectures of Milton H. Erickson.* New York: Irvington.

Rossi, E., & Ryan, M. (Eds.) (1991). *Creative Choice in Hypnosis. Vol. 4. The Seminars, Workshops, and Lectures of Milton H. Erickson.* New York: Irvington

Rossi, E., & Ryan, M. (Eds.) (1992). *Creative Choice in Hypnosis. Vol. 4. The Seminars, Workshops, and Lectures of Milton H. Erickson.* New York: Irvington.

Rossi, E. & Smith, M. (1990) The Eternal Quest: Hidden rhythms of mindbody healing in everyday life. *Psychological Perspectives*, 22, 146-161.

Rössler, O. (1971). "A system theoretic model of biogenesis. *Z. Naturforsch*, 26b, 741-746.

Rössler, O. (1976). An equation for continuous chaos. *Physics Letter.* 57A, 397-398.

Rössler, O. (1983). Deductive prebiology. In Rolfing, K. (Ed.) *Molecular Evolution and the Prebiological Paradigm.* New York: Plenum.

Rössler, O. (1987). Chaos in coupled optimizers. In Koslow, S., Mandell, A. & Schlesinger, M. *Perspectives in Biological Dynamics and Theoretical Medicine.* New York: Annuals of the New York Academy of Sciences, Volume 504.

Rössler, O. (1992 a). The future of chaos. In Kim, J. & Stringer, J. (Eds.) *Applied Chaos,* 457-465. New York: Wiley.

Rössler, O. (1992 b). Interactional bifurcations in human interaction — A formal approach. In Tschhacher, W., Schiepek, G. & Brunner, E. (Eds.). *Self-*

References

Organization and Clinical Psychology: Empirical Approaches to Synergetics in Psychology. New York: Springer-Verlag.

Rössler, O. (1994a). Micro Constructivism. *Psysica D*, 75: 438-448.

Rössler, O. (1994b). Endophysics — Descartes taken seriously. In Atmanspacher, H. & Dalenoot. G. (eds.) *Inside Versus Outside.* Berlin: Springer-Verlag.

Rössler, O. (1995). An introduction to chaos. *International J. of Intelligent Systems.* *10,* 5-13.

Rumelhard, D. (1995). Affect and neuro-modulation: A connectionist approach. In Morowitz, H. & Singer, J. (Eds.) *The Mind, The Brain. and Complex Adaptive Systems.* New York: Addison-Wesley.

Ruzyla-Smith, P., Barabasz, A., Barabasz, M., & Warner, D. (1995). Effects of hypnosis on the immune response: B-cells, T-cells, Helper and Suppressor cells. *American Journal of Clinical Hypnosis,* 38, 2, 71-79.

Sacededote, P., (1982). A Non-Statistical Dissertation about Hypnotizability Scales and Clinical Goals: Comparison with Individualized Induction and Deepening Procedures. *The International Journal of Clinical and Experimental Hypnosis.* 30(4):354-376.

Sackeim, H. (1982). Lateral asymmetry in bodily response to hypnotic suggestions. *Biological Psychiatry,* 17(4), 437-447.

Saito, T. & Kano, T. (1992). The diurnal fluctuation of hypnotic susceptibility. *The Japanese Journal of Hypnosis.* 37, 1, 6-12.

Sanders, S. & Mann, B. (1995). The effects of light, temperature, trance length and time of day on hypnotic depth. American J. Clinical Hypnosis. 37, 3, p. 43-53.

Sapolsky, R. (1990). Stress in the wild. *Scientific American,* January, 116-123.

Sapolsky, R. (1992). *Stress, The Aging Brain, And The Mechanisms of Neuronal Death.* Cambridge: MIT Press.

Sarbin, T., & Coe, W. (1972). *Hypnosis: A Social Psychological Analysis of Influence Communication.* New York: Holt, Reinhart & Winston.

Scharrer, E., & Scharrer, B., (1940). Secretory cells within the hypothalamus. *Research Publications of the association of Nervous and Mental Diseases.* New York: Hafner.

Schmitt, F. (1984). Molecular regulators of brain function: A new view. *Neuroscience, 13,* 991-1001.

Schrodinger, E., (1944). *What is Life?* New York, Cambridge.

Schumaker, J. (1991). (Ed.) *Human Suggestibility: Advances in Theory, Research and Application.* New York: Routledge.

Schwartz, J., Stoessel, P, Baxter, L., Karron, M. & Phelps, M. (1996). Systematic changes in cerebral glucose metabolic rate after successful behavioral modification treatment of obsessive-compulsive disorder. *Archives of Psychiatry, 53,* 109-113.

Sehgal, A., Rothenflush-Hilifiker, R., Hunter-Ensor, M., Chen, Y, Myers, M., and Young, M. (1995). Rhythmic Expressions of timeless: A Basis for Promoting Circadian Cycles in period Gene Autoregulation. *Science*: 270:3 p. 808-810.

Selye, H. (1976). *The Stress of Life.* New York: McGraw-Hill.

Selye, H. (1982). History and present status of the stress concept. In L. Goldberger, & S. Breznitz (Eds.), *Handbook of Stress* (pp. 7-20). New York: Macmillan.

Shapiro, F., (1995). *Eye Movement Desensitization and Reprocessing: Basic Principles, Protocols, and Procedures.* New York: Guilford.

Shashoua, V. (1981). Extracellular fluid proteins of goldfish brain. *Neurochemistry Research, 6,* 1129-1147.

Shaw, R. (1984). *The Dripping Faucet as a Model Chaotic System.* Santa Cruz: Aerial Press.

Shawe-Taylor, J. & Shawe-Taylor, M., (1996). Consciousness as a linear phenomenon. *Consciousness at the Crossroads of Philosophy and Cognitive Science.* Maribor Conference, 1994. Thorverton, England: Imprint Academic, pp. 32-38.

Sheehan, P. (1995). The effects of asking leading questions in hypnosis. In Burrows, G. & Stanley, R. (Eds.) *Contemporary International Hypnosis.* p. 55-62. New York: Wiley.

Shor, R. & Orne (1962). The Harvard Group Scale of Hypnotic Susceptibility, Form A. Consulting Psychologists Press, Palo Alto, California.

Siegel, B., (1986). *Love, Medicine and Miracles.* New York: Harper & Row.

Siegel, B., (1989). *Peace, Love and Healing.* New York: Harper & Row.

Siegel, B., (1993). *How to Live Between Office Visits.* New York:Harper Collins.

Siegman, A. & Feldstein, S. (1979). Ultradian biorhythms in social interaction. In Siegman, A. & Feldstein, S. (Eds.) On Time and_Speech. p.57-70. New York: Erlbaum.

Smith, A. & Nutt, D., (1996). Noradrenaline and attention lapses. *Nature, 380, 6572,* pp. 291.

Smith, L. & Thelen, E., (1993). *A Dynamical Systems Approach to the Development: Applications.* MIT Press, Boston, Massachusetts.

Sommer, C. (1990). The ultradian rhythm and the Common Everyday Trance. Paper presented at the 32nd Annual Scientific Meeting, March 24-28, Orlando, Florida. (Published in this issue of *Ericksonian Monographs.)*

Sommer, C. (1993). Ultradian Rhythms and the Common Everyday Trance. *Hypnos,* 20, 135-140.

Spiegel, D., & Barabasz, A. (1988). Effects of hypnotic instructions on P300 event-related-potential amplitudes: research and clinical implications. *American Journal of Clinical Hypnosis,* 31, 11-16.

Spiegel, D., Bloom, J., Kraemer, H. & Gottheil, E. (1989). Effect of psychosocial treatment on survival of patients with metastatic breast cancer. *Lancet,* October 14, 888-891.

Spiegel, D., Cutcomb, S, Ren, C. & Pribram, K. (1985). Hypnotic hallucination alters evoked potentials. *J. Abnormal. Psychology.* 94, 249-255.

Spiegel, H., & Spiegel, D. (1978). *Trance and Treatment: Clinical Uses of Hypnosis.* New York: Basic Books.

Spanos, N. (1986). Hypnotic behavior: A social-psychology interpretation of amnesia, analgesia, and "trance logic." *Behavioral and Brain Sciences,* 9, 449-503.

Spanos, N. & Chaves, J. (1989). *Hypnosis; the cognitive-behavioral perspective.* Buffalo: Prometheus Books.

Sperling, G., (1960). The information available in brief visual presentations. *Psychological Monographs, 74* (Whole No. 498).

Stam, H. & Spanos, N. (1980). Experimental designs, expectancy effects, and hypnotic analgesia. *Journal of Abnormal Psychology, 89,* 751-762.

Stephan, K., Fink, G., Passingham, R., Silbersweig, D., Ceballos-Bauman, A., Frith, C., Frackowiak, R., (1995). Functional anatomy of the mental representation of upper extremity movements in healthy subjects. *J. Neurophysiology, 73,* 373-385.

Stonier, T. (1990). *Information and the internal structure of the universe.* New York: Springer-Verlag.

Strogatz, S. (1986). *The mathematical Structure of the Human Sleep-Wake Cycle: Lecture Notes in Biomathematics, 69.* NY: Springer-Verlag.

Strogatz, S. (1994). *Nonlinear Dynamics and Chaos.* NY: Addison-Wesley.

Sturgis, L. & Coe, W. (1990). Physiological responsiveness during hypnosis. *The International Journal of Clinical Hypnosis, 38,* 3, 196-207.

Sturis, J., Polonsky, K., Shapiro, E., Blackman, J., O'Meara, N. & Van Cauter, E. (1992). Abnormalities in the ultradian oscillations of insulin secretion and glucose levels in Type 2 (non-insulin-dependent) diabetic patients. *Diabetologia,* 35:681-689.

Sudhof, T. (1995). The synaptic vesicle cycle: a cascade of protein-protein interactions. *Nature, 375,* 645-653.

Swanson, J. & Kinsbourn, M. (1979). State-dependent learning and retrieval: methodological cautions and theoretical considerations. In Kihlstrom, J. & Evans, F. (Eds.) *Functional Disorders of Memory.* New York: Wiley.

Tache, J., Morley, M. & Brown, M. (1989). *Neuropeptides and Stress.* New York: Springer-Verlag.

Takahashi, J. & Hoffman, M. (1995). Molecular Biological Clocks. *American Scientist,* 83:2, pp. 158-165.

Tellegen, A. & Atkinson, G. (1974) Openness to absorbing and self-alternating experiences ("absorption"), a trait related to hypnotic susceptibility. *Journal of Personality and Social Psychology, 33,* 142-148.

Thelen E. & Smith L., (1994). *A Dynamical Systems Approach to the Development of Cognition and Action.* MIT Press, Boston, Massachusetts.

Thom, R., (1972). *Structural Stability and Morphogenesis.* New York, Addison-Wesley.

Thom, R., (1983). *Mathematical Models of Morphogenesis.* New York: Wiley.

Tinterow, M. (1970). *Foundations of Hypnosis.* Springfield, Ill: C. C. Thomas.

Tipler, F. (1995). *The Physics of Immortality.* New York: Doubleday.

Todorov, I., (1990). How cells maintain stability. *Scientific American, 263,* 66-75.

Tschacher, W., Schiepek, G. & Brunner, E. (1992). *Self-Organization and Clinical Psychology: Empirical Approaches to Synergetics in Psychology.* New York: Springer-Verlag.

Tsuji, Y., & Kobayshi, T. (1988). Short and long ultradian EEG components in daytime arousal. *Electroencephalography and Clinical Neurophysiology,* 70, 110-117.

Turner, J., Dewerth, M. & Fine, T. (1993). Effects of flotation REST on salivary Iga: Presented at the Fifth International Conference on REST investigation, Seattle, Washington, February.

Unterwegner, E., Lamas, J., and Bongartz, W. (1992). *Heart-Rate Variability of High and Low Susceptible Subjects During Administration of the Stanford Scale, Form C.* in Bongartz, E. (Ed.), (1992). *Hypnosis: 175 Years after Mesmer: Recent Developments in Theory and Application.* Konstanz: Universitatsvergag.

Vallacher, R. & Nowak, J., (1994). *Dynamical Systems in Social Psychology.* New York: Academic Press.

Van Cauter, E., Desir, D., Decoster, C., Fery, F., & Balasse, E. (1989). Nocturnal decrease in glucose tolerance during constant glucose infusion. *Journal of Clinical Endocrinology and Metabolism,* 69(3), 604-611.

Veldhuis, J., & Johnson, M. (1988). Operating characteristics of the hypothalamo-pituitary-gonadal axis in men: Circadian, Ultradian, and pulsatile release of prolactin and its temporal coupling with luteinizing hormone. *Journal of Clinical Endocrinology and Metabolism,* 67(1), 116-123.

Veldhuis, J., King, J., Urban, R., Rogol, A., Evans, W., Kolp, L., & Johnson, M. (1987). Operating characteristics of the male hypothalmo-pituitary-gonadal axis: pulsatile release of testosterone and follicle-stimulating hormone and their temporal coupling with luteinizing hormone. *Journal of Clinical and Endocrinological Metabolism,* 65, 65-929.

Waldrop, M., (1992). *Complexity: The Emerging Science at the Edge of Order and Chaos.,* New York: Simon & Schuster.

Wallace, B., (1993). Day persons, night persons, and variability in hypnotic susceptibility. *Journal of Personality and Social Psychology,* 64, 827-833.

Wallace, B. & Kokoszka, A., (1995). Fluctuations in Hypnotic Susceptibility and Imaging Ability over a 16-hour period. The International Journal of Clinical and Experimental Hypnosis, 16, 1, 7-19.

Wallace, B., Turosky, D. & Koloszka, A., (1992). Variability in the assessment of vividness, *Journal of Mental Imagery,* 16, 221-230.

Watkins, J. (1978). *The Therapeutic Self.* New York: Human Sciences Press.

Weingartner, H. (1978). Human state dependent learning. In B. Ho, D. Richards, & D. Chute (Eds.), *Drug Discrimination and State-Dependent Learning,* 361-382. New York: Academic Press.

Weinstein, E. & Au, P. (1991). Use of hypnosis before and during angioplasty. *American Journal of Clinical Hypnosis,* 34, 29-37.

Weitzenhoffer, A. & Hilgard, E., (1967). *Revised Stanford Profile Scales of Hypnotic Susceptibility,* Consulting Psychologists Press, Palo Alto, California.

Weitzenhoffer, A. (1971). Ocular changes associated with passive hypnotic behavior. *The American Journal of Clinical Hypnosis,* 14, 102-121.

Weitzenhoffer, A. (1980). Hypnotic Susceptibility Revisited. *The American Journal of Clinical Hypnosis, 22*, 130-146.

Werntz, D. (1981). Cerebral hemispheric activity and autonomic nervous function. Doctoral Thesis, University of California, San Diego.

Werntz, D., Bickford, R., Bloom, F., & Shannahoff-Khalsa, D. (1981). Selective cortical activation by alternating autonomic function. Paper presented at the Western EEG Society Meeting, February 12, Reno, Nevado.

Werntz, D., Bickford, R. & Shannahoff-Khalsa, D. (1982). Selective hemispheric stimulation by unilateral forced nostril breathing. *Human neurobiology, 6*, 165-171.

Werntz, D., Bickford, R., Bloom, F., & Shannahoff-Khalsa, D. (1982a). Alternating cerebral hemispheric activity and lateralization of autonomic nervous function. *Human Neurobiology, 2*, 225-229.

Werntz, D., Bickford, R., Bloom, F., & Shannahoff-Khalsa, D. (1982b). Selective hemispheric stimulation by unilateral forced nostril breathing. *Human neurobiology, 6*, 165-171.

West, M. ed. (1987). *The Psychology of Meditation.* Oxford: Clarendon Press.

Wever, R. (1984). Toward a mathematical model of circadian rhythmicity. In Moore-Ede, M. and Czeisler, C., (Eds.) *Mathematical Models of the Circadian Sleep-Wake Cycle.* (p.17-79). New York: Raven Press.

Wever, R., (1988). Order and disorder in human circadian rhythmicity: Possible relations to mental illness. In Kupfer, D., Monk, T., & Barchas, J. (Eds.). *Biological Rhythms and Mental Disorders.* New York: Guilford.

Wever, R. (1989). Light effects on human circadian rhythms: a review of recent Andechs experiments. *Journal of Biological Rhythms, 4, 161-185.*

Wever, R. & Rossi, E. (1992). The sleep-wake threshold in human circadian as a determinant of ultradian. In Lloyd, D. & Rossi, E. (Eds.) *Ultradian Rhythms in Life Processes: A Fundamental Inquiry into Chronobiology and Psychobiology,* (pp. 307-322). New York: Springer-Verlag.

Wheeler, J. (1994). *At Home in the Universe.* Woodbury, New York: American Institute of Physics.

Woody, E., Bowers, K., & Oakman. (1992). A conceptual analysis of responsiveness: Experience, Individual differences, and context. In Fromm, E. & Nash, M. (Eds.), *Contemporary Hypnosis Research* (p. 3-33). New York: Guilford Press.

Woody, E. & Bowers, K. (1994). A frontal assault on dissociated control. In S. J. Lynn & J. W. Rhue, (Eds.), *Dissociation: Clinical, theoretical and research perspectives* (p. 52-79). New York: Guilford Press.

Yapko, M., (1989). *Brief Therapy Approaches to Treating Anxiety and Depression.* New York, Brunner/Mazel.

Yapko, M., (1990). *An introduction to the Practice of Clinical Hypnosis.* New York, Brunner/Mazel.

Yerkes, R. & Dodson, J., (1908). The relationship of strength of stimulus to rapidity of habit formation. *Journal of Comparative Neurology and Psychology*, 18, 459-482.

Zeig, J., (1985). *Experiencing Erickson: An Introduction to the Man and his Work.* New York: Brunner/Mazel.

Zeig, J., (1994). (Ed.) *Ericksonian Methods: The Essence of the Story.* New York: Brunner/Mazel.

Zeig, J.. & Gilligan, S., (1990). *Brief Therapy: Myths, Methods and Metaphors.* New York: Brunner Mazel.

Zilboorg, G., & Henry, G. (1941). *A History of Medical Psychology.* New York: Norton.

Zurek, W., (1990). Complexity, Entropy and the Physics of Information Complexity — A Manifesto. In Zurek, W. (Ed.), *Entropy and the Physics of Information: The Proceedings of the 1988 Workshop on Complexity, Entropy and the Physics of Information held May-June, 1989 in Santa Fe, New Mexico.* New York, Addison-Wesley.

Index